W.S. Gilbert and the Context of Comedy

To what extent is a great comic writer the product of his time? How far is he (or she) influenced by factors of personal psychology upbringing and environment? To what extent is the writing actually part of a long continuum in which there is continuity within change and change within continuity? *The Progress of Fun* considers principally the last of these areas, focussing on the case of W.S. Gilbert and challenging the frequently held view that he is pre-eminently a typical Victorian. This it does by tracing his roots back to Ancient Greek comedy and to the various comedic developments that have dominated Western Europe thereafter. Also included is a careful examination of the constraints and limitations that in various forms have long affected comedy-writing, and an evaluation of Gilbert's particular skills and legacy within the ongoing process. The whole is a suitable prelude to a second volume (*Pipes and Tabors*) which will consider genre in W.S. Gilbert, again relating it to comedic precedents and the universally timeless within the particular.

Richard Moore is a university lecturer and teacher in adult education with a Cambridge University doctorate on the subject of Christianity and Paganism in the Victorian Novel. He has at various points been a civil service executive, a vice principal in secondary education, and a leader of seminars on topics as diverse as Roman Comedy; the Puritans and Creative Literature; literary Waste Lands; and the Literature of Gardens. He is also a creative writer, responsible for over a hundred dramas and numerous libretti for comic operas and musical farces, several of them performed in the schools and colleges where he has taught.

Currently, Richard Moore is preparing more work on the Victorian Theatre while running seminars and literary courses in Newcastle, Berwick upon Tweed, and Pitlochry. His other interests are nature conservation, social and dynastic history, and the detective fiction of the Golden Age. He lives in the Scottish Borders, alternating with the southern Highlands and is a keen follower of Scottish countryside interests.

Routledge Studies in Nineteenth-Century Literature

For more information about this series, please visit: https://www.routledge.com

W.S. Gilbert and the Context of Comedy
The Progress of Fun

Richard Moore

Routledge
Taylor & Francis Group

NEW YORK AND LONDON

First published 2019
by Routledge
605 Third Avenue, New York, NY 10017

and by Routledge
2 Park Square, Milton Park, Abingdon, Oxon, OX14 4RN

First issued in paperback 2021

Routledge is an imprint of the Taylor & Francis Group, an informa business

Publisher's Note
The publisher has gone to great lengths to ensure the quality of this reprint but points out that some imperfections in the original copies may be apparent.

Library of Congress Cataloging-in-Publication Data
A catalog record for this title has been requested

ISBN 13: 978-1-03-209225-6 (pbk)
ISBN 13: 978-1-138-31108-4 (hbk)

Typeset in Sabon
by codeMantra

This book is dedicated to my parents, still with me in the eternal moment.

Contents

Acknowledgements

The writing of this book would have been impossible without the aid of several friends and supporters. In particular, I should like to thank my niece Susannah Curran and friend Cian McHugh for much practical advice; my inspiration Rosslyn Bowers for ordering and collating many books for background research; and my Lord High Everything Else John Stewart Ward for overall encouragement, not least in supplying me with endless cups of tea when I was working in the small hours.

In addition to the above, I owe a debt of support to many people, not least my unseen support team at Routledge, New York, and those in England, where Bryony Reece has been especially helpful. Others to whom I owe an ongoing gratitude are J. Derrick McClure, editor of the *W.S. Gilbert Society Journal*, and Andrew Crowther, Honorary Secretary of the *W.S. Gilbert Society*. Finally, in terms of general encouragement I should like to pay tribute to my sister, Christine Nuckey, my very good friend Wendy Culverwell, numerous members of the Berwick Educational Association, and all those I teach in Newcastle, Berwick, and Pitlochry. Also supportive from another dimension were my parents, who first inspired my love of literature and an eclectic range of music and to whom I dedicate this and all future texts.

Introduction

Take a look at W.S. Gilbert's early comedy, *On Guard*, and your eyes may light on the following passage:

MRS. FITZOSBORNE: Now that you've joined, we shall have such fun.
KAVANAGH: You're very good to say so.
MRS. FITZOSBORNE: Oh no! Indeed, I mean it.

Clear enough certainly but what exactly does 'fun' mean? Ben Jonson in his *Ode to Himself* lamented that his own 'dainty age' could not endure reproof and that he had better, therefore, maintain the high ground rather than serving as page-boy to the Stage which he labels a strumpet. Presumably, he is implying that in the early 17th-century satire can no longer count as 'fun' at all. Not only will the wolf's black jaw devour it. The dull ass's hoof will give it a kick. Fun must henceforth be harmless and borderline mindless. Otherwise, the comic playwright will be destroyed for his efforts.[1]

The range of comedic possibilities goes, of course, far beyond satire. But in Gilbert's case, satire is an essential ingredient. This applies even though he also tells us that life is a pudding full of plums from which care must be banished as a benumbing canker.[2] Possibly, fun should be a mix: it should combine sheer exuberant high spirits with a critical stance lambasting the follies of the age. The latter may be conveyed in the context of the former. Equally, the satirical point may itself be expressed in a surreal semi-patter-song scenario providing its own *joie de vivre*. Such applies the fable of the King who promoted everybody, leaving no such thing as a commoner, and of the monkey that deliberately and consciously decided to become Darwinian Man.

Follies of the age may, of course, also have a timeless element, and this perhaps is a vital ingredient in its appeal. Sometimes, a point made by one of Gilbert's satirically conceived characters nonetheless seems to sort with his own comedic position. When, for instance, Lady Blanche tells us that

The present as we speak becomes the past.
The past repeats itself and so is future.

Gilbert might be referencing his own conviction that comedy in its
motifs, viewpoint, and assumptions is both cyclic and repetitive.
Equally an apparently new and semi-surreal scenario may reference
age-old mythical ideas and practices. When Ko-ko devises a plan to
let Nanki-Poo live for a month like a fighting-cock before being executed as a sacrifice to the Mikado's decree and Titipu's future existence, his creator is drawing on the ancient idea of the scapegoat
sacrifice. According to Frazer, every year on the 14th of March, a
man clad in skins was led in procession through the streets of Rome,
beaten with long white rods, and driven from the city. He was called
Mamurius Veturius, that is, 'the old Mars' and the ceremony took
place on the day preceding the first full moon of the old Roman year.[3]
An animal variant explaining the term is described in the Old Testament (Leviticus 16:7–10). Here, we learn of two goats to be chosen
by lot: one to be 'for YHWH', and to be offered as a blood sacrifice, and the other to be the scapegoat to be sent away into the
wilderness.

The linking of old ideas with later comic scenarios is quite common
in Gilbert. In *The Grand Duke*, the crafty Ludwig unhesitatingly offers himself as a scapegoat substitute for the fury of Rudolph's subjects.
Though this is actually part of an ingeniously conceived scam, it references other ideas of a victim-alternative. When in 1591 Shah Abbas the
Great was warned by his astrologers that a serious danger impended, he
attempted to avert the omen by abdicating the throne and appointing
a certain unbeliever named Yusoofee, probably a Christian, to reign in
his stead. The substitute was accordingly crowned, and for three days
allegedly enjoyed not only the name and state but also the power of the
king. At the end of his brief reign, he was put to death, the decree of the
stars being fulfilled by this sacrifice. Abbas then re-ascended his throne
in a highly propitious hour, being promised by his astrologers a long and
glorious continuance.[4]

The linking of sacrifice with substitution and seasonal renewal is
only one of many areas in which Gilbertian comedy touches on long-
exploited *motifs*, legends, and stories. *The Grand Duke* indeed has both
the seasonal *and* the sacrificial elements. But this is not so much a book
about myth as about the incursion of its ideas and symbols into a long
comedic line. The essence of the thesis is that, as well as being a 'classic
Victorian', Gilbert is part of continuous self-renewing trends in the history of theatre comedy. This partly dictates not only what is included but
also what is excised. Biography will necessarily take a second place. It
will, however, be referenced when – as in the treatment of identity – the

dramatist's own somewhat traumatic childhood has a direct bearing on his theatrical output.

There are only two more caveats. The first one is that this is a book about comedy. It is not a study of the Victorian Theatre *per se* and takes little account of Gilbert's serious works. Gilbert is not solving the problem of the human condition. He is amusing us with it. It is in the *process* of this (and perhaps as a by-product) that he reveals to us his own jaundiced, if buoyant, response to the way human beings – and in particular the Victorians – think, feel, conduct themselves and live.

The second point is a reinforcement. It is a reminder that Gilbert, though distinct, is not unique – that his *oeuvre* is part of an ongoing theatrical process. Few writers bubble up out of nothing and, as Lady Blanche well knows, the past repeats itself, eventually becoming the future. It is, however, a *modified* future, since in comedy, as in life, time is a three chorded note with the bass note modifying the middle one, and both in turn variously affecting the accumulated effect of the top.[5]

It is still possible to enjoy Gilbert without an academic input. Humour is universal and, in order to work, has to be appreciated spontaneously rather than by the perusal of footnotes. Nonetheless, there is, I think, a gain in placing a comic writer in context, and particularly when the writer (as I claim) is as much a transitional figure as a time-bound Victorian. Eventually, I plan to produce another volume covering the genres in which Gilbert worked. In the meantime, it is his context that is central. It is by a consideration of this – by looking too at the dramatist's own temperament and talent and the constraints placed upon them – that we are able more fully to codify and finally evaluate the total creative achievement. That is the background. It is the setting and web of influences from which the individual works shine forth.

* * * * * * * *

Notes

1 Jonson implies that opponents and critics will destroy him if he dares to use comedy as a vehicle for social critique.

2 *The Gondoliers*, in *The Complete Annotated Gilbert and Sullivan* (ed. Bradley, O.U.P., 2016 edition), p. 965.

3 Frazer adds: 'As the ceremony took place on the day preceding the first full moon of the old Roman year (which began on the first of March), the skin-clad man must have represented the Mars of the past year, who was driven out at the beginning of a new one. Now Mars was originally not a god of

war but of vegetation. For it was to Mars that the Roman husbandman prayed for the prosperity of his corn and his vines, his fruit-trees and his copses; it was to Mars that the priestly college of the Arval Brothers, whose business it was to sacrifice for the growth of the crops, addressed their petitions almost exclusively; and it was to Mars, as we saw, that a horse was sacrificed in October to secure an abundant harvest'.

4 J.G. Frazer, *The Golden Bough, A study of magic and religion* (Project Guternbug Release: January 2003), Section XXV: *Temporary Kings.*

5 *New Yorker*, 1 March 2012, *Walking with Arthur Miller.*

Prologue
The Life and Times – A Gilbertian Sketch

The Life

W.S. Gilbert was born on 18 November 1836, at 17, Southampton Street, Strand, London, the son of a recently retired naval surgeon who later became a novelist. His mother, who on the maternal side was of Highland Scottish descent, was Anne Morris, daughter to Dr. Thomas Morris, under whose tutelage his father had learned the bases of surgery. An interview in the *Strand Magazine* in October 1891 includes a picture of a young Gilbert at the feet of his old grandfather, listening to his theatrical and other tales, the claim being that the old man had known Dr. Johnson, David Garrick, and Sir Joshua Reynolds. The impression given is that all this refers to his paternal grandfather. As the relevant William Gilbert died in 1812, the illustrated old gentleman must, however, be the non-theatrically minded Dr. Morris.

Apart from possibly spurious accounts of a kidnap in Naples, the young W.S. Gilbert next appears as a schoolboy in Boulogne (1842). This is before attending the Western Grammar School, Brompton (1846), and Great Ealing School (1849) where he became head boy at sixteen. In 1853, he enrolled in the Department of General Literature and Science at King's College, London, and in 1855 entered the Inner Temple as a student of law. The removal to France relates probably to his father's financial difficulties, later in 1844–1845 augmented by a particularly traumatizing court case. Still, the acquisition of fluency in the language – enhanced by briefly living there – may certainly be considered an advantage.

In 1857, Gilbert gained the qualification of Bachelor of Arts and in the same year passed a competitive examination for a clerkship in the Education Department of the Privy Council Office. He also began two decades of service in the militia, his relationship with the army being, in his own mind, linked with the military experience of his maternal forbears.[1]

1858 is significant as the year in which W.S. Gilbert first appeared in print. He did so with a translation of the laughing song from Auber's *Manon Lescaut*, performed as an item in the Promenade Concerts. More important, however, was the beginning of his contributions to *Fun*, a new rival magazine to *Punch*. This was facilitated by the inheritance in 1861 of £300, which had happily enabled him to resign the incredibly boring clerkship.

Gilbert was called to the bar in 1863, the year in which he published *My Maiden Brief*. He was by now trying out a number of written styles and (equally important) identities, not least the *Comic Physiognomist*. In 1865, he contributed briefly to *Punch*, and in 1866, he wrote *Dulcamara,* the first of five operatic burlesques. This was the year in which he joined the northern circuit as a barrister, earning only seventy-five pounds in two years. He had also started writing *The Bab Ballads*, later (from 1869) to be captioned as such in *Fun*.

Meanwhile, on 6 August 1867, Gilbert had married Lucy Agnes Turner. The marriage has been exhaustively analysed by David Eden whose own view of Gilbert is of a narcissistic bullying personality, with a retarded emotional and sexual development. There may indeed have been an element of infantilism and maternal substitution. By about 1872, he is writing to his wife as 'dear old lady' or 'My Darling Old Girl'. He is also signing off 'Ever your devoted husband, A BOY'.[2]

The emphasis on youth could be merely playful. It may link with a self-mocking vanity as regards his retained good looks. However, since Lucy was nearly twelve years younger than her husband (she was born on 14 November 1847), it also feeds in to what we know of his love of inversion, and topsy-turvy relationships. Significantly, in *Topsyturveydom* (1874), mothers are considerably more youthful than their progeny.

The early creative years show Gilbert following but refining existing burlesque and pantomime traditions. More interestingly, he also shows a marked penchant for imaginary other worlds, fairy *motifs*, and juggling with metaphysical concepts such as time. Overall, there is a mix of the innovative and adherence to conventional formats. His work with the German Reeds reflects both. Essentially, it helped hone a respectable decorous form of witty musical entertainment, aimed specifically at middle-class family audiences.

The middle-class mode remains key to much, but not all, of Gilbert's writing. The obsession with other worlds, the childlike propensities, the occasional manic high spirits, and the latent radicalism: all of these suggest a more complex, in some ways conflicted, personality. We also have to remember the constraints imposed by the low repute of theatre in Non-Conformist and some Anglican Establishment circles. 'Good God ... you have let that child go to a playhouse', was the shocked reaction of Emily Soldene's favourite uncle when he saw the eight-year old future Carmen dancing innocently with her shadow.[3]

The key date in terms of the creative life is probably that of the first meeting between Gilbert and Sullivan. This occurred at a rehearsal for a shortened version of *Ages Ago*, with the composer Frederic Clay making the introductions. The encounter is usually dated to 13 December

1869 and involved Gilbert (apparently) flooring Sullivan with a pedantic invented question of music theory.[4] Two years later, John Hollingshead brought the pair into creative partnership with *Thespis,* first produced at the Gaiety on Boxing Day, 1871, and incorporating Fred Sullivan, the composer's elder brother, in the cast. Sullivan then returned to 'serious' music with a *Te Deum* for the recovery of the Prince of Wales, an oratorio *The Light of the World,* and (in lighter vein) incidental music for *The Merry Wives of Windsor.* Gilbert busied himself with an assortment of musical and non-musical pieces, including *Happy Arcadia* (1872), *The Wicked World* (1873), *Sweethearts,* and *Topsyturveydom* (1874). He did, however, write two song lyrics for Sullivan settings, these being *Sweethearts* (linked with the play) and *The Distant Shore.*

Gilbert's last contribution to *Fun* was *Rosencrantz and Guildenstern* (1874). It was shortly after this that he and Sullivan began their twenty-one-year association under the impresario Richard D'Oyly Carte. The latter's father (another Richard) was the inventor of a new kind of flute, the founder of *The Musical Dictionary,* and the husband of a Welsh woman descended from the old Norman family of D'Oyly or D'Ouilly. A trained musician and occasional composer, Carte always felt a closer affinity with the charming, genially convivial Sullivan than with an often bombastic, prickly, and dogmatic W.S. Gilbert.

Gilbert's temperament has over the years been subject to much discussion and considerable vilification. The *Era* in 1897 claimed that 'Mr. Gilbert's abnormal self-esteem has, with advancing years, developed into a malady'. Seven years earlier, Sullivan wrote (with exasperated punctuation), 'How I have stood him so long! I can't understand!' In 1896, after conducting the première of the last collaboration, *The Grand Duke,* he decamped to Monte Carlo, writing, 'I arrived here dead beat, and feel better already. Another week's rehearsal with W.S.G. and I should have gone raving mad. I had already ordered some straw for my hair'.[5] Even after a comparatively friendly collaboration, Gilbert could darken the picture. When a song previously cut from *Fallen Fairies* was restored without authorial consent, an infuriated Gilbert attempted to apply for an injunction to prevent its ever being sung again.

The greatest creative disappointment in Gilbert's writing career was the failure of some of his serious and (he thought) poetical dramas such as *Broken Hearts.* He was also convinced that his best work included his social problem, human dilemma pieces such as *Brantinghame Hall* and *Charity.* Conversely, he despised (or affected to despise) the works that had brought him the greatest acclaim, writing in 1893 to Maud Tree, 'I don't think I am a vain man or I shouldn't have so poor an opinion of what I do'.[6] The infamous carpet quarrel of 1890 over Carte's handling of finances may have soured him further. It involved his bringing a successful legal suit against the impresario.

After the relative failure of the (actually very interesting) *Grand Duke*, Gilbert never fully regained the height of his former public celebrity. There was a strong sense that he was a tired dramatist rehashing mechanical old tricks. Nonetheless, he gained the recognition of a knighthood in 1907 and was still, to a degree, innovative in works such as his final piece *The Hooligan* (1911). This last play is a short character study in which the law confronts the individual with the force of Kafkaesque nightmare. The protagonist's mix of desperation, self-justification, self-pity, and impotent vengefulness shows the writer to be far more psychologically acute than the *Commedia dell'arte* origins of some of his work might suggest.

The death of Gilbert, like his temperament and personality, has received a very varied response. Like the hooligan Solly, he suffered heart failure, this time after apparently seeking to dive to the aid of a young lady (Ruby Preece) in difficulty swimming in his lake. David Eden reminds us that Gilbert – suffering from a weak heart – had been repeatedly warned about the dangers inherent in the lake – yet he bathed there up to three times a day, often urging his female guests to join him. Maybe he *intended* to die there or perhaps he looked on the lake as a destiny to be embraced or defied. In the *Daily Graphic,* the account of his death was tweaked. In reality, the elderly male Gilbert was bathing with a pair of nubile young girls. In the *Graphic,* the girls are standing on the bank, fully clothed, one then pluckily wading in to seize hold of him when he gets into difficulties.[7]

Gilbert's relationship with young women is another area that lies outside the scope of this book. Nonetheless, it has its interest. David Eden thinks that, in a quasi-paternal, perhaps idealizing way, he fell in love with Nancy McIntosh, the first Princess Zara, who ended up living in his household as a substitute daughter. Yet Eden also thinks of Gilbert as prurient, suggestive, and keen to titillate. Rupert Christiansen with casual crudeness goes further. To him, Gilbert is merely a 'classically terrible old sexist'.[8] This may be set against the memories of his niece, Mary Carter, who recalls him as 'the kindest and most human of uncles'.[9] She, of course, is retrieving pre-pubescent memories. She is not accessing the man who revelled in his 'flirtorium' or indeed the litigious bully we encounter in some of the law-suits.[10]

The many aspects to Gilbert do not preclude some distinct elements. One is his hyper-sensitivity to criticism and his dislike of being challenged, a trait which perhaps explains his tendency to relax with less critical children and with his various exotic pet animals. Another is his obsession with detail and his anally retentive impeccable neatness. Most notable of all is a sense of maternal rejection, associated with the childhood trauma of being sent in 1841 to live with his Aunt Julia and Uncle Seton.[11] This – linked with a distressing law-case centred on inheritance – also involved jealousy of his cousin Francis (aged four) who went with him and was far the more pampered. He was, after all, the delicate child of a dying father, Joseph Mathers Gilbert, who in November was to expire of consumption at the home of Gilbert's parents.

The other key characteristic is the need for retreat – the compulsion to discover or make a more beautiful world. An illustrated interview in the *Strand Magazine* (2 October 1891) commences with the line 'Mr. Gilbert lives in a little land of his own', going on to describe the ivy-covered mansion, the bee hives, the vineries, and the astronomical observatory.[12] This was Graeme's Dyke (or Grim's Dyke), an estate where there was 'nothing wanting to complete his miniature kingdom' and where a deep sense of concealment was achieved by a range of winding paths, diminutive forests, and secluded valleys.

The Gilbert of withdrawal is also the Gilbert who hates blood-sports and who doubts whether he has ever killed anything that was not making itself actively objectionable, though not so much through humanity as through awe at the wonderful mechanism of life.[13] Yet he was no recluse. He travelled extensively (as, for instance, on a three months' pleasure-trip to India straight after the opening of *The Gondoliers*) and was actually staying in Egypt at the time of Sullivan's death. Hence always there is a duality. In Gilbert, we see a man who is both solitary and gregarious, kind and vicious, considerate and bullying, generous and parsimonious. In his version of *Great Expectations,* Pip at one point says to Estella, 'You speak of yourself, as if you were someone else'.[14] Gilbert too has more than one voice. Identity in him is multifaceted. No two critics have matching views of this man. There is no art to pluck out the heart of the mystery that is W.S. Gilbert.

His Times

Since it is the contention of this book that Gilbert was more than a typical Victorian, I shall not belabour attempts to make him one. However, a few points are worth making, one being that his own dualities and pluralities often reflect a wider Zeitgeist. Side by side and often conflated in the Victorians are a sense of thrusting developmental progress and of decline – of expansionist confidence, on the one hand, and, on the other, of loss, shrinking vitality and an ebbing away of traditional certainties.

The sense of decline is very often expressed physically. It is seen in neurasthenia, nervous debility, and (in a sometimes-artificial form) in the greenery-yallery mode of the attenuated aesthetes. But, beyond that, the smallness of the human is something of a literary obsession. In *Two on a Tower*, Thomas Hardy explains in a preface that his intention was to 'set the emotional history of two infinitesimal lives against the stupendous background of the stellar universe'. From a subjective human perspective, the infinitesimal may seem more relevant – even more important – but from the point of view of the immensity we are mere pinpricks. This and aesthetic lassitude are not entirely new *motifs*. One of the twenty-nine-year old Coleridge's letters includes the melancholy announcement 'Sinking, sinking, sinking, I feel that I am sinking!'[15] Still, to link this with cosmic indifference is a largely new development. Gilbert in *To the Terrestrial Globe* suggests in miniature something similar, the main impression being of cosmic indifference.

The fear of meaninglessness is often itself related to temporal concepts. In *Dover Beach,* there is a strong sense of the sadness of ages, combined with a melancholy impression of everything – including religious faith and assurance – running down.[16] Such a shrinking of the sea of faith opposes the idea developed in *Dombey and Son* of a sea that is linking and eternal. Gilbert's sense of elegiac loss can be felt in lyrics such as *The World Is but a Broken Toy.* More personal in tone is the mood of *Eheu! Fugaces!* which presents the heavenly hope more as an increasingly urgent need than a trusted reality.

Eheu! Fugaces! presents us with an old man 'praying with all his breath'. He has been 'careless enough' in his youth and, though often at church (because the rector was his employer), only pretended to pray. This kind of double 'make believe' is no longer adequate, yet with death approaching, he finds the Book of the Earth far more instructive than any former teaching from the Bible. The *motif* of the *Ruddygore* madrigal – 'life is lovely all the year' – here ends on a grave-mound, a sense of the natural seasonal processes yielding to a far sadder note of inevitable decay.[17]

In addition to confident assertion and melancholy disillusion, Gilbert has a third mode: that of ironic (actually subversive) complacency. One example is Lord Mountararat's linking of brainless Establishment inactivity with the glories of Elizabethan sea-power and Wellington's land victories, here presented as if the inactivity and the glories presuppose each other. The odd thing is that Gilbert did still retain a very strong sense of patriotic endeavour and of militaristic and naval pre-eminence. In an interview in *Cassell's Magazine* (20 March 1900), we learn that 'Mr. Gilbert is at the moment preparing his next work – a labour of love – the book on the Crimea'. Apparently in his youth, the dramatist had been destined for the career of a Royal Horse Artilleryman, but the war ended before he could obtain his commission. The Crimea, however, 'has always been to him a kind of field of romance'. Indeed, 'when he visited it last year, he found from his voracious reading on the subject that every memorable spot was as familiar to him as if he had actually been there before'.[18]

The sense of opportunity denied, linked with the longing for a cause to believe in, may suggest that Gilbert's cynicism is that of the disappointed idealist. In this, he does link with his age which – albeit hardly uniquely – straddled hope and fear, confidence and doubt. The rather hollow tones of the hope and confidence are heard in lyrics such as

Tennyson's *Ode Sung at the Opening of the International Exhibition* (1862) and the 1887 *Ode for the Queen's Jubilee*. The former begins:

> UPLIFT a thousand voices full and sweet,
> In this wide hall with earth's inventions stored,
> And praise th' invisible universal Lord,
> Who lets once more in peace the nations meet,
> Where Science, Art, and Labor have outpour'd
> Their myriad horns of plenty at our feet.

The latter praises:

> Fifty years of ever-broadening Commerce!
> Fifty years of ever-brightening Science!
> Fifty years of ever-widening Empire!

Tennyson himself said that he wrote a great deal of it in the beautiful metre of Catullus, *Collis o Heliconii*. This failed to impress William Morris who informed his daughter Jenny: 'I am sorry poor old Tennyson thought himself bound to write an ode on our fat Vic's Jubilee ...'.[19]

The expansionist confident mode can be replicated many times. The 1886 *Colonial & Indian Exhibition Ode* features the regular repetition of the line *Britons, hold your own*, with a strong sense of the 'Imperial whole' which is personally protected by the deity. This is writing for public consumption on a ceremonial occasion, and perhaps we should applaud its idealism. But always there is an obverse side. According to *Dover Beach*, when religion was still intact, the world was dressed. It appeared furled in the folds of a bright girdle. Now with faith receding, it lies increasingly stripped and bleak. In this condition, the only hope lies in human love and interpersonal fidelity. Even so, we remain on a darkling plain swept with confused alarms, amid the night-time clashing of ignorant armies.

Whether Gilbert felt the 'struggle and flight' of these armies is debatable. In his (longish) short story *Johnny Pounce*, he includes a moving depiction of the much-hallowed Crimean veterans but also shows the tricks and contrivances involved in enlistment and has a contemptible officer cad as a major character. In *Dover Beach*, the reference is probably to a passage in Thucydides, describing the battle on the Epipolae, the cliff above Syracuse. This was a contest in which friend could not be distinguished from foe, and Diomilus and 300 of his men were ignominiously slaughtered.

The melancholy note may in Gilbert be counterbalanced by various factors. One obviously is black humour. Another is fortitude, as applies in Dame Carruthers' representation of the Tower of London. A third is wondering puzzlement, devoid of the elegiac. In *The Yeomen of the*

Guard, the Tower, 'unliving and undying', continues impervious to the pain, loss, and slaughter for which it is the medium even while being the city's guardian and bulwark. In *The Mikado*, there is another mode. The schoolgirls, awed by the great world, and wondering whether its pleasures and palaces are evanescent fantasies, are not so much elegiac as anticipatory. Their chorus bespeaks a trembling on the threshold of adulthood and a step to the brink of the unknown.[20]

i.

The melancholy strain in Victorian intellectual thinking may be seen as a necessary corrective. *Something*, after all, is needed to balance the mirror opposite of arrogance in the face of a buoyant imperialist expansion. One of the challenges here was that of evolutionary theory, but so too were archaeological discoveries, suggesting other cultures, other times, and the sweeping away of entire civilizations. In Egypt, in the 1880s, William Flinders Petrie was the first to make a fully comprehensive study of the Great Pyramid. Earlier, and nearer home, William Cunnington (1754–1810) began his Wiltshire excavations in about 1798, leaving a considerable mark on the works of Thomas Hardy.

The idea of the decay of Empires predates Queen Victoria, as is clearly indicated by Shelley's *Ozymandias* (1818). But in Gilbert's day, there was also a more local sense of undermined potency. Hardy's *A Tryst at an Ancient Earthwork* tells us:

> We can almost hear the stream of years that have borne [past] deeds away from us.

and, in relation to dead souls:

> There arises an ineradicable fancy that they are human voices ... the lingering air-borne vibrations of conversations uttered at least fifteen hundred years ago.[21]

This is the sort of writing that stresses both vulnerability and a lingering semi-ghostly endurance. The result is both like and unlike *Ozymandias* where a sense of time-challenges includes an emphasis on an ultimate barren and negative emptiness.

The changes wrought over time are a very common Gilbertian *motif*, whether treated quizzically (as in *Topsyturveydom*) or – as in *Utopia Limited* – ruefully in a time-based comic song.[22] Another linked mode is to mock other times and historical figures, as happens in the waxworks scene in *Robert the Devil* where to the tune of *A fosco cielo* (from *La Sonnambula*) characters such as King John, Richard 111, and Mary Tudor step forth to complain about being remodelled and re-cast (in a double sense). The way in which the King John transmutes from the noble William Wilberforce to the worst of English monarchs focuses Gilbert's enduring preoccupation with identity.[23] It is also a wry burlesque comment on the reinterpretation and reappraisal of actual historical figures, one example being Boadicea who, largely neglected in the Middle Ages, was treated as an unwomanly aberration in a 1753 Richard Glover play and later (via Smollett) became increasingly hailed as a national inspiration.[24]

Boadicea's Victorian makeover has its relevance in that the less than heroic maidens of *Princess Ida* can be seen inverting the trend of the inspirational female warrior. Gilbert was interested in the Iceni queen, not least because she had associations with his own dwelling. One interview, describing 'a little tour' round his grounds, refers directly to the fact that the edge of Gilbert's property is 'the ancient boundary of the Kingdom of Casivellaunus [sic], whose capital was at Verulamium'. This prompts Gilbert to comment: 'It is only about a mile from here ... that Boadicea killed herself to escape the attentions of the Roman General'. Such at least, he says, is the tendency of the 'old story' which is clearly of considerable personal interest.[25]

It is not my contention that *Princess Ida* necessarily draws on Boadicea, though Lady Blanche's eccentric warlike accoutrements may hint as much. But Gilbert's quizzical duality of response certainly offsets the increasing veneration of the warlike heroic female. Princess Ida is noble, but she is also misguided. Like most people with a mission, she is devoid of proportion, limited in common sense, and unwilling to accept the venial weaknesses of the less committed. By contrast, the Victorian Boadicea was becoming an icon. Her very name, meaning 'Victory', became associated with that of the Queen. Gilbert, always suspicious of inflated adoration, often undercuts it, notably at the end of *The Pirates of Penzance* where the pirates' instant yielding to the intoning of the royal name becomes more a matter of burlesque than of a genuine patriotic sentiment.[26]

The fact that Gilbert could mock an institution does not mean that he had anarchistic intentions. It is rather a case of seeing a church by daylight and, in Empire terms, hoping that Britain really is, or may be, all that she professes.[27] The contrary mode – that of inflated uplift – is encapsulated in the vast bronze sculptural group of Boadicea in her war-chariot that from 1856 adorned the Thames Embankment. The embodiment of martial prowess, the lady here personifies two aspects: (a) the nation at its most maternally protective and (b) the Britannia-figure, spear in hand, who defends British Liberty against all comers.

ii.

However much the British Empire may have re-invented Boadicea, scientific advances – as well as declining faith – were steadily undermining traditional assumptions. Gilbert himself was not opposed to the benefits of science. At Grim's Dyke, a cupboard to the left of a 'beautiful Chippendale bookcase' contained a telephone which not only communicated with the general system but had a special wire to the Savoy. The whole of the house from the kitchens to the roof was lit by electric light, and a steam-engine, a dynamo-engine, and accumulators had infiltrated the basement. The impression here is of all mod cons, aesthetically co-ordinated, but developmental progress has its downside. In *Sweethearts,* the spreading town covering a once-rural vista seems a subject for regret. In *Patience,* the Elysian Fields are an unattainable fantasy. Beyond Grim's Dyke's winding walks, diminutive forests and secluded valleys, an ugly commercial world might well be inclined to build on them, if only it could get the chance.[28]

The ugliness of contemporary life is well attested in the Pre-Raphaelite and Aesthetic repudiations. Burne Jones' angels are, as he said, a defiance of, and protest at, the factory buildings increasingly disfiguring the landscape.[29] More metaphysically, a sense of decline is almost certainly – if rather ironically – augmented by scientific advance. Charles Lyell's *Principles of Geology* (1830–1833) has as its central argument the view that 'the present is the key to the past' – a point prefiguring some of Lady Blanche's cross-time links, as indeed those in T.S. Eliot's *Burnt Norton.* Lyell's main point is that ancient geological remains could, and should, be explained by reference to geological processes now in operation. The book is also notable for being one of the first to use the term 'evolution' in the context of biological speciation.

The geological interest can be felt not just in science but also sometimes in the arts. William Dyce's *Pegwell Bay*, exhibited at the Royal Academy in 1860, shows looming cliffs, a shell-strewn beach and isolated figures – actually members of the artist's family – fishing independently, dwarfed by their environment. Significantly, in the sky, unseen by the fishers, is Donati's comet, first observed in June 1858. This too evokes the immensities of time and space. It hints at a growing sense that the universe is not fixed but unstable and moving to eventual collapse.

How far Gilbert worried about human littleness is impossible to determine. His frequent reference to *little* maids and *little* men does miniaturize human beings but is complicated by being interwoven with concepts of charm and, in the female case, with a safe distancing from adult sexuality. We do know that he himself was wilful, dominant, and controlling. Jessie Bond tells in her memoirs that he refused to think about or even concede her marriage: 'That was so characteristic of him; anything he did not want to happen, or wish to believe, had no existence in his mind'.[30] Perhaps, he found it unsettling to conceive of anything that reduced or outflanked him. The martinet with the cruel wit, tight-lipped dignity, and explosive temper would find a disposing God hard enough, but a random uncaring Universe – one possibly in terminal decline – if taken personally, might seem considerably worse.

The unsettling aspects of geological excavation are not simply a retrospective assumption. Ruskin refers to the 'dreadful hammers' of the geologists chipping away at the rocks and in 1851 remarks that he hears their clink at the end of every Biblical verse. The impression is (a) of excavation chipping away at biblical assertion and (b), latently, of a loss of hope. The mood is reflected in the opposite (melancholy) face of Tennyson whose poem *Despair* led the atheist Edward Alveling to state that 'All freethinkers owe a debt of gratitude' to the poet. Also relevant is the latter's prose play *The Promise of May* (1882) which was interrupted frequently during the soliloquies about modern man's freedom from ethical constraint, the noisiest protests emanating from the Marquess of Queensbury who claimed that it distorted freethinking views.[31]

The sense of lost assurances leading to loss of hope is mirrored in much late Victorian literature. In *Jude the Obscure,* the doctor's fashionable interpretation of the death of Little Father Time is that it reflects 'the coming universal wish not to live'. The individual pathology is associated with the growing sickness and degeneracy of a generation. Significantly, physicists such as William Thompson (1824–1907) were from the early 1850s making studies of the rate at which the sun's energy was being drained. The conclusion was that eventually it would burn itself out, though estimates of when varied from mere decades to millions of years.[32]

The idea of running down is often held in tension with evolutionary progress. 'The time must come', wrote Thomas Huxley in 1891, 'when evolution will mean adaptation to a universal winter, and all forms of life will die out, except such low and simple organisms as the Diatom of the arctic and Antarctic ice'.[33] One view of Gilbert might be that he is fully aware of this, his response being to laugh in the face of dissolution and chaos and play up the absurdity in everything. His own treatments of evolution are ingeniously farcical. Lady Psyche divides the genders, concluding that Darwinian Man, far from being made in the image of the Creator-God, is in essence a shaved monkey. Her song actually works in two ways: it gives an unflattering picture of the Victorian male, while also showing up the scientific ignorance of the feminist singer, who is herself of the same biological genus.

The loss of human assurances can be countered in various ways. One is quite simply that of denial. Another is to seek compensation in an illustrious family pedigree, and a third – more satirically – is to accept but subvert the whole concept. The last two are what happens in Pooh-Bah for whom it becomes a matter of pride to be able to trace oneself back to the most primitive and brainless of organic matter. The mirror opposite is the *kudos* that General Stanley seeks to find in purchased ancestors and that Mabel (in a surviving but excluded lyric) finds in a probably fictitious ancestral relation.

The downside of evolutionary progress was the sense that, though taking us to a peak of perfection, it might also reach a tipping-point into decline and collapse. H.G. Wells' *The Time Machine* (1895) not only includes a climactic vision of the end of the world. It also has a sociological implication, its underground ape-like Morlocks being emblematic of a deprived lower caste workforce, while the Eloi, attenuated to near-lifelessness, suggest the declining aristocracy. In them, we see a class that had long exploited the underlings now becoming their food-prey, reduced to an effete, indolent and essentially apathetic helplessness.

H.G. Wells' Morlocks have something in common with Gilbert's resentful hooligan. They are an underclass worm that has turned. The difference is that Gilbert's Solly is not so much a representative of a lower-class workforce as of a social type – the individual tipsy lout gathered from the gutter.[34] His victim status is seen in his oppressive dream. The Judge – not the hooligan – here becomes the monster, his two arms stretching forth from his red robes growing longer and longer until they reach a quarter of a mile, at which point they clutch the hooligan round the gullet, squeezing him till he is virtually throttled. The surreal horror is increased by the presence of a nightmare crowd. These nod in harmony as if saying, 'Just so; we quite agree; go on'.[35]

Gilbert's awareness of an underclass can be seen throughout his works, not least in his play-adaptation of *Great Expectations,* where one of the main characters, Magwitch, has been brought up to be 'a varmint'. The more cosmic elements meanwhile go beyond individual deprivation. In *The Time Machine*, the eventual end-of-the-world scenario is entirely chilling. Menacing reddish crab-like creatures slowly wander the blood-red beaches chasing enormous butterflies in a world covered in simple lichens. Making short jumps through time, the Traveller sees Earth's rotation gradually cease. The sun grows larger, redder, and dimmer, and the world falls silent and freezing as the last degenerate living things die out.[36] Obviously, Gilbert in his comedy never enters upon such realms, but the thought of his terrestrial ball rolling on through pathless realms of space is almost equally chilling.

The idea of a brutalized Yahoo workforce seeking a cannibalistic revenge obviously has no part in the world of comic opera. But even comparatively mild social comment is, in Gilbert, regarded as suspect. The magazine *Truth* considered Strephon's '*Fold Your Flapping Wings*' entirely inappropriate for the clown, while *The Theatre* lambasted the author for utilizing the entire libretto as the vehicle for conveying 'a feeling protest on behalf of the indigent, and a scathing satire on the hereditary moiety of our Legislature'.[37] Actually, such *motifs* add substance to the fairy elements, which can be regarded as an ingeniously original way to filter challenging material. In any case, Gilbert is not always on a radical soapbox. In *Utopia Limited*, it is precisely because everything is socially so easy and conditions are (ironically) so Utopian that rebellion is finally fomented.

The idea of a too-perfect society really suggests one with too much input from an over-intrusive state. The opposite is suggested by Samuel Smiles, whose *Self-Help* (1859) promulgated the view that society is like a series of ladders up which the virtuously self-reliant can rise to prosperity.[38] In 1861, Smiles published an article from the *Quarterly*, renamed *Workers Earnings, Savings, and Strikes*, where he claimed that poverty in many instances is caused by habitual improvidence.[39] He quotes a workman earning 50s–60s a week (above the average pay of bank clerks) who is content to inhabit a miserable ill-sited single room simply because of 'carelessness'. Gilbert is aware of such things but tends (as in Strephon's song) to blame lack of education and a bad upbringing. Ideal worlds of fairy fantasy are the other face of this interest. They are an escape and a comfort, with the further advantage of allowing him, as monarch, to dictate all the rules.

The desire for order mixed with fantasy may relate to Gilbert's dislike of ragged or inconclusive endings. In 1901, he tells William Archer, 'In real life no curtain descends to tell you that the story is at an end. In point of fact, in real life the story never *does* end'. However, in literature, at least he wants a few certainties, not least some indication of what becomes ultimately of the characters.[40] Evidently, he wishes that life also had clearer pointers. Despite outward complacency, he has an underlying sense of the chaos beneath the controlled.

Gilbert's neat tidiness of construction was by the end of his life seeming theatrically outmoded. But it was never fully superseded, besides which his use of certain mechanical devices and stock characterizations later fed into the more mechanistic modes of the Theatre of the Absurd. Seeing the ridiculousness of the world's man-made forms, Gilbert inverts them as if in a pre-emptive strike before they invert themselves. Another possibility is that this is a childlike defiance of adult actualities – one in which Gilbert, the BOY gets his revenge on adults, not least for having insisted he grow up.

One clear point about Topsyturveydom is that it combines Gilbert's adherence to a sense of structure with a wish for defiance or escape. Structure exists but is subversive. It enables a personal mastery of retreat from reality. In addition, it is sometimes minatory. By inverted reflection, the topsy-turvy landscape mirrors an insufficiency or hypocrisy in existing norms.

Though something of a Gilbertian trademark, topsyturveydom is in fact far from entirely his own invention. In *Aucassin et Nicolette*, a French mediaeval *chantefable*, the King of Torelaore is found in childbed while his wife is away fighting in the army. Nicolette (a French name) is a Saracen, while Aucassin (al-Kassim) is French. In a parody of *amor de lonh* (distant love) the troubadour is actually the disguised female Nicollette seeking her adored young man. Battles are waged with cheese and apple projectiles, wars here being fought *with* food, rather than being part of trade-wars over it.

Gilbert's topsy-turvy vein undoubtedly looks back to the *Aucassin* mode. But there is a difference since, as well as literary parody, he offers a considerable implication of social critique. It is true that, in his more anarchic moments, even Gilbert can sometimes invoke chaos. But latent too is a psychological need for order. Topsyturveydom as a kingdom is contained. It is a controlled indulgence. There is no sense that Gilbert for ever wants to stay there. Far more than the *Aucassin* poet, W.S. Gilbert retains a wider adherence to the definitive structures of his world.

iii.

The need for order has in Gilbert another aspect. It also implies a need for *sense*. Nonsense for him has two facets. Sometimes, it is a release from the self-imposed constraints. But it can also be an indulgence which paradoxically shows how much he values its obverse. In *The Astounding Adventure of Wheeler J. Calamity*, the opening line is 'I cannot say how it came to pass but I found myself at the bottom of the pond!' This is Absurdist, yet is set again a background which is only an exaggerated version of a life-denying Victorian reality. Calamity's dissenting evangelical background offsets what happens to him when (tipsy from unwonted liquor) he falls into the pond, entering the upside-down word of irreverent ill-regulated burlesque.[41]

Escape from reality – whether disconcerting or life-affirming – can take numerous forms, one being an escape into history and/or into an idealized version of the national past. Gilbert's mode here is to tend more towards the universal and timeless. In *The Yeomen of the Guard,* both collaborators wanted a piece that was human and emotionally straightforward 'with no topsyturveydom or deliberate anachronism in the writing'. They also wanted to prove that 'English is (next to Italian) the very best of all European languages for singing purposes'.[42]

Gilbert's relatively limited interest in historical comparatives may derive from mistrust of the Mediaevalizing tendency of the aesthetes and Pre-Raphaelites. But attitudes *to* the past are, in Gilbert, frequently glimpsed. In *Patience*, Bunthorne pours scorn on those who are eloquent in lauding Queen Anne's (very dull) glory-days or in tracing the last days of culture to the Court of Bonaparte's Empress. In *The Mikado,* there is another variant. One category on Ko-ko's little list consists of those who praise every century but this and every country but their own.[43] The caveat is that it is always dangerous to take the view of a character as the view of his creator. Gilbert, we know, took full advantage of the costuming and staging opportunities of Victorian aestheticism. He was well read in classical and other history. One omission is in the area of historical folklore. He neglects (for instance) the resurgent interest in a folk-hero (non-pantomime) Robin Hood. In stage terms, he shows little affinity for the attractions of Arthurian myth.

The rebirth of interest in English historical legend may itself have sociological implications. Like Burne Jones' angels, it was partly a counterblast against increasing industrialism, utilitarianism, urbanization, and the scientific challenge. Man, the most highly evolved human species, may be increasingly powerful, but, like Hardy's Henry Knight, he is also hanging from an evolutionary cliff, facing eventual extinction.[44] This perhaps encouraged a retreat. It leads into folk-myth, fairy story and the misty notion of a heroic semi-legendary past. The reaction is understandable. It is not easy hanging by your finger-lips onto life, limb, and European civilization – particularly with the sea (from which life emerged) pounding below, and your own eyes staring helplessly into a cliff-face embedded with the fossils of the long extinct.

iv.

The above suggests one aspect of the Victorian *Zeitgeist*. But we should not overstate the pull of the past. In 1873, in a paper delivered at a Cambridge conference, the economist Alfred Marshall claimed that progress was at hand: given adequate education and suitable occupations, the working class could progress 'till the official distinction between working man and gentleman has passed away'. Admittedly, even *he* feels that the labour-intensive repetitive work of working men tends to keep their characters rude and coarse. But his outlook is optimistic. The time will come when, by occupation at least, every man will be a gentleman. In the meantime, there are gradations. Some – but not all – occupations demand and supply powers and activities of mind that directly promote culture and refinement. These, elevating even the naturally coarse, can stimulate sympathy and fellow-feeling 'with men far off and near'.[45]

The idea of amelioration is appealing but not all-embracing. Even Marshall admits the existence of Gilbert's tipsy louts and hooligans, not to mention a raft of workers whose work coarsens and dissatisfies. Numbing and repetitive, it produces precisely the unrest and physical cravings that 'hound a man .... to his undoing'. As for the naturally unregenerate, they are beyond salvation. Thomas Hardy refers to crowds of Londoners as 'a molluscous black creature' having nothing in common with humanity, throwing out 'horrid excrescences and limbs' into neighbouring alleys.[46] Here, one question is whether London is the monster spawning similar offspring or whether it is the people who have spawned the monster that is the city.

From considerations of socio-economic realities – and particularly from the toil and sweat of urban and industrial ugliness – one escape is into theatrical spectacle and another into myth-making and fantasy. Gilbert himself often railed at the sort of elaborate effect that required endless setting up and taking down, one example being the fountain which so annoyed him in *Harlequin, Cock-Robin and Jenny Wren*.[47] This is not to deny that the spectacle mode had a long history. At the Vauxhall Gardens on Tuesday 30 May 1786, there was the first of a large number of military fêtes. On 18 May 1787, the Season opened with a Subscription Masquerade. On 6 August 1801, there was a 'Splendid

Gala, involving a Grand Oriental Car, richly decorated with trophies, and drawn by elephants', while in 1816, the sensational Madame Saqui walked on the high wire, accompanied by music and fireworks. By Gilbert's day, things were changing. There was competition from the music-halls, and Vauxhall itself was becoming more profitable as building land.[48] But a sustained taste for masques, pageants, and chivalric entertainments remained, reaching its Edwardian zenith under two leading 'pageant-masters', Louis Napoleon Parker and 'the man who staged the Empire', Frank W.T.C. Lascelles.

The pageant mode had itself a strong historical basis. One example is Sullivan's 1864 cantata, *Kenilworth, A Masque of the Days of Queen Elizabeth*, performed first in Birmingham and later in the same year at the Crystal Palace. This looks back to a real event when Robert Dudley, aiming at matrimony, entertained the Queen at Kenilworth Castle with a nineteen-day Arthurian entertainment, costing an alleged £1,000 per day, and featuring (for instance) the spectacular emergence of the Lady of the Lake, attended by two water nymphs, floating towards the Queen on a false island surrounded by blazing torches.[49] One insertion in the Sullivan piece is a lengthy love-duet based on the opening scene of Act 5 *of The Merchant of Venice*. More widely, the text draws on Scott's 1821 novel, contemporary accounts circa 1575, Shakespearian blank verse, and the librettist Henry Chorley's own additional fiction.[50]

The *Kenilworth* pageant mode was not an isolated event. It continued into and beyond the *fin de siècle* years, being referenced in Sullivan's *Ivanhoe* (1892) and *Victoria and Merrie England* (1897) and reaching patriotic heights in Edward German's *Merrie England* (1902). Folklore elements meanwhile arise in Thomas Hood's *The Plea of the Midsummer Fairies* (1871), Sullivan's *King Arthur* music (1895), and the 1892 Robin Hood drama, *The Foresters,* which has a (bad) libretto by Tennyson who had also tried his long-winded hand at historical drama in works such as *Queen Mary* (1876), *Harold* (1876), and *Becket* (1888). The first was longer than *Hamlet,* the lavish and enlarged orchestra needed for it requiring the removal of numerous seats, for which Tennyson himself offered to cover the cost.[51]

The vogue for historical drama may have helped the success of *The Yeomen of the Guard,* but Gilbert himself was not entirely satisfied. He felt with regret that the public still preferred topsy-turvy scenarios, and later declined the chance of being the librettist for *Ivanhoe.*[52] Where he *does* seem to draw on historical precedent is in his use of *motifs* of acting and historical revolution. This is seen, for instance, in *The Grand Duke,* drawing possibly on the 1848 European revolutions which in February led to the flight of Louis Philippe, abdicating in favour of his nine-year-old grandson, and fleeing in a cab under the pseudonym Mr. Smith.

The *Grand Duke* link relates mainly to Germany, one notable casualty being Wagner (forced to flee into exile from Dresden, going first to Paris and then Zürich) and another Ludwig 1 of Bavaria whose open relationship with an Irish dancer and actress, Lola Montez, caused widespread scandal. Lola's attempts to launch liberal reforms through a Protestant prime minister had not only outraged the state's Catholic conservatives. It had prompted student demonstrations in demand for constitutional reform. Also notable is the later 1886 abdication and mysterious death of the theatre-loving Ludwig 11. The big difference is that Ludwig 11's opulent rule was entirely unlike that of Gilbert's penny-pinching Grand Duke, at one time called Wilhelm (after the German Kaiser) and ruling not Bavaria, but Hesse-Halbpfennig.

The name Ludwig for Gilbert's low comedian is itself of interest. Perhaps, it was randomly chosen, but equally, it may have been transferred, for topsy-turvy or politically expedient reasons, from two deposed monarchs to a leading light in the conspiratorial party. Whatever the truth, it is intriguing to relate *The Grand Duke* to a wider context of revolutionary uprisings. One example is that of Russia whose Nihilists, in March 1881, would assassinate Czar Alexander 11. More significant, however, is a revolution in Belgium, for which Daniel Auber's *La Muette de Portici* (1828) served as an incendiary signal. Like *The Grand Duke*, *La Muette* has a King for a Day *motif* and a plot linked with disrupted marriage. In *The Grand Duke,* the unpopular Grand Duke is preparing for an ultimately thwarted marriage to the enormously wealthy Baroness von Krakenfeldt, while the Lisa-Ludwig marriage is also threatened. *La Muette* actually starts with a marriage, but it brings only misery to the heroine who is discarded in favour of a more politically and hierarchically appropriate union.

Though linked, *La Muette* and *The Grand Duke* are certainly not blood-brothers. One difference is that Auber's plot has nothing to do with an acting company. Another is that Gilbert's rejected Lisa (a *seconda donna*) is not ousted till the end of Act 1 and even then is not willingly jettisoned. What does link and add interest to both is the incorporated political element. This has a long history, as shown by Dryden's *Albion* and *Albanius*, which bases the hero and his supporters quite clearly on the Stuart dynasty. One pointed aspect is the political allegorizing of the Tory message and denigration of the Whigs. The enemies here include a figure representing the Earl of Shaftesbury 'with Fiend's Wings, and snakes twisted round his body'. Adding to his discomfort he is 'encompassed by several fanatical rebellious heads, who suck poison from him, which runs out of a tap in his side'.

v.

Albion and Albanius (1680–1685) is in the court masque tradition but is also the first *full-length,* all-sung English opera. By the 19th century operatic political issues were increasingly censored but an undercurrent of subversion survived. In terms of plot, *La Muette* is loosely based on the historical uprising of Masaniello, a Neapolitan fisherman, who in 1647 rebelled against Spanish rule, part of the impetus being the seduction and abandonment of his mute sister, Fenella, by Alfonso, son of the Neapolitan Viceroy.[53] The climax comes when, against the backdrop of an erupting Vesuvius, Alfonso makes a march on the city against the people. Masaniello, king for a day but dying of poison, falls in the act of saving the life of Elvira, Alfonso's bride. Fenella thereupon leaps into an abyss, while the fugitive noblemen again take possession of the city.

The interest for us of this melodramatic scenario is the combination of theatre, revolution, and political unrest. The backdrop for *La Muette* was a celebration – in subservient Belgium – of the fifteen-year reign of the Dutch King William 1. The opera was to be the crowning glory of a three-day festival, the trouble being that the King's anticipatory announcements met with open plans for revolt.[54] Gilbert's Rudolph himself clearly fears assassination, talking of being 'deposed tomorrow and perhaps blown up with dynamite'. This allows Ludwig to seize on his alarm, implying, whether truthfully or not, that the revolt does indeed involve an intended killing.[55]

The above links should not blind us to big differences. Unlike Ernest's theatrical company, there is no proof that the cast of *La Muette de Portici* were part of a revolutionary conspiracy. On the other hand, like the Dummkopf company, they *did* know revolt was likely. Prior to the performance the *Courrier des Pays-Bas* issued a coded call for attendees to leave prior to the opera's fifth act. This was to be a trigger for the uprising. The most commonly cited moment for the exodus is during or after the second act duet *Amour sacré de la patrie*. This is reinforced by a contemporary account telling us that when Masaniello (Lafeuillade) launched into the invocation '*Aux Armes!*' the public could no longer be restrained.[56]

So what does all this suggest? One answer is that it does at least hint at a climate. What *The Grand Duke* does is to tap into links between the stage and revolution – links which applied not only in the Belgium of 1830–1831 but also in the Bavaria of 1848 through the involvement of the *actress* Lola Montez. That said, *The Grand Duke* as a whole is not primarily political. When the King for a day lengthily extends his rule, it develops into a comically surreal Bacchanalia. It also incorporates elements of the *Commedia dell'Arte* and aspects of ancient seasonal myth. Taken as a whole, these are no bad guide to the playwright's priorities. Gilbert is aware of the current of his times. He both draws on and subverts many of the aspects. But his main debt is not socio-historical – not to politics, not to science, not to economics, and certainly not to moral philosophy. It is, rather, to a long-standing mythological and comic tradition – a tradition that it is now time to explore.

* * * * * * * *

Notes

1 For more on the Sutherland link, see Eden, David, *W.S. Gilbert – Appearance and Reality* (Sir Arthur Sullivan Society, 2003), pp. 34–39. Gilbert's maternal relations were of higher social standing than the paternal ones, his grandfather – despite alleged literary connections – having been a grocer in Commercial Row, Blackfriars, London.

2 Quoted in Pearson, Hesketh, *Gilbert, His Life and Strife* (London: Methuen, 1957), pp. 33–34. See also Eden, *W.S. Gilbert – Appearance and Reality*, p. 103.

3 Soldene, Emily, *My Theatrical and Musical Recollections* (London: Downey and Co. Ltd, 1897), p. 5. An exception was that as a child Emily was allowed to attend Phelps' Shakespeare productions at Sadler's Wells. See Stedman, Jane W., *Gilbert Before Sullivan* (London: Routledge and Kegan Paul, 1969), p. 4.

4 For full details, see Crowther, Andrew, *Gilbert of Gilbert and Sullivan* (History Press, 2011), p. 84. Crowther quotes How, Harry, *Illustrated Interviews: Mr. W.S. Gilbert*, p. 340.

5 For the sources of these views, see *The Era*, 16 October 1897 ('*Mr. Gilbert and Mr. Grundy*') and Sullivan's Diary, 6 May 1890, quoted in Ainger, Michael, *Gilbert and Sullivan: A Dual Biography* (O.U.P., 2002), p. 310. Sullivan's outburst after *The Grand Duke* can be found in a letter to Burnand, 12 March, 1896, quoted in Jacobs, A, *Arthur Sullivan* (O.U.P., 1984), p. 367. For the *Fallen Fairies* contretemps, see Crowther, *Gilbert of Gilbert and Sullivan*, p. 230.

6 W.S. Gilbert to Maud Tree (16 June 1893), quoted in Pearson, Hesketh, *Beerbohm Tree* (Greenwood Press, London; based on 1956 edition). pp. 74–75. Also in Crowther, *Gilbert of Gilbert and Sullivan*, p. 236.

7 Eden, *W.S. Gilbert – Appearance and Reality*, pp. 110–111. The inquest returned the girls to the water. In the *Daily Graphic* one rushed to the house for help while one – also fully clothed – waded into the water from the shore.

8 *Daily Telegraph*, Interview with Mike Leigh, 1 February 2015.

9 Letter to the *Daily Telegraph*, 6 January 1956.

10 See Eden, *W.S. Gilbert – Appearance and Reality*, pp. 159–221.

11 See Eden, David, *A Tale of Two Kidnaps* (Sir Arthur Sullivan Society, 1988), p. 14. Julia was the sister of Catherine Gilbert who was the mother of Francis. Julia's husband was Seton Laing (1810–1887), an indigo broker. It was he who acted as 'next friend' to Catherine and her children as plaintiffs in the law case concerning her children's custody.

12 How, Harry, *Illustrated Interviews, No. IV: Mr. W.S. Gilbert* (Strand Magazine, 2 October 1891), pp. 330–341.

13 Archer, William, *Real Conversations. Recorded by William Archer. Conversation V – with Mr. W.S. Gilbert* (Pall Mall Magazine, 25 September 1901), pp. 88–98. See also *The Critic*, 39 (1901), pp. 240–250, reprinted in Archer's book *Real Conversations* (1905), pp. 106–131.

14 W.S. Gilbert, *Great Expectations* (Dickens Dramatized Series of Plays, Theatre Arts Press, 2015), p. 32.

15 Letter to Davy. Monday 4 May 1801. The doctor blames irregular gout with nephritic symptoms.

16 Arnold, Matthew, *Dover Beach* in *The Collins Book of Best-Loved Verse* (Harper Collins, 1992), p. 9, ll. 15–20.

17 *Ruddygore*, in *The Complete Annotated Gilbert and Sullivan*, pp. 705–707.

18 Salaman, Malcolm C., *William Schwenck Gilbert: 'The Man, The Humorist, the Artist'*. *Cassell's Magazine*, 20 March 1900. pp. 413–421.

19 Quoted in Henderson, Philip: *Tennyson, Poet and Prophet* (Routledge and Kegan Paul, London and Henley, 1978). Nowadays, the Imperial Institute is no more. Only the Patriot-Architect's white, green-domed tower survives as a landmark to a departed age.

20 *The Mikado*, in *The Complete Annotated Gilbert and Sullivan*, p. 577.

21 Hardy, Thomas, *A Tryst at an Ancient Earthwork*; *Detroit Post*, March 1885.

22 *Utopia Limited*, in *The Complete Annotated Gilbert and Sullivan*, pp. 999–1003.

23 W.S. Gilbert, *Robert the Devil* (W.S. Gilbert Archive), pp. 24–25.

24 Smollett, Tobias, *History of England* (1757). The frontispiece here has an illustration produced by Charles Grignon, based on the work of Francis Hayman, showing the queen bare-breasted, wearing a chain-necklace, and carrying a wicker shield, a spear, and a hare. See Hingley and Unwin, *Boudica: Iron Age Warrior Queen* (Hambledon Continuum, 2003), pp. 143–144.

25 Wentworth, Henry, '*Mr. W.S. Gilbert at Grim's Dyke*', *Graphic*, 17 November 1906, p. 637 et seq.

26 More on Prince Albert's interest will appear in a book I am currently writing on Gilbertian *motifs*, the relevant section being entitled, *Time and History*. For the yielding of the pirates, see *The Pirates of Penzance* in *The Complete Annotated Gilbert and Sullivan*, p. 261.

27 *Utopia Limited*, in *The Complete Annotated Gilbert and Sullivan*, p. 1079.

28 *Patience*, in *The Complete Annotated Gilbert and Sullivan*, p. 295.

29 See *Guardian* 23 December 2006. A famous photographic portrait taken by Barbara Leighton at the time he was working on *The Star of Bethlehem* shows the elderly artist balanced on the ladder with his huge resplendent Christmas angel in the background. It seems as if Burne Jones is about to be swept up in her great wings to join the heavenly host.

30 Bond, Jessie, *The Life and Reminiscences of Jessie Bond* (London, Bodley Head, 1930), p. 201.

31 See *Modern Thought,* January 1882, pp. 7–10, and Smith, Elton Edward, *Tennyson's 'Epic Drama'* (University Press of America, 1997), p. 22.

32 See Ruskin, John, letter to Henry Acland, in *The Works of John Ruskin*, ed. E.T. Cook and Alexander Wedderburn, Library Edition, 39 volumes (London, 1903–1912), Volume 36, p. 115. For Hardy's *Jude the Obscure*, see especially Part 6, Chapter 2. For William Thompson, see Sharlin, H, *Lord Kelvin, The Dynamic Victorian*, Pennsylvanian State University Press, 1979, p. 112.

33 Huxley, Thomas, *The Struggle for Existence in Human Society, in Evolution & Ethics, and Other Essays* (London, 1895), p. 199.

34 *Iolanthe*, in *The Complete Annotated Gilbert and Sullivan*, pp. 434–436.

35 W.S. Gilbert, *The Hooligan, Century Magazine*, LXXXIII (November, 1911), p. 99.

36 Wells, H.G., *The Time Machine* (Heinemann 1895). See especially Chapter XI.

37 Quoted in Bradley. *The Complete Annotated Gilbert and Sullivan*, p. 436.

38 Smiles, Samuel, *Self-Help* (Part 1 of 7). The opening quotes J.S. Mill: 'The worth of a State, in the long run, is the worth of the individuals', and Disraeli: 'We put too much faith in systems, and look too little to men'.

39 For more on this and other miscellaneous writings, see *The Autobiography of Samuel Smiles, LLD*, ed. T. Mackay, 1905, New York edition.

40 Archer, *Real Conversations,* pp. 88–98.

41 Printed in *Fun Christmas Number*, 1865.

42 Letter to William Archer (5 October 1904), quoted in Crowther, *Gilbert of Gilbert and Sullivan*, p. 183.

43 *The Mikado*, in *The Complete Annotated Gilbert and Sullivan*, p. 573. The *Patience* reference is on p. 293.

44 Hardy, Thomas, *A Pair of Blue Eyes*, Chapter 22.

45 See Reisman, David, *Alfred Marshall: Progress and Politics* (Routledge Revivals, 15 April 2011), p. 19.

46 Quoted in Ford, Mark, *Thomas Hardy, Half a Londoner* (Belknap Press, Harvard University Press, 2016), p. 19.

47 Extract from A.E. Wilson *Pantomime Pageant* (Stanley Paul and Co., 1947. n.l.a.), quoted in *W.S. Gilbert and Pantomime* in *It's Behind You* (Internet Download).

48 See *Vauxhall Gardens, 1661–1859: Full Chronology*. Internet website.

49 For more on this, see www.elizabethan-era.org.uk (Elizabethan Masques). Torches were a feature of many popular pageants and entertainments. Mummers, for instance, would enter the Great Halls of nearby aristocrats with loud blasts from trumpets and drums and the blaze of many torches. Over the years dialogue was added to the mummer's plays but the element of disguise continued and the identities of the performers were concealed.

50 See C.D. Booklet Sir Arthur Sullivan: *The Masque at Kenilworth* (Symposium Records, 1999) for more details on this and other pageants.

51 Henderson, Philip, *Tennyson, Poet and Prophet* (Routledge and Kegan Paul, London and Henley, 1978), pp. 167–168, 173.

52 See 'Blank, Blank!! THE NEW OPERA AT THE SAVOY. A CHAT WITH MR. GILBERT' (*Pall Mall Gazette*, 3 December 1889, reprinted in *Chicago Tribune,* 29 December 1889, p. 17 et seq.

53 Fenella is named from Sir Walter Scott's novel *Peveril of the Peak*, a work revolving round a 1678 Popish plot and featuring a similarly named deaf and dumb dwarf.

54 The advertised revolution did not follow the course of the operatic one. In the opera Masaniello, though shrinking from murder and unnecessary cruelties, leads the rebels to such effect that the city magistrates present him with the royal crown, proclaiming him King of Naples. Then, after being poisoned, he is assailed by the counter-revolution, dying nobly as stated. The Belgian case ended with a less dramatic scenario. An 1830 London Conference recognized Belgian independence, leading to the installation next year of Leopold 1 as King of the Belgians. (See Renieu, Lionel, *L'Histoire des Théâtres de Bruxelles: depuis leur origine jusqu'à ce jour* (Duchartre & Van Buggenhoudt, 1928), p. 744.)

55 *The Grand Duke,* in *The Complete Annotated Gilbert and Sullivan*, p. 1129–1131. It is important to note that the ending sets Rudolph back in place, so the topsy-turvy dispensation is ousted, albeit with a new Grand Duchess instead of the intended Baroness.

56 The lyrics include the lines: 'Mieux vaut mourir que rester misérable! Pour un esclave est-il quelque danger? Tombe le joug qui nous accable, Et sous nos coups périsse l'étranger! Périsse l'étranger!' The singers owe their country their life and their country owes liberty to them.

Part 1

Modes, Forms, Theories, and Origins

What is comedy? Can we define it? Broadly speaking, the answer is yes. However, there is no precise quick summary. James Robinson Planché calls his version of *Beauty and the Beast* (12 April 1841) a 'grand comic, romantic, operatic, melodramatic fairy extravaganza'. His first stage work *Amoroso, King of Britain* (Covent Garden, 1818) was announced as a 'serio-comick bombastick operatick interlude'. Obviously here the title parodies itself. But even the (slightly) less flamboyant ones cover more than one aspect. *The Discreet Princess; or The Three Glass Distaffs* (Olympic, 26 December 1855) is 'A new and doubly moral though excessively old melodramatic fairy extravaganza'. More soberly, *The Camp at the Olympic* (7 October 1853) is 'An introductory extravaganza and dramatic review in one act'.[1]

It may seem odd to start a work on Gilbert with reference to another playwright, but my whole point is that Gilbert was part of an ongoing stream. Planché himself drew on 18th-century burlesque, gradually reducing the element of critical parody (e.g. of Italianate operatic stage styles) and increasing fanciful elements. He defined his later work as embodying the 'whimsical treatment of a poetical subject'. This marks a development from (for instance) Henry Carey's *Dragon of Wantley* (Haymarket, 1737) which is a 'straight' burlesque of Italian opera. Another Carey mode is that of the burlesque 'tragical tragedy' *Chrononhotonthologos*. This not only parodies 18th-century theatre bombast but also constitutes part of an intermittent tradition of nonsense-writing, later continued by Gilbert.

The above takes us straight into the heart of the Victorian stage. It does not, however, help in tracing ultimate origins. Here, the key point is that the Greek word *komos* (from which we get 'comedy') is linked with *komodios*, an actor or singer in the revels. The Old French *comedie* simply means 'a poem', but the word also incorporates *aoidos*, 'singer, poet', from *aeidein*, 'to sing'. This in turn relates it to *oide*, which gives us the word 'ode'.

It is worth stressing these musical links, not least because they are often so central to Gilbert. The second act of *The Grand Duke* is, except in its lack of bawdry, essentially a *komos* – one in which the chorus become increasingly wild and drunk led by Ludwig who is linked with Komos (Comus), the god of revelry, merrymaking, and festivity. Even the rhymes are rather unruly, 'Corybantian mani*ac kick*', for instance, finding itself paired with 'Dionysiac or *Bacchic*'. This too emphasizes wildness, appropriate to Komos, who was son and cup-bearer to the wine-god Dionysos, himself an exponent of sensuous abandon.[2]

Ludwig as play-acting Grand Duke has much in common with the play-acting *komodios*. The focus of a wine-drenched orgy of feasting and revelry, he marks the obverse of the real ruler's regime of elaborate ceremony, a near-starvation diet, and parsimonious economy. Yet Gilbert nearly always inverts or modifies his originals. For one thing, Ludwig is hen-pecked by his *prima donna* Grand Duchess and pursued by importunate others. For another, he himself admits the inconveniences of Ancient Greek modes. Compared to this, the original Komos seems to have been a thoroughly wild lad. Generally, he was depicted in one of two ways: either as a winged youth or as a *satyriskos* (child-satyr) with balding pate and asses' ears. Philostratus (*Icon.* i. 2) describes him as he appeared in a Neapolitan painting, drunk and languid after a repast, his head sunk on his breast. For fear lest the flames of his torch come too near, he bends his lower left leg over towards the right, holding the torch out on his left-hand side.[3]

The hint of danger in revelry exists in comedy from the first. Sometimes – as in the flame reference above – it suggests a possibility of burning up – of exceeding safe behavioural limits. There can also be hints of anarchy, as applies to some extent in Ludwig's usurping court. In that case, the irony is that everyone is strictly ranked according to company precedence. There is hierarchy within abandonment. Elsewhere, abandonment itself is suspect. Noting that Komos has his head bent forward and his face in shadow, Philostratus interprets an implied moral: 'The moral, I think, is that persons of his age should not go revelling, *except with heads veiled*'. Perhaps the idea is of a too precocious indulgence. Perhaps it is that neither the reveller nor others should see or even admit – their potential excesses.

The caution advocated above suggests a latent preference for the Greek ideal of *sophrosyne* with its notions of temperance, moderation, prudence, and self-control. But early accounts of the *komos* tend to be purely factual. Hesiod's *Shield of Herakles* links *komos* with wedding festivities, as applies in the Act 11 opening chorus of *The Grand Duke*. Pindar describes *komoi* as taking place at the city festivals, while Demosthenes (admittedly rather more judgmental) mentions their occurring after the *pompe* and *choregoi* on the first day of the Greater Dionysia.[4]

One notable thing is that, for Philostratus, there seems to be a developed sense of unnaturalness. It is true that there is tenderness in the description of the god's crown of roses which are painted 'fragrance and all'. But he also mentions 'the castanets and the flute's shrill note and the disorderly singing'. Peals of laughter (he says) rise up; women rush along with men, wearing men's sandals and garments 'girt in strange fashion'; men 'put on women's garb and ... ape the walk of women'. In the 19th century, Gilbert will rail against men in women's clothes, but he will also show himself fascinated by identity changes and gender confusion. A good example occurs in *Happy Arcadia*, where the treatments, though tantalizing, are far less pornographically overt.[5]

There is no doubt that the *komos* was a risqué affair. Unlike the rest of the Dionysiac celebration, it lacked a chorus leader, had no script, and (apparently) managed without any rehearsal. In the performance of Greek victory odes for winning athletes (the so-called *epinikia*), the choral singers often present themselves as *komasts* or extend an invitation to join the *komos*, as if the formal song were a preliminary to spontaneous, often obscene, revelry. It is true that a few *komoi* were expressly described as *semnoí* ('modest', 'decent') but perhaps the exceptions suggest an alternative rule.

Whatever form they took, *komoi* were not much in line with Victorian requirements. In December 1867, the *Tomahawk* defined true comedy as 'a real picture of human Nature, lighted up with brilliant flashes of wit'. It was a form of 'teaching under cover of genial satire, a true lesson from the book of life'.[6] Actually, Victorian burlesque and pantomime were vibrant rather than gentle, sometimes becoming overblown and vulgarized. But even then they lacked the full anarchic formlessness of most of the *komoi*. In the Neapolis painting, vibrancy yields to weariness: 'Their crowns are no longer fresh. Crushed down on the head on account of the wild running ... they have lost their joyous look'. The flowers, too much handled, seem to wither before their time. Hands beaten like cymbals resound in a (presumably unpleasant) noisy unison.

Noise and vulgarity are rarely a Gilbertian concomitant. But the *Tomahawk's* insistence on geniality remains, in Gilbert's case, questionable. Seymour Hicks labelled him 'incapable of geniality, especially in the company of men'. Horace Hutchinson recalls his delight in employing a mordant wit, without showing signs of aggression in his face.[7] In the *Athenaeum*, the 1868 *Bab Ballads* edition is damned for offering the dreariest and dullest fun we have ever met with. 'The poems have no real humour nor geniality, nor have they the broad farce of burlesque'.

The idea that Gilbert's comedy is not quite in the orthodox genial mode is suggested sometimes by Gilbert himself. 'Am I destined to revolutionise the art of comic writing?' he writes. 'Am I the man who is to write the burlesques and extravaganzas of the future? Are the managers and editors of light literature doomed to fall at my feet in humble obeisance?' This, however, is hardly a credo or mission-statement; it is a joke at his own expense. Beyond that, there is nothing revolutionary in what he plans to offer. Fun in the sense of light burlesque entertainment is still at the core. There is even a hint that it will be a fairly statically conceived, non-developing, genre: 'Is it to me that society at large must look for its amusements for the next (say) forty years? To these questions I unhesitatingly reply, "I am! They are! It is!"'[8]

My own view is that we should not take Gilbert's teases at all seriously. His comedic vision actually did develop, and the boasting mode of the above shows him yet again inventing a self-satirizing persona. Possibly, the egotism is a reality. Possibly, it is simply here parodied by being taken to excess. But Gilbert, like Evelyn Waugh, conveyed even the serious aspects of life through the vehicle of jokes. One oddity is that he combined a free-wheeling surreal sense of absurdity with a strong element of rigorous control. Even at their zaniest, his works usually have a remorselessly logical underpinning. There is ample evidence of his determination that, once honed and refined, his texts should stay largely inviolate.

Compared to the Gilbertian control, the early Greek drama was a rather more fluid experience. Admittedly, it is now difficult to re-create exactly how it developed, but it is quite possible that originally much was improvised, some of the two-way dialogue deriving from banter exchanged between processional revellers and watching bystanders. Such invention and interpolation – combined with a fairly limited range of characters – was to continue well into the *Commedia dell'Arte*. Nor did it stop there. Victorian low comedians also often improvised and 'gagged', though Planché, and later Gilbert, vigorously opposed this tendency.

Planché's own comic works come in three main modes. First, there are those using figures from Greek or Roman mythology parodying classical drama. Second are works derived from fairy tales, owing much to Charles Perrault. Third, there are the 'dramatic reviews' (again French-derived), defined by the playwright as 'a running commentary on recent metropolitan events'.[9] Gilbert incorporates all these but is most distinctive in his parodying of current theatrical modes and *motifs*, one example being the sentimentalized orphan. In Watts Phillips' 1869 play *Not Guilty*, not only does Alice Armitage describe herself as 'an orphan ... without a friend'; Jack Snipes, the convict with the heart of gold, describes how he went to the bad and became a thief, purely to support a little boy orphan. This, eliciting the comment, 'Poor fellow!' looks forward to a direct parody treatment in *The Pirates of Penzance*.[10]

i.

Apart from the concept of *komos*, the biggest influences on Gilbert's comic mode are the *Commedia dell' Arte* and (in particular) the Harlequin character. As a boy, Gilbert admired the agile Harlequin and despised the mischievous Clown but later this changed. Clown became for him 'a good fellow, whom it would be an honour to claim as an intimate companion'. Harlequin by contrast now seemed 'a rather tiresome muff who delayed the fun while he danced in a meaningless way with a plain, stoutish person of mature age'.[11] Later still, there was another variant. Not only was Gilbert concerned at the lack of retribution or accountability for Clown's anarchy. He also came to deplore the glaring difference between Clown and Harlequin as characters and the often rather seedy actors who embodied them.

The origins of Harlequin are not distinct but one pre-*commedia* theory links him with the mischievous devil or demon in French passion plays. This originates with an Old French term *harlequin* or *hellequin*, first attested in the 11th century, by the Anglo-French chronicler Orderic Vitalis (1075–circa 1142). Vitalis records the story of a monk who, while wandering at night on the Normandy coast, is pursued by a troop of demons led by a masked, club-wielding giant. Known as *familia herlequin* (or sometimes, *familia herlethingi*), these are probably a French version of the Germanic Wild Hunt, still known in France as the *Mesnée d'Hellequin*. Also linked is the English figure of *Herla cyning* ('host-king'), probably referring to Woden and further related to the German *Erlkönig*, derived not from 'elf-king' but from King Herla.[12]

The anarchic, disruptive origins of the Harlequin character link him with the wilder aspects of the Greek *komoi*. But he is far more sinister. Originally, he is a black-faced (sometimes red-and-black faced) emissary of the devil, arising from the smoke of hell chasing the damned souls of evil people into his own Underworld. Also relevant is hairiness. In the play *Le jeu de la feuillée* (circa 1276), Crokesot, the messenger of Hellequin and the Underworld, is described as *hurepiaus*. This links with the words *herle* and *hair*. It relates to the idea that demons had hairy faces linking too with *hure* from the Old French for the head of a boar, wolf, or bear.[13]

The hairy bestial aspects of the harlequin figure can be related to the Greek satyrs (σάτυρος *satyros*) accompanying Dionysos. Usually, these are shown with hairy goat-like features and a permanent erection. Early artistic representations may also include horse-like legs, though in black-figure pottery of the 6th-century B.C., human legs are more common.[14] The emphasis on fecundity suggests a common comedic *motif*, though in the satyr play, the treatment is strikingly bawdy. Rather like 18th-century pantomime, such plays were short tailpieces, one such being performed in counterpoint to each of the trilogy of tragedies in the Athenian Dionysia.[15]

The idea of the creature who is half-beast, half human has, like comedy itself, both a joyously liberating and a shadow side. In Harlequin's case, this includes a murderous possibility. In an evolved story based on a hint in *Genesis*, Lamech, Cain's grandson, shoots an arrow at a hairy goat-like man whom he thinks to be a beast, only to find out that this is his grandfather. He has thus shot 'Hairy Cain', the first murderer,[16] with 'Harlequin' as a derivative. Compared to this, goat-like satyrs are relatively amiable. Lovers of wine and women, they roam to the music of pipes (*auloi*), cymbals, castanets, and bagpipes, chasing the maenads with whom they are carnally obsessed. Later, the chase *motif* will become dominant in the Harlequinade, with an anarchic but less obviously lustful Clown taking over some of the satyr-play's zest. Before this, in late classical art, there seems to have been a double effect. The faun-satyrs may be shown dancing with graceful nymphs, but the dance itself – the *sikinnis* – on their part is still grotesque and orgiastic.[17]

The alleged but unproven links between satyrs, Cain and Harlequin, may be too much for many readers. But there are plenty of other etymological choices. In Cantos XXI and XXII of Dante's *Inferno*, there is a devil by the name of Alichino, while in a 1514 French manuscript (written in Latin), the French demon Herlequin is first fully identified by the harlequin name. Norse links, meanwhile, suggest a connection with Old High German ancestral ghosts, the *Hella cunni*, kinsmen of Hel, the goddess of the Underworld. Hel was a daughter of Loki, associated with tricks and mischief. One fairly strong possibility is that these became corrupted into the black devil who is a Harlequin derivative in mediaeval mystery plays.[18]

The various possibilities about Harlequin's origins make them more a 'Great Possibility' than actual fact. But the Harlequin of Victorian Pantomime must have come from somewhere, and here we do have a few clues. In 1262, a character called Hellequin appeared as a masked and hooded devil in *Jeu de la Feuillée* (*The Play of the Bower*) by Adam de la Halle. Then – probably – he infiltrates the Mystery plays as a black devil.[19] Later in the 16th century, he becomes a known Italian *commedia* figure. In this transformation, he seems to have been introduced by Zan Ganassa who is mentioned in 1568 as the leader of a troupe in Mantua. The character was then popularized in Paris in 1584–1585 by the Italian actor Tristano Martinelli, becoming a stock character – and increasingly an agile and graceful dancer – after Martinelli's 1630 death.[20]

Not just Harlequin but all the *commedia* figures have a doubtful chronology. *Il Dottore*, for instance, is first recorded as a comic foil to Lucio Burchiella's *Pantalone* in 1560 but undoubtedly existed earlier. Harlequin by this time was also acquiring a clear but not entirely fixed personality. Generally, he is a cheat and a liar and, though athletic and agile, is cowardly in the face of violence. The cowardice is obviously comedic but rather challenges yet another theory of his origins – namely that his name derives from a 9th-century knight, Hellequin of Boulogne, who died fighting the Normans.

The route from demon or murderer to Harlequin or Arlecchino includes many other variants. Frequently, he dresses in women's clothes and advises Columbine on every detail of make-up and fashion. In one 18th-century Dutch scenario, he is depicted as the 'mother' of a child.[21] Almost certainly what Gilbert found most appealing was not this but the magical aspect. A Harlequin sheet printed in 1824 shows the character as a magical enchanter, leaping through a mirror which is presumably a hole in the scenery. In other respects, his story by now is one of pursuit, he and Columbine being kept apart by the girl's father, Pantaloon, upon whom his servants play various tricks.

It was John Rich who made the chase scene – in which Pantaloon is joined by his servant Clown – into a key pantomime feature. To introduce it, Harlequin was equipped with a slapstick or wooden bat with which he would knock down hinged flaps in the scenery, thence taking the characters to numerous locations, all controlled by his magical implement. Among Gilbert's further suggestions is the idea of constraining the character according to the classical unities. In *A Stage Play*, he goes further, giving us a plot involving a Harlequin who takes holy orders in order to be accepted as a suitable fiancé for the daughter of an Archbishop. Later, elements of this will resurface in *The Fairy's Dilemma*.

The importance of Harlequin to Gilbert might not have been so great but for Joseph Grimaldi (1778–1837). He refigured the Harlequinade, introducing (for instance) butter slides and sausages which suddenly come to life. With his bizarre nonsense songs, Grimaldi also changed the entire clown role. From stupid, loutish 'feed' he became a comic grotesque, complete with white face and red cheeks, a pie-crust frill, baggy trousers, a cavernous mouth, and an elastic, intensely expressive countenance. Here even the elasticity suggests liberation. Later Buttons' comic routines and the re-invented Dame's glorious absurdity would both have roots in Grimaldi's slapstick excess.

It is not only Clown and Harlequin who caught the young Gilbert's imagination. Early in 1863 he contributed a series on *The People of the Pantomime*, beginning with the Pantomime Demon (King Alcohol) and including the Pantomime Monarch, Prince, Servant, and the Comic Business, many of whom were already going out of fashion. In the case of Alcohol, this is attributed to the ridiculous over-enthusiasm of the total abstinence party. Nowadays Alcohol's demon cohorts (Djin, Wiski, Brandi and others) have been usurped by Envy, Hatred, Malice and other more inward passions. Meanwhile, the abstinence party has overdone its case so much as to render temperance ridiculous. The demon's more bibulous cohorts are indeed regarded by the 'lightly disposed' as rather convivial fellows, just right for the good fellowship of a party.

The two-part separation between the Harlequinade and the preceding play first finds full expression in *Robinson Crusoe* (1781), a pantomime featuring Guiseppe Grimaldi as Harlequin Friday and an Italian actor, Carlo Delpini as Crusoe himself. Later 19th century changes include the growth in importance of the transformation scene, and eventually the reduction of the final Harlequinade. Usually, during the transformation, key actors would take off the giant head masks that they had worn for the main story and reveal themselves as the main *commedia* characters. Increasingly, however, the transformations became events in themselves, trick objects being inverted to alter their nature, and elaborate scenery flown in on wires or spectacularly changed by means of more flaps.

ii.

The influence of the *Commedia* can be felt quite often in Gilbert's characterizations. Columbine, for instance, looks forwards to the lively pert soubrette exemplified in Pitti-Sing, Tessa, and (more seriously) Phoebe Meryll. It is the sort of thing also found in Polly in *Not Guilty*, where the on-off comic love relationship with Triggs, the lawyer's clerk, shows her pulling the strings, appearing wayward but actually remaining entirely virtuous.

There is no doubt that – outside the penny gaffe and the music hall – virtue was far more of a prerequisite than in the original *Commedia*. But in pantomime, at least liveliness and anarchic zest certainly remained a feature. Pantomime, for the mid-Victorians, suggests a piece based on a nursery story or folk tale, in which the main characters are eventually changed into those of a riotous Harlequinade. Other forms are different. 'Review' means (roughly) 'revue' in its literal sense: a further look at recent happenings. Burlesque, employing similar techniques, extends its subject matter to include contemporary plays, operas, news events, or anything else reducible to travesty. *Burletta*, meaning 'little joke', is a brief comic opera with strong elements of (sanitized) *Commedia dell'arte* farce.[22]

The difficulty of knowing how to define comedy is in part an acknowledgement that there are numerous types. City comedy, dating back to Aristophanes, and more recently familiar from Ben Jonson, Samuel Foote, and Arthur Murphy, is a different genre from romantic comedy with its emphasis on the magical, the exotic, the faraway, and transformative. Also infinitely varied is the manner of *playing*. One of Planché's demands as stage manager (=director) was that even in extravaganzas the characters be played straight.[23] This too was not new. Recalling John Gay's *The What D'ye Call It* of 1715, Dr. Johnson remarked that 'Mr. Cromwell, who could not hear what was said, was at a loss how to reconcile the laughter of the audience with the solemnity of the scene'.[24]

The treatment of the comic as serious was later to be a trademark Gilbert technique. Perhaps, both he and the Wilde of *The Importance* had read Planché's Preface to *High, Low, Jack and the Game* (Olympic, 1833) which attributes the play's success to the performers not attempting to be funny 'but acting it as seriously as possible'.[25] The other (non-Gilbertian) requirement was sentiment. Laughter was to be caused by pleasure *in*, and sympathy *with*, innocent or benevolent goodness, combined with eccentricity or absurdity. An unidentified critic quoted in Edgar Pemberton's *Life of Tom Robertson* praised that playwright for finding 'Like all genuine humorists … the source of humour to be very near the fount of tears'. This links back to the 18th-century *Comédie Larmoyante* and to the Cult of Sensibility brilliantly mocked by Jane Austen.[26]

The genteel sentimentality of mid-Victorian comedy makes even its stock types very different from those of the (much more improvised) *Commedia*. The hostile *Athenaeum* review of the *Bab Ballads* stresses the need for fellowship. 'To have real fun you must have a real human heart ... fun requires sympathy quite as much as sentiment'. Absent here is the *grotesquerie* of characters such as Pantaloon with his oversized hooked nose, grubby goatee beard, slippers, and skullcap.[27] Humour requires a quaint but sympathetic insight 'into the most contradictory moods and tenses of human nature'. It must suggest 'a power of love for all human things inspiring and underlying the sense of whimsicality'.[28]

The above requirement certainly is not the main feature of the *Bab Ballads*. According to the review, they 'do not contain a single thread of interest, nor a spark of feeling. The illustrations are painful, not because they are ugly, but because they are inhuman'. James Ellis regards the poems as being pre-pubescent, matching the 'Bab'/Baby alias of the author. They are addressed to the child in each of us, though not as a redemptive force – not a Little Nell or Tiny Tim – but as a half-naïve, half demonic anarchist.

However we regard Gilbert's babies, there is no doubt that the child in the adult is a common comedic ingredient. In *She Stoops to Conquer*, Tony Lumpkin is a lusty overgrown child-booby, immature but essentially genial and harmless, as suggested by the diminutive 'kin' in his surname. In *The Importance of Being Earnest*, there is a more sophisticated variant. Algernon, confronted in Act 3 by Lady Bracknell, becomes no more the airy irresponsible prankster but the constrained temporarily obedient schoolboy. At the same time, his repetition of a 'thank you' formula to Lady Bracknell is latently subversive.[29] The tone of grateful respect hints at sardonic mockery, a point suggested by the young man's demure echoing of Cecily's own politely decorous obedience.

iii.

The child in the adult is, then, a common comedic *motif*. But there are many variants in the treatment. The Gilbertian child is not constrained but exuberant. His spite and vengefulness are selfishly asocial.[30] Possibly, this is a reflection of Gilbert's dysfunctional childhood. Possibly, it suggests a mix of splenetic impotence with a wish-fulfilment mode of active defiance. But it could equally be not so much deliberately cruel as a matter of anarchic, subversive high spirits, looking forward to Evelyn Waugh, Joe Orton, and Ben Elton. What is odd is that many critics find Gilbert not so much splenetic as cold. In his review of *The Importance*, George Bernard Shaw writes, '... There is a scene between the two girls in the second act quite in the literary style of Mr Gilbert, and almost inhuman enough to have been conceived by him'.[31] Presumably, he is thinking of *Engaged*, though whether he found that play equally 'adulterated by stock mechanical fun' is not recorded.

Shaw is not alone in remarking a lack of empathy, a common consensus being that Gilbert can be whimsical and tender but is not naturally warm-spirited or generously expansive. Seymour Hicks' view was that he was double-sided: though not genial, he *did* love to amuse pretty ladies. Mrs. Alec-Tweedie was convinced that 'most of his conceited remarks were uttered in a spirit of fun'.[32] One complication is that in his published persona, he often appears aggressive, pompous, contemptuous, and snobbish. So, he does in his 'breakthrough' article for *Fun* (17 January 1863), *The Shoeblack and the Crossing-Sweeper Nuisance*, linked perhaps with a cartoon from *Punch* for 26 January 1856 showing a middle-class man importuned for money by a gaggle of boys employed to sweep horse manure and other filth out of the way.

The crossing-sweeper scenario is certainly indicative. In Dickens, it allows for the pathos of Jo. In Gilbert, it is an excuse for (comic) pontificating:

> Having occasion, sir, in pursuance of my daily avocation – that of a clerk in the War Office – to traverse the distance between my chambers in Clement's Inn and my office in Pall Mall pretty frequently, I feel myself in a position to protest as an interested party, against a public nuisance which you should undertake to abate.[33]

Here, the tone undercuts any validity we might have been tempted to attribute to the message. The man is a self-satisfied windbag, such pomposity and impercipience being the hallmark of many of Gilbert's literary personae.

The circumlocutory mode is not the only one. Sometimes, it is combined with direct insult, as, for instance, when the 'Comic Physiognomist' signs off after eighteen episodes of his first series expressing the supremest contempt for the British Public glorying in the fact that his impenetrable incognito allows him full rein to say so. The public, he asserts, do things because they are told to do them. The C.P. tells them to go home and go to bed and be ashamed of themselves, and he hasn't the slightest doubt but that they will do it.[34] The effect looks towards the comic rudeness of the opening chorus of *The Mikado* which deliberately flies against all the usual conventions of welcoming and informing your audience. Still, it is no surprise that Gilbert's dining club associates called him the *enfant terrible*. It helps explain why he had to found his own club simply to achieve the popularity of membership.[35]

iv.

The question of Gilbert's comic tone is a matter of dualities. Is he, in a spirit of irony, assuming an entertainingly rude persona for our delight or is he *really* the egocentric, vaunting, insensitive, and disdainful figure he projects? Perhaps, he is both. Perhaps, the mask allows him to say what he really thinks but for which he needs a whimsical cover. Sometimes, the insults and rudeness are humanized by Sullivan's music, as in the graceful *Silver'd is the Raven Hair* where the tension between melody and words produces an effect of rueful but stoical pathos. Elsewhere, one wonders whether comedy is for him a medium of self-revelation or an escape. Certainly, there is a sense of strain in trying to marry the workaday material adult world with the childhood realm of alternative fantasy and dream.

The desire to create and depart to alternative worlds is often illustrated. In *Getting Up a Pantomime* (*London Society*, 1868), Gilbert suggests that adult trauma is deeply rooted in the unhappiness of the child. Yet paradoxically, it was the childhood world that gave him the greatest enchantment. The words Harlequin, Columbine, Pantaloon, and Clown have, he says, an agreeable magic carrying us back to the most miserable period of existence – early childhood. The theatre was a 'mystic building'. It offered 'incomprehensible beings of all descriptions' holding 'astounding revels', none of them accounted for, but together making 'absolute realizations' of a fairy mythology which he had almost incorporated with his religious faith.[36] Such unmixed enchantment is the equivalent to Eliot's penny world behind the screen. Perhaps, resentment at its loss led to a reaction. Perhaps, it explains the mordant, disillusioned joke of imparting rudeness to a Chorus of Japanese when the Japanese at the Knightsbridge exhibition had been always so impeccably polite.

The love of childhood theatre trips is not in itself so very unusual. It has strong links with the concept of the circus in *Hard Times*. But in *Hard Times*, the industrial world of grim, dehumanized polluted Coketown is itself an inverted circus, while the real circus – tawdry and unsophisticated though it be – offers the tinsel and glitter of escape. In Gilbert, escapist worlds tend more to be fairy ones and even these may become tarnished. In *The Wicked World* (story version), Fairyland is polluted by the arrival of men. In *The Fairy's Dilemma*, an intended removal to the Realms of Radiant Rehabilitation is preceded by terrible indignities, making a mockery of fairy-based transformational possibilities. Another tendency is for the magical to be treated as prosaic and the nostalgic tinged with the unpleasant. In *The Astounding Adventure of Wheeler J. Calamity*, the 'magical' Realm of Burlesque exists at the bottom of a pond and, far from being a place of release, imposes on its unhappy evangelical visitor a demand to crack jokes, speak in rhyme, and digest meaning from things said in the most unruly of unmanageable metres.

Wheeler Calamity's story is, of course, a jest. We revel in the killjoy's discomfiture. But sometimes, effects are more complex. In *The Wicked World*, only the absence of men allows contentment to be fully sustained. In the story version of *The Fairy's Dilemma*, there is not even an ideal to start with. Nostalgia exists side by side with a deflationary mockery of something beloved. First printed for Christmas, 1900, the tale features a fairy – Fairy Rosebud – who has been brought up under the tutelage of a stout but experienced old hand, now 'long retired from the active exercise of the profession'. Unfortunately, many of the taught accomplishments are not congenial to the matter-of-fact Rosebud. While Calamity was expected to come up with endless puns and instant rhymes for words such as 'month', 'silver', 'orange', 'bismuth' and 'writing-desk', Rosebud has to talk in rhyming decasyllabic couplets, while working her magic for ungrateful or disagreeable people. The one comfort is that considerable freedom is allowed: 'A syllable or two more or less than the academic allowance ... is regarded as no serious lapse'. There is also a 'liberal latitude' permitted in the matter of rhyme.[37]

The main comic dichotomy in The *Fairy's Dilemma* is that fairies, expected to be charming airy sprites, are in fact the reverse. They are 'very commonplace people', regarding their activities as 'ridiculous and unmeaning drudgery'. In this particular case, the task is to oppose the Demon Alcohol whose demonism is given the usual accoutrements but is treated by Rosebud with tolerant dismissiveness. The demonic lair is festooned with horrors. It includes huge toads, slimy lizards, big dusky bats, gigantic hairy spiders, beetles with human legs and arms, and numerous speckled snakes. But, as the Fairy puts it, 'The Demon himself I rather liked'. She only wishes he might have killed the black beetles. One technique here is understatement, and another is a kind of comic bathos.[38] The undercutting is not unlike that in A *Midsummer Night's Dream*, where the noble tragical story of *Pyramus and Thisbe* is made ludicrous by the use of inappropriate vocabulary, crude alliteration, and juvenile rhymes in a context of anguished lamentation.

There is, however, one important difference. *Pyramus and Thisbe* includes ridiculous inflated rhetoric. Gilbert prefers understatement. Bottom's 'Quail, crush, conclude and quell!' is the bathetic climax of a lament which is really a fourfold alliterative exclamation of a single idea. Gilbert's bathos works differently. When Rosebud announces the intention to thwart the Demon's abduction of a maiden, the result is merely a mildly ruffled annoyance, with the added joke that Rosebud (by what she calls a 'dodge') forces the demon to supply a concluding obligatory rhyme.[39] This raises the question of whether Gilbert has his own theory of comedy, the answer being probably not, though he does insist on the need to build up to a suitable act-climax.[40] His own view of theatre attendance is simple: people go, 'not in order to think, but to be amused'. In more serious contexts, the aim is equally straightforward: it is 'to have their feelings worked upon by a series of dramatic events', appealing principally to the eye and incidentally to the ear.[41]

v.

The above – plus the observation that plays which neglect such aims will probably fail financially – hardly suggests propaganda for the inculcation of higher virtue or a more generous social outlook. Gilbert *does* write serious plays, and even the comic ones have serious moments. But mostly, he undercuts preaching, sometimes, as in the hilarious *Vice Triumphant*, suggesting that any deducible moral is of entirely vicious and anti-social tendency. The context here is of an aged curate writing to *Fun* to protest that the modern sensation drama is totally misguided. It represents vice as ending up punished, whereas in real life the reverse occurs. This leads the writer to vow nobly in old age, to go in for a course of 'hideous and blood-curdling wickedness' beginning with the writing of his own sensation drama in which vice will be entirely and unrepentantly successful.[42]

Mockery of sentiment and associated moral lessons is a Gilbertian commonplace. In *The Fairy's Dilemma*, Rosebud ruefully admits that she 'condemned the mortals to their present disreputable course of life' only in order that she and the Demon might escape from their personal inconvenient difficulties.[43] One effect is to repudiate the idea of a correlation between stage conduct and behaviour in wider society – a tendency which goes against an earlier Victorian aim to make the stage the source of a kind of radiant restorative beam. The epithets most commonly applied to Planché's plays were 'delightful', 'beautiful', 'brilliant', and 'graceful'. The lyrics were 'as faultless in tone, tact and taste, as they were rhythmically perfect'. T.W. Moncrieff, who wrote *Life in London*, claimed that Planché always wrote in white gloves. Edward Fitzball added that 'For my own part, I always seemed to entertain an idea that he lived on honey and nectar'.[44]

The above should not be taken too far. Some of the comments are tongue-in-cheek, and there was already plenty of boisterousness on the pantomime and vaudeville stage. Nonetheless, there remained a sense that legitimate theatre had a responsibility for decency, morality, and sometimes spiritual uplift. It was this kind of moral assumption that in 1918 led to the sensational Maud Allan libel trial. Here, a projected performance of Wilde's *Salome* had been denounced as the Cult of the Clitoris. It was libelled as likely to encourage lesbianism, social decadence, international spying, and the demoralization of the British war effort.[45]

Mistrust of drama – and particularly satirical comedy – has, of course, a long history, the idea being that practitioners were latently supporting the vices they ridiculed. Jeremy Collier's *Short View of the Immorality and Profaneness of the English Stage*, published in 1698, proclaimed the thesis that 'the business of plays is to recommend Virtue, and discountenance Vice'.[46] Nothing, said Collier,

> can be more disserviceable to Probity and Religion, than the management of the Stage. It cherishes those Passions, and rewards those Vices, which 'tis the business of Reason to discountenance. It strikes at the Root of Principle, draws off the Inclinations from Virtue, and spoils good Education.

Actually, a counter-tendency had already been felt. At the opening night of Colley Cibber's *Love's Last Shift* (Drury Lane, January 1696), spectators had been genuinely surprised by the unexpected spousal reconciliation of the close. The joy of seeing this, 'spread such an uncommon rapture of pleasure in the audience that never were spectators more happy in easing their minds by uncommon and repeated plaudits and honest tears'.[47]

Not everyone today accepts the potency of smiles and tears. George Taylor's edition of plays by Samuel Foote and Arthur Murphy insists that the 18th-century sentimental vogue was 'a theatrical fashion that counted for a smallish number of plays'.[48] Nonetheless, *Love's Last Shift* did *itself* mark a shift. Acting the part of a high-class prostitute, Amanda, wife to the absent and profligate Loveless, invites him into her luxurious home, treats him to a night of passionate bliss, and next morning confesses her identity. Loveless is so impressed by her faithfulness that he instantly becomes a reformed character.

Against those restored to wholesome values, there were plenty of plays highlighting the degenerate and effeminate. This is a type developed from the *macaroni*, shading in real life into the more restrained but still fashion-obsessed Beau Brummell. To the *Oxford Magazine* in 1770, the creature is 'a kind of animal, neither male nor female, a thing of the neuter gender', that 'talks without meaning ... smiles without pleasantry ... eats without appetite ... rides without exercise ... [and] wenches without passion'.[49] On stage, this unprepossessing and often malicious type is embodied in Sheridan's Sir Benjamin Backbite, but he has quite a long previous history, much of it associated with flamboyant foppishness. George Etheredge's *The Man of Mode* (1676), Aphra Behn's *The Town Fop* (1676), and Vanburgh's *The Relapse* (1696) look forward to 'beau' comedies such as Mary Pix's *The Beau Defeated* (1700), and George Farquhar's *The Beaux' Stratagem* (1707). One aspect of the playing was affected vocal intonation. This foreshadows the later aesthetic mode whereby (for instance) 'lily' becomes 'li-*ly*' (rhyming with 'die') as in the Act 2 Finale of *Patience*.

The affected beau appears sometimes in Gilbert. He has his more highly spiced variant in Bunthorne and, as regard Frenchified exquisiteness, in the flamboyant Prince of Monte-Carlo. Bunthorne, like the beaux in *The Beaux' Stratagem*, is not so much foolish as conducting his own elaborate scam. But the true macaroni is silly and ridiculous. In *She Stoops to Conquer*, young Marlow, dupe of a trick whereby he has mistaken a gentleman's house for an inn, fears that he will be stuck up in caricature in the print shops as *The Dullisimo Maccaroni*.[50] More generally, a life-theatre overlap, often linked with foppish behaviour and/or faux transcendental thought, has many variants.[51] One is Burnand's The *Colonel* based on Jean François Bayard's 1844 play *Le mari à la campagne*. This links a mockery of transcendentalism with a satirical treatment of aesthetic sham. Earlier the part-time playwright Sir Lumley Skeffington (born 23 March 1771) had become so famous for excess polish that in one of Gillray cartoons, he is represented by a huge black boot.[52]

Skeffington's style was essentially a continental one. Avowedly copied from Paris, it made the macaroni into a painted puppet, a 'French toy'. Gilbert's aesthetic variant is seen in the marionette-like performance of the three leading dragoons, posing as aesthetes, in *Patience*. Actually, by his day, marionette theatre was considerably down-at-heel. Most of it involved travelling companies playing in rickety wood-and-canvas tents, the repertory favouring melodrama and farce and the emphasis being on special effects.

The Victorian marionette theatre, linked with *commedia* archetypes, can be glimpsed behind other Gilbert creations, such as Pietro's travelling troupe in *The Mountebanks*. Nita here is a tightrope dancer, one of the marionette theatre's special effects. Other highlights included dragons spewing fire and skeletons scattering and reassembling under the influence of hidden magnets. At the time of *Thespis*, a contemporary engraving showed a dragon costume, with a huge fanged head mentioned nowhere in the libretto but presumably from the ballet. Real marionette troupes were meanwhile having a hard time, selling hot peas, potatoes, and chocolate to supplement their meagre income and voyaging as far as Probolingo, Java, in pursuit of audiences.[53]

The decline of puppet theatre does not negate its comedic (and other) influence. Occasionally, Gilbert's own plays became adapted for marionette theatre as applied with *Creatures of Impulse*.[54] *Punch* specifically refers to the 'marionette-like accuracy' the playwright demanded in imitation of his own directorial style.[55] In the 18th century, puppets and marionettes were a satirical belittling mainstay. One example was that of Henry Fielding, who, attacking Samuel Foote, had one of his own star puppets dubbed Puppet-Fut – 'Grocer and Mimick'. The insult was completed by the labelling of Foote as a 'failed actor' – one who 'impersonates, badly, others'.[56]

The degeneration of marionette theatre is only one of many examples of change within continuation. In other areas, the changes might include considerable bowdlerization, as applies with *The Relapse*, re-modelled by Sheridan as *A Trip to Scarborough* (24 February 1777). Elsewhere, the development was not so much towards sanitization as parody. Gilbert's burlesque treatment of Meyerbeer's *Robert le diable* has a climax where the devil-figure descends not into Hell like the original Bertram (and indeed Don Giovanni) but into the Chamber of Horrors to be immortalized as a waxwork.

Another area mocked by Gilbert is that of high sentiment, a mode given an impetus by the playwright Richard Steele, whose first published work, *The Christian Hero*, is 'an argument proving that no principles but those of religion are sufficient to make a great man' (1701). Then, on 7 November 1722, he gives us *The Conscious Lovers*, a work built on the idea that sentimental comedies 'make us approve ourselves more'.[57] Denis Diderot doubtless agreed. His own *Paradox of the Actor* claims that the great actor is guided by his intelligence, not his emotion. His other – almost opposite – point is that sentimentalism helps spectators remember that all nature is inherently good.[58]

Diderot's view is that great acting is characterized by a complete absence of feeling. The actor's art involves creating the *illusion* of it. This – relevant to *The Grand Duke* – includes the idea that, if a great actor were to become too emotional, he would not be physically capable of sustaining a long run. Besides, the surges of feeling would lead to unpredictable or uneven performances. Sometimes – as increasingly in Falstaff and in the *Lovers' Vows* scenes of *Mansfield Park* – the sheer ability to act may suggest a morally bankrupt or selfishly Protean personality.[59] The opposite view was that intellectually conceived comedy could retain a moral aim, but that this is achieved by exhibiting characters from whom audiences should take warning.

Pierre Beaumarchais is another writer with a moral angle. In an essay published in 1767, he explains that the purpose of sentimental comedy is to offer a more immediate interest and more direct moral lesson than tragedy and a deeper meaning than comedy alone. Noisy laughter is the enemy of thought. Sentimental comedy allows a more silent sympathy and thought-provoking contemplation in tears. Beaumarchais's own bourgeois-set prose-drama *Eugénie* (1767) includes a damsel in distress, a rake's progress towards reformation, a secret marriage, a paternal figure hovering between authority and tenderness, a virtuous deserter at risk of being executed, and a passionately humanitarian plea against duelling. The essay also references the John Rich mode. It includes an advocacy of *jeux d'entr'acte* or *actions pantomimes* – passages of mute acting to be performed by some of the *dramatis personae* between the acts.

One of Beaumarchais' ideas is that prose is the best dramatic medium. In the essay, he praises sentimental comedy for doing away with verse and rhyme, these tending to obscure the meaning at the expense of truth.[60] Another argument is that laughing at other people merely distances the amused audience from the objects of the mirth, the danger being that we will become more interested in the rascal than the honest fellow. What Gilbert would have made of this is debatable. His known views refer less to moral results than to the *nature* of the comic mode which, for him, should treat the absurd and fantastic with the gravity of an apparently reasonable logic. But, for all his cynicism, the Savoy operas do suggest something of Laughing Comedy's vibrant life-affirming intention. In a 1773 essay titled *A Comparison between Laughing and Sentimental Comedy*, Goldsmith invokes the classical definition of comedy through Aristotle and Terence, insisting that comedy is meant to expose the vices rather than the distresses of man. Our 'best efforts' indeed are now exerted 'in these lighter kinds of composition'.

Goldsmith's essay had its own threefold agenda. It was written partly as a puff for *She Stoops to Conquer*, partly to anticipate some possible critical objections and partly to exaggerate the author's own originality. But this – like Richard Steele's private tendency to drinking, duelling, and manifest debauchery – does not necessarily negate the viability of his theatrical theory. The sentimental school conceived of human beings as essentially good but capable of being led astray by bad example. Gilbert suggests the reverse. He exploits the 'interested motives' in even the most apparently charitable of acts, one example being the plaint of his aged curate whose lifetime of virtuous conduct has led to no triumph at all.[61] The joke here is that 'triumph' is conceived not at all in religious or moral terms. It is purely a matter of self-indulgent material prosperity.

Between Steele and Gilbert, Goldsmith occupies a middle way. His comedy is less cynical than Gilbert's but eschews the rarefied mode of the higher sensibility. Comedy, Goldsmith tells us, is defined by Aristotle to be a picture of the frailties of the lower part of mankind. This distinguishes it from tragedy, which is an exhibition of the misfortunes of the great. One corollary is that low life and middle life 'are entirely its object', not least because this reduces the sense of significant loss. It is inappropriate to make too much of the comparatively limited, hardly earth-shattering fall of a low- or middle-ranking character. Terence, we are reminded, always judiciously stops short before he comes to the downright pathetic; yet even *he* is reproached by Cæsar for lacking the *vis comica*. Better to ally ourselves with Boileau for whom comedy will not include or even admit of tragic distress.[62]

Gilbert has his own links with Boileau, not least in his keen metrical sense and high opinion of Horace and Juvenal. Yet his more direct antecedents are undoubtedly English. Ian Bradley suggests that he stands in the English satirical tradition stretching back to Jonathan Swift (who was actually Irish).[63] It is a tradition, he says, which lampoons and parodies the major institutions and public figures of the day while remaining 'firmly within the Establishment' displaying 'a deep underlying affection' for the objects of its merciless attacks. My own view is that such writers were more cynical – that Gilbert in particular supported the institutions mainly as being necessary to shore up the fabric notwithstanding the fact that they are part-built on a collusive sham.

Although Gilbert does relate to various 18th-century satirists, his writing is hardly in the mode of the Augustan heroic couplet. One reason is that he liked so much to vary his metres. Another is that he enjoyed quirkiness which was part of a nonsense tradition. In *The Astounding Adventure of Wheeler J. Calamity*, there is much discussion of the word 'tomfoolery' which has no matching rhyme in the singular but may be rhymed with 'Toolieries' (Tuilleries) in the plural. This is the sort of word coinage or word distortion that we find in the elaborately flippant literary games of the universities and Inns of Court. It also gives us the 'Cabalistic Verse' prefaced to *Coryat's Crudities: Hastily gobled up in Five Moneth's Travels (sic)* (1611), the book itself being an eccentric account of Thomas Coryate's European tour.

Coryat's Crudities is mainly memorable for the responses. Not only was it mockingly patronized by Prince Henry. It was introduced by laboriously facetious mock-encomiums from fifty-six poets, including John Donne and Ben Jonson. Within this is one verse by Sir John Hoskyns which, beginning with reference to 'waves of brainless butter'd fish', has a note of visual and verbal surrealism strikingly anticipating Gilbert.[64] Like Hoskyns, Gilbert saw words as almost lithe and live elements. Like him, he is alert to their capacity to deceive. By contrast, sentimental comedy embraces honesty, though this may itself be an illusion. Apart from its novelty, Goldsmith attributes its success to a tendency to flatter every man in his favourite foible. Almost all the characters are good and exceedingly generous; they are 'lavish enough of their tin money on the stage', and though they want (lack) humour, all 'have abundance of sentiment and feeling'.

The danger in the above is an absence of verisimilitude. It renders a picture of life that is slanted and unrealistic. So, for that matter, does tragedy. 'The pompous train, the swelling phrase, and the unnatural rant are', he says, 'displaced'. They have given way to 'that natural portrait of human folly and frailty, of which all are judges, because all have sat for the picture'.[65] Goldsmith's objection to the sentimental strain is mainly moral. If the characters do happen to have faults or foibles, the spectator is taught, not only to pardon, but to *applaud* them. He will exalt them in consideration of the goodness of their hearts. A better mode is to contain criticism within the fun. This looks towards Gilbert's Jack Point, a jester who aims to trick us into learning with a laugh.

Gilbert's mistrust of the emotional mode does not mean that he sees no place for sentimental comedy. Indeed, he writes one, *Sweethearts*, in memory of his friend Tom Robertson. But his art is essentially one of witty exposure, of nailing hypocrisy, of dissecting the (apparently) charitable action, sometimes with the addition of a kind of surreal but forensic cruelty. In *Gentle Alice Brown*, the heroine has:

> ... helped mamma to steal a little kiddy from its dad
> ... assisted dear papa in cutting up a little lad,   ˙
> ... planned a little burglary and forged a little cheque,
> ... [and} slain a little baby for the coral on its neck.

This – devoid of repentance or uplifting moral, and including a devastating critique of Roman Catholic priestly hypocrisy – is the opposite of the sentimental strain.[66] It makes Gilbert more a Ben Jonson than a Cibber, more of a Goldsmith than a Steele.

vi.

We have seen, then, that Gilbert follows the more hard-headed of his comedy-writing predecessors. But I am not saying that he has no heart or is ignorant of life's frequent juxtaposition of laughter and tears. In *Princess Ida*, a boisterous scene of high farce as the young noblemen dress up as blue-stocking novitiates gives way to a moving quartet, later to be sung at Sullivan's funeral. Perhaps, indeed, the world really is a broken toy. Perhaps, 'fairest days' do include shade with the sun.[67] Nonetheless, at the end of the day, it is better to be surrounded with wealth than love, and there is a macabre delight to be gained from Alice's story satirizing inverted family values and the greed and hypocrisy of a major world religion.

The more savage aspects to Gilbert's wit are seen particularly in the *Bab Ballads*. In *The Baby's Vengeance*, the 'innocent child' dreams that the ticking of the clock is one of the Fates. He imagines each tick as a sharpened knife used to 'snick off' bits of his hated rival. *The Yarn of the 'Nancy Bell'* goes further still. Here, we get an Ancient Mariner resorting – in a kill-or-be-killed situation – to a jovial kind of cannibalism, all of it registered in the mode of a lugubrious hornpipe.

The *Nancy Bell* mode in some ways reflects the dehumanizations of clown-humour and pantomime. But equally, it looks forward to writers such as Evelyn Waugh and Edward Gorey.[68] In Gilbert's case, macabre humour is often augmented by buoyant rhythms, but there may also be a clever use of an almost nursery-like tone. In Alice's story, the use of words such as 'dear' (dear papa) and 'little' (little burglary) add a note of the faux genteel, also suggesting a whimsical awareness of an appealing naughtiness rather than any sense of serious transgression.

The elimination of the sentimental is not always to be advocated. Even Goldsmith allows that if people find delight in weeping at comedy, it would be cruel to abridge them in that, or any other, innocent pleasure. On the other hand, if we are permitted to make comedy weep, do we not have an equal right to make tragedy laugh? May we not, for instance, 'set down in blank verse the jests and repartees of all the attendants in a funeral procession'? This may remind us of the deliberately comic allusion to fireworks promised as a celebration of Nanki-Poo's execution[69] and of the hilarious tonal shifts in works such as Stoppard's *The Real Inspector Hound*.[70] The latter again mixes the decorous with the macabre, as when a genteel card-game ritual takes place over an intermittently concealed body, the whole set to the tune of brooding passions and murderous jealousies in the players.

The exaggeration of modes, and juxtaposition of incompatible ones, is nothing new. It is the essence of Viola's swaggering as a boy and of the erstwhile Puritan killjoy Malvolio's simpering with love while haughtily parading in yellow stockings. But in Gilbert and his successors, effects become extreme. One example is his parodic mini-version of Boucicault's

Jezebel (*Fun*, 24 December 1870), where the innate absurdity of apparently serious drama (or melodrama) is highlighted by two things: (a) gross exaggeration and (b) the omission of bridge passages:

Act 1: Room in GEORGE D'ARTIGUES' House at Bordeaux.
[Enter MADAME D'ARTIGUES. Her long skirt and her tightly-done hair show what a bad character she is.]
MADAME D'ARTIGUES: – I am a female fiend, but I have reasons of my own for not wishing this to be generally known.
[Enter George, her husband]
GEORGE: – My wife, here is Alfred Ravel, a navy surgeon, and an old friend of mine.
MADAME D'ARTIGUES: *[aside]* – I will poison him! *(Aloud)* I welcome you, sir. *[Starts]* Ha! That *face*!
RAVEL: *[recognising her]* – Ha! *That* face!
GEORGE: – Let us hie to the gaming-table, and play fiercely.
RAVEL: – We will!
[Exeunt GEORGE and RAVEL]

Here, the absurd concentration of intense dramatic effects and self-declamation is the opposite of the sentimental. It makes extreme emotion a mechanical act, using it specifically for burlesque and satirical purposes.

vii.

If the mockery of the sentimental mode is part of Gilbert's theatrical inheritance, so too is that of the stately historical drama. Here, one common comedic target is a simultaneously over-simplified and over-artificial exposition. In *The Critic, or A Tragedy Rehearsed*, Sheridan has Mr. Dangle innocently asking, 'Mr. Puff, as he knows all this, why does Sir Walter go on telling him?' Puff's answer is that the less inducement a character has to tell us things, the more we ought to be obliged to him. In his parody of *The Frozen Deep*,[71] Gilbert also mocks theatrical artifice, in this case covering inappropriate reactions, excessive use of coincidence, and a jostling of various characters to explain themselves:

LUCY: – It's a long story – I will tell you all about it.
MRS. STEVENTON: – No – don't – some other time. I also have a long story to tell. It takes twenty minutes, but, nevertheless, I will give it to you.
LUCY: – Spare me!
MRS. STEVENTON: – Never! *[Tells her a long story that lasts twenty minutes. Any jumble about the Arctic regions, polar bears, and second sight will do.]*

All this looks forward to the expository mode of *The Real Inspector Hound*, where Birdboot considerately tells us, 'I'm a family man devoted to my homely but good-natured wife', and Mrs. Drudge offers reams of guide-book exposition, much of it on the telephone.[72]

viii.

The mockery of unlikely dialogue makes a point about wider comedic aims. In both Gilbert and Stoppard, it is a means to undercut any sentimental or other emotional intensity. Mocked too is the artificiality or clichéd conventionality of stage setting. In Gilbert, the ruined chapel of General Stanley is a typical Gothic adjunct made funny because he has bought it complete with ancestors. In Stoppard, humour attaches to Mrs. Drudge's unlikely upper-class tones in telling us of the 'lovely old Queen Anne house', situated, we are later told, near cliffs yet somehow also in the Essex marshes. More extreme examples may mock both unlikelihood and the very nature of staging itself. In Gilbert's *Jezebel* parody, 'the scene is shifted for no necessary reason from Bordeaux to South America and from South America to the Rhine'. What is even more remarkable is that 'all the characters turn up together in different quarters of the globe without any sufficiently ostensible reason for doing so'. In *The Frozen Deep*, after the action has moved from the Arctic to Newfoundland, Clara remarks, 'Suppose we should come across the explorers from the North Pole! Wouldn't that be a coincidence?' The response is: 'It would indeed. Ha! Here they are!'[73]

The abandonment of likelihood in the interests of surprise and/or stage spectacle could sometimes prove a burden. In Planché's case, scrupulous realism of historical setting became doctrinaire antiquarianism. Spectacular excess (including excess of buffoonery) led to his being 'clowned, as well as painted, out of existence'.[74] Fortunately, such faults gave Gilbert much comic leverage. In *Jezebel*, Crystal lands at the 'rather vague address' of a Sea Port in South America, this being possible because 'dramatists always seem to regard South America as a compact little colony'. Rather than offering anything in the nature of how or why, she opens with: 'I am a bigamist'. Eventually, the plot is resolved by multiple bigamies. These provide the 'valuable moral lesson – that bigamy is no moral crime if your first wife is a bigamist too'.[75]

The above inversions and distortions of likelihood have other adjuncts, sometimes leading to a wider Absurdist breaking of barriers. In *The Real Inspector Hound*, two theatre critics become bound up in the play they are watching, and the phrase 'the real Mc.Coy' (generally meaning 'the genuine article') morphs into either an unseen character within the play or possibly a false identity of Moon, the second stringer. Gilbert also takes the metaphorical literally or the abstract as actual. In *The Mountebanks*, the line 'He's got a way with him' leads into the response 'Has he got it with him now?'[76] Mockery of complex identity meanwhile occurs in his burlesque version of Watts Phillips's *Nobody's Child* (*Fun*, 28 September 1867):

PATTY: – My uncle, Peter Grice, is Postmaster of St. Arven. Joe, the village idiot, is our servant. Lewcy Tregarvon, my foster-sister, is the daughter of Sir Robert Trevargon, a long-haired, horsemanship-looking bart. Captain Dudley Lazonby was formerly engaged to Miss Lewcy, but is now thrown over for George Penrhyn. Now you know all about us.

Here, what is mocked is both the plethora of relationships and the unlikelihood of anyone in real life ever reeling them off to us.

The matter of identity is in comedy crucial. Many farces in particular depend on mistakes and confusions of identity or on people playing – or being taken as – other people. Such applies, for instance, in Gogol's *The Government Inspector*, Gilbert's *His Excellency*, and (in its more comedic scenes) Da Ponte's *Don Giovanni*. The Absurdist complication in Gilbert is that, like Stoppard, he often interleaves the play world with the real one and the dream life with a form of reality. In *The Wicked World*, every earthly character has a fairy-world equivalent. Psychologically, they are opposed, but their interrelated worlds and identical names suggest simultaneously created parallel levels of existence.

If identities can be double, so too can mockery. There can be burlesque both of a device *and* of its failure to convince. In Gilbert's parody of *The Great City*, Arthur Carrington sets everything going with the following:

ARTHUR C: – I am here to meet Edith, who is coming by train from Canterbury. I will not go and meet her on the platform, but I will wander about in front of the Charing-cross Hotel. What more natural than that I should avail myself of this opportunity to remark, with much melodramatic action, that I am disinherited by my uncle in favour of Jacob Blount, M.P. because I get drunk? [*Wanders about the Strand*][77]

Such artificial exposition is frequently replicated. In the parody *Tame Cats*, Mrs. Langley announces, 'I am a grass-widow' and 'my husband is in India. I am carrying on a flirtation with a person named Wedgwood'. In *Jezebel* Madame d'Artigues shows her evil nature by telling us in an aside: 'Don Quixote is my lover – I want to marry him first and poison him afterwards'. She then briefly wonders where she has put her cyanide of prussic strychnine, only to find it instantly and promptly add it to her husband's light claret.[78]

The mockery of stage conventions and bad writing reinforces the sense of a continuing tradition. Essentially, comedy has a fairly small stock of *motifs* and devices. There is disguise; there is overhearing; there are misinterpretation, eavesdropping, mistaken identity, impersonation, and cross-dressing, but really, it is the *mode* of treatment that marks out a particular school. Gilbert's mode is robust and anti-sentimental. It follows Goldsmith who in his essay increasingly denigrates insipidity and languor. In Gilbert's characters what is funny is not only their mania for self-revelation but also the fact of *what* they are prepared to reveal – everything from sadism and a love of gratuitous violence to a serial killer tendency.[79] Also notable is a complete lack of internal moral conflict, as in this from *Lost at Sea*:

JESSOP: – The cheque was honoured by no other than Walter Coram himself! What shall we do? He will he down upon us directly.
RAWLINGS: – We must murder him![80]

Here, the dark humour is gained by the rapidity of the decision and the direct unadorned nature of its utterance.

ix.

The repudiation of the sentimental has in Gilbert many aspects. But perhaps, the most important is a matter of language-use. Where in sentiment is irony? Where are epigrams and puns? Where are the dichotomies exploited by wit? We look in vain for the latent *implied* prurience of the chapel-elder in *The Fairy's Dilemma* or the obvious buoyancy of Wilde's recently widowed Lady Harbury.[81] One notable point here is the way comedy writers cross-pollinate and borrow. In *The Pirates*, Ruth, asked to make a confession about Frederic's origins, tells us that her mind has long been gnawed by the cankering tooth of mystery, so she had better *have it out* at once. This gives us the germ of a little scene in *The Importance* where Algy also speaks of 'having it out' and Jack accuses him of talking like a dentist.[82] Later, Cecily's account of her internal struggles over whether or not to agree to an engagement with the wicked but absent Ernest recalls Gilbert's Lord Chancellor telling us of his long interior struggle over whether he may or may not marry Phyllis. Both are classic comedic treatments of people deciding, apparently reluctantly, to do what they really desire and intend all the time.[83] Gilbert's own borrowings include whole characters. Pooh-Bah (though much more cleverly developed) derives from Planché's Baron Factotum, the 'Great-Grand-Lord-High-Everything' in *The Sleeping Beauty in the Wood*.[84]

There are other areas of comparison, notably those of style and technique. The playing of Wilde's more comic scenes owes much to Gilbert's approach. It must not be vulgarly done – no sitting on pork pies, for instance[85] – and the characters must take themselves very seriously, however absurd the arguments they posit. The reverse mode is that of sudden exuberance – of a kind of anarchic *joie de vivre*. Sometimes, this has led to criticism. 'If Saphir I choose to marry', we are told, is too lively for aesthetes and their would-be partners. This misses the point that the would-be aesthetes were only *pretending* in order to win back their ladies.[86] Exhilaration is appropriate, as is a sense of relief at casting off the gloomy aesthetic pretence. Besides, the audience enjoys lively dance numbers. To have too many doleful trains of aesthetically gloomy characters would undermine the comic momentum.

There are two final points. One is that Gilbert's *motifs* of change and reversal reflect something wider. Linked with topsyturveydom, they imply that life faced head-on is simultaneously painful, serious, and ridiculous. Fun is gained by inverting it. The paradox is that this only highlights the absurdities of the norm. Pooh-Bah's outrageous family pride is ridiculous. It is, after all, invested not in a glorious samurai warrior but a protoplasmal primordial atomic globule.[87]

The other point is that Gilbert (like Wilde) knows that comedy may have its own unorthodox value system. In the parody *of Lost at Sea* (*Fun*, 2 October 1869). Walter Coram is less obsessed by love, life, and death than by preserving his shirts and socks. He not only loves these items. He is also considerate. He would not for the world 'put them to the inconvenience of coming round the Cape with me if it could be avoided'. This can be compared to Miss Prism's admittedly more important handbag. Whether this had handles or not becomes – at a time of suspense – material for a kind of inconsequential exasperated joke. Besides, Miss Prism has missed it greatly. It has been a 'great inconvenience' being without it all these years.[88]

The link between Gilbert and these other writers has many facets. But essentially, it lies in this: in viewing life from a deflationary comic perspective. All see humour in human pretension and human vanity; all have a strong sense of the hidden motives underlying personal conduct. When Lady Harbury's hair goes *gold*, we expect the word 'grey' or 'white'. The implication is that she is pleased at her husband's death and already dyeing her hair to attract new men. At the core are two things: the wit of verbal substitutions and the literal interpretation (or re-interpretation) of common expressions. 'Mrs. So-and-so was very pretty once', somebody once said to Gilbert. 'Yes, but not twice', replied Gilbert, thereby simultaneously showing both the alleged 'heartlessness' and the comic dexterity of his thinking.[89]

* * * * * * * * * * * *

Notes

1 Preface to *Sleeping Beauty in the Wood* (billed as an Extravaganza, rather than a burletta). Quoted in Roy, Donald ed., *Plays by James Robinson Planché* (CUP, 1986), p. 28.

2 Dionysos (or Dionysus), the son of Zeus and Semele, was rescued from ashes when Semele was burned to death in Zeus's radiance. He was then held in

Zeus's thigh, re-born from there, and entrusted to Ino, sister of Semele and wife of Athamas. Jealous Hera drove them mad, leading to his being handed over to the nymphs of Mount Nysa from whence in part he gets his name. One theory is that Dionysos was originally a beer god and that the word 'Tragedy' derives from the Greek word for a spelt or grain used in beer-making. The usually interpretation, however, is that the word means 'Goat-song' and he is now best remembered as the god of the vine.

3 Philostratus the Elder, Icon i. 2 (trans. Fairbanks). See also the entry in the *Dictionary of Greek and Roman Biography and Mythology* (Smith, William. Reprint, publ. Forgotten Books, 13 September 2018).

4 Demosthenes: *Speeches* (21.10) Demosthenes upbraids the brother-in-law of Aeschines for not wearing a mask during the *komos*, as was the custom (*On the Embassy* 19.287). Christiane Sourvinou-Inwood in *Tragedy and Athenian Religion* (Rowman and Littlefield, 2003) quotes Demosthenes complaining that Epikrates at the Dionysia procession behaved badly, as though participating in a *komos* (p. 70).

5 *Happy Arcadia* in *Gilbert before Sullivan*, ed. Jane Stedman (London, Routledge and Kegan Paul, 1969).

6 The *Tomahawk* was a weekly *Saturday Journal of Satire*, published between 1867 and 1870, price 2d, edited by Arthur à Beckett. Matt Morgan was its principal artist. Its contributors included Frederic Clay.

7 Hicks, Seymour, *Between Ourselves* (Cassell, 1930), pp. 49–50; and Hutchinson, *Portraits of the Eighties*, p. 257. The latter, originally published in 1920, is available through Kessinger Publishing (30 October 2007).

8 Gilbert in *Fun*, September, 1865, p. 27 (*Fun* (1861–1901), Bodleian Library, Archived 2007-02-06 at the Wayback Machine. The magazine was founded by H.J. Byron (21 September 1861) and in 1901 was absorbed into *Sketchy Bits*.

9 Roy, ed., *Plays by James Robinson Planché*, p. 30.

10 Phillips, Watts, *Not Guilty* (Forgotten Books, Reprint of Robert M. De Wit, 1869 edition), pp. 45, 22. Compare *The Pirates of Penzance* in *The Complete Annotated Gilbert and Sullivan* (1996 edition, pp. 221–225.

11 See *Fun*, 16 January 1864, p. 181, where Gilbert calls Clown's antics 'a vacant and unreasonable enjoyment'. See also *Getting Up a Pantomime*, p. 51, referenced in Crowther, *Gilbert of Gilbert and Sullivan*, p. 19.

12 The Herla-Erl link is widely accepted, but there are other possibilities. The Erlkönig's name translates literally as 'Alder King'. It has also been suggested that *Erlkönig* is a mistranslation of the original Danish *elverkonge*, which does mean 'king of the elves'.

13 For more on this, see Lima, Robert, *Stages of Evil – Occultism in Western Theater and Drama* (University Press of Kentucky, 2005).

14 Gantz, Timothy, *Early Greek Myth* (The Johns Hopkins University Press; Reprint edition, 19 June 1996), p. 135.

15 The only complete remaining satyr play is *Cyclops* by Euripides, though we do have fragments of Sophocles' *Ichneutae* (*Tracking Satyrs*). *Cyclops* mixes the myth of Dionysus's capture by satyrs, with the well-known episode of Polyphemus, the cannibal cyclops found in the *Odyssey*.

16 See Melinkoff, Ruth, *The Mark of Cain* (University of California Press, 1 July 1992), p. 71.

17 See *Wikipedia*, Entry under *Satyr*.

18 O'Brien John, *Harlequin Britain* (John Hopkins University Press, 2004), pp. 118–137.

19 As E.K. Chambers noted in the 1930s, the devils in miracle plays frequently 'wore vizards or were, like the bad souls themselves, painted black'.

20 Mystery and miracle plays are mainly associated with England, but there are some continental ones. The *Miseri d'Elx* is still played on every 14 and 15 August in the Basilica de Santa María in the Spanish city of Elche. The prohibition of theatrical plays in churches by the Council of Trent eventually threatened to interrupt yearly performances, but in 1632, Pope Urban V111 issued a special permit for their continuation.

21 In *The Marvellous Malady of Harlequin*, the Dutch artist Peter Schenk shows Harlequin injected in the bottom by a doctor and bearing a son. See Fischer, Lucy, *Cinematernity: Film, Motherhood, Genre* (University of Princeton, 19 April 2016), p. 125.

22 Roy, ed., *Plays by James Robinson Planché*, p. 30.

23 Ibid., Preface to *High, Low, Jack and the Game*.

24 Quoted in Eden, David: W.S. Gilbert *–Appearance and Reality*, p. 130.

25 Roy, ed., *Plays by James Robinson Planché*, p. 30.

26 Pemberton T. Edgar, *The Life and Writings of T.W. Robertson* (London, 1893), p. 234.

27 Pantaloon is a devious, greedy Venetian merchant. Columbine, usually his daughter, is (rather oddly) also a serving-girl with charm, wit, a sharp tongue, and higher aspirations. In 1558, she had a lucky escape when Pope Sixtus V issued an edict forbidding women from appearing on stage. Improvisation was not considered legitimate theatre, hence escaping the veto.

28 *Athenaeum*, 10 April 1869. The *Athenaeum* was a literary magazine published in London, from 1828 to 1921.

29 Wilde, Oscar, *The Importance of Being Earnest* Act 111, final scene.

30 See Ellis J. ed., *The Bab Ballads* by W.S. Gilbert (Harvard Paperbacks, 30 April 2003), p. 14.

31 *Saturday Review*, 23 February 1895, lxxxix, pp. 249–250.

32 Alec-Tweedie (Ethel Brilliana Tweedie), *Me and Mine* (1930), p. 95. Quoted by Eden, *W.S. Gilbert – Appearance and Reality*, p. 123. The full title is *Me and Mine, A Medley of Thoughts and Memories*.

33 *Fun*, 17 January 1863, p. 173.

34 *Fun*, 5 March 1864, p. 252.

35 This was 'The Serious Family'. They met in Gilbert's Chambers. The annual subscription was two guineas, but Gilbert was exempted on the understanding that he should supply a rump steak, a joint of cold boiled beef, a Stilton cheese, whisky and soda, and bottled ale, every Saturday night for the rest of his life.

36 *London Society*, January, 1868, pp. 50–51. For childhood's penny world, see Eliot's *A Cooking Egg*, in T. S. Eliot, *Poems* (New York: Alfred A. Knopf, 1920), pp. 22–23. E546 A753 1920a Fisher Rare Book Library. Poem available online at Representative Poetry Online).

37 *The Fairy's Dilemma* in *The Lost Stories of W.S. Gilbert*, ed. Peter Haining (Robson Books, 1982), p. 229.

38 Ibid., p. 231.

39 Ibid., p. 232.

40 *How They Write Their Plays: Mr. W.S. Gilbert* in *St. James's Gazette*, 23 June 1893. Gilbert says that an audience will often pardon a feeble, wearisome act for one dramatic climax at its conclusion.

41 Gilbert's review of Dr. Westland Marston's *Life for Life*, in *The Illustrated Times*, 13 March 1869.

42 *Fun*, 11 November 1865. Wilde indirectly makes the same joke when Miss Prism defines fiction as the good ending happily and the bad unhappily: 'That is what fiction means'.

43 W.S. Gilbert, *The Fairy's Dilemma*, p. 243.

44 Fitzball, Edward, *Thirty Five Years of a Dramatic Author's Life*, 2 vols. (London, 1859), pp. 11, 28.

45 For more on this, see *The Maud Allan Affair* by Russell James (*Remember When*, 2008) and Hoare, Philip, *Oscar Wilde's Last Stand* (Arcade Publications, 1998).

46 Collier, Jeremy. *A Short View of the Immorality and Profaneness of the English Stage*, ed. Yuji Kaneko (London: Routledge, 1996; first published 1698). See also Cordner, Michael, *Playwright versus priest: profanity and the wit of restoration comedy* in *The Cambridge Companion to English Restoration Theatre*, ed. Deborah Payne Fisk (Cambridge University Press, 2000).

47 Davies, Thomas (1784). *Dramatic Miscellanies* (IIIrd ed.). pp. 411–412.

48 Taylor, George, ed., *Plays by Samuel Foote and Arthur Murphy* (C.U.P., 1984), Introduction, p. 1.

49 *The Oxford Magazine*, 1770, quoted in Shipley, Joseph Twadell, *The Origins of English Words: A Discursive Dictionary of Indo-European Roots* (JHU Press, 1984), p. 143.

50 Goldsmith, Oliver, *She Stoops to Conquer*, Act 1, Scene 2 (London, 1773, British Library, Shelfmark: DRT Digital Store) p. 643.e.4. (6).

51 See, for instance, the Court dress in *The Grand Duke*, Act 11, and the costumes hired from a Jewish costumier by the Prince of Monte-Carlo. In *Middlemarch*, Mrs. Cadwallader links Jewish identity with old clothes merchants (Eliot, George, *Middlemarch*: Book V111, *Sunset and Sunrise*, chapter lxxxiv). Her husband considerately cuts off the remark that will hint at Will's Jewish identity.

52 For Skeffington and other dandies, see Woodeforde, J., *The Strange Story of fake Hair* (London: Taylor and Francis, 1971), p. 40. The dress typically entailed squeezing the figure into a very tight, long-tailed coat with pastel-coloured breeches, a suffocating stock, and wigs allegedly 'a yard high'. The effect – including jewelled shoes, a quizzing-glass, at least one snuff-box, numerous rings, make-up, a muff, a fan and a floral bouquet – was a theatrical pose in itself.

53 For more on this, see McCormick, John, *Victorian Marionette Theatre* (*Studies in Theatre History and Culture*) (University of Iowa Press, Paperback – 30 November 2004.)

54 W.S. Gilbert, *Creatures of Impulse: One-act Play for Marionettes*, Federal Theatre Project (U.S.), National Service Bureau, 1938, 30 pages.

55 See Stedman, Jane W., W.S. Gilbert, *A Classic Victorian and His Theatre* (O.U.P. 1996), p. 217.

56 Kelly, Ian, *Mr. Foote's Other Leg* (Picador, 2012), p. 127. Samuel Foote had already run satirical puppet shows. Fielding, on 26 March 1748, offered a rival treatment, using Mrs. Fielding's 'large Breakfasting Room' as a venue to avoid problems of censorship and intervention by the Lord Chamberlain. See also Murray, Venetia, *High Society: A Social History of the Regency Period, 1788–1830* (Viking, 1998), p. 45. In the 18th century, various operas were composed for puppets; Alessandro Scarlatti wrote works for Cardinal Ottoboni's theatre in Rome, as did Joseph Haydn for Count Esterhazy. Powell's Covent Garden puppets attained celebrity by parodying the vogue for Italian opera, and Henry Fielding, Samuel Foote, and others presented puppet shows to burlesque contemporary fashions.

57 Steele, Richard, Epilogue to *The Lying Lover* (London, 1703). Available in *The Plays of Richard Steele*, ed. Shirley Strum Kenny (University of Nebraska Press, 1968).

58 Diderot's essay was not published in full till 1830 but an earlier shorter version appeared in Grimm's Correspondence Littéraire (1770). In 1883,

Chatto and Windus published a version with a preface by Henry Irving. The essay consists of a dialogue between two speakers in which the first speaker espouses the views of Diderot on acting. Included is reference to Mlle. Clairon who could experience emotion when portraying a character for the first time, but in repeat performances, she would be in complete control of her emotions. Diderot also gives an example of theatrical discipline, quoting Garrick who could run a gamut of convincing emotions very much by sheer intellectual control of his craft.

59 Fanny also has more specific concerns. For a dependent girl in whom gratitude is a key element, it is wrong to perform a play of which her absent uncle would strongly disapprove. In addition, rehearsals allow indefatigable scenes of passion between her cousin, Maria, and the flirtatious Henry when Maria is actually engaged to somebody else.

60 Beaumarchais, Pierre Augustin Caron (Paris, 1767): *An Essay on Serious Drama.*

61 King Gama (said by Gilbert to be based on himself) tells us: 'A charitable action I can skilfully dissect And interested motives I'm delighted to detect'. The aged curate is the one in *Fun,* 11 November 1865.

62 Quoted in Goldsmith's Essay. This appeared in January 1773, before *She Stoops* was produced at Covent Garden on 15 March.

63 For Ian Bradley's view, see Bradley, Ian. *W.S. Gilbert:* 'He was an Englishman'. *History Today,* Vol. 61, Issue 5, 2011.

64 Serjeant John Hoskins (1 March 1566–27 August 1638) was an English poet, scholar of Greek, lawyer, judge, and politician. He was expelled from Oxford University partly because the authorities did not appreciate his biting satire. In 1614, in parliament, he spoke his mind about the Sicilian Vespers and consequently was imprisoned for a year in the Tower of London. Early in 1638, when as a judge he was attending assizes, 'a massive country fellow trod on his toe'. Gangrene set in and, despite amputation, he died in August that year, aged seventy-two.

65 Goldsmith, Oliver, *An Essay on The Theatre; or, A Comparison Between Laughing and Sentimental Comedy.*

66 *Fun,* VII, 23 May 1868. *The Yarn of the Nancy Bell* also appeared in *Fun (Fun* n.s. II – 3 March 1866).

67 *Trial by Jury* in *The Complete Annotated Gilbert and Sullivan,* p. 23.

68 R.C. Harvey: *Edward Gorey and the Eccentric Macabre* in *The Comic Journal, Toucan,* 24 September 2014. Edward Gorey (1925–2000) published over one hundred of his own works and has illustrated works by Gilbert and Sullivan among others. *The Edward Gorey House* biographical website quotes the *Washington Post* (undated): 'Not enough praise has been awarded to Gorey's superb prose. He possesses the ear of a great parodist ... a distinctive vision that is nobody's but his own'.

69 *The Mikado* in *The Complete Annotated Gilbert and Sullivan,* pp. 592–593.

70 Stoppard, Tom, *The Real Inspector Hound* (Faber and Faber, 1970 edition), pp. 19, 27. The play draws on Stoppard's experiences as a Bristol theatre reporter. The critics watching the play increasingly find their personal desires and obsessions interwoven into their bombastic and pompous reviews: 'Already in the opening stages we note the classic impact of the catalytic figure' ... 'Sometimes I dream of Higgs' ... 'Sometimes I dream I've killed him'.

71 The original was written for amateur performance in 1857 by Wilkie Collins and Charles Dickens, partly in response to the abortive expedition to find the North West Passage. Dickens was directly involved because the widow of the expedition leader, Sir John Franklin, sought his help when the men disappeared. Gilbert's review (*Fun,* 17 November 1866) draws on an 1866

revision. Apart from the coincidences and elaborate expositions, he particularly mocked the ludicrous treatment of snow ['Enter the SHIP'S COM-
PANY. A party in a white cap heaps a shovelfull *(sic)* of snow on each as he
enters. They expostulate'.].

72 Tom Stoppard: *The Real Inspector Hound*, pp. 12, 15, 17.
73 *Fun*, 17 November 1866.
74 Granville Barker, Harley, *Exit Planché – Enter Gilbert*, in *The Eighteen
    Sixties*, ed. J. Drinkwater (Cambridge, 1932), p. 127.
75 Parody review of *Jezebel* by Boucicault, printed in *Fun*, 24 December 1870.
    The play had started its run at thee Holborn on 5 December.
76 W.S. Gilbert, *The Mountebanks* in *Original Plays by W.S. Gilbert* (Chatto
    and Windus, 1941), p. 359.
77 This comes from Gilbert's first burlesque review of an Andrew Halliday
    play. *The Great City* opened at Drury Lane on 22 April 1867. The parody
    dates from 11 May *(Fun)*. It includes the interesting stage direction 'They
    garrotte each other'.
78 *Fun*, 24 December 1870.
79 *Fun*, 24 December 1870.
80 *Fun*, 16 October 1869. Parody review of *Lost at Sea* by Boucicault and
    Byron (Adelphi, 2 October 1869). *Fun*, 24th December, 1870. He will be
    down upon us directly' means 'He will expose us at once'.
81 Wilde, Oscar, *The Importance of Being Earnest*, Act 1. Dialogue of Alger-
    non and Lady Bracknell. Available in many editions – e.g. *The Importance
    of Being Earnest and Other Plays* (Oxford Paperbacks, 2008).
82 Wilde, Oscar, *The Importance of Being Earnest*, Act 1. Dialogue of Alger-
    non and Jack.
83 W.S. Gilbert, *Iolanthe*, Act 2. Lord Chancellor's speech beginning: 'At first
    I wouldn't hear if it – it was out of the question. But I took heart. I pointed
    out to myself that I was no stranger to myself; that, in point of fact, I had
    been personally acquainted with myself for some years.' (*The Complete
    Annotated Gilbert and Sullivan*, p. 441. Compare Cecily in Act 11 of *The
    Importance.*)
84 The piece derives originally from Charles Perrault. For *Sleeping Beauty*,
    Planché himself said, 'I was requested to furnish one solid versification of the
    many versions of fairytale to accompany the illustrations by Richard Doyle'
    (J.R. Planché, November 1865).
85 George Grossmith in his *Reminiscences* (*A Society Clown*, Chapter V1,
    pub. Arrowsmith Britsol Books, 1888) tells us that Gilbert 'very properly
    objects to any business being interpolated without his sanction, especially
    if its sole object is merely to raise a laugh, and thereby stop the action of
    the piece'. It is here that he quotes Gilbert's dislike of Jessie Bond's pushing
    Grossmith so hard that it caused him to roll over. When Grossmith pointed
    out that he got an enormous laugh by it, Gilbert replied, 'So you would if
    you sat on a pork-pie'. Gilbert, like Buster Keaton, realized the advantage of
    dead-pan 'straight' playing even in the most slapstick of comedy.
86 The (to my mind) misguided view of the inappropriateness of the quintet
    comes from *A Most Ingenious Paradox, The Art of Gilbert and Sullivan* by
    Gayden Wren, (O.U.P., 2006), p. 109.
87 W.S. Gilbert, *The Mikado*, Act 1. The humbling of family pride becomes an
    Act 1 running joke, as in the trio 'I am so proud' where the mortification –
    again claimed as a moral stance – is actually a self-serving excuse for the
    preservation of his life.
88 Wilde, Oscar: *The Importance of Being Earnest*, the dénouement scene in
    Act 111.
89 Hicks, S., *Between Ourselves*, pp. 49–50.

Part 2
Literary Context

From Aristophanes to Shakespeare

Comedic origins and traditions are rather like the striations on a shell and particularly on a scallop. The later has so many lines of convergence that it is often worn by pilgrims to indicate the completion of the journey to the shrine of St. James in Spain. The same applies with many of the most familiar comedic *motifs* which are regularly recapitulated even when apparently deriving from a number of discrete sources. Significantly, the scallop shell is not only a Christian icon. A symbol of light and couch of sea deities, it combines various traditions. In Christianity, it represents salvation and is sometimes used to sprinkle baptismal waters. But the shrine of St. James was originally the shrine of the Goddess Bridgette, the Celtic version of Aphrodite. The scallop itself was associated with the goddess Venus born of the sea and carried to shore on a shell. Scallop shells are also a symbol of the Hindu version of Aphrodite, the goddess Lakshmi born from the churning of the ocean, consort to Vishnu, and the embodiment of beauty, grace and good fortune, which she also bestows on believers. Her four hands represent the four goals of human life: *dharma* (righteousness), *kāma* (pleasure and love), *artha* (prosperity) and *moksha* (liberation and spiritual values).

The varying developmental lines are not always, of course, derived from different traditions and cultures. Sometimes, one line splits and divides as applies with the various developments of Aphrodite. There is also the fact that some comedic modes do not so much branch off as seem to come to a dead end. When Plautus died, his epitaph suggested the end of an era:

> postquam est mortem aptus Plautus, comoedia luget,
> scaena est deserta, dein risus, ludus Iocusque
> et numeri innumeri simul omnes conlacrimarunt.
> After death befell Plautus, comedy mourned,
> the stage was deserted, then laughter, play, joke
> and all of countless measures wept together.

The fact that, according to Aulus Gellius, the above was written by the playwright himself does nothing to negate the idea of an irreplaceable loss.

The end-of-the-line idea is not in fact ultimately valid. Plautus continued to exert influence well into the period of the *Commedia dell'Arte* and beyond. One key factor was that he was the only Latin playwright of the period – aside from the later Terence – whose works survive in the manuscript tradition. An incredible 130 comedies are ascribed to Plautus, the vast majority of which were already in antiquity labelled spurious. The ones that have come down to us are fortunately the ones labelled authentic by the antiquarian and grammarian Marcus Terentius Varro. Others were likely to be authentic but, on account of uncertainties, had ceased to be copied in late antiquity.

The above raises a significant question: namely, how far back one should go. In Gilbert's case, the answer seems to be to the Greeks. Edith Hamilton called him a mid-Victorian Aristophanes. So did Walter Sichel, who wrote a 1911 essay on the subject. Gilbert himself was well aware of lines of comedic origin, but often he mocks the idea both of continuity and of veneration of his forbears. The Shakespeare who used Plautus as a source for *The Comedy of Errors* is admired by Gilbert but can also be mocked. One proof of this is the following anecdote:

> Here's a good story about W.S. Gilbert: he was talking with a Shakespeare enthusiast once, and to bait the man, he said that the Bard's plays don't even make sense. Take this, for instance. 'I would as lief be thrust through a quickset hedge as cry "Plosh!" to a callow throstle'. The man explained that it was very simple, really. It meant the speaker would rather be shoved into a thornbush than disturb a singing bird. 'But what play is that from?' he asked.
>
> 'None', replied Gilbert. 'I just made it up. And jolly good Shakespeare it is too'.

Here, the links and vagaries within the comic tradition offer fortuitous connections. Having read the above, it is fun to recall that in *Sir Lancelot Greaves,* Smollett introduces a 'most stubborn and vicious' carthorse called Gilbert – one that 'once threw Crabshaw into the middle of a quickset hedge'.[1]

i.

Chance links, then, there certainly are. But there is no doubt that Gilbert emerges from a distinct historical context, reaching back at least to the aforementioned Aristophanes. So, what is the nature of Ancient Greek comedy and where, speaking generally, are the significant links?

Greek Old Comedy plays are essentially high-spirited romps. Composed of song, dance, personal invective, buffoonery, and parody, they gradually took on a six-part structure: an introduction, in which the basic fantasy is explained and developed: the *parodos or* entry of the chorus; the *agon or* ritualized debate; the *parabasis,* in which the chorus addresses the audience on contemporary issues and hurls scurrilous criticism at prominent citizens; a series of farcical scenes; and a final banquet or wedding. The chorus often were dressed as animals, while the characters wore street dress and masks with grotesque comedy features.

The satirical and musical aspects in Gilbert obviously suggest a link. As Gilbert mocks world-weary poets and airy aesthetes in *Patience*, as he lampoons metaphysically-minded Romantics in *Tom Cobb*, and particular politicians in *The Happy Land*, so Aristophanes in *The Clouds* (423 B.C.) mocks Socratic intellectual pretension and the misuse of philosophical argument. Another link is an interest in the theatrical process itself. *The Frogs* (405 B.C.) offers a satire directed chiefly against Euripides but also considering the whole experience of Tragic Drama. In Gilbert's *Comedy and Tragedy,* the central conceit is the duality of the comedy-tragedy masks, while the lady's own role-play suggests the tantalizing overlap when a real person becomes an acted part.

One of Edith Hamilton's arguments is that Aristophanes speaks to the follies and foibles of his nation *at a particular period*. By contrast, Shakespeare's world is timeless, undated, and replete with a universal zest. Is this true? The ill-wishing pompous Malvolio is almost certainly based on the Puritan but lovesick Sir William Knollys. Polonius suggests William Cecil, his advice to Laertes being drawn from a letter written by Cecil to his son.[2] The critic is on stronger ground in asserting that Gilbert did not have the freedom of caricature permitted to Aristophanes. When he introduced Gladstone, Robert Lowe, and Acton Smee Ayrton into *The Happy Land*, the work was immediately censored.[3]

It is true, then, that Gilbert lacked Aristophanes' freedoms, but even here, we can to some degree demur. The anti-German tone of *The Grand Duke*, with its puny mean-minded ruler, seems almost dangerously topical. It taps into the anti-German feeling resulting from the defeat of the Jameson Raid (29 December 1895–2 January 1896) which had prompted the German Emperor to send a telegram of congratulation to Kruger, the Boer President. Still, Gilbert has to be careful, renaming his Wilhelm as Rudolph (with a temporary possibility of Max) for fear of too obvious a correlation with Queen Victoria's grandson. One of Edith Hamilton's points is that, unlike Aristophanes, Gilbert was working 'in the safest and most comfortable world mankind has ever known'. But the censorship suggests no-go areas, while songs such as Strephon's admittedly cut 'Take a wretched thief' hardly suggest authorial complacency.

Perhaps, the main link between Aristophanes and Gilbert lies in the exposure of hypocrisy, pretension, and sham. In *Thesmophoriazusae,* Aristophanes almost immediately introduces two contrasting types – one with the lofty air that befits a Poet and Philosopher and one with the cheerful easy-going latitude of the easily impressed. This has two Gilbertian aspects. First, the windy rhetoric looks forward to Lady Blanche's metaphysical maunderings and, second, the scene looks to Gilbert's balancing of opposite types – Minnie and Belinda in *Engaged*, for instance, and Matilda and Caroline in *Tom Cobb*.[4] In the Aristophanes play, Herakles' account of horrors involved in the journey to Hades is set against Dionysus' colloquial mock-bravado and the luggage-carrier's concern about his dogsbody role:

> And I'm the donkey in the mystery show.
> But I'll not stand it, not one instant longer.[5]

Here again, comedy is created by different tonal registers and the single-minded maintenance of each character's juxtaposed viewpoint.

ii.

The use of comic juxtapositions is a well-tried comic device. But sometimes, there are closer links. In the *Plutus*, a slave Carion meets an unnamed politician, who tells us he is Supervisor-General of all things public and private, his qualification for the job being that he *wanted* it.[6] Hamilton relates this to the get-rich celebrity schemes of the Duke and Duchess of Plaza Toro but a closer link might be with the proud, equally greedy Pooh-Bah. In both writers, satire of the real and material may also be couched in a context of fantasy lands and surreal environments. Lands of clouds and birds become Gilbert's *Topsyturveydom*. This inverts everything with the implication of upside-down structures and priorities in real-life party politics.

The *Topsyturveydom* format is very much in the mode of illogical logic and the logical illogical. The country itself is a land 'where everything is conducted on principles the very reverse of those' in England. People are born elderly and grow younger until they become infants. They start out wise and gradually forget everything, until at last their minds are a perfect blank. Folly is honoured, wisdom is despised, true beauty consists in making yourself ugly, and people walk on the ceiling with their heads on the floor. As in Samuel Butler's *Erewhon*, the real objects of satire are the institutions and conventions of the Victorian present. But Gilbert is more like Aristophanes in showing the subversion especially through the medium of kings, princes, gods, and statesmen. In *Thespis*, the gods themselves are decrepit. Mercury, the celestial drudge, though unacknowledged, carries out most of their functions, including those of an illiterate Minerva. Then, when actors take over, conditions actually deteriorate. Such a mix of intellectual satire and buffoonery might have amused Aristophanes, though, given his cultural context, his ridicule of the Olympians is far more directly subversive.

The links and differences between Gilbert and Aristophanes are partly a matter of scale. When Aristophanes inverts the relations of gods and men, it is the gods of tragedy – Zeus the King, Hermes the messenger, Prometheus the rebel – that he references. Gilbert, lacking an equivalent, limits himself to debasing and ridiculing contemporary politicians. That said, the two playwrights are alike in investing their inversions with a spirit of carnival[7] – one which paradoxically gives an ultimate sanity of perspective, for there is 'no doubt that the right-side-up is the real one'.[8]

Another link is the element of the magical and Absurdist, invested by Gilbert with a more picturesque ambience. In *The Pirates of Penzance,* the Cornish police march into a ruined chapel by moonlight. A chorus of girls appears in peignoirs holding lighted candles. There is an irrelevant but charming song about the fickle wind as a wooer. More in the Aristophanes mode is the satire. In *The Pirates,* this relates to issues of heredity by purchase. It can be related to Aristophanes' (rather stronger) attacks on the new rich, whom Chremylos labels 'temple-breakers, orators, informers and knaves'.[9]

The attacks on the new rich are frequent in the *Ekklesiazousai*, though the wealthy generally get a pasting. More sympathetic is Isokrates who, in the *Antidosis*, tells us that nowadays wealthy men have to defend themselves for being rich as if it were the worst of crimes.[10] One of Gilbert's twists is to suggest that morality, courage, and virtue can themselves become a purchased inheritance, as applies with General Stanley's ancestors who are to prove inspirational to Mabel. Perhaps, one source here is Julian who in *Misopogon* ('Beard-hater') writes:

> For just as in the case of plants it is natural that their qualities should be transmitted for a long time, or rather that, in general, the succeeding generation should resemble its ancestors; so too *in the case of human beings it is natural that the morals of descendants should resemble those of their ancestors.*[11]

iii.

Gilbert's satire of bourgeois pretensions is not in itself original. Chaucer has long before satirized those guildsmen's wives who like to have their mantles 'roialliche ybore'.[12] But latently, there is more than simple one-upmanship. In contemplating ancestry, Gilbert (like Hardy in *A Laodicean*) taps into a sense of the need for supportive structures in a post-evolutionary, shifting world. This sense of shift may also encourage a new take on *motifs* of identity and false seeming. In *Amphitryon,* the plot depends on two counterfeits: (a) the god Jupiter sleeping with Amphitryon's wife in the guide of her husband and (b) Mercury adopting the guise of the slave Sosia. This calls to mind Gilbert's *Happy Arcadia* and *The Gentleman in Black*, in the first of which people find themselves encased in other people's bodies, while in the second there is a comically sinister exchange of souls.

There are numerous variants of the above. One is for a godlike and mortal identity to conflict, as occurs in *Thespis*. Daphne, for instance, becomes Calliope, the muse of fame, and is hence married to Apollo. However, in mortal life, the actor playing Apollo is married to Nicemis, who is now the moon and hence Apollo's sister. What adds to the fun is that all this Greek mythology is according to a sanitized family edition and that sometimes relationships overlap. Such applies with mortal Pretteia, playing the immortal Venus, who has to juggle the fact that Venus had two 'marriages' with gods now played, respectively, by her own father and grandfather. More metaphysically, in *The Gentleman in Black,* we encounter a form of transubstantiation with two swapped souls (really, personalities) each residing in the other's physical appearance.

The Gentleman in Black is a good example of some of the limitations under which Gilbert had to labour. His 'Gentleman' is described within the play as 'the king of the gnomes'. Almost certainly Gilbert would have liked to make him the devil but felt constrained against it. To make matters worse, the *Era* (22 May 1870) then accused him of plagiarism. It also informed us that, it is 'quite unnecessary to make our readers acquainted with the alias of the Gentleman in Black, seeing that it is never mentioned to ears polite'. Apparently, a very dark 'dash' is an indicator in the programme, but 'the author has striven hard to show that the gentleman in question is not always so black as he is painted'.[13]

The difficulty of treating the devil does not preclude his appearing elsewhere. We find him, for instance, in the 1898 Sullivan-Pinero-Comyns-Carr opera *The Beauty Stone* where he appears to an ugly, crippled girl called Laine, who mistakes him for a holy friar. The message of the piece is that beauty is inward and/or in the eye of the beholder, but ultimately the devil is more a disillusioned than an alarming figure. The incorporated mode of the sinister joker looks back to the mediaeval mystery plays and to early dramas such as *Gammer Gurton's Needle* where we read:

> Saw ye never Friar Rush
> Painted on a cloth, with a side-long cow's tail.
> And crooked cloven feet, and many a hooked
> nail?

and:

> Look even what face Friar Rush had, the devil had such
> another.[14]

More seriously, as early as the fifth century living tableaux were introduced into sacred services, linking drama with Christian (and devilish) concepts.

These were later superseded by part-vernacular forms, one being *Quem Quaeritis?* (circa 930), a dramatised liturgical dialogue between the angel at the tomb and the women who are seeking Christ's body.

One thing worth noting is that these early performances were something of a hybrid, being given in Latin, but preceded by a vernacular prologue and synopsis spoken by a herald. The writers and directors were probably monks, and the pieces were not necessarily solemn. One French example – referenced in Walter Pater's *Denys l'Auxerrois* – included a liturgical game enacted in the Cathedral every Easter Monday, members of the clergy performing a ritualized dance, while tossing a ball and singing the *Victimae paschali laudes* to organ accompaniment. In 1210, there was a clampdown. Suspicious of the increasingly popular miracle plays, Pope Innocent III issued an edict forbidding clergy from acting on a public stage. Thereafter the organization of the dramas moved to town guilds, vernacular texts replacing Latin, non-Biblical passages being added, and eventually whole cycles being performed on Festival Days. Then, in 1534 in England, the whole genre was banned following the establishment of the Anglican Church.

Despite the vicissitudes, mediaeval drama was a buoyant and popular form, known for its zaniness and a blend of the bawdy profane with the spiritually exalted. Whereas Gilbert feels obliged to re-jig his Black Gentleman, the devil in a mediaeval play may be both named and treated as a buffoon, as he is in the York Barkers' Pageant, *The Creation and the Fall of Lucifer*. This pattern reaches a bawdy and anti-clerical zenith in a drama called *Mankind* (circa 1470) which is unique among moralities for its juxtaposition of serious theological matters with colloquial (sometimes obscene) dialogue.

Generally speaking, the cycle plays present a divine comedy. The contrast is between a final serene spiritual joy and the coarseness of earthly merriment. The comic is at best a shadow. At worst, it is a perversion of the prospect of heavenly bliss. In Gilbert, there is often a sense of reality as the 'shadow of a shade', but religious application is generally absent. What do linger are certain stock types and *motifs*. Lucifer, in *The Fall of Lucifer,* is in the tradition of the Roman *miles gloriosus* – a tradition inverted in Gilbert in the dialogue before 'In Enterprise of martial kind' (*The Gondoliers*) and sketched lightly in the plot of *Creatures of Impulse*. In the latter, the coward Peter becomes unwillingly courageous as the result of a curse from a malevolent fairy. Meanwhile, Sergeant Klooque, a professional soldier, is made unwillingly to keep ducking and backing off, lamenting 'I shall lose my reputation! I shall be branded as a coward!'[15]

The mediaeval treatment of braggadocio and arrogance usually ends in collapse. In Lucifer's case, it culminates in the ultimate turnabout – a slapstick episode in which the lesser devils batter him. Rather similarly, in *Creatures of Impulse,* the malevolent fairy is herself routed when all her victims turn upon her, carrying out – against her – the undesirable behaviour with which she has afflicted each in turn. In mediaeval comedy, effects tend to be broader, as, for instance, in the Wakefield Cycle's account of Cain and Abel, where Garcio the ploughboy acts as comic foil to the loutish, undisciplined Cain. Also lively is Noah's wife in the Chester version of *Noah's Flood.* This woman is not evil – she is, after all, spared from the Flood – but she is disobedient to her husband, who, unlike her, understands the Almighty's intent. On the Ark, she boxes Noah's ears. She is willing to risk destruction at the hands of God for the earthly pleasures of gossip and wine.

The treatment of Noah's wife is archetypal. She is the long-standing comic type of the unruly wife. Gilbert's Duchess of Plaza Toro is a more refined wifely equivalent – one who has made the sex war literal, changing from a dominated weaker vessel to a warship galleon in full sail. Compared to *her,* Noah's wife is merely foolish, but this is not entirely a matter of gender bias. A masculine equivalent is Joseph in the Coventry play of the Annunciation. Unaware of God's plans for Mary, Joseph denounces her, only to be the butt of laughter when he has to come crawling back.

Perhaps, the richest humour in the Cycle plays takes place in *The Second Shepherd's Play.* Here, there is a two-part structure, heavily skewed towards the comic tale of the shepherds and Mak the sheep-stealer. Mak's very entrance is accompanied by an affected accent that the shepherds denounce as the silly chap putting on airs. The mockery of his speech (he pretends to be a yeoman sent by a lord) is one branch of the verbal humour found (for instance) in the apostrophes and transcendental utterances of Bunthorne and the high-flown attitudinizing of the materially threadbare Effinghams. In Italy, the *Commedia dell'Arte* had long exploited linguistic jokes the name *Zani* being taken from Bergamo and incorporating a northern dialect form of the name *Giovanni.*

Gilbert quite often uses dialect forms, not least the cockney mode used throughout *A Clown's Story* and *The Hooligan,* and the Scottish and Lincolnshire forms in *The Man o'Airlie* and *Lost in London.*[16] The most complex case is that of *The Grand Duke*'s Julia Jellicoe. Here, the point is that the part – that of an English actress working in a German theatrical company and ostensibly speaking German – was originally played by a Hungarian with a strong Middle European accent whose associates (speaking impeccable English) were treated as speaking High German. In Aristophanes, dialect from outside Athens is often used comedically. Such applies with the Scythian in *Thesmophoriazusae,* but even better is the Megarian mode used in the *Acharnians.* Here, strong dialect-use suggests that the whole scene of the father selling his daughters as pigs should be read as a parody of Megarian farce.[17]

iv.

The jokes to be obtained from language and tone can, of course, be augmented by music. In *The Grand Duke*, this applies in the mock-Italianate nature of Julia's hypocritical *prima donna* histrionics in the Act 1 Finale and in the exaggerated French accent of the Act 2 singing Herald. In earlier comedy, however, it is speech which is paramount. In *The Second Shepherd's Play*, Coll, the first shepherd ('primus pastor') does not revel bucolically but complains about the (typically English) cold weather, his own poverty, and the arrogance of the local gentry. Gib, the second, is equally rueful, complaining first about the weather and then about the plight of married men, among whom he is peeved to include himself.

The humour in *The Second Shepherd's Play* is a vernacular version of the lugubrious type found in Ko-ko's response to the plan for wooing Katisha, and the rueful Pooh-Bah declining lunch before execution. In the operas, dialect is comparatively rare, though *The Sorcerer* does include a delightful Mummerset mode in the wooing of man and maid under the love-philtre's influence. Elsewhere, a darker metropolitan world may be evoked, as when Josephine, in the middle of her love-crisis, envisages living in dark and dingy rooms in a noisy desolate back street.[18] This is contrasted with the luxurious home of her father – rich in antiques and with 'everything that isn't old from Gillow's' – a colloquial reference to a firm made rich by the lucrative West Indies trade.

Gilbert's limited use of social comment is matched by an even more limited use of sexual innuendo.[19] But one area where he does recapitulate both classical and mediaeval modes is in the comic *motif* of the baby-exchange or child-substitution. Gilbert's *Baby's Revenge*, published in *Fun* on 16 January 1869, tells of a cradle-swap made by one baby (Paley Vollaire) at the expense of another (Frederick West). *H.M.S. Pinafore*, *The Gondoliers* and *The Gentleman in Black* all include swapped babies, in the first case owing to a muddle, in the second to a mismanaged kidnap, and in the third to a deliberate move.

The Gilbertian treatments take various forms. In *The Gondoliers*, Don Alhambra deliberately steals what he thinks is the baby Prince of Barataria only to find that his foster-mother has exchanged him with her own baby. In *The Gentleman in Black,* effects are more calculated: the peasant babe creeps from his clothes-basket, quietly removes the sleeping baby baron, and swaps them about.[20] Here, the fact that a child effects the substitution makes it not so much funny as semi-macabre.

Much of *The Gentleman in Black* plot can be related to Gilbert's real-life sense of childhood displacement. But here, the point is the link with the cuckoo-in-the-nest or baby-substitute plot found also in the *Second Shepherds'* play and in European folklore. One allegedly true story from the Breslau area tells us that in about 1580, a female harvest-worker had her baby removed and replaced by one from the devil which sucked her milk so greedily and howled so inhumanly that she knew it was alien. When she beat the substitute hard with a switch, it screamed so loudly that the Devil appeared, returning her own stolen child, and taking his own back with him.[21]

The Breslau story has its own relevance to *The Gentleman in Black*. Gilbert takes the idea of a black devil-figure but transfers the actual child-swap to the agency of a baby. A variant treatment involves a farcical incursion. In *The Second Shepherds' Play*, Mak agrees to make camp with the shepherds. Then, once they are asleep, he casts a spell to keep them so, before proceeding to steal one of their animals. At home, this leads to the plan to disguise the sheep as a human baby, the fact that the lamb and good shepherd are Christian symbols adding more black comedy piquancy.

The farcical humour of Mak's dealings offsets the later Christian adoration of the Christ-child. But there are also blended ambiguous treatments. In Walter Pater's *Apollo in Picardy*, one central episode has an itinerant labourer, Apollo/Appolyon, clad in animal skins, bringing a bleating lamb to Midnight Mass on Christmas Eve. He is the Greek god, but he is also a Bunyan-derived devil. In addition, the lamb may be a Christian or pagan symbol. It may be an image of salvation or a sacrificial offering. In Greek myth, Apollo is not only the sun-god but also guardian of flocks and herds. This means the lamb in the Christian building may be under his pagan protection, making the effect doubly ambiguous.[22]

However we regard Apollo's lamb, *The Second Shepherd's Play* clearly uses the sheep incident for comedy. Gill herself is in the existing tradition of the nagging but resourceful wife. Firmly believing that Mak will be hanged for the theft, she comes up with the plan of putting the sheep in an empty cradle and pretending it is her newborn. Not only that. She will claim to be loudly and painfully in labour with its twin, so that the shepherds will quickly abandon any search. When they do go seeking, Gill decides to brazen it out, even going so far as to say that, if she is lying, she will actually eat the 'child' in her cradle (as indeed she intends).

The substitute child idea has many comedic and indeed serious variants. In *The Second Shepherd's Play,* the resolution comes with the shepherds' second visit. Realizing that they have failed to bring any gifts to Gill's 'baby', they go back to Mak's dwelling, remove the swaddling clothes, and recognize their sheep. Elsewhere, there may be more fanciful treatments, as in *Jane Eyre*, where the heroine (offsetting her plainness) strikes her master as a fairy sprite or a changeling, fairy-born, and mortal-bred. Another possibility is for apparent substitution not to be initially known to those most affected. This – found in *The Gondoliers* – also applies in Euripides' *Ion*. Secretly giving birth to a child, Creusa (raped by Apollo) leaves it in a basket, along with some trinkets, expecting that it will be devoured by beasts. Apollo, however, sends Hermes to bring the boy to Delphi where he grows up unwittingly as an attendant at the temple.

This particular Creusa story ends happily. But there are also some shadows. The Chorus, recalling the story of the daughters of Cecrops and Aglauros, reminds us that children born of mortals by a god's agency are fated to suffer. So too are those of mixed mortal-fairy heritage, as applies in comic vein to Strephon, another shepherd character, who is literally and physically a half-breed. More seriously, child-substitutions are nearly always dangerous. In traditional Welsh stories, the changeling child (*plentyn cael*) initially resembles the human it replaces, but gradually grows more vicious and uglier. One way of identifying it is to cook a family meal in an eggshell. The child will exclaim in surprise and then vanish, to be replaced by the original human infant.[23]

The opposite of expulsion is adoption, and here Gilbert provides more parody variants. In *Ruddygore,* the baby Rose Maybud has been left with a book of etiquette at the workhouse door but is somehow taken in by her aunt. In *The Gondoliers,* the drunken gondolier acquires – or thinks he acquires – a kidnapped baby prince but is unable to tell it from his own son. These twin *motifs* – those of abandonment and the re-moved noble – occur in many myths. Such applies with Paris on Mount Ida (suckled by a bear) and with the Persian Cyrus who is left on a wild mountain side, rescued by the royal herdsman (sometimes a bandit) and raised in safety. In one Assyrian story, a fish-goddess falls in love with a beautiful young man, gives birth to a half-mortal daughter, abandons the child in the wilderness, and then kills herself in shame. The baby is fed by doves and survives to be found and raised by a royal shepherd, growing up to become Semiramis, the great Warrior Queen of Assyria.[24]

Gilbert's parodies of baby-swap and kidnaps are more generic than specific. This is one difference from the Mak story which clearly references Moses in the bulrushes and the placing of the God-child Jesus in the manger. More secularly comedic are *motifs* of mislabelling and wrong identification. Plautus' *Menaechmi* – itself the basis for *The Comedy of Errors* – has numerous mistakes of identity linking it loosely with *The Gondoliers*. In the opera, the dénouement reveals that the prince was actually not stolen away at all as his wet nurse had substituted her own infant. This extra twist complicates the double-identity *motif*, providing the impetus for a happy ending.

v.

Whatever the source, Gilbert's fascination with the idea of swapped identities provides considerable comic potential. In *The Baby's Vengeance,* one resentful infant cheats the other out of his fortune. Possessed of an intrusive foster-brother (as in *The Gondoliers*), he changes places, only on the point of death to reveal the plot and suggest a swap back.

Since he has run through his entire fortune while the poorer hard-working one has dutifully scrimped and saved, this will be yet another blow to the subservient victim. The whole thing mocks the idea of a Tiny Tim childhood innocence, offering a different emphasis from the *Menaechmi* where stock *characters* are more central than any mockery of sentimental stock *responses*.

Stock characters – such as the pedant, the fop, and the braggart – are, however, often exploited by Gilbert. *The Menaechmi* has several: the parasite, the comic courtesan, the comic servant, the domineering wife, the doddering father-in-law, and the quack or fraudulent doctor. As for the plot, this too strikes familiar chords. In *The Gondoliers*, Don Alhambra seeks out the Palmieri brothers, thinking one is really the prince. Unable to tell which it is, he arranges for both to rule jointly. In *The Menachmae*, when the separated twins are grown to manhood, Menaechmus of Syracuse sets out in search of his brother. This leads to comic confusions when the questing twin arrives in Epidamus, unaware that his identically named brother actually resides there. Here again separated or removed babies are a mainspring, brothers are a main *motif*, and it is confusions of identity which drive the farcical plot.

There is one further thing to stress here, which is an emphasis on dress and disguise. In the Cornish *Death of Pilate*, Pilate knows that he will escape punishment as long as he is clad in Christ's robe. When his secret is discovered, he attempts to fast-talk his way out of surrendering the garment, one excuse being that of not wishing to appear naked before the Christ figure. Ironically, this is true spiritually as well as physically. But the emphasis on clothing suggests wider literary links, found seriously in plays like *Macbeth* and comically-satirically in Gilbert's *Eyes and No Eyes*, and Andersen's *The Emperor's New Clothes*.[25] In *Princess Ida*, the Princess' mock-heroic view of chaos is partly of her neophytes wearing clashing colours and having clothes that come undone at inconvenient moments. When Casilda is first told she is the reigning Queen of Barataria, her first thought is that she has nothing to wear.

Casilda's response to rapid elevation may nowadays seem a male sexist jibe. But – apart from the comic bathos – the main point is of human beings defining themselves – and their institutions – by appearance. Rather similarly, the liberating Court Dress of Ludwig's *Troilus and Cressida* company tells us something about the regime's shedding of muffled-up inhibitions. It implies that ceremonial may be a sham, a cover, and a mask, below which – as in the original *Troilus* – lies hollowness.[26] Elsewhere – as also in *Troilus* – there may also be savage possibilities, offering humour juxtaposed with horror. A good example occurs in the Wakefield *Herod the Great*, where the braggart soldiers associated with the slaughter of the innocents are a grimmer version of the *miles gloriosus*, a figure also lurking behind Shakespeare's Falstaff and Parolles.

Parolles with his hollow drum has another relevance. It was possibly he who gave Gilbert the idea of Luiz as the 'private drum' to the Plaza Toros. In Parolles' case, it symbolizes a windy lack of substance – a noise that is bombastic but hollow. Hence, it is appropriately ironic that Parolles ('Words') should be brought low by words which are as meaningless as his own protestations of virtue.[27]

The above mingling of the comic and serious shows how often a double effect may exist. So it does in some Gilbertian works – notably *Comedy and Tragedy* but also some of the operas. Both *The Mikado* and *The Yeomen* include sadistic and cruel elements, made more piquantly comic by the Mikado's scrupulous tone of reasonable politeness and the Assistant Tormenter's lugubrious sense of his work ruining his love-life. One notable point in the *Yeomen* is that religion is carefully eschewed. There is no speaking part for a Tower Chaplain and no reference to the religious turmoil resulting from the King's Great Matter.[28] Where the piece is more like the Mystery Plays is in the blending of the comic and macabre. In mediaeval drama, the comically dark side is provided less by pessimistic gloom than by a deliberately overdone rant. This is packaged with more localized satirical comment – as in the complaints about taxation, the abuse of the poor, the problems of dysfunctional marriage, even sometimes the bleakness of cold northern weather.

Leaving aside the everyday aspects, ranting is easy to exemplify. Satan in the York play of the temptation of Jesus opens with a full-blown villain's rant which not only reminds us of Pharaoh's and Herod's raving in three earlier pageants but by its sheer rudeness reduces his fearsomeness. A variant is for us to be invited to collude with villainy, as happens in *Richard III* where we may feel almost gleefully privileged to be included in his devilish soliloquized plots.[29] Rather similarly, in *Mankind* the villains goad the audience into paying money to persuade the devil Titivillus to appear, thereby implicating us joyfully in his wickedness.[30]

Not all villains, even in the Mystery Plays, are entirely devilish. The Wakefield pageant offers a Herod who is an arrogant egotist, esteeming himself above all other rulers, but fearing a greater king sufficiently to lead to the ordering of horrible atrocities. By the end, this counsel has been reduced to the ironic, 'Be not *too* cruel'. This may remind us of elements of grim concern in *The Mikado*, as when the potentate, thinking his son dead, calls Ko-ko a 'poor fellow' for having zealously produced the tiresome result of killing him.[31] Glee in detailing gruesome punishments here again combines with affected solicitude, the lack of paternal grief further augmenting the comic potential.

The underplaying of horror, only to augment it, is a very common comedic device. The Wakefield Herod (like that of *Jesus Christ, Superstar*) evinces a certain whimsical charm – one that ironically brings his evil into sharper focus. Gilbert too enjoys an interweaving of comedy with the cruel and macabre. Gentle Alice Brown is actually a child killer   she has slain a little baby for the coral on its neck. As for the Mikado's sadistic revelling in boiling human flesh, this actually reflects real Mediaeval and Renaissance punishments. When the cook Richard Roose (or Rous) was accused in 1531 of attempting to poison Bishop Fisher, he was locked in a chain over a cauldron of boiling water, hoisted in and out, and thus 'poached still alive'. This was indeed a punishment to fit the crime. Yum-Yum's anticipation of burial alive seems almost mild by comparison.

vi.

The comedy that includes the macabre relates partly to the idea of completeness. For the mediaeval mind, the idea of *comedy* includes the *divine* one. Happiness lies in going beyond this vale of tears and reaching Heaven. Tragedy is a matter of being in the state of separateness from God. Plays such as *Everyman* offer a transformation from tragedy to divine comedy, from doom to salvation, but the comedy, in a simpler sense, may still include the macabre, not least because it is part of the unredeemed condition of a fallen life.

Leaving aside the theological aspects, there is no doubt that cruelty and pain may have an amusing aspect. So, they do in Gilbert, where they are, in any case, offset by numerous factors. One – in the musical collaborations – is the humanizing effect of melody.[32] But also life-affirming are charming stage spectacle and sometimes an element of sheer high-spirited exuberance. Gilbert loves to use contrasts of setting, as in *The Pirates* where we move from sunny seashore to night-time ruined Gothic chapel. He also revels in attractive but bizarrely opposed group-juxtapositions, as in *Patience* where the fact that the soldiers perform aesthetic droopiness with military precision is part of the joke.

There is another point about Gilbert's stage pictures which is that, when the macabre or devilish *are* introduced, they are usually undercut. In *The Sorcerer,* the semi-surreal is set against the everyday world of business normality. Parodying both Weber's Wolf's Glen and Balfe's *Satanella*, Gilbert gives us a middle-class tradesman – a family sorcerer – performing incantations with flashing fire round a teapot. Even when he goes down to the fiery realm of Ahrimanes, he does so throwing up a flurry of business cards. Here, it is the element of commercial business franchise that adds humour, another variant being *Ruddygore*'s professional bridesmaids, parodying the over-eager amateurs in Weber's *Der Freischutz.*

vii.

In addition to a combination of opposites, comedy has its own long-standing stock range of *motifs.* Among those exploited by Gilbert are spying and overhearing, disguise, cross-dressing or dressing up, pride or pomposity going before a fall, the inversion of social norms, the adoption of false identities, and clashes of Youth and Age. Often spying and overhearing lead to a mistaken interpretation of the import, while clashes may include clashes of cultures, temperaments, and sometimes (as in *Much Ado About Nothing*) of feminine and masculine modes. There may also be comic clashes between low life and refinement or education and ignorance. Nearly always there will be problems of love and the hurdles to be overcome in obtaining it.

Among the physical ingredients, one of the most familiar is the aforementioned clothing. In *Lysistrata,* the removal and re-donning of clothing – by the choruses over an extended period (ll. 614–1023) and by the two peace delegations when they first meet (ll. 1074–1096) – is a major feature of the second half design. In *Clouds,* the contrasting ambitions of Pheidippides' parents for their son involve one seeing him driving a war-chariot in a fine robe (*xystis*) and one imagining him driving home a flock of goats in a leather smock (*diphtheria*). Later examples include the Puritan Malvolio cavorting in his yellow stockings and Ludwig in his Greek *chiton* and Louis Quatorze wig. When in *She Stoops to Conquer* Kate Hardcastle is mistaken for a barmaid, the mistake is partly because of the simple, non-fashionable dress she adopts, by pre-arrangement with her father, every evening.

The significance of clothes is various. They can be a symbol of changed character, a means of changing it, or an incongruous source of jokes when the outside appearance conflicts with the individual essence. In *Princess Ida*, the young men's donning of girl-graduates' academic robes leads to their being taken by the Princess for would-be novitiates. Here, the deception is soon discovered but sometimes, as in *Le Bourgeois Gentilhomme* (1670), an elaborate disguise can be a means of exposing the foolish pretensions of those who believe in it. In *The Grand Duke*, the clothes for the supernumeraries acting as the Prince of Monte Carlo's suite are hired 'from a very well known costumier'. Here, the treatment is a satire on two things: Gilbert's so-called Adelphi guests (i.e. rent-a-crowd extras) and the falsity of a kind of theatrical power-point self-presentation.

Dress, disguise, and false appearance do not, of course, dominate all comedic plots. But one thing that does is an obligatory happy ending. This is not to say that even in the sunniest of works there may not be serious elements. Themes of the biter bit, or the malcontent humiliated and thwarted, extend from a humiliated Malvolio to Gilbert's King Gama. There may also be an element of the unresolved, as when Malvolio departs vowing revenge 'on the whole pack of you'. Later, the daily rain referenced by Feste suggests a mode of smiling through tears – very different from the zany speed of mounting confusions where the comedy veered towards farce.[33]

The momentum of farcical developments depends often on people being put in impossible conditions. Such applies in *Twelfth Night*, whose various rivalries, jealousies, and anticipated comic duel find echoes (though without the gender-confusion) in Gilbert's *The Palace of Truth*. Occasionally, other Shakespeare plays are referenced. Ko-ko in *The Mikado* offers a comic reduction of the *Measure for Measure* scenario, having been sentenced to death for flirting, as opposed to Claudio's fornication. The joke here is that the locals, fearing general vulnerability, have appointed him headsman on the understanding that, as he is the next on the list, he must first decapitate himself. This is comedy on a knife-edge of disaster which is the obverse of the pleasure evoked in the treatment.

Spiralling disaster is only feasible if there is a norm to set against it. According to K.J. Dover, 'the normal man' in Aristophanic comedy 'takes as much as he can of song, dance, food, drink, sex, sleep and good company' – these being ideally augmented by honour, recognition, reputation, and material prosperity. Gilbert limits the sex and makes more of the dangers. In *The Mikado*, keen to fulfil the tyrant's demand, Ko-ko invents an execution, only to find that his alleged victim is the disguised heir apparent. Before this, the suggestion had been that Ko-ko should execute himself, even an unsuccessful half-decapitation being better than nothing.[34]

viii.

The idea of increasingly impossible conditions usually continues until the dénouements. Such applies in both *Twelfth Night* and *The Mikado*, where the untying of the knots depends on a character returned apparently from the dead. In both too, there is a real element of danger. In *Twelfth Night,* Duke Orsino expresses himself willing to sacrifice the lamb he loves on the altar of his jealous emotions, making it perhaps surprising that Viola should ultimately accept him. Gilbert treads more warily. In *The Mikado*, death, pain, and the more macabre elements are either treated surreally or with a practicality that reduces their terrors. This applies in the discussion of Ko-ko's self-decapitation, made comic by the down-to-earth responses of his associates who treat the problem as a matter of troublesome civic business.

This brings us to the matter of language – and in particular tone and vocabulary. In *Le Bourgeois Gentilhomme*, Turkish in the final farcical ceremonials is replaced by *Sabir*, a pidgin language used as a lingua franca in the Mediterranean Basin. Elsewhere, an amusing effect is achieved simply by understatement in the vernacular. In *The Mikado*, the prospect of burial alive is comically undercut by the bathos of Yum-Yum's response ('It's such a stuffy death'). A near-opposite is the use of grisly language when we expect something pleasanter. In the epilogue to *Troilus and Cressida*, rather than bowing and appealing charmingly for applause, Pandarus, dying, announces that he will bequeath to us his terminal syphilis.

The comedy of spiralling difficulty is often combined with another common *motif*, that of testing. By it, weak mortals are made to reveal their weakness, fools their folly, and grosser souls their crudity, while romantic heroines such as Viola prove their loyalty, integrity, humanity, and tenderness. In Gilbert, there is a more satirical approach. Sweet Rose Maybud is tested in love many times, not least when, in the middle of her wedding, her betrothed turns out to be an accursed bad baronet. But a swiftly adjusting selfishness sustains her. She re-takes an inferior choice, only to revert as soon as the curse is lifted. This is all part of a wider take on human vices and hypocrisies. Ben Jonson's aim in *Volpone* and *The Alchemist* is to 'mix profit with your pleasure' by exposing generic human follies. Sir Philip Sidney in his *Apologie for Poetrie* (circa 1580) tells us that comedy is 'an imitation of the common errors of our life which he (the dramatist) representeth as the most ridiculous and scornful sort that may be'.

Compared to Shakespeare, Ben Jonson is urban, mercantile, and anti-romantic, making him in some ways more in line with Gilbert. But Gilbert does ultimately celebrate the triumph of love, also retaining a genial streak, not least in the presentation of his rural Cornish policemen, who – incompetent, endearing, and distinctly non-heroic – have some links with Dogberry and Verges. The cowardice *motif* – seen variously in Falstaff, Sir Andrew Aguecheek, Parolles, and Bob Acres – is yet more familiar. One variant is Peter, in *Creatures of Impulse*, who maintains that in danger all men are equally frightened, but that some – unlike him – have the power of concealing it. When, cursed by the Bad Fairy, he is made to seem permanently keen to hit people, the apparently reckless bravado belied by his craven way of discussing it.[35]

In addition to characters acting against the grain, most comedy plots include another feature, which is that of over-reaching. This applies, for instance, in *His Excellency*. Here, in a developing vortex of deception, most of the characters become increasingly deluded and cheated, but the Governor's maniacal addiction to practical-joking founders on the fact that the man he thought to be the false Regent is actually the real one. Such a comic come-uppance links back to many earlier – sometimes part-serious – examples. In *Volpone,* the fall of the parasite Mosca arises from two factors. One is the falling out of the two chief plotters. The other is structural, depending on such a spiralling of plot and counter-plot that it becomes impossible to keep the various strands apart.

The defeat of an over-reaching Mosca links with another comic *motif*: that of the over-ambitious subject or servant. An early incarnation is Plautus' astute, quick-witted trickster slave. He in the *Commedia erudite* turns into a less potent figure, only to regain centre stage in the

Commedia dell'Arte, though without the *servus callidus*' quick intelligence.[36] Gilbert seems to prefer the quick-witted original, as in the case of Ludwig who – though initially foolish in exposing the conspiracy – gains the grand duchy by a trick in which he encourages his social superior to collude.

Not all ambitious servants are tricksters. A variant is for the servant to be merely ambitious, or for the role to be, not servile but merely that of an inferior in a hierarchy. The former applies with Malvolio; the latter with Gilbert's jealous Lady Blanche. Blanche is unusual in not coming to grief for her aspiration, though, of course, she considers herself born to rule and socially superior to her leader. In Mosca's case, the result is different. The over-reaching is the cause for a sundering of interests which alone could have held the various plot strands together.

The continual reuse of the same *motifs* does not mean that all comedy has a similar ambience. Jonson's comedies belong mostly to the mercantile world of Jacobean London. Romantic comedies are less anchored, often featuring exotic and semi-magical events, remote and beautiful locations, shipwreck, piracy, marvellous escapes from imminent death and hazards boldly encountered. Gilbert's quirk is to combine the magical and imaginary with the *anti*-romantic and frequently political. In *The Wicked World*, Chaos comes to Fairyland when mortal (sexual) love is imported. In *The Happy Land*, the political target is popular government, brought in by representations of real-life political figures.

One common adjunct of Romantic Comedy is melody and song. Lively jolly music denotes a zest for life combined with robust animal spirits. Refined lyrical airs seem to hale forth the soul, while also suggesting the fuller, more gracious capabilities of the spirit. Gilbert offers scope for both, but his view of life possibly became more jaundiced with age. In *The Mikado,* the trio of schoolgirls are roguishly upbeat: 'Life is a joke that's just begun'. In *Utopia,* limited the jokes is on us: 'Comes at last the final stroke. Time has had his little joke'. The quizzical ending of the latter opera is notably cynical. Government by party, we are told, involves a never-ending quarrelsome unravelling which nonetheless is a paradoxical source of England's greatness. All may be managed by the manipulations of rival puppet-masters pulling the Establishment strings.

ix.

Pulling the strings is one thing. But the above is not to suggest that Gilbert developed a new theory of comedy. Generally speaking, comedy celebrates life and laughter. There is a movement from death to life, war to peace, destruction to creativity, barrenness to procreation. All this applies in Gilbert, as does a more subtle awareness of life's vicissitudes, of the passing of time, of wind and weather. Gilbert's broken toy mode is the poignant face of this. The more sardonic is Paramount's song on the farce we call life which 'teems with quiet fun' but remains nonetheless a dispiriting business.

In some ways, it might seem that sickness and decay are antithetical to comedy zest. But there are many exceptions. In the Old French *fabliau* of *Les dues Anglois et l'ane*, a sick Englishman asks for a meal of lamb but owing to linguistic misunderstanding is given donkey, making him laugh so heartily that he is cured. In *Volpone,* the protagonist feigns debility in order to dupe greedy fortune-hunters, while in *Le Médecin malgré lui,* Sganarelle discovers that Lucinde is only feigning illness as a means to avoid an unwelcome marriage. Gilbert's variants include a feigned incapacity that becomes real (in *The Mountebanks*) but a more important treatment is that in *The Grand Duke* where a debilitated en-feebled runt of the Saxe-Coburgs is set against the unfettered liveliness of Clown-Ludwig's counter-movement. Mean-minded, humourless, and stingy, Rudolph gets ill though living too low. He replaces human vitality with a charade of elaborate ceremonial which itself illustrates the hollowness and shallow base of ritualized authority.

The debility and sickness of Rudolph (set against Ludwig's ebullience) includes an element of Winter-Spring, Age-Youth dualities. This too is not new. In the tragic-comic *The Old Law, or A New Way to Please You* (published 1656), Duke Evander of Epire has promulgated a law that mandates a programme of euthanasia: every man who reaches the age of eighty, and every woman who reaches sixty, will be put to death, thrown from a cliff into the sea. The cynical, heartless Simonides is delighted, looking to a speedy inheritance. The virtuous Cleanthes is conversely appalled. What makes a link with Gilbert is the centrality of the law and the ability to find humour within the grim or gloomy. *The Old Law*'s comic-grotesque dance of Old Women (like some scenes in Bennett's *Allelujah!*) is an assertion of the life-force even in adversity. Rudolph's Act 1 *habañera* with the Baroness is a Gilbertian variant, perfectly combining rueful comedy with a certain degree of eccentric self-parodying high spirits.

x.

High spirits or even zaniness are a good way of retaining a residual buoyancy. But equally powerful may be simple good nature. Eventually, in *The Old Law*, this leads to a *Measure for Measure* type of trial-scene where we learn that the Duke's harsh law involves a public test of virtue. The old people supposedly executed are in fact still alive. The good younger couple and the elderly pseudo-victims are promoted to be judges, with appropriate correction for the guilty. Such cases of the biter bit and a restoration of moral authority often occur in Gilbert. One example comes in *The Gentleman in Black* where the wicked baron is comically degraded.[37] A less jolly one occurs in *His Excellency* where, at the end of a sarcastic speech apparently in the Governor's favour, the Regent permanently reduces him to the ranks.[38]

Reversals and table-turning are, then, a comic corrective. But this does not always remove darker shadows. *The Yeomen of the Guard* includes a jeering, molesting mob; a torturer who discusses his art at considerable length; and the probable death of the jester main character.[39] Perhaps, the opera is best glossed as a romantic tragic-comedy, but in fact comedy often accommodates such material. In *Volpone*, the old fox is admittedly only feigning debility, but the society in which he lives is as deformed as his pets. Venice, its laws and institutions – apart from two cipher good characters – is sick of a deep-seated moral decay. Here, as in *The Old Law* and far more than in Gilbert, images of deafness, impotence, cruelty, and decline stretch the comical frame almost to breaking point.

xi.

Even dark material, of course, has its limits. At the end of *Volpone*, the Senate (notwithstanding some members' worldly ambitions) expels corruption and restores good government. Even before that, the wit and inventiveness of the protagonist have charmed and added buoyancy. One reason why we can laugh with him is that for much (not all) of the time he is duping rogues. But perhaps too the buoyancy itself is attractive. Such applies with Falstaff – airy in his wit, extravagant in his invention, and all the more piquantly so because of his physical clumsiness. The danger is that many comic protagonists, delighting in their own corrupt ingenuity, go too far. Vitality may be an expression of the life-force – it may overflow the belt of rule and the limitations of time and space – but too much abundance had better be curbed.

Curbing can occur in various ways. Sometimes, it happens of its own accord. A joke will play itself out. This is a realization of Gilbert's amoral practical-joking Governor who faces the exhaustion of his mine of jocularity while also learning that such jokes always recoil on their perpetrator. On the other hand, without jests – or indeed cakes and ale – life is diminished. At the end of *Henry IV, Part Two*, the beadles who arrest the low-life characters are thin things, half-starved in appearance, contrasting with the overflowing abundance of Doll Tearsheet who has stuffed cushions up her front in an attempt to appear pregnant. The effect is semi-symbolic. When the cushions fall out it is as if something of the abundant life-spirit of the Eastcheap Tavern – even of Merrie England itself – is being expelled.[40]

The curbing of comic licence is in *Henry IV*, a necessary expedient. Doll is, after all, only an ageing tart and Falstaff, coarsened by greed and inflated by pride, would dangerously have commanded the law. Gilbert too recognizes the need for order and at least some residual forms of hierarchy. Don Alhambra's song of the King who makes everybody equal suggests that total egalitarianism merely makes for a kind of general loss. Individual distinction and significance are eradicated and rational valuations subverted. This is an idea also canvassed by Walter Pater in *Gaston de Latour.*[41] Besides, uniform equality is a mirage: when people have to obey other people's orders, equality is out of the question.[42]

If equality is a false hope, anarchy may be a temptation. Carnival for instance has many advantages. A vital release in itself, it is also a useful way of siphoning off those excess energies and resentments that need a temporary outlet but cannot be allowed unrestrained continuance. The Feast of Fools referenced in Pater's *Denys l'Auxerrois* allows for a strictly time-bound period of topsy-turveydom, seen also (despite Ludwig's attempt to extend it) in *The Grand Duke.* In many ways, Ludwig's court is itself a Feast of Fools. In *Thespis,* the actors' reign as incompetent gods similarly suggests the dangers of an unregulated or confused dispensation.

The above does not negate some irony. Under Ludwig's manic rule, the laws of theatrical hierarchy and engagement contracts are actually *enforced.* In *Thespis,* it is the need for actor-gods to conform to their mythical history which conflicts with more natural human arrangements. One further complication is that all this can be manipulated. Julia, falsely claiming to loathe the part of Grand Duke's wife, is actually exploiting her own 'cherished dream' agenda. In the Feast of Fools, this does not apply, but there is even more disruption. Revelling clergy elect a burlesque Lord of Misrule, preside over the divine office wearing animal masks or women's clothes, sing obscene songs, swing censers that give off foul-smelling smoke, play dice at the altar, kick balls about, and otherwise parody the liturgy of the church. Afterward, they take to the streets, howling, issuing mock indulgences, hurling manure at bystanders, and – significantly – staging scurrilous plays.

The burlesque upturning of an existing dispensation is seen in many Gilbert works, sometimes – as in *Topsyturveydom* – with the burlesque version presented as a separate parallel entity. This is not to say that all alternatives are opposites. In *Sacred Folly*, Max Harris rewrites much of the traditional interpretation of the Feast of Fools, stating that it developed in the late 12th and early 13th centuries as a dignified alternative to rowdy secular New Year festivities. It recalls Mary's joyous affirmation that God 'has put down the mighty from their seat and exalted the humble'. This still, however, leaves us with the King for a Day, which in Ludwig's court involves a willed overturning of the values of economy, rigid formality, and dietary constraint. The difference is that Ludwig is not a Holy Fool – he is a secular one – a Lord of Misrule – who has to be curbed. In his case, the curbing comes from a technical quibble. Other treatments may be different. They may show a free-wheeling abundance and dangerous recklessness forced to submit to time and evanescence – to a sense of inevitable decay.

The sense of both *defying* and having to *accept* time passing is exemplified particularly in *Twelfth Night*. Not only is the last song elegiac. The earlier 'Come away, death' – also sung by Feste – sets a dark
shadow over the winter sun, adding its own comment on the desperate
revelling of the Toby Belch set. In Gilbert, several arias use the imagery
of darkness, winter storm, and loss, two fine examples being Princess
Ida's 'I built upon a rock' and 'Sorry her lot' from *H.M.S. Pinafore*. In
the latter, images of encroaching dark over wastes of waters[43] temporarily deepen the shadows. In *Much Ado,* the threatened darkness is
so great that it requires the introduction of a larger-than-life Dogberry
and starveling Verges to provide a double act to keep the comedy light
flickering.

Overall, the richest forms of comedy are probably those where the
shadow of night lies latent in the sunshine. Viola expresses her love
by innuendo – she is almost deprived of a voice but manages to con-
vey it obliquely to us while her beloved remains oblivious. Beatrice's
mother cried at the birth but 'there was a star danced and under that
was I born'.[44] The pathos, if not the poetry, looks to Gilbert's Mad
Margaret – the violet in a bed of more desirable roses. A borderline
sentimental version is his pantomime fairy-dancer whose tawdry stage
performance becomes *really* fairylike when she ministers unselfishly to
her drunken father in their poverty-stricken slum.[45]

The pathos within comedy should not be exaggerated. Quite often
a bitter-sweet main plot will be offset by a livelier, more farcical sub-
plot, the two gradually becoming intertwined. Meanwhile, a more
knockabout fun may intrude in the form of accidents. Elopements by
night may be interrupted; items may be lost or left behind; escaping
people may be seen or leave evidence of their departure. In *The Barber
of Seville,* a ladder for elopement is removed. In Act 2 of *The Marriage
of Figaro*, disguise, confusion, and the use of sign-language contribute
to a whole host of comic cross-currents.[46] Pace here is of the essence
but the undercutting of human endeavour can also occur in less frenetic
moments, as when Mabel, told she is to be separated from Frederic from
the 1870s till 1940, sings plaintively 'It seems so long'.[47] The opposite
(non-bathetic) mode is that of ridiculous inflation. In *The Grand Duke,*
the pettiness of the penny-halfpenny state of Pfennig Halbpfennig is actually highlighted by the Grand Duke's ostentatious displays of ritual
ceremony. Julia's parody mad-scene – a brilliant depiction of a woman
who strangles her apparent love-rival, then goes mad on discovering that
the dead woman was her lover's aunt – is notable for both inflationary
and bathetic comic effects.

There is, of course, a more philosophical aspect to the madness of
love, and this too finds frequent expression. Shakespeare's Theseus
combines the idea of love-lunacy with the assertion that the experience
can nonetheless lead to rhapsodic insights.[48] His Rosalind makes the

love-madness link part of the universal human condition.[49] One drawback is that it can be so destabilizing. In *Ruddygore,* Mad Margaret,
abandoned by Sir Despard, and replete with floral references, become
a parody not just of a crazed Ophelia but also – judging from her flute
obbligato – of Donizetti's *Lucia di Lammermoor.* Here and elsewhere,
Gilbert's treatments include two other things. One is a sense of the pathos within the parody. The other is an awareness of the counterbalancing sanity in wit. If, as Theseus claims, the visions of love are a mingling
of the revelatory and the hallucinatory, then wit is the voice of the rational. It offsets both the airy flights of fancy and the despair of the
rhapsodically forlorn.

The value of wit as a corrective and a challenge is reflected in Shakespeare and Gilbert alike. In characters such as Beatrice, wit is a both a
weapon and a defence. It is also a direct sign of the clear-sighted sanity
of a girl who can see a church by daylight. In *Patience*, this sanity – and
its value – are wittily endorsed by the *author.* Such applies when the absurd wail of a poet's heart ('Oh hollow! Hollow! Hollow') is equated by
the heroine with the *View Halloo* of a Cumbrian hunting-song.[50]

The downside of wit lies in its abuse. In Falstaff, it is increasingly used
for self-seeking mercenary ends. It connotes a lack of moral principle.
So, it does in *His Excellency* where it is the last refuge of the 'played-out
humorist'. Opposed to this is Jack Point's observation that an accepted
wit is regarded as including a joke even in mundanely saying 'Pass the
mustard'. More seriously, Beatrice shows the limitations of clever jocularity in commanding 'Kill Claudio'. Here, she abandons wit altogether,
expressing female solidarity in an uncompromising challenge to a man
whose own love for her will be gauged by his response to it.[51]

Whatever its form, one of the principal features of wit is that it exploits a dichotomy. There will be an opposition between what is said
and what is thought, what is stated and what is implied, how things *are*
and how things *seem*. Sometimes too, the joke will depend on subtle differences of meaning, as in Gilbert's remark about the woman who was
pretty once where 'once', meaning 'at some period in past time', transmutes into 'on one occasion'.[52] In comedy, generally such doubleness
can sometimes make a serious point. When Beatrice says that she gave
Benedict a single heart for his double one, she is implying his infidelity –
his claiming a truth to her which his conduct belied. Elsewhere, wit
can be an ingredient in a more surreal duality. In *His Excellency,* the
Governor forces the hussars to perform their drills in the form of a ballet dance. Here, the wit – visually played out – lies in the very concept
of yoking together two aspects which would normally be regarded as
incompatible.[53]

The Gilbertian tendency to undercutting itself involves a dichotomy.
Rose Maybud's selfishness is couched in the language of the Old Testament. She regularly uses 'thee', 'thy', and 'thou', favours the archaic third

person singular, and makes much use of 'Lo' and 'Behold'. This – partly satirizing the artificiality of melodrama dialogue – also gives a false quasi-religious moral seriousness to what is actually a career of fairly ruthless self-advancement. Of course, Rose 'loves' Robin, but her only soliloquy on the subject is made deliberately abrupt morphing from the idea of his being 'hallowed' to the admission that he would be no worse than anybody else. The whole treatment goes against the romantic bias in Shakespearian comedy, yet many of the plot devices (such as indirect confession of love and languishing in secret) are almost identical.

The revelation of love by indirect means is shown in Gilbert when Rose and Robin consult each other about alleged friends who are actually themselves. This matches Viola in *Twelfth Night* confessing her love by self-identification with an imaginary other – one who never told her love and whose history is a blank. In this case, the wistfulness does not preclude the possibility of cheekiness, swagger, and even bawdry. The girl's overacted cockiness as Cesario is itself an aspect of comic dichotomy, as is the joke when – faced with the prospect of a duel – she ruefully refers to the 'little thing' (a penis) that could make her tell how much she lacks of a man.[54] A much stronger example is Shakespeare's concealing of a four-letter word in the letter prepared for Malvolio. This is quite alien to Gilbert but the common-sense element is common to both.

The variety within the romantic comedy heroine is usually brought out by particular plot developments. Such applies with Beatrice when Hero is dishonoured and with the frequently burlesqued Princess Ida when she taps a genuine depth of despair at the failure of her hopes. Not all Gilbert's heroines undergo such developments. Rose Maybud, with her selfish materialism and inappropriate charities, is satirically conceived throughout. But Gilbert is aware that comedy is at its most piquant when there is an undertone of aspiration leading to possible failure and loss. It offsets the overall tendency to celebrate life, health, and harmony. It challenges ideas of Spring after Winter, procreation, fecundity, and growth.

Against the sense of possible loss and transience, there is one other key comic ingredient, namely an almost opposite sense of human empowerment. Sometimes – as in Lady Bracknell's comments on health – this endows the human spirit with abilities and control mechanisms which it does not actually have. Sometimes, Time itself is transcended. This again suggests a duality. Comedy (unlike farce) often registers loss, decay, and deliquescence, but generally it rises above it. Even in the dark-hued *Measure for Measure*, there is selflessness and compassion, not least when Isabella makes the supreme humanitarian gesture of joining Mariana in pleading for Angelo. In Gilbert, love also ultimately wins through, but his comedy, though high-spirited, is perhaps more latently anarchic. The main plus is that the spirit of mirth still triumphs. Care is a benumbing canker. It is hence to be resisted. Ultimately, Gilbert's comedy is on the side of life. It dissipates pains it encounters. It ends with a bargain called love.[55]

* *

From Shakespeare to Gilbert

Gilbert was born in 1836. This is not quite Victorian, and indeed, 18th-century theatrical traditions still exerted an influence. So, what *was* the condition of post-Shakespearian drama? One point to stress is limitation. By the beginning of the 19th century, there were still only two main theatres patented to mount spoken drama in London during the winter season. Other theatres were permitted to show comedy, pantomime, or melodrama, which then had a musical concomitant.

Initially, the licensing of the patent theatres marked a liberation from earlier restraint. Public entertainments had been banned under Cromwell, and it was Charles II himself who issued letters patent to Thomas Killigrew of the King's Company, Drury Lane, and to William Davenant of the Duke's Company, Lincolns Inn Fields.[56] In 1662, there were revisions allowing performance rights to actresses. One notable feature was an emphasis on adaptation. In 1662, for instance, Davenant staged *The Law Against Lovers*, a heavily adapted version of *Measure for Measure* incorporating various characters from *Much Ado About Nothing*.

Broadly speaking, Davenant was more innovative than Killigrew, being notable for reviving works by John Fletcher and his collaborators. The other big factor was the infiltration of a French influence. Years later in *A Hornpipe in Fetters*, Gilbert would complain of two critical assumptions: (a) that French plays are innately superior to the English[57] and (b) that Old Drama must be better than new. In *Old Plays and New Plays* (1873), he points out that, of nearly 4,000 plays produced between 1700 and 1800, 3,950 are now unknown, except perhaps by name. Of the remaining few, only thirty-five are still being produced. Of these, he estimates eleven could justifiably be considered classics.[58]

The influence of French and other European writing has a long history. The 1662 production of Sir Samuel Tuke's *The Adventures of Five Hours*, based on Calderón's *Los Empeños de Seis Horas*, was the first great hit of Restoration drama. By the time of Davenant and Killigrew, Corneille and Racine had already established the neo-classic standard for tragedy, and Molière, Quinault, and others were steadily supplying the English with comedy plots. The first French opera, *Cadmus and Hermione*, by Lully and Quinault, performed in Paris in 1673, crossed the channel almost immediately, influencing Dryden in his own attempts. Sometimes, the plots of Calderón or Lope de Vega came to the English at second-hand through French versions, while the romantic, semi-historical romances of Madame Scudéry and the Countess de la Fayette afforded a second supply of story material.

The French influence, though often resented, was difficult to avoid. Gilbert himself often adapted French works, ranging from Offenbach's *Les Brigands* to *Le Roi Candaule*. The latter was described in the programme as 'a very free and easy version of the highly successful Palais Royal Farce', itself by Henri Meilhac and Ludovic Halévy. Gilbert's version, *The Realm of Joy,* was, however, more than just a quick translation. He rewrote parts of it, making it apply to a topical event in which he had personally been closely implicated.

Le Roi Candaule is set in the box lobby of a theatre where an immoral play is being performed. In Gilbert's version, the play is politically rather than sexually scandalous, making a clear reference to *The Happy Land*, which Gilbert had co-written earlier the same year and which was still running on the new play's first night. *The Happy Land* had been briefly banned by the Lord Chamberlain because of its political satire – hence the references in the French-based play to 'the Lord High Disinfectant'. *The Realm of Joy* was nodded through partly to stem the controversy. The Examiner of Plays (William Donne) thought the piece utterly *incorrigible*. Nonetheless, prompted by the Lord Chamberlain, he did pass it.

i.

Even in the early days, serious drama was not entirely reliant on speech, being interspersed with singing or dancing, presumably to prevent non-stop gravitas. Meanwhile, there *were* new developments. The late 17th century was a period of intense rivalry among London's actors, and in 1695, there was a split in the United Company, which had been formed in 1682 with the merger of the King's Company and the Duke's. Dramatist and architect John Vanbrugh seized the opportunity and in 1703 acquired a former stable yard for the construction of a new theatre on the Haymarket. This eventually became the centre for Italian opera. Another nearby venue was the First Haymarket Theatre or Little Theatre built by John Potter and opening on 29 December 1720, with *La Fille a la Morte, ou le Badeaut de Paris*, performed by the Duke of Montague's 'French Comedians'. The theatre was closed under the 1737 Licensing Act, but in 1758, Theophilus Cibber obtained a general licence under which Samuel Foote, supported by the Duke of York, was allowed to exhibit plays each year from May to September during his lifetime.

It was the Licensing Act of 1737 which had given the Lord Chamberlain the statutory authority to veto performances. Not only could he ban any new play or any modification to an existing one. Theatre owners could be prosecuted for staging a play (or part of one) that had not received prior approval. By Gilbert's day, this had been replaced by the Theatres Act, 1843, by which the Chamberlain could only prohibit performances when of the opinion that 'it is fitting for the preservation of good manners, decorum or of the public peace so to do'. Earlier still, control was mainly a matter of the royal prerogative. In the 1620s and 1630s, the influence of the French queen Henrietta Maria directly encouraged more French incursions into English drama.

The French influence is seen not just in plays' subject-matter but in the performers. Actresses, for instance, first appeared on the English stage in 1629, when a troupe of French players, male *and* female, attempted to give performances at Blackfriars. According to a letter addressed by Thomas Brande to William Laud, Bishop of London, the public was indignant. The French actresses were 'hissed, hooted, and pippin-pelted from the stage'. The writer 'did not think they would soon be ready to try the same again'. As a matter of fact, they reappeared a few weeks later at the Fortune and Red Bull theatres but again not successfully. The Master of the Revels, 'in respect of their ill luck', kindly returned a portion of the fees which they had had to pay for their licence.

The French fiasco was long remembered but the idea of female performers (as opposed to boys trained by older male actors) continued to gain currency. In 1632, Lady Strangelove, in Brome's comedy, *The Court Beggar*, was made to say: 'The boy's a pretty actor, and his mother can play her part: women-actors now grow in request'. In 1633, Prynne opposed this, bringing out his *Histrio-Mastix*, in which he stigmatized all 'woman-actors' as 'monsters', calling their performances 'impudent', 'shameful', and 'unwomanish'. Gilbert had no great problem with cross-dressing actresses. In *On Guard*, the part of Guy Warrington was played by Maggie Brennan, who had appeared as Peter in *Creatures of Impulse*. In *The Princess* (1870), Hilarion, Cyril, and Florian and King Gama's three sons were all enacted by women.

The employment of actresses in male roles does not prevent Gilbert from railing against transvestism when it involves men dressing as women. 'To my thinking, Mr. Clarke, or any other actor in girls' clothes is not a pleasant sight', he writes in an *Illustrated Times* review.[59] An article in the following year (15 May 1869) goes further: 'It is a disgrace to the stage that men are suffered to wear women's clothes and pad themselves in imitation of women's figures'. Oddly, Gilbert himself allows male to female cross-dressing in *Princess Ida*, but here the robes are academic ones and the men's masculinity remains deliberately obvious.

The arrival of the actress was especially signalled by Davenant's *Siege of Rhodes*, a piece performed in 1656 at Rutland House, before a paying audience, with a cast including Mrs. Coleman as *Ianthe*. The work was an opera, written to Davenant's text by five composers, Davenant achieving permission from the Puritan government by calling it

'recitative music'. When it was published in 1656, it was under the equiv-
ocating and indigestible title:

> The siege of Rhodes made a representation by the art of prospective
> in scenes, and the story sung in recitative musick, at the back part
> of Rutland-House in the upper end of Aldersgate-Street, London.

The 1659 reprinting changes one detail, giving the location *at the Cock-
Pit in Drury Lane.*[60]

ii.

After *The Siege of Rhodes,* the advance of the female grew apace. When,
on 8 December 1660, Killigrew mounted a representation of *Othello*
with a female Desdemona, a prologue by Thomas Jordan drew strong
attention to the special attraction:

> I come, unknown to any of the rest.
> To tell the news; I saw the lady drest –
> The woman plays to-day; mistake me not,
> No man in gown or page in petticoat.

By Gilbert's day, men in gowns were more of a rarity. They were mainly
low comedians playing harridan wives, mothers, dames, and occasionally historical characters such as Joan of Arc or Queen Elizabeth.

The above was not universally pleasing. Surely (said Gilbert), to any
person of taste, there must be something 'utterly repulsive' in the appearance of a man 'dressed, padded, and painted in imitation of a woman,
with pink stockings and embroidered underclothing'.[61] But there were
plenty of other reasons for objecting to play-going. A letter of 1826
from Prince Pückler-Muskau to his wife is scathing about the state of
the English drama: 'The striking thing to a foreigner in the local theatres here is the unheard-of roughness and coarseness of the audience.
It means that, apart from the Italian opera … the higher classes rarely
visit their national theatre'.[62] In the 1660s, theatre-going was more
fashionable, because more newly re-introduced, but men-woman cross-
dressing was not part of the attraction. According to Jordan (who disdains 'men-actresses'):

> Our women are defective, and so sized
> You'd think they were some of the guard disguised;
> For, to speak truth, men act, that are between
> Forty and fifty, wenches of fifteen:
> With bones so large and nerve so incompliant,
> When you call Desdemona, *enter* giant.

Here, the writer is thinking of men in serious roles and is being satirical rather than serious. Nonetheless, Gilbert would surely have concurred.

As far as the 17th century is concerned, another key event occurred in June 1661. This was a public performance of *The Siege of Rhodes* at Davenant's theatre, with Mrs. Davenport as *Roxalana* and Mrs. Saunderson (Betterton) as *Ianthe*. By this time, prejudice against 'women-actors' had abated to the extent that in1664, Killigrew produced his comedy, *The Parson's Wedding*, with women in all the parts. Another change was more directly linked to the Continent. Much French drama remained in rhyming couplets and Roger Boyle, Earl of Orrery (1621–1679) seems to have had the doubtful glory of re-introducing this into England, writing at least four tragedies on historical or legendary subjects. Actually in France, by the 1620s, the French royal court had grown tired of tragedy, preferring the more escapist tragic-comedy, but the theatre-going still public preferred the former.

Whether in France or elsewhere, one notable feature of 17th-century theatre was the degree of cross-fertilization. Theoretical precepts would derive from Horace and Aristotle, augmented by modern commentaries from Julius Caesar Scaliger and Lodovico Castelvetro. Plots favoured Seneca, Plutarch, and Suetonius but might also draw on French, Italian, or Spanish short stories. By the middle of the century, Sophocles and Euripides were also becoming significant, while Spanish playwrights such as Pedro Calderón de la Barca, Tirso de Molina, and Lope de Vega were being widely adapted. The Pastoral was especially associated with Spain and Italy. French comedy favoured farce, the satirical monologue, and the mode of the Italian *Commedia dell'Arte*.

One important French voice was the dramatist Pierre Corneille. One of his contentions was that the stage – in both tragedy and comedy – should focus on noble people who should never be depicted as vile or doing reprehensible actions. Such ideas, best seen in his three *Discours du poème dramatique* (1660), were to have a direct influence on Dryden. So was his point that what happens on the stage must be necessary, not coincidental, not resulting from some sudden change of mind, and not involving the intervention of the *deus ex machina*.

Corneille's stress on necessity includes one corollary: that transitions from one scene to the next should not be abrupt. What he was really arguing for was greater logic in developments, but logic is itself a loaded term. In Gilbert, the emphasis will be on the quirks and quibbles within a logical set-up, as when being half a fairy becomes a literal bodily split. In *The Grand Duke*, the logic of the law not only requires the random drawing of playing cards but even the contesting of their painted values.

The arbitrary aspects of logic are well seen in *Ruddygore*. Here, the fact that suicide is itself a crime makes refusal to fulfil the witch's curse (leading to automatic death) a crime in itself. This obviates the effect of the punishment. By *not* committing a crime one is in fact actually committing one.

Another of Corneille's views is that on-stage narration should be limited, events previous to the action being used as little as possible, and exits and entrances made plausible. Here, what he is really doing is developing the classical doctrine of verisimilitude and unity[63] – the sort of thing mocked by Gilbert in *A Consistent Pantomime* and in Pooh-Bah's insistence on verisimilitude in the fleshing out of an increasingly implausible narrative. Elsewhere, the joke is on a *lack* of verisimilitude (and unity). Gilbert's parody of Henry Neville's adaptation of *Les Misérables* (*The Yellow Passport*) highlights the fact that it takes four acts and ten years of pursuing Jean Valjean for his pursuer Javert finally to discover that he has absent-mindedly been carrying his pardon in his pocket.[64] In his burlesque of *The Long Strike* (*Fun*, 29 September 1866), the policeman informs us: 'The best way to detect a murderer is to let everyone go whom you suspect'. This then leads to the stage-direction: *[Lets every one go whom he suspects. Tableau.*

iii.

Although generally favouring the unities, even Corneille admits that too strict an adherence may be counterproductive, as (for instance) in Aeschylus' *Agamemnon* where the fall of Troy and the King's return occur within minutes. This too strikes a chord with Gilbert who often mocks the violation of likely time sequences and in *A Sensation Novel* introduces the character of Gripper, a permanently late detective. In one scene, he enters in disguise as a Grand Turk, only to be upbraided by Lady Rockalda, with the brusque 'You're late, Gripper'. The reply suggests that sensation detectives always *are* late. If they were not, the novel 'would come to an end long before its time'. The other implied joke is about the disguise *motif*. Gripper takes so long putting on his totally unconvincing disguises that he is unlikely ever to be on time for anything.[65]

In Corneille's view, the best solution for dramatic time is to leave it indeterminate. All acts should, however, cover a similar amount of story time, though the fifth may be allowed the privilege of acceleration. Gilbert makes fun of such logical sequencing (a) by telescoping time within a played scene or (b) by using the interval time as a kind of short-term reality. The first occurs in his parody of Edmund Falconer's *Oonagh*, where the time taken to bury a body is not left to the interval but condensed within the action:

SOMEBODY: Here is a person called Peery Clancy. We will bury him, and cut off his ears!
ALL: We will! *[They bury him, all but his head, and cut off his ears.*

The second applies in *A Sensation Novel* where the dramatized action is itself an interval. In the largely unseen novel, Ruthven is detested by

Alice, but fortunately, at the end of each volume, they can be themselves, shaking off their imposed 'detestable attributes', to appear for an hour or so in their true light.[66]

The feasibility and likelihood required by Corneille are mocked in Gilbert by their absence. In his parody of *A Hero of Romance*, Victor (as in the original) is accidentally locked in the ruined tower of Elfen with the lady Blanche. To avoid compromising her, he then gallantly leaps out, an act exaggerated here into 'a sheer fall of at least twelve thousand feet'. In the next act, he reappears to tell the audience, 'Saved by a miracle! Not so much as a scratch'. On stage his fall was allegedly broken by projecting ivy. *The Tomahawk*'s variant is for Victor to jump merely a couple of hundred feet, after telling Blanche, 'Nay, start not; among my many accomplishments I number athletics'.[67]

iv.

Corneille's legacy to the English is difficult to quantify, but he certainly exerted influence. One of his contentions was that tragedy deals with affairs of state such as wars and dynastic marriages, while comedy deals with love. Another was that tragic work need not always have a tragic ending and that plays should never show evil being rewarded or nobility degraded. This was challenged by Vanbrugh, and later by Gilbert, but endorsement of the iambic couplet rhyme was more successful, possibly unfortunately so since it often became stilted and monotonous. Roger Boyle's methods usually involved taking a semi-historical story, filling it with bombastic sentiments, giving the strutting figures iambic rhyming pentameters, and labelling the result 'heroic drama'. This was still being satirized in Gilbert's day, one linking bridge being Sheridan's *The Critic*.

Not all heroic drama was despicable. Dryden for one praised its excitement, its perpetual bustle and commotion. But too often the rhetoric gave a sense of inflation overlying a barren emptiness. Pepys called Boyle's *Guzman* 'as mean a thing as had been seen on the stage for a great while'.[68] More enjoyable were the parodies, one being *The Rehearsal*, mocking *The Conquest of Granada* and featuring Dryden as Bayes in reference to his being poet laureate. Though condemned as 'scurrilous and ill-bred', this piece, like Gilbert's burlesques, served usefully to puncture the pretentiously overblown.[69]

Restoration Comedy was generally very different. It consisted of works that were clever, polished, and ingenious, suggesting mainly the rather blasé sophistication of a coterie of the fashionable world, with a knowing (often French-derived) sexual emphasis. The women, for the most part, are lovely and pert, some – especially the older ones – showing a cynical wit. This is a type Gilbert is to exploit but ultimately humanize in Mrs. Fitzosborne,[70] though the constraints of moral censorship limit the scope of his epigrams.

The Restoration comic world also shows an Italian influence. Duped husbands and fathers are a more sophisticated form of the dull, stupid *Pantalone*. The companions of the main protagonists – the busybodies, gossips, amorous widows, and jealous wives – reflect the intrigues and intriguers of Italian court comedy. Sometimes, there is a sense of ennui – of a jaded palate needing ever more stimulation, so it is hardly surprising that the world-weary cynicism and moral laxity led to a reaction. Jeremy Collier, writing from a clergyman stance, denounced not only Congreve and Vanbrugh, but Shakespeare and most of the Elizabethans. Three points especially drew forth his denunciations: the so-called lewdness of the plays, the frequent references to the Bible and biblical characters, and the criticism, slander, and abuse flung from the stage upon the clergy.

In Gilbert's day, concern for the above was still in force. No clergy figure arrives in Utopia to be displayed and partly satirized as a Flower of Progress, and even appealing ones can be denounced. The *Monthly Musical Record* complained, for instance, at the comic depiction of a clergyman in *The Sorcerer*, commenting that 'the earnest, hard-working, and serious Clergy should not be made the subject of sneering caricature upon the stage'. Worse came from Lewis Carroll who in 1888 wrote:

> That clever song 'The pale young curate', with its charming music, is to me simply painful. I seem to see him as he goes home at night, pale and worn with the day's work, perhaps sick with the pestilent atmosphere of a noisome garret where, at the risk of his life, he has been comforting a dying man – and is your sense of humour, my reader, so keen that you can laugh at that man?[71]

Clearly, one had to tread a careful line in the satirical vales of Victorian burlesque.

v.

The would-be constraints imposed on Gilbert did have some happy effects. If not Rival Curates, it did give us Rival Poets. But this would still have displeased Collier. Not only did he advocate barring any Desdemona, however chaste, from showing her passion. In comedy, *any* ridicule or satire should be barred except that against persons of low quality. One big trouble (he said) was that playwrights glorified all the sins, passions, or peculiarities portrayed in their characters. Here, he had royal support, shown in the *nolle prosequi* (immunity from prosecution for earlier offences) granted by William III. Meanwhile, Congreve and Vanbrugh were among the playwrights now being persecuted, fines also being imposed on some of the most popular actors and actresses.

The campaign against 'vice and profaneness' was quite long-lived. It provoked a pamphlet war, lasting sporadically until about 1726. In 1698, the English critic John Dennis wrote a piece titled *The Usefulness of the Stage*, and John Vanbrugh a more light-hearted *Short Vindication of The Relapse and The Provok'd Wife from Immorality and Prophaneness* (sic). One of Vanbrugh's accusations was that Collier was more upset by unflattering theatrical depictions of clergymen than by any actual blasphemy. But some writers certainly took the matter seriously. William Congreve refuted Collier's allegations in his *Amendments of Mr. Collier's False and Imperfect Citations* (1698). Thomas D'Urfey in *The Campaigners* (1698) gave his riposte on the stage. This only led Collier to fire back with his *Defence of the Short View* (1699). Eight years later, Edward Filmer offered a counter-movement in *A Defence of Plays*.

However one views Collier's strictures, the fact remains that there was a step-change. By the end of the 17th century, the Restoration comic style had collapsed, giving way to the sentimental mode beginning in 1696 with *Love's Last Shift*. Possibly, the swelling of public opposition was due to a surfeit. But under King William and later Queen Anne, there was also the beginning of a stricter moral infiltration. Collier's insistence that the playwright's *business* is to recommend virtue, and discountenance vice is almost the opposite of that in *The Double-Dealer* (1693). Here, Congreve tells us: 'It is the business of a comic poet to paint the vices and follies of humankind'.

One first result was the decline of the French influence. Frenchmen and the French-influenced English still appeared but were usually an object of satire as happens with La Nippe in *The Lord of the Manor* (1780) and all the darned Mounseers who were a butt of the nautical melodrama satirized in *Ruddygore*.[72] On the other hand, French influences *did* lie latent. Gilbert himself often borrowed French material, complaining that English writers write tame plays because French subject-matter is denied them. Not only does an English audience not like conjugal infidelity. A duel cannot be introduced 'since it is no longer an English custom'.[73]

Gilbert's objections are later to be reinforced more trenchantly by Shaw, but his own are eloquent enough. Many dramatic critics, he laments, have recently discovered 'that satire and cynicism are misplaced in comedy', meaning that the 'propriety of repartee is to be estimated by the standard of conversation in a refined drawing-room'.[74] He even seems to envy the greater freedom of Sheridan, though the latter is a poor example, having himself bowdlerized *The Relapse*.

Whatever the constraints on English drama, there is no doubt that French influence revived. *The Ticket-of-Leave Man* (1863) by Tom Taylor is a four-act melodrama, based on a French drama, *Le Retour de Melun,* and the first to introduce a significant detective (Hawkshaw) of a type later to be satirized by Gilbert. *Narcisse*, another of Taylor's plays, also has a foreign provenance. It is adapted from a play by Brachvogel, based on Goethe's translation of Diderot's novel *Le Neveau de Rameau.* By the time of the London opening (Lyceum, 17 February 1868), Brachvogel's version had already been played in America, initiated by Daniel E. Bandmann (1840–1905), an actor-manager considerably admired by Gilbert.

Apart from foreign factors, the rise of the actress can also be dated well back into the 17th century, often leading to augmentations, as in Dryden's revised *Macbeth* where Lady Macduff gains numerous extra passages.[75] Also increased was the spectacular element and the taking of theatre into the provinces. After Davenant's death (April 1668), Betterton collaborated with his widow in organizing three consecutive (and profitable) summer seasons in Oxford starting in 1669. Later from 9 November 1671, a move into Dorset Garden theatre allowed the Duke's Company to produce many of the spectaculars, operas, and semi-operas that would become the hallmark of Restoration opulence.[76]

Another point was the gradual widening of performance opportunities. One key date here is 1695 when, after some disagreements, Betterton obtained a licence from William III, to form a new company at the old theatre in Lincoln's Inn Fields, later (in 1720) moving to Covent Garden. Thereafter, there were other proliferations. Not only did Samuel Foote's Haymarket fill the gap left by the patent theatres' summer closures. In 1768, the Theatre Royal, Bath, got its patent; in 1772, the Theatre Royal, Liverpool, opened its doors; and in 1778, the Theatre Royal, Bristol, achieved patent status.

Provincial theatre could in fact be quite adventurous. One striking piece was *Mahomet, a* five-act tragedy written in 1736 by Voltaire, and staged in Liverpool on 5 June 1772. The play is a study of religious fanaticism and self-serving manipulation based on Muhammad's ordering of the murder of his critics. The dramatist – in language unacceptable today – described the play as 'written in opposition to the founder of a false and barbarous sect'. Presumably, it was staged in the 1741 translation (really an adaptation), completed by John Hoadly, first performed in 1744 and published by a certain A. Donaldson in 1759.

The patent theatres obviously had most of the advantages. But actually, even in London, there was pressure to expand. In the early years of the 19th century, the modern West End began to emerge when the Lord Chamberlain's Office partially broke the monopoly by allowing a few *burletta* licences. This was really a permission to perform plays with music in small theatres along the Strand such as Jane Scott's *Sans Pareil* (1806), later to become the *Adelphi*, furnishing the notorious supernumeraries who became Gilbert's much satirized Adelphi guests.[77] One of the *Adelphi*'s sensational aspects was that on 16 December 1897, the actor William Terriss was stabbed to death while entering.[78] The Gilbert link is that Terriss' daughter was the actress Ellaline Terriss, who, with her actor-manager husband Seymour Hicks, was a regular guest at Grim's Dyke. At Gilbert's prompting, Hicks – in collaboration with

George Edwardes – wrote a melodrama, *One of the Best*, based on the recent Dreyfus trial, and intended to star his father-in-law. The *Adelphi* opening (21 December 1895) was a great success, the piece running for well over a year.

The middle-class ambience of Seymour Hicks was not, earlier in the 19th century, a prevailing trend. Far from being limited to serious drama, shows at Covent Garden and Drury Lane now included lion-taming in cages and battles on horseback. This was despite a growing celebrity status for some performers, notably Lewis and Quick who appear as characters in Jane Austen's *Love and Friendship*. Democracy meanwhile was certainly at work in the structure. There were two royal boxes, a huge gallery, and on the ground the pit where people came and went, leaping over the backless benches. Meanwhile, in the saloons and lobbies men-about-town could easily expect to meet prostitutes who got in at special prices with a season ticket.

The above is important because it helps to explain Gilbert's later attempts at sanitization and good order. In the decades before his birth, most aristocrats were far too fashionable to arrive at the theatre on time: 'The votaries began to drift in after the first act, and ladies of pleasure from the interval'.[79] Even in the newly re-opened Theatre Royal, audiences remained rowdy. When in 1809 the Duke of York took his seat, people yelled out 'Dukey!' and 'My darling!' (a reference to his mistress who had illegally sold army commissions). When Macduff played by Charles Kemble killed Macbeth (John Kemble), there were roars of 'Well done! Kill 'im, Charley!'[80]

Another of Gilbert's crusades was the imposition of more unity on an evening's entertainment. This certainly seemed apposite. A poster dated Monday 5 February 1838, advertises *Richard III* featuring Charles Keane 'to conclude with (35th Time) a New Grand Comic Christmas Pantomime' called *Harlequin Jack a Lantern*. There is also reference to a farce called *Our Mary Ann*, which, having been received 'with shouts of Laughter and Applause', will be repeated 'Three Times every Week', including on 8 February when it will share a bill with two works: Auber's 'Grand Historical Opera' *Gustavus III* and the ubiquitous *Jack-a-Lantern*. Throughout the 18th century, this wide-ranging, essentially libertarian tradition had been commonplace but, by the late Regency period, a new decorum was jostling with it. In her autobiographical jottings, Lady Sarah Lennox mused that, compared with the time of her youth (the 1760s), language was becoming bowdlerized. Anna Laetitia Barbauld writes that 'in our more refined age (1813) we do not call a *spade* a *spade*'. Modern women 'go into fits at the bare mention of breeches'. They would expire at the dinner table 'if you were to name the thigh of a chicken'.[81]

The new prudery is partly allied to the Cult of Sentiment, which in turn relates to the French *Comédie Larmoyante*. But a concern for linguistics had arisen long before the later Georgian period. In the aftermath of *Les Précieuses Ridicules,* we have in 1756 the hilarious afterpiece *The Kept Mistress* or *The Mock Orators,* whose sub-plot (featuring Mrs. Love-phrase) directly mock the new-fangled fashion for 'oratory'. This – airy nonsense disguised as metaphysical thinking – is the sort of thing later to be ridiculed in the Effingham family in Gilbert's own *Tom Cobb*. By the mid-Victorian period, much of the theatre's earlier boisterousness had diverted to the rowdy Music Hall, but even this reflected social divisions. In the song *What cheer (or Watcher!), 'Ria!'* (1885), a woman green-grocer is mocked by her friends in the gallery simply for sitting with the swells in the stalls, leading to a series of disasters which seem a mockery of her own presumption.

The segregation of clientele had admittedly long been a contentious issue. It was indeed one of the causes of the so-called Covent Garden Theatre Wars of 1809, themselves a reflection of the avowed libertarian-ism of the British theatre-going public. Mr. Punch here is important. He embodied a Briton's right 'to spit, swear, take his clothes off, drink to ex-cess and conduct his life as he saw fit'. In 1826, Prince Pückler-Muskau called him 'a perfect symbol of the Englishman'. Both are wooden and heartless, but the puppet, like his public, 'conquers everything by his invincible merriment and humour, laughs at the laws, at men, and at the devil himself'.[82]

The question of whether Punch's activities really constitute comedy is debatable, but the black humour certainly looks towards *Gentle Alice Brown*. Punch is a sadist. He kills his wife and baby, taking up with a buxom mistress and brooks no interference with his destructive liberty. Though an Italian immigrant, it is he who punishes all the bogey-men of the popular British imagination: mothers-in-law, bailiffs, creditors, doctors, parish overseers, policemen, and officious meddlers. In this, as Pückler-Muskau noticed, he 'shows in part what an Englishman is, in part what he wishes to be'. Charles Dickens' Quilp is a version of this iconic figure and so (some might add) is the irascible, uncompromising W.S. Gilbert.

The black comedy of the Punch scenario is aided by various aspects. One is the lack of flexibility. Since the puppets are carved from wood, their facial expressions cannot change. They are stuck in the same exag-gerated pose, this helping to deter any sense of realism and to distance the audience. The use of the swazzle also helps to create humour, as does the swazzled sound of Punch's voice making more eccentric the intrinsic cruelty. The popularity of the character is reflected in a transcript to be found in Henry Mayhew's *London Labour and the London Poor* in which Punch eventually kills Satan with his cudgel, crying, 'Bravo! Hor-ray! Satan is dead. We can now all do as we like!' This resembles one of Gilbert's inverted moral endings but to Dickens Punch was both harm-less and invigorating, his main point being the spectator-satisfaction involved in seeing likenesses of men and women so knocked about, without any pain or suffering.[83]

vi.

Whatever we make of Mr. Punch, there is no doubt that questions of liberty and licence pervade English theatre and letters. *Mansfield Park* probably derives its title from William Murray, first Earl of Mansfield famous for denying the legality of keeping slaves in England. Sterne's *Sentimental Journey* tells us that liberty is a 'thrice sweet and gracious goddess'. Such views (from 1768) are later to be called into question by the indiscriminately destructive effects of the French Revolution, but the freedom of the Briton (and especially the Englishman) does echo down the ages, particularly in the British tar – Gilbert's soaring soul, 'as free as a mountain bird'. In The *Kept Mistress* – where freedom ironically includes impressment – it is the bluff members of the British Navy who carry off the egotistical and ridiculous First Orator, the implication being that British honesty and independence will have no truck with fancy speech and affected pontificating. The other side of the coin is the sentimental one. Already in *As You Like It,* Jacques had combined cynicism with a strong strain of romantic melancholy. Later, this will resurface in the English comedies of Colley Cibber and Sir Richard Steele, and the French ones of Pierre-Claude Nivelle de la Chaussée popularizing the lachrymose mode.

One key sentimental work is Steele's *The Conscious Lovers* (Drury Lane, 7 November 1722) achieving an initial run of eighteen consecutive nights. Its French counterpart, the *comédie larmoyante*, was exemplified in works such as *La Fausse Antipathie* (1734), leading naturally to the domestic dramas of Diderot and Sedaine. To Voltaire, all this was deplorable. The *comédie larmoyante* was a proof of the inability of the author to produce either comedy or tragedy. Oddly, however, he himself produced a play of similar character in *L'Enfant prodigue.*[84] More widely, there was the oddity that robust common sense existed side by side with neurasthenia, and Romanticism marched both beside and within the Gothic.

Why the age was so disparate is debatable. Some might argue that it was excessive over-refinement that made the taste for the Gothic necessary. It was a kind of indulgent excess needed to stimulate an otherwise jaded palate. Gilbert's take on the sentimental strain is, unsurprisingly, one of mockery. In *Tom Cobb*, the poverty-stricken Effinghams claim credit by reaching at the height of lofty metaphysical abstraction. It is their way of avoiding self-blame for their poverty. In *Patience,* lofty language is again ridiculed. One example comes in Lady Angela's response to Grosvenor's cautionary jingle 'Teasing Tom was a very bad boy'.[85] Here, in the reference to retribution like a poisèd hawk, effusive rapture mingles the moralistic with the rhapsodic mode, both suggesting an element of artificiality in the process.

The mockery of the sentimental school is most effective when it is embedded in a strong character contrast. Such applies in *Tom Cobb* when Caroline Effingham visits her down-to-earth Irish ex-school-friend, telling her of a romance initiated through the effects of the printed page. One aspect is a contrast between Matilda's laconic directness and Caroline's gushing rhapsody. Another is the use of undercutting detail – elements such as the hardly poetic name of the *Surrey-suburban Journal*, the defection of the beloved, and Caroline's mercenary recourse to the law.[86] In *His Excellency* (1894), there is another variant. Here, the two daughters of the Elsinore Governor join their father in a series of heartless humiliating jokes, which eventually will rebound back on them. What is most interesting, however, is that, even when they soften, they fight against it, particularly in relation to the tricking of their suitors:

THORA: *[sighing]* – Oh, Nanna, they're good fellows! I wish it was all real.
NANNA: No use wishing, dear. We'd better try and forget all about them *[Looking off.]* Oh – look! All the people coming to get married!
THORA: Poor people. We – we must go and find our bridegrooms!
NANNA: Poor bridegrooms! It's…it's a capital joke! *[about to cry]*
THORA: Capital! *[Looking at Nanna's face]* Why, a real tear, I do believe!
NANNA: *[holding it on her finger]* – Yes, it's real this time.
THORA: *[examining it]* – Funny, isn't it?
NANNA: Very amusing!
THORA: Put it back. *[Nanna does so]* All right now?
NANNA: *[brightly]* – All right now![87]

Here, the bright words belie the inner unhappiness suggesting a war between innate cynicism and the dawning of emotional commitment.

vii.

Gilbert's distrust of emotional display is not without precedent. Early Victorian farces often adopt the boisterous, anti-romantic mode, one example being Joseph Coyne's *How to Settle Accounts with Your Laundress* which takes us far from the sentimental love-duty mode found for instance, in the Truemore-Sophia scenes in *The Lord of the Manor*. Here, Trumore tells Sophia: 'A passion for our country is the only one that ought to have competition with virtuous love – when they unite the hearts, our actions are inspiration'. He then launches into an aria about imbibing fire from the girl's eyes to give courage to conquer or expire. Even quite cynical plays succumb to the sentimental strain.

Bulwer-Lytton's *Money* 'employs the manipulation and manoeuvring of a Congreve comedy against a background of Victorian materialism'. Unfortunately, however, the influence of Dickens and Thackeray (and, we might add, the late 18th century) is reflected in the 'calculated sentimentality of the love-interest'.[88]

How far then was Gilbert satirizing an ongoing theatrical and novelistic tendency? One key event was the trial of James Hackman, a young soldier-clergyman, who in 1779 was indicted for the murder of Martha Ray, the opera-singing mistress of the Earl of Sandwich. In *Love and Madness: A Story Too True*,[89] letters attributed to Hackman reflect the idea of the heart as a vessel of supreme emotion – palpitating, passionate, extreme in highly tuned sensibility. One odd fact is that William Wordsworth used the name Martha Ray in his poem *The Thorn* where a peasant woman, deserted and left pregnant by her lover, has become mad through her grief. This – driving her to infanticide – looks forward to George Eliot's Hetty Sorrel and (without the illegitimate child) to Gilbert's Mad Margaret. The other aspect is psychological-scientific. Erasmus Darwin, obviously not referencing peasant fatalism, saw love's madness as a new condition. To him, it is a consequence of the leisure, refinement, and taste that were made possible by modern society.[90]

The Mad Margaret mode is, of course, a melodrama parody. But high sensibility was often linked with madness and excess. Modern abundance has led to 'a proliferation of desire, the elevation of feeling and heightening of sensibility in ways that were unheard of in less developed societies' ... 'Where the savage feels one want, the civilised man has a thousand'. This, the view of Thomas Trotter, means that 'everything within view is calculated to prompt his desires and provoke his passions; no antidote is opposed to suppress the one or to moderate the other'.[91] Gilbert's satire is directed less to this than to the more lofty attenuations. Both the Effinghams and the rapturous maidens float on a high cloud of aesthetic-metaphysical pseudo-enlightenment. Both, however, have links with earlier manifestations. The mature Lady Louisa Stuart recalled that at the age of fourteen, she was afraid 'she should not cry enough to gain the credit of proper sensibility'. Hazlitt called the rage for it 'a do-me-good, lack-a-daisical whining make-believe'. In 1811, the journalist Hewson Clarke makes another point, linking it to a prudery whereby one day Society will ban 'every object that seems to bear a Phallic outline', not least rolling-pins and pokers.[92]

The theme of imposed prudery and acted emotion is a recurring one in Gilbert. Bunthorne, the fleshly poet, confesses in soliloquy that his Mediaevalism, and by implication his Hellenism, are an affection. They are 'born of a morbid love of admiration'. Lady Sophy lectures daily to the Utopian Maidens on the proper mode of courtship, shunning all 'unrehearsed emotions' in favour of a refined (but calculated) ritualistic display.[93] In real life, it was not calculation but *feeling* that was stressed, but the tangle of affectation with real attempts at a higher sensibility could have confusing results. Sir William Harrrington, walking in Bath in a public garden, was so overcome with wordless emotion that he felt compelled to throw himself face down in a flower bed. Another gentleman was so overwrought with anxiety about the health of his schoolboy son that, rather than taking a post-chaise to see him, he sat down and composed an elegy.[94] Meanwhile, in Parliament, Charles James Fox (1749–1806) burst into floods of tears over a political quarrel with Burke (1729–1797), who then started weeping himself. When the Prince Regent refused to extend a sinecure to Sheridan's son, the playwright-father made a hysterical scene, 'crying and shrieking' most bitterly.

The cult of sensibility and its theatrical offshoots would eventually morph into the limp and clinging mode referenced by Gilbert's Lady Jane. But another mode was the hysterical frenzy of a Julia Jellicoe mad scene. The Prince Regent 'cried by the hour' over Mrs. Fitzherbert, rolling on the floor, striking his forehead, and tearing his hair. He also bombarded her with sentimental letters – one of forty-two pages – and feigned at least one blood-soaked suicide attempt.[95] The opposite face was a tendency towards a fashionable melancholia and hypochondria. In *Patience,* the twenty lovesick maidens 'sighing and burning and clinging and yearning' are characterized by the naively down-to-earth dairymaid, as never seeming quite well. This apparently is the transcendentalism of delirium. It is an acute accentuation of the most supreme ecstasy which the earthy might mistake for indigestion.

The link from Regency hypochondria to the art and times of the mature Gilbert can be found partly in medical literature. Thomas Trotter in *A View to the Nervous Temperament* (1807) introduces us to a new modern race of 'Samuel Sensitives'. As an experienced naval doctor, he is appalled by the feeling that people at home have degenerated into fops and weaklings, all the more debilitated by the reading of novels.[96] In literature, such morbidly degenerative effects (reinforced here by inbreeding) are seen in *The Fall of the House of Usher*. Later, Gilbert's Lady Jane (probably named for Jane Morris) will equate exalted love with both high aesthetic feeling and morbid debilitation.

Whether real or psychosomatic, the idea of over-strained nerves taps into another factor: the idea of too much artiness being psychically dangerous. In *Patience*, the rapturous maidens, transfigured by a love which is also a cultural aspiration, sob, sigh, and (according to Patience) have red, sore eyes. In an 1869 letter from Henry James to his invalid sister, he presents Jane Morris' own silent invalidism as a kind of embodiment of Pre-Raphaelite art. The lady is described as languishing in purple, [a] dark silent mediaeval woman with her mediaeval toothache.[97] One implication is of an element of personal self-creation – perhaps of playing up to an image. Another is of unhealthy self-absorption. Shaw once said of Jane that 'She did not take much notice of anybody, and none whatever of Morris, who talked all the time'.[98]

viii.

The Regency obsession with ill-health is notable in itself. But it may also suggest links with the new prudery which – given a Victorian twist – was to impose a strong limitation on Gilbert's ability to deal frankly with sex. In *Creatures of Impulse,* the sexually inhibited and shy Pipette is cursed by a malevolent fairy but only to the extent of having to go round *kissing* everyone. Compare this with Feydeau's *A Flea in the Ear,* and we soon realize that we are in a world of Victorian bourgeois respectability. Ultimately, it morphs into Lady Sophy, a virgin blessed with 'Respectability enough for Six', who even after conferring four parts upon her pupils, still retains, a considerable balance compared to the King. As finally conceived, she is a blend. A type of Victorian self-repression, she also look back to an earlier prudery mocked in the idea that 'no horses but mares and geldings should enter a town nor any unchaste idea inflame the bosom of a single virgin'.[99]

Lady Sophy's strictures are actually unfair as the King has been forced to write his own libels. But the main point is that this is by now a parody. The lady's prudery is already old-fashioned. One complication is that there were in the Regency some popular and quite specific volumes about bodily pleasure. *Aristotle's Compleat Master Piece* (first published in 1684) advised us to have sex early and often: 'it eases and lightens the body, clears the mind [and] comforts the head and senses'. It also expels the melancholy so damaging to the sensitive soul.

In terms of the theatre, one interesting aspect is an overlap of metaphors. Aristotle's image is of a woman as a ship to be boarded. This is the complete opposite of the stalwart defence of British womanhood in countless marine dramas which, however, also use ship metaphors for the beloved object. Gilbert's Rose Maybud may be a 'tight little, slight little craft', but she is also a prim one. On becoming engaged she allows one kiss as apparently sanctioned by her Book of Etiquette. This parody treatment may be contrasted with the following from a poetical Aristotle where the craft represents the male sex organ:

> Now my infranchis'd hand on every side,
> Shall o'er thy naked polish'd iv'ry slide ...
> I shall enjoy thee now, my fairest; come
> And fly with me to love's Elysium.
> My rudder with thy bold hand, like a try'd
> And skilful pilot, thou shalt steer, and guide,
> My bark in love's dark channel, where it shall
> Dance as thy bounding waves do rise and fall,
> Whilst my tall pinnace in the Cyprian straight (=strait)
> Rides at anchor and unloads the freight.[100]

Here, the treatment seems more salacious than informative, with the phallic male dominance offering the reverse of Hewson Clarke's suggestion of a need to hide the pokers.

ix.

The use of seafaring imagery for male-female relations dates from well before the Regency, by which time – and after – it is frequently purloined for nautical drama. Ralph Rackstraw in *H.M.S. Pinafore* calls Josephine not only the fairest bud that ever blossomed upon the tree of a poor fellow's wildest hopes but also 'the figurehead of my ship of life – the bright beacon that guides me into my port of happiness'. The tree reference links with Douglas Jerrold's *Black-Eyed Susan* where William, expecting to die, recalls an old aspen growing near the church porch where he and his beloved Susan first locked arms (like branches) and he himself cut a little bough as a memento. William's mind is like a faithful compass (or beacon) pointing him always towards Susan. Her face is a figure-head over which the white flag of pallor spreads itself when she is wrongly informed he has drowned.[101]

Another common theatrical *motif* is the dandy – the buck and the blade, briefly introduced into *Ruddygore* where the treatment is rather sanitized. The bucks and blades – prepared to be the bridesmaids' 'slaves for the moment' – show neither the attenuated nor the more robustly hectic aspects of the traditional Regency buck. They are nothing like the 'Hopes of the Country', a group of bored Cambridge undergraduates whose principal enjoyment was driving too fast and knocking out lamps. Nor do they resemble the Four-in-Hand Club, one of whom had his front teeth removed so he could spit like a coachman.[102]

The relevance of the roaring boys lies here in the theatrical spin-offs, one of them derived from a monthly publication by Pierce Egan under the title *True History of Tom and Jerry; or the Day and Night Scenes of Life in London.* A smash hit in 1821 at the *Adelphi,* it led to copycat versions appearing all over London. During the 1821–1822 season, it appeared at ten theatres always to overflowing houses. The serial was so popular that it was still being reprinted in 1871.

The *Adelphi* version of Tom and Jerry ran uninterruptedly through two seasons and led to spin-offs (some burlesque, some serious) as far asunder as Wales, Scotland, America, and the West Indies. One thing this highlights is the lack of effective copyright law. Another is the prevalence of plagiarism, with contemporary writers such as Tom Dibden and Douglas Jerrold often producing their own versions. According to the Adelphi impresario, Dukes and Dustmen were equally interested in the theatre performance.[103] This was the obverse face of a snobbish stuffiness found in institutions such as Almack's, a club ruled over by seven alarming ladies with strict rules to force people into conformity and to keep out the unfashionable.

The stiff, formal, prosy conversations at Almack's were a dull version of the 'elegant high-society talk' referred to by Tessa in *The Gondoliers.* They seemed designed to remind people that interesting dialogue was impolite. But the hypocrisy, the rituals and the scandal-mongering offered great theatrical opportunities, notably in the plays of Sheridan which remained popular throughout the Victorian period. Here again, dress was important. Tilburina and her confidante hilariously wear a different quality of material for their mutual mad scene. Lady Teazle shows her temporary corruption by abandoning her pretty linen figured gown.[104] Gilbert's own variants take many forms. In *Utopia Limited*, the Utopians' desire for English fashions parodies the vogue for French couture. In *Princess Ida*, the bluestocking girls who are told to forswear fashion actually wear beautiful Pre-Raphaelite gowns.[105] Later, the miserly threadbare Grand Duke will blaze with cheap but showy decorations. These – combined with an obsession with elaborate ceremony – boost a false (but not costly) sense of his and his duchy's importance.

There is no doubt that in the 19th century, a person's rank could be suggested by dress and deportment. But there were complexities within the mix. The Regency dandy regimented taste in a calculated reaction against the exuberance and perceived effeminacy of the Macaronis. Beau Brummell allegedly spent hours getting his boots black, shining them with the froth from champagne. Captain Kelly martyred himself by rushing into a burning building to retrieve a favourite pair of the same article.[106] Gilbert's use of dress and appearance usually involves mocking ridiculous fads and fancies. In *Patience*, Lady Jane, referencing the new London School of Design, is deeply offended by the dragoon's brilliant uniforms: 'Red and yellow! Primary colours! Oh, South Kensington!' She is also patently faux-mediaeval, though her idea of the Early English is anything but.[107] Later, the soldiers' valiant attempt to win back their erstwhile fiancées will take the form of adopting aesthetic dress and mannerisms. Here, as with Sheridan's Lord Foppington, but more deliberately incongruously, clothing reinforces the satirical points.

The effeteness of the theatrical Lord Foppingtons may seem to look forward to Bunthorne. But here there is a difference. For one thing, Bunthorne is as much highly spiced as effete. For another, Gilbert is very careful to tread warily as regards any hint of homosexuality. One of Patience's functions is to prove the poets' heterosexual credentials. Through her, Grosvenor is allowed to admit that he is beautiful. When Bunthorne and Jane plot to sabotage his popularity, one remedy is to make him cut his curly hair. Indirectly, this reinforces the theatricality of appearance. Beau Brummell, in the army for a brief time, resigned allegedly because officers were obliged to follow the old-fashioned practice of powdering their hair. When someone asked him the address of his hairdresser, he replied, 'I have three', the first responsible for the temples, the second for the front, and the third 'for the occiput'.[108]

Grosvenor's position as a trustee for beauty is (he claims) a hideous duty. It involves endless persecution by adoring ladies. In real life, some, of course, sought it. One example is that of 'Romeo' Coates, a man who covered his coat, shoes, and wig with diamonds and achieved a local fame by reciting Shakespeare in Bath drawing-rooms.[109] His persuasion of one of the local theatre managers to let him play Romeo was, however, a mistake. When he eventually walked on, he was dressed more like a clown than a lovesick Veronese, wearing scarlet tights, a sky-blue coat, a Charles II wig, a top hat, an enormous cravat, masses of real diamonds, and an idiotic grin. Nor was this all. In the balcony scene, he produced a snuff-box, took a pinch himself, and offered the same to a bewildered Juliet. The highlight (after many had departed) was his death. Here, the treatment was so ludicrously absurd that the gallery members called for an encore.[110]

The antics of Romeo Coates suggest an extreme form of Gilbert's Ludwig. It reminds us of his appearing in a *Troilus and Cressida* costume, wearing a huge Louis Quatorze wig. The more serious point is the link between theatre and public display. The foppish Sir Lumley Skeffington (author of a Drury Lane *Sleeping Beauty*) looks towards men such as Oscar Wilde and Max Beerbohm who headed a kind of dandy renaissance. Gilbert himself was no dandy, but he had a strong sense that display can be a matter of social prestige, a theatrical joy, and a semi-political statement. On the first night of The *Grand Duke*, the exquisite costumes of blue, violet, mauve, grey and grass-green, and the Herald's bold red, white, and black tabard (with playing card *motif*) delighted the eye, the *Troilus and Cressida* dresses in particular being hailed as cleverly mocking the current devotion to Greek costume.[111] Meanwhile, the zany surrealism of Ludwig's French wig suggests the pantomime sham of his whole court. It can be set against two other theatrical aspects: (a) Rudolph's threadbare garb, blazing with its meretricious medals, and (b) the hired costumes of the Monte Carlo suite, exhibiting a whole job-lot of inappropriate effects.

The conjoining of clothing with social pretension often suggests an underlying falsity. Gilbert's Prince of Monte Carlo has recently been released from debt by inventing an arbitrary game of chance. The roulette ball, the card, and the dice reinforce a sense of social distinction as a game and a sham, reinforced by the fact that the Prince's so-called noble escort are supernumeraries from the Theatre Monaco dressed by a Jewish costumier. Here, the joke is at the expense of the *Adelphi* extras, whom the Prince instructs on appropriate gestures in the manner of an old-style actor-manager. This can be set against other 'clothing' treatments, one being the semi-pathos of the out-at-elbows threadbare Effinghams.

The Effinghams are psychologically rather interesting, for in their case, inflated pompous speech seems almost a compensation for material failure. This is shown when the aged patriarch (possibly based physically on Dickens' Mr. Casby) addresses his son Bulstrode for whom life itself is 'one protracted misfit':

> My boy, sneer not at these clothes. They have been worn for many years by a very old, but very upright man. Be proud of them. No sordid thought has ever lurked behind that waistcoat. That hat has never yet been doffed to vicious wealth. Those shoes have never yet walked into the parlours of the sinful.[112]

Here, the hint is that the Effinghams are not very far above the level of the man in the Music Hall song *When These Old Clothes Were New*. The latter traces descent from life as a swell to preparing for death in a new (but hated) pauper's suit.[113]

Songs such as *When These Old Clothes* allow no scope for parody. But comedy does regularly exploit clothing to amusing effect. In *Love and Friendship,* Laura's comment on the blue white-streaked sky is enough to distress Sophia by reminding her cruelly of Augustus' satin striped waistcoat.[114] Much the same applies with hair 'Why', asks Gilbert's Tom Cobb, 'do benevolent people have such long hair? Do they say to themselves, "I am a benevolent person, so I will let my hair grow", or do they let it grow because they are too benevolent to cut it off?'[115]

The rarefied concerns of hair and dress in the Regency period prompted a reaction. Spurred by the French Revolution and international war, there was a counter-movement extolling the virtues of British courageous manliness, jostling with romantic melodrama (notably Sheridan's *Pizarro*) and a new vogue for plays about industrial unrest. Not all the state-of-the-nation themes were seriously treated. George Colman's comedic *John Bull, or The Englishman's Fireside* (Covent Garden, 5 March 1803) proved so popular that its characters and situations were adapted for Moncrieff's *Reform, or John Bull Triumphant* (1831). The latter referred back to a 1780 print, also called *John Bull Triumphant*, and showing a bull tossing a Spaniard into the air, with France at America standing terrified, an amused Dutchman watching, and the Earl of Bute, Lord North, and Lord Mansfield attempting to hold it back. Equally ironically, an 1833 wood-engraving shows a different, emaciated John Bull sitting in his room on a chair, shivering with a policeman just outside the window.[116]

The popularity of the original George Colman play is directly validated by Elizabeth Inchbald who, in her own edition, denies that the multitude are always wrong in their verdicts.[117] In an era dominated by a concern with the Rights of Man, the playwright actually pays tribute to the virtue of tradesmen and the labouring class, the action being driven by bankruptcy, bad loans, bad investments, and a perverted class-consciousness that values aristocratic rank above honesty and integrity.

The action concerns Mary Thornberry, the daughter of Job, a poor brazier, and in love with Frank Rochdale whose father Sir Simon (great grandson to a miller) has arranged for him to marry a lady of quality. The catch is that this lady is the daughter of Lord Fitz Balaam who has accumulated vast debts and requires a payment of £40,000 as a stipulation in the marriage contract.

Although clearly on the side of the honest poor, Colman's play does include an element of *noblesse oblige*, not to mention a sense that wealth is a necessary commodity. Much of this – and indeed the plot – finds echoes in Gilbert's *An Old Score*, where Ethel Barrington, the niece of Colonel Calthorpe, becomes a bargaining chip for marriage with a wealthy Bombay merchant. This is a man whom the now heavily indebted Colonel had once helped out of penury. Marriage would settle the debt. The big difference is that the merchant, James Casby, refuses to pay the debts in the manner required of him.

Another main character in the Colman play is a certain Peregrine (denoting *traveller*). He has lost his own fortune of £100,000 in a shipwreck off Penzance but nonetheless rescues Job from undeserved financial ruin by the repayment of a thirty-year-old loan of ten guineas with accumulated interest. This debt-repayment again looks to *An Old Score*, albeit with a different treatment. In Gilbert's play, Calthorpe inherits money and a title from a relative, Lord Ovington, but is proved to have once forged Casby's name as guarantor to several loans. Casby wipes out the old score by paying these on Ovington's behalf. In Colman's play, it is Peregrine who is the Good Samaritan. Not only does he bring Frank and Mary together. He also reveals that he is the elder brother of Sir Simon and thus – in another inheritance plot – the rightful heir to the Rochdale estates.

x.

The political and social elements in Regency theatre did not prevent its remaining rather a hybrid. Edward Keene, playing Macbeth might, for instance, give way in the second part to *Aladdin*.[118] Meanwhile, the patriotic boost given by the French Wars is both celebrated and mocked, the latter, for instance, in *The Critic*, where, in literary terms at least, British pluck and the heroic past are vigorously lampooned. A slightly earlier tendency is to set British naval valour as a standard against folly, affectation, and debilitating faddishness, as happens in *The Kept Mistress*. This, satirizing rhetorically oratory, was performed at Drury Lane on 10 April 1756, almost certainly as a 'benefit' for Richard Yates (1706–1796), a low comedian famous as a speaking Harlequin.

The significance of rhetoric to British culture is that, by the end of the 17th century, it evoked a double reaction. On the one hand, it retained a high status, being closely associated with history, poetry, and the so-called *belles letters*. On the other hand, it came under attack from adherents of the new science, who claimed that it promoted factionalism, and obscured the truth. Such arguments, lying behind Locke's *Essay Concerning Human Understanding* (1690), made *perspicuity*, or *clarity*, the new watchword. But even this was not enough. By the 1750s, a complete psychological or epistemological theory of rhetoric had arisen, focusing on its powers of mental persuasion, and using the elocution movement as a tool to deliver it.

The influence of the oratory movement is well seen in Lord Chesterfield's pronouncements on the *Art of Speaking* (1739) and George Campbell's *Philosophy of Rhetoric* (1776). Gilbert himself often mocks by imitation the exalted convoluted language found in works such as *Pizarro*, but his straight mode is one of eloquent condensation. Robin Oakapple's 'Oh my forefathers' speech was, he says, originally three pages long before being honed down to its most eloquent essential requirements.[119] As far as *The Kept Mistress* is concerned, what distinguishes it from endless other afterpieces is its refusal to accept prevailing dramatic convention.[120] The first title summarizes the main plot, featuring a comedy of Restoration type depending on a love-intrigue. The second – *The Mock Orators* – suggests satire of a kind reaching back to Ben Jonson, while also referencing Samuel Foote. In the end, love is brought safely, if belatedly, within the bounds of marriage. It comes, however, without the parallel expectation of fulsome reform, recantation, moral didacticism, or regret.

The *Mock Orators* plot of *The Kept Mistress* reminds us of other comedies of ridiculous language, not least the aesthetic utterances of Gilbert's *Patience* and the pretentious absurdities of *Les Précieuses Ridicules*. Widow Lovephrase is sorely infected by the new-fangled rhetorical obsession and, by way of cure and catharsis, is mocked to her face by an impersonator aping the modes of an oratorical master. He then deprives the widow of her only daughter while she herself is eventually matched with the unattractive Ringworm. The linguistic quibble of the daughter's excuse – said to come of 'logic chopping' – gives the play a strong Gilbertian quality. So too does the anti-romantic tendency. Though in Gilbert love usually triumphs, this is not inevitable. In *Creatures of Impulse*, he deliberately avoids a romantic tie-up ending. In *The Grand Duke*, Julia only takes Ernest on sufferance.

Another Gilbertian aspect is tonal. It is the hint of anger and aggression beneath a light, witty surface. In *The Pirates of Penzance* (original version), the *Hymn to the Nobility* is more mordant than genial. In *The Kept Mistress*, the professional con men who have tried to capitalize on the elocution craze are exposed without mercy. The device for this dénouement is an interventionist Royal Navy which silences the first Orator, gagging him and forcing him into the service. Verbal persiflage and ornate rhetoric are suspect. Though ironically involving a press gang, they run counter to British traditions of common sense, few words, and personal liberty.

The Kept Mistress is a good example of a piece which is both Gilbertian and not Gilbertian. Like Gilbert in *Patience*, the author mocks a current fad while adopting an anti-romantic tone. Like him, he pours scorn on inflated rhetoric. But the closing song with its reference to past naval heroes such as Drake and Blake is played straight whereas in Gilbert it might well be used in the service of satire. This certainly applies in songs such as *When England Really Ruled the Waves*, in the presentation of Richard Dauntless, and in the Boatswain's anthem to the glory in being born English. Unlike the cowardly Dauntless, the British seaman in *The Kept Mistress* is the honourable upholder of an ancient tradition.[121] This is linked to the stalwart British manly character, associated in turn with a respect for ancient liberties.

xi.

The respect for liberty is in British theatre a watchword. 'In Britain we freedom shall find', sing the 1756 sailors. 'We'll not be enslaved, nor enslave'. But this avowed libertarian spirit could transmute into violent outbursts, as was later to happen in the Covent Garden Theatre Wars of 1809. One innovation in the new Covent Garden (built after fire destroyed the old one) was the inclusion of enclosed private boxes, which were to be let by the year. Previously, even the King's box was let to the public on nights when he was absent.

The abhorrence of the new Covent Garden dispensation suggests the radicalism within early 19th-century theatre. The new 'snug retreats' evoked 'moans and hisses'. This, however, was merely the *hors d'oeuvre*, for in the six days of the theatre remaining open, the play became merely a dumbshow, with men and women standing on the benches, shouting, singing, blowing horns, and ringing dustmen's handbells. Banners appeared demanding a return to 'Old Prices' and slogans were hurled such as 'No snug retreats' and 'Damn your pigeon holes'. On Saturday 23 September, the new theatre was temporarily closed. That night, a coffin was borne through the pit (the stalls) marking the demise of the New Prices.

The rioting of 1809 may well have had a retrospective influence on Gilbert. Certainly, he was always wary of audience volatility. One stimulus at Covent Garden was simple economics. People were furious that public pleasures were ceasing to be affordable. But the lower classes also resented no longer being able to see the intricacies of aristocratic behaviour. There were even two 'Old Prices Dances', one, involving forming circles and banging each other's walking sticks, called, for no very apparent reason, 'The Rattle-snake Minuet'.

The violence of the Covent Garden Riots had a happy outcome. Prices for admission to the pit were lowered to 1808 levels, and following further riots, the private boxes were removed. But the whole escapade puts paid to the idea that everyone in Regency cultural life was decorous and stylish. Even those who rarely visited the theatre might declare themselves 'by God. bloody fond of a riot'. Interestingly, in the newspapers, 'bloody' and 'God' were edited, showing that decorum had a place even in barbarity.[122]

So how, then, should we view the pre-Gilbert theatre? One point is that there were very different audience components. The sentimental comedies were, for instance, written to appeal both to the rising bourgeois middle class and (later) to adherents of the higher sensibility. So too were the new forms of tragedy. In 1731, George Lillo made tragedy more domestic by using middle-class characters in *The London Merchant*. Similarly, in Europe, Gotthold Ephraim Lessing's *Miss Sara Sampson* (1755) was a deliberate attempt to shake off French Neoclassical influence and produce a truly German genre – the so-called *bürgerliches Trauerspiel*.

Another point is one of sheer expansion. Throughout the 18th century, the theatre grew as a vehicle for popular entertainment, with many smaller playhouses being opened to accommodate the growing number of plays. At the beginning of the century, Paris had three theatres. By 1791, there were 51. In London, it is true, there was a hitch. The growth of playhouses was discouraged by the Licensing Act of 1737, which gave the Lord Chamberlain extensive powers to censor all plays and to uphold the monopoly of the two patent theatres. Theatre managers, however, found a way around this. They re-labelled their programmes, filling them out with musical items. Similar laws in Paris were evaded by unlicensed actors. These played in *forains*, the illegal theatres of the fairgrounds.

Outside London, the spread of theatres royal in provincial towns gave new importance to the touring circuits, which – as in the case of David Garrick – became valuable training grounds. Garrick is also important for developing a more naturalistic style of acting that became widely influential. As manager of the Drury Lane Theatre, he introduced concealed stage lighting and (like Voltaire in France) stopped the practice of spectators sitting on the stage. Oddly, at the time when Garrick was being buried in Westminster Abbey French actors, under penalty of excommunication, still had to be buried in non-consecrated ground.

It was in comedy, however, that the 18th-century influence on Gilbert is strongest. Goldsmith in *She Stoops to Conquer* (1773) signalled a return to hearty laughter. Sheridan revived the comedy of manners in *The Rivals* and (especially) *The School for Scandal* (1777). In France and Italy, the most interesting developments were literary applications of the *Commedia dell'Arte*. Banished by Louis XIV, the Italian actors were back in 1716 under the name *Comédie-Italienne*. This time they softened their style to suit prevailing taste, finding a sympathetic writer in Pierre Marivaux.

In Italy too, *Commedia* was being redefined. Carlo Goldoni replaced the improvised dialogue with fully written texts, achieving popularity around 1745 with *Il servitore di due padrone*. Carlo Gozzi, on the other hand, allowed his actors plenty of opportunity for improvisation. He mixed fairy-tale fantasy and realism in a type of play he called *fiabe*, the best-known example being his 1761 piece *L'amore delle tre melarance* (*The Love of Three Oranges*). In France, comedy was also on the rise, reaching an exuberant peak in *Le Barbier de Séville* (1775) and *Le Mariage de Figaro* (1784).

For Gilbert, the resurgence of the *Commedia dell'Arte* was to be a notable influence. So too was a curious offshoot of Roman pantomime introduced into England by John Weaver and John Rich, drawing on a familiar story or classical legend in verse, but interspersing harlequin scenarios. Here – foreshadowing later transformations from main play to Harlequinade – the tricks and adventures were mimed, being danced to appropriate music.

The pantomime mode is, together with burlesque, perhaps Gilbert's biggest source-base, used with both affection and ridicule. Perhaps, he is himself rather like his own Pantomime Prince. This fellow has a bitter, bitter sorrow at his heart. He knows that his destiny is either (a) to grow up, outside the play, to be big-headed, unjust, red-faced and detested or (b) to be changed within it into a harlequin, dancing endlessly, jumping through windows and 'converting sensible business announcements into irritating puns'.[123] Gilbert himself seems to have been torn between the sensible and the nonsensical. He was a juggler of the normal *and* the inflated, of the everyday *and* the fantastical. It was part of his theatrical past. It was also his *now* and *to come*.

* *

The Post-Regency and Victorian Period

The State of the Theatre

Gilbert was one-year-old at the time of Victoria's accession, but his birth was by no means a watershed, and it came at a time when the theatre was in crisis. In 1832, a Select Committee had been specifically formed to enquire into theatrical decline, the report blaming incompetent management, the low salaries of actors, excessive production costs, religious scruples, and even late dining hours. On the other hand, all was not lost. An 1832 account tells us that in the past fifteen years new theatres have opened in a number of towns, including Aberystwyth, Blackburn, Sheffield, Warrington, Thetford, Douglas, Perth, Loughborough, and Barnstaple. There is also a London business boom with the opening of five new venues, including the Grecian Theatre, specializing in light opera, the West London Pavilion for melodrama and comic songs, and the Albion in Windmill Street, again offering melodrama. Simultaneously, the newly opened Cremorne Gardens ('fêtes and outdoor entertainments') was much heralded. It was 'likely to rival provision at the Vauxhall', pleasure gardens of this sort now being 'a very popular source' of London entertainment.[124]

The trouble in all the above lies in an absence of quality. It is interesting to hear that Mr. Lanza's singing rooms in New Road 'have been converted into the new Clarence Theatre with an interior designed to look like a Chinese Pavilion', but few new plays of substance are being produced. Terry Otten writes of 'senile plots, pseudo-Elizabethan techniques, melodramatic claptrap, stock characterisations and bombastic language'.[125] Audiences too were dwindling. In 1850, entry costs had been reduced so that they were often cheaper than in 1800. Increasingly, only niche markets were guaranteed financial success.

There were, however, counter-trends. One of Tom Robertson's assets was association with the Queen's Theatre, renamed the Prince of Wales, and progressing from 'Dust Hole' to 'Gold-Dust Hole'. This involved a mild gentrification later to be recapitulated and enhanced at the Savoy. Under Marie Wilton, the Dust Hole's floors were carpeted, the chairs in the boxes were upholstered and antimacassars were introduced. Lord Leighton wrote of the place: 'I think your theatre is quite the dandiest thing I ever saw'.[126] According to Daniel Barrett, the house was soon 'thronged with intellectual and cultured adherents, many of whom were by no means theatre-goers as a general rule'.[127]

The gentrification of the theatre is sometimes linked with the siphoning off of poorer social categories now attending the Music Hall, the Penny Gaffs, and various circus and variety entertainments. This view is rather simplistic – even at the Savoy the (generally less affluent) gallery contingent could be riotous – but it contains some truth. One admonitory example was Charles Somerset. He had once written popular melodramas for the Surrey, Adelphi, and Olympic but was later reduced to producing two-act dramas for twenty-five shillings apiece. Finally, he was seen standing before the Mansion House with a label round his neck, declaring: 'Ladies and gentlemen, I am starving'.[128] Meanwhile, at the Britannia, George Dibdin Pitt's *burlettas* such as *The Cricket on the Hearth* (1846) were coining only a mere thirty shillings, while pantomimes, melodramas, and domestic dramas, which in the 1840s had been making three pounds apiece, in 1850 saw this reduced to two.

The parlous financial state of much London theatre was shared in the provinces. In about 1846, Sam Wild, proprietor of a portable theatre travelling round the northern counties, paid Charles Somerset two guineas each for a series of three-act canine plays, based around Nelson, Wild's performing dog. This is slightly better than some London rates, but animals too could have a bad time. One (admittedly amusing) story relates to a production of *Don Quixote* for which Henry Irving advertised for a thin, hungry-looking horse. The first horse-owner who appeared was arrested for cruelty to animals. The second claimed that his horse had already appeared on stage but tended to cause distress among actors by violently breaking wind. 'Ah', said Irving, 'not only an actor but a critic as well'.[129]

Gilbert's attitude to theatrical poverty is never fully clarified, but he did contribute to charitable support ventures. Meanwhile, the Savoy Operas were carefully tailored to appeal to an affluent middle class. Possibly, the rather harsh reviews of *Engaged,* combined with the comparative failure of *The Ne'er-Do-Well,* encouraged a greater focus on audience expectations. One reason why he disparaged his Savoy libretti was that they afforded a rather vulgar commercial success while being (so he said) notably easy to write.[130]

The eventual resurgence of British theatre was partly due to Tom Robertson. He – one of Gilbert's comparatively few male friends – was regularly praised for his 'bright, sparkling dialogue, his home truths, his kindly affections (= playful suggestions) of cynicism, his similes, and his keen appreciation of the little weaknesses' of our everyday world.[131] This, however, was no great intellectual breakthrough.[132] To William Archer, the contemporary theatrical appetite was for a recorder, not a moralist-propagandist. He is expected to give in his work, 'not yet a judgement or an ideal, but a *painting*'.[133]

Gilbert himself admired the Robertson approach. He praised the way he gave life and variety to his plays by breaking up the scenes with 'all sorts of little incidents and delicate by-play'. But there were also detractors. To Henry Arthur Jones, Robertson was deficient because he never attempted the 'seizure and presentation of a movement of national thought'. Robert William Buchanan agreed: 'When Robertson loomed above the horizon, the world prepared for something cosmic, only to discover that what it imagined to be a sun was a sort of gigantic tea-cup'. W.B. Yeats believed his only real achievement to be that of 'substituting real loaves of bread and real cups of tea for imaginary ones'.[134]

i.

The move in the theatre towards gentility had a direct effect upon Gilbert. Yet at the same time, he was steeped in tradition, retaining, for instance, an anarchic 'Clown' element, generally diverted into burlesque and parody. In the meantime, popular entertainment was increasingly under threat. One sign of this was the decline of Bartholomew Fair, a great institution, granted a charter by Henry I, and indirectly referenced in *The Old Curiosity Shop* (1840–1841). By the 1840s, the fair had become more like a carnival than a market. Attractions when Wordsworth attended in 1815 included albinos and Red Indians, ventriloquists, wax-works, and a learned pig which, blindfolded, could tell the time to the minute and pick out any specified card in a pack. In 1825, William Hone enjoyed the living skeleton, an elephant which uncorked bottles, a glass-blower in a glass wig blowing teacups for threepence apiece, and baby crocodiles being hatched from eggs by steam.

The point here is that the fair's loutishness, drunkenness, and vul-garity had aroused growing middle-class disapproval. It was attracting too many thieves and muggers, and the City's increasing restrictions were lowering the profits. In 1840, the City Solicitor's report to the Market Committee complacently related St. Bartholomew's decline to the March of Progress. The lower ranks are 'fast changing their habits, and substituting country excursions by rail roads and steam boats, and other innocent recreations, for the vicious amusements of the description which prevailed in Bartholomew Fair'. Other reports echoed this. The Fair has 'fallen into a bad odour'. It 'has been voted a public nuisance'. The general opinion is 'it will never be held again'.[135]

The disparagement of working-class pleasure did not go without chal-lenge. Dickens opposed it, and some reports did admit the need to pro-vide 'something of an amusing and instructive kind' in its place. The catch was that this should be in 'a more convenient locality', one ex-ample being the seaside, later to be a major venue for Punch and Judy whose first surviving printed script (1827) was based on a show by trav-elling performer Giovanni Piccini, illustrated by George Cruikshank, and written by John Payne Collier. Even this was sanitized in subsequent Victorian treatments.

The importance of the Bartholomew Fair case to Gilbert is twofold. In the first place, he has to take account of an increasing civic prudery with associations of moral rearmament. Second, and rather in opposition to this, he is at pains to assert a continuing allegiance to fairs, strolling play-ers, and a mountebank ambience. Elsie Maynard, Jack Point, Nita, Bar-tolo, and Pietro all stem from the world of the travelling showman, and many of his comic plays have associations with *Commedia dell'Arte*. At the same time, he *does* sometimes despair of popular (lack of) taste, one example coming in a verse in *Fun* (28 October 1865), where he appears appalled at the vulgarity of contemporary audiences and their addiction to visual slapstick.[136] So he does in *Pantomimic Presentiments* where he wonders when (or if) there will ever again be anything approaching true novelty. He also lambastes the lengthened transformation scene, which was a comparatively new development.

Gilbert's dislike of theatrical vulgarity may seem to mix oddly with his own anarchic high spirits, but he almost always places limits on free-wheeling possibilities. Music Hall is particularly disparaged, partly because it bespeaks a potentially riotous *urban* working-class culture. Gilbert's English strollers emanate from a more rural world as suggested in Elsie's excised but apparently self-referential song featuring maidens tripping over the lea.[137] Actually, strolling players did not have a particularly easy time. Usually, they performed in Inn Courtyards, but the authorities were often hostile, their play of Robin Hood in particular being sometimes seen as subversive. In 1572, this, plus a fear of plague, led to their being banned. Henceforth, the only actors allowed to perform around the country were those employed by noblemen, as in a sense (long before 1572) happens to Elsie and Jack.

Gilbert's concern to limit theatrical vulgarity is in part a matter of his own psychology. As an English gentleman, albeit an irascible one, he disdains low effects, balancing a love of the theatrically exuberant with an almost anally retentive penchant for control and discipline. In addition, he wishes to elevate the low repute of the acting profession. In the key year of 1832, Joseph Grimaldi Junior had died. Alcohol combined with 'excessive debauchery' had finished him at thirty. Gilbert was acutely aware of such dangers. Fun needed strict regulation. Possibly, his allusion to 'Poor Old Joe' in *Harlequin Wilkinson* alludes not just to the popular music hall song but also to the Grimaldis, Joey by now having become a generic clown nickname.

The danger implicit in the Grimaldi case spurred actor-managers to tighter controls. It was one of many examples of excessive drinking and irrational behaviour infuriating theatre management while rapidly alienating the public. For Gilbert, the *genre* was tired. It was a case of:

> Seedy sprites forever vaulting, seedy metre ever halting,
> Men of 'property' cobalting eighteen-penny devil's face;
> And the foolish culmination in a weary 'transformation'
> Whose complete elaboration takes a twenty minutes' space.[138]

This sets the tone of what to avoid. Fun must rise above such predictable uniformity. It must contain lively high spirits within a tightly constructed witty artefact, concentrating most typically on colourfully treated oppositions between incompatible modes of life.

ii.

The regaining of theatrical originality depended partly on its directors. Regardless of how we rate Tom Robertson, it was he who, according to Gilbert, invented stage-management. Help was provided by the Bancrofts who gave him considerable creative freedom, rewarding him with a nightly sum (now known as a royalty), ensuring regular and fair earnings, rather than a modest flat fee. Some argue that this involved a certain elitism – that the success of the Bancroft-Robertson trio relied on 'the regular attendance of a privileged audience' able to pay much higher than normal admission prices.[139] One reason why writers like Robertson and Gilbert could not afford to be *too* original was that theatre could not rely on a compliantly encouraging audience. It was financial success that made literary plaudits possible.[140]

The constraints suggested above do, however, require a caveat. As shown by the reaction to *The Happy Land*, Victorian audiences – even middle-class ones – could be surprisingly appreciative of lampoons, caricatures, and the politically subversive. Much more restricted were areas of sexuality while even duelling, still available as a *motif* for the French, is considered in England outmoded. In *The Grand Duke*, Gilbert cleverly manages to subvert the limitations. Here, the duel becomes a bloodless one with playing cards, and Ludwig is claimed by a succession of brides, each claiming they have sole contractual right to him.

Gilbert's irritation at the freedom and supremacy of the French drama is fairly obvious. In *A Hornpipe in Fetters* (*Era Almanack*, 1879), he attacks the critical assumption that French plays are automatically superior, adding that, if the English write tame plays, it is because they must dance in the fetters of the Lord Chamberlain, colluded in by the English audience.[141] One irony here is that new plays were often translated French imports. In *Nicholas Nickleby,* Mr. Crummles, wanting a piece quickly, takes a roll of papers from a table-drawer and tells the hero: 'Just turn that into English, and put your name on the title page'. This reflects the Dramatic Copyright Act which ensured that it was cheaper to adapt foreign plays than to startle the world with new ones written in English.[142]

The popularity of French imports accounted for some notable English hits, as, for instance, Tom Taylor's *The Ticket of Leave Man* (1863) based on *Le Retour de Melun*. But the French influence could in its way be equally limiting. Théophile Gautier, speaking of Eugène Scribe, questioned how 'an author without poetry, lyricism, style, philosophy, truth or naturalism could be the most successful writer of his epoch'.[143] Also often criticized was Victorien Sardou, for whom George Bernard Shaw came up with the dismissive term 'Sardoodledom'.[144] Sardou's own advice to young playwrights wishing for success was to 'Torture the women!' This should be a main plank of any play construction.

The vogue for Scribe was in part a reaction against the Romanticism of plays by Victor Hugo, Alexandre Dumas, Alfred de Musset, and George Sand. By the 1840s, a new 'Theatre of Common Sense' was arising, involving a tight plot and a climax occurring close to the drama's end. Such sudden dénouement revelations are both used and mocked in *Engaged* and *The Importance of Being Earnest*. One recurrent device is the use of letters or papers falling into unintended hands or discovered after being missing.

The well-wrought French *pièce bien faite* should in some ways have appealed to Gilbert. In his *Appeal to the Press* (*Era Almanack and Annual*, 1873), he laments how parts are inappropriately 'written up' or 'cut down', according to the needs or whims of particular actors. Responding to Boucicault's *Jezebel*, he writes of the structure: 'A very confused and wholly improbable story with a wholly unnecessary second act'. Boucicault himself cheerfully acknowledged his limitations. His response to critical snubs for *The Poor of New York* is: 'I can spin out these rough-and-tumble dramas as a hen lays eggs. It's a degrading occupation, but more money has been made out of guano than out of poetry'.[145]

The willingness to be a successful literary hack is a significant admission. Charles Reade banked £2,000 for *Drink*, adapted from Zola's *L'Assomoir*, and European works in translation were often remarkably good box office. Great acting, of course, helped. After Squire Bancroft saw the dress rehearsal for Beerbohm Tree's English version of *Fédora* (1893), he wrote ecstatically of Sarah Bernhardt's performance.[146] Shaw meanwhile had proved prescient about another Sardou piece, *La Tosca*: 'Such an empty-headed ghost of a shocker', he wrote. 'Oh, if it had but been an opera!'[147]

iii.

The constraints on, 19th-century English theatre did not, of course, only affect Gilbert. But they did mean that he had to plough a different sort of furrow from (say) Meilhac and Halévy and the later Georges Feydeau. There is in Gilbert little use of a *demi-monde* scenario or of the frivolous, frank unsentimental mode of the Parisians boulevardiers. What *is* shared is a tendency to remove people out of their natural comfort zone. Can-can girls appear in the Underworld; scarlet-uniformed soldiers are engulfed by greenery-yallery aesthetes; peers find themselves assailed in Arcady by the sprites of Fairyland. The big difference is that the Boulevardiers take their rather epicurean world with them or, if they stay, remain generally unregenerate.

The unregenerate aspect is well seen in *La Vie Parisienne*. Here, a courtesan sings sardonically of the *bachanale* that roars nightly in the fashionable Café Anglais. It is a rite that lasts until the exhausted revellers order tea and stagger home, 'drunk with champagne and pretended love'.[148] Gilbert does differently. *The Sorcerer* gives us tea in the form of a village carouse and a magically induced love that has no effect on married people. In his comedy, sexual rules are never fully transgressed, a point well illustrated in his witty but sanitized adaptation of *Le Roi Candaule*.

The Move Towards Splendour

The harsh and often restrictive conditions of the Victorian Theatre might so far seem to suggest a depressing picture. But there is also another more exhilarating side. Augustus Harris' view was that earlier in the century financial constraints had made the Harlequinade often shoddy and inadequate. Now, spectacular theatre must be the trysting-place of all the arts. Art, he says, is 'a very extravagant and lavish mistress', thereby heading off claims of overblown excess.[149]

Increasing extravagance had another concomitant. It often enhances the link between the outdoor pleasure-ground and the escapist world of theatrical entertainment. Masquerades, for instance, frequently featured characters from pantomimes, while the staging of pantomimes within the Vauxhall Gardens was relatively frequent. The 1828 offering was *Harlequin in the Bottle* followed in 1829 by *The Yellow Dwarf of Harlequin Knight of the Lion*. In all cases, lighting was a key adjunct. An 1826 article in *The Times* refers to the Vauxhall's brilliancy of artificial illuminations, and the range of additional lamps highlighting (among other things) the motto 'Long live our gracious patron'.[150] An early undated 19th-century newspaper clipping tells us: 'The great object of admiration was the fifteen hundred glass lamps, which were lit up suddenly on the approach of darkness',[151] giving 'a brilliant appearance to the alleys and avenues of trees' and very much prefiguring the Victorian pantomime mode.

The light-dark mode occurs frequently in Gilbert and not always for fun. Princess Ida bids Minerva to endow with sight the unillumined eyes of her girl-neophytes. Lisa, despairingly crushed at the loss of Ludwig, responds in the simple childlike terms of day becoming night. In the Victorian transformation scene, the emphasis is on the reverse. Percy Fitzgerald recalls a host of gauzes lifting slowly, one behind the other, to give tantalizing glimpses of the Realms of Bliss. As the clouds and concealing banks begin to part, a few 'divine beings' arise. These are then augmented by a pyramid of lovely ladies seen mounting slowly, radiant in beauty as a stream of lights 'in every colour and from every quarter' create the richest possible effulgence.[152]

The climactic effect of the pantomime transformation scene is characteristically mocked by Gilbert. In *The Fairy's Dilemma*, the Radiant Realms have a telegraphic address: Realms. In *Harlequin Wilkinson*, they are reached to the accompaniment of an organ voluntary. *Thespis* meanwhile turns the whole concept on its head. First, the transformation is not to a new place but to an existing one hitherto obscured by fog. Second, it is effected, not at a comparatively late point but almost immediately after the opening chorus. Third, what is revealed is disintegration. The scene that meets us is of shattered columns, overgrown with ivy; entrances to a ruined temple; fallen columns littering the stage; and three broken pillars lying about.

The above may, it is true, seem picturesque, but the context marks the satirical intention. Even when the fog has cleared, nothing magical ensues. Mercury may shoot up from behind a precipice, but he carries nothing more glamorous than several parcels and appears 'very much fatigued'. Also notable is the lack of any fairy element. Instead, we have an elderly Diana, wrapped up against the cold with a respirator, and Apollo appearing as a degenerate, elderly buck. This, plus the colloquial chat sustained both before and after the transformative moment, completely reverses the currently popular aims of glamour, magic, awe, and excitement.

Gilbert's ability to create an interesting theatrical effect, while also undermining it, is an early example of his love of dual possibilities. It is a *coup de théâtre* which nonetheless mocks conventional expectations. Percy Fitzgerald writes of the transformation scene's climactic revelation of the empyrean in which some 'fair spirit' rises aloft 'in a cloud among the stars'. *In Thespis* the stars, seen only through fog, are actually *dispersed* and, instead of a motionless tableau, we have Mercury popping up like a jack-in-the-box. Even the dawning light hardly matches the usual radiance. In the Drury Lane *Humpty Dumpty* (1891), scores of little electric lights twinkled from the petals of lilies and convolvulus adorning the dancers. In the wedding scene of *Dick Whittington* (1894), the set was apparently decorated with more than 4,000 individual lamps.[153] Perhaps this – as much as the reference to *Aladdin* – explains the call for 'No lamps' in *Harlequin Wilkinson*.

Traditionally, transformative effects have another aspect. They are often linked with the possibility of regaining a more beautiful and chivalrous outlook. In the 1900 *Sleeping Beauty and the Beast*, the Prince is on fire for a romantic mission, a desire which the Fairy Queen seems more than willing to support. His fear that it is too late to save beauteous damsels, overcome evil magicians, and traverse a world full of fairies and witches leads to:

FAIRY QUEEN: Not so! True chivalry's not dead but sleeps
And every heart some sweet romance still keeps;
The wish to be a hero still endures –
Wouldst truly like to test how strong is yours?[154]

This can be contrasted with *Iolanthe* where the Queen, though similarly encouraging, transports Strephon *not* to some heroic never-never land but into the Houses of Parliament.

The *Iolanthe* scenario is partly a satirical response to Boucicault's *Babil and Bijou* – a work with a Prologue in which we learn that a fairy, Melusine, loved a mortal shepherd, Lancelot, the union producing a half-fairy daughter. Unfortunately, the working-classes in fairyland – gnomes, imps, jins *(sic)* and pixies – have revolted and expelled Melusine's fairy court. Gilbert changes the gender of the fairy child, makes *him*, not his father, the shepherd, and turns an *expulsion* from the fairy domain into an *invasion* by the House of Peers. Later the act of opening the Peerage to competitive examination, will not so much take us back into an enchanted mediaeval dream-world as lead us out of it. The only monster to be quelled will be that of Parliamentary privilege, the working-classes meanwhile being benefited by Strephon's own legislative agenda. Here, opening the Peerage to competitive examination, he will not so much take us back into an enchanted mediaeval dreamworld as lead us out of it. The only monster to be quelled will be that of Parliamentary privilege.

Gilbert, then, mocks Victorian theatre's escapist dreams. Yet he does to some extent share them. In *Princess Toto*, the song of the two worlds suggests the superiority of the ideal dream state. A degree of yearning for a non-jealous romantic love, and a life of chivalric virtue, lies behind the wistful disillusion of *Broken Hearts* and *The Wicked World*. In comedy, the joke lies in the clichéd nature of the material and the inadequacy of the realization. The satirical *What Is a Burlesque?* ridicules both the ingredients and the rendition, suggesting all the pitfalls of hackneyed material, inadequate performance, and insufficient funds.[155]

Gilbert's own attitude to escapist spectacle was a mixed one. The Drawing Room scene in *Utopia Limited* was clearly intended to be lavish, notwithstanding *The Times* reviewer's criticism of the ladies' dresses.[156] But in story-form, spectacle can be mocked without fear of disappointing an audience. In *The Fairy's Dilemma*, the confrontational encounter between the Demon and Fairy Rosebud ends ('you will be surprised to hear') with a step dance. This shows Gilbert doing two things: (a) making dance-spectacle bathetic and (b) satirizing irrelevant introduced material. 'It is', says Rosebud, 'another anomaly of my calling that we have to be ready with extemporized parodies of all the commonest music-hall songs of the day'. This includes duets 'even when the duettists are on the very worst of terms'.[157]

Fairy Rosebud's aggrieved response to spectacle and fairy-magic is a typical Gilbertian undercutting. But that does not make him impervious to the value of spectacular surprises. The *Troilus and Cressida* processional chorus opening *The Grand Duke*'s Act 2 makes for a striking entry. In Act 2 of *The Gondoliers,* the ducal party's entry, magnificently dressed, preceded by retainers, and accompanied by loudly braying brass, is devised as the opposite of their low-key Act 1 arrival. Many Victorian dramatists similarly exploit contrast, sometimes in a more juxtaposed form as, for instance, when Jack Worthing appears in deep mourning for an Ernest who has just arrived in exuberant health. In more serious mode, this may give us another effect: that of the double tableau. At the end of Act 2 of Watts Phillips' *Not Guilty*, the background is first filled with warders presenting muskets to rebellious convicts. Then, after the Curtain has fallen, it rises again 'almost as rapidly', to show the main villain in custody and the convicts 'sullenly forming into file under the menacing attitude of Warders'.

The double tableau is not a Gilbertian mode, but he does often offer switchbacks. In *Patience,* the Act 1 Finale includes many surprises.

First, there is Patience's sudden eruption in acceptance of Bunthorne and then the (deliberately lower key) entry of Grosvenor, leading to the mayhem and *furore* of the maidens' sudden romantic re-alignment. This – disorientating everyone and providing an example of unity in opposition – can be set against over-dramatic and unlikely reversals elsewhere. One example comes in *Not Guilty* when the villain Silas, last seen on Dartmoor as a disgraced prison-warder, appears in India to the raising of Venetian blinds announcing: 'It's like my luck! Escaped at the hazard of my life from Australia, that land of kangaroos to the land of curry-powder, and only to find myself as usual out of the frying-pan into the fire – cursed luck!'

The *Not Guilty* example is rather a hybrid. Possibly, the intention is half-humorous, but the piece is called 'a drama', and Silas himself has entered 'haggard, ragged and wounded'.[158] Such amazing, almost unmotivated moves from one country to another are parodied throughout in *Princess Toto*, but elsewhere the unexpected surprise or unforeseen arrival will be limited to key moments. One example is the *coup de théâtre* of Luiz's sudden appearance 'crowned and robed' in *The Gondoliers,* offering a kind of mini-transformation scene without the gradual process. The opposite technique is to undercut striking effects already achieved. In the same opera, the haughty grandeur of the Act 11 ducal entry is undercut by the distinctly low-key republican reception it elicits.[159]

The low-key effect in which the only bell rung was the visitor's is the reverse of the embodied spectacular found (for instance) in the pantomime transformation scene. When William Beverley introduced a 'fan effect' – scenery collapsing sideways and inwards to reveal a view from behind – audiences literally gasped. So, they did at the *parallèle*, a rising platform on which were ranged about twenty fairies, mermaids, water-nymphs, angels, or mythical sprites, opening out like an inverted umbrella or huge blossom. The whole thing required windlass-operation, but it was the weight of the figures themselves that caused their support-base to sink.[160]

The emphasis on the visual was often at the expense of verbal distinction or even felicity. But there was a certain irony in the return to speechless display. Originally, the mimed approach was partly dictated by the 1737 Licensing Act giving a duopoly which in London allowed the use of the spoken word to be limited to the two patent theatres. What influenced the changes was the passing of the Theatre Regulation Act (1843), abolishing the duopoly. This allowed for the advent of the rhyming couplet, the almost endless recourse to pun and wordplay, the lengthening of the pre-Harlequinade opening, and the scope to comment satirically on current events.

Although eventually vulgarized, Victorian pantomime did have strong supporters. William Archer, translator and champion of Ibsen, admits in *The World* (1893) that 'the full glory of the mimic world' did not burst upon him until he saw a Drury Lane pantomime, *Beauty and the Beast*. Pantomime, he says, is 'a national institution', an *invaluable* art-form, far superior to the French *revue*, 'allowing scope for poetry, fantasy, parody, satire, sense, nonsense, the most ingenuous nursery babble, and the most penetrating criticism of life'. It also has the immense advantage over burlesque, that it does not necessarily involve the degradation of anything noble or beautiful. The folklore in which it finds its traditional subjects presents indeed 'just the requisite blending of the graceful with the grotesque'.[161]

i.

The championing of graceful pantomime must be taken with a pinch of salt, not least when we reflect on Lewis Carroll's particularly admiration of young pre-pubescent girls as a symbol of innocence.[162] But there is no doubt that the combination of beautiful staging with a moral message won over many intellectually-minded attendees. John Ruskin rejoices that audiences can submit themselves for an hour or two to 'that golden light, and song, and human skill and grace' which contrast so much with modern industrial 'smoke-blackness, and shrieks of iron and fire'. What he deplores is the fact that these same enthusiasts can return to the underground railroad so cheerfully.[163] Gilbert is more quizzical. On 20 February 1864, taking the persona of an allegedly shocked theatre-goer, he demands of the *Fun* Editor why nothing is done to make the Harle-quinade obey the classical rules of the Unities. Why, too, is the confiding shopman's business invariably transacted on the pavement? We don't find Mr. GRAVES, of Pall Mall, striking bargains with 'parti-coloured customers' outside his shop-door. Here, it is the real-life detail that adds to the humour. Henry Graves was a purveyor of fine prints with elegant showrooms. He would make a fine butt for an anarchic Clown if there really *were* a reality-make-believe mix.

The blending of artifice with reality (or sometimes vulgarity) is seen more in vaudeville than pantomime. But when it *does* happen it will not please all attendees. Ruskin's abhorrence for the cigar-smoking girls in *Ali Baba and the Forty Thieves* (1867) is based not just on his dislike of smoking but also on the total desecration of womanhood he descries in it. It is the opposite face of the grace and innocence seen in pieces such as *Jack in the Box* (1874) where young child dancers performed as buttercups and daisies.[164] Children appearing as birds, dolls, elves, squirrels, butterflies, cats, and so forth were indeed a regular pantomime feature. Ruskin, in his account, contrasts the smoking minxes with the charm and innocence of an eight-year-old dancer performing a *pas-de-deux* with a pantomime donkey. The downside was that her 'perfect grace, spirit, sweetness and self-forgetfulness' won applause from no one but himself.[165]

ii.

The vulgarization of visual display can in part be attributed to Augustus Harris – the man whose father (similarly named) produced *Ali Baba*. Gilbert himself deplored their inclusion of novelty acts and music hall celebrities. Among the stimuli for his late return to the *motif* of the Harlequinade were (a) a wish – often farcically treated – to reassert a link between the pre-transformation and post-transformation scenes and (b) a desire to remind the audience of what modern pantomime was in danger of losing. Augustus Harris' own self-justifications were that he was catering to an increasingly sophisticated and more educated audience.[166] Later another tack was to justify the modern lavishness as in keeping with the luxurious spirit of the age.

It would be absurd to suggest that the Victorians alone heaped spectacle on drama. Even in the early 18th century, there had been an excess of lavishness, causing fears that members of the working class might want to share in the voluptuousness.[167] In Gilbert, apart from the dislike of vulgarity, there was perhaps a further factor. One of Gilbert's realities is that life is a meaningless joke – that no amount of spectacle can disguise the awful aloneness of the human condition. This – treated with lugubrious humour in King Paramount's song – is a strong counterweight to escape into fabulous dreamworlds. By 1911, even this is changing. According to Jimmy Glover, musical director at Drury Lane, 'We live in an age of splendour, luxury and comfort. Therefore the best in spectacular display, in talent, in music and interpretation is provided'. Here splendour and spectacle are seen as part of the fabric of a contemporary lifestyle. The real is the spectacular, not (as for Gilbert) a condition from which we may seek to escape.[168]

The Absence of Ideas

The need to keep attracting a notably fickle public has for Gilbert a number of implications. One is that he has to decide whether to go with the tide or maintain originality and risk neglect. Another question concerns the advisability of including a social message. The poor reception accorded to Strephon's *Fold Your Flapping Wings* suggests a public reluctant to be lectured and awakened to a wider imaginative empathy.[169] On the other hand, a song is only a song. Perhaps Strephon's aria is merely an opportunity for a ballad, useful to give the character the spotlight, slow the pace, and change the mood after the high jinks of a riotous trio.

The truth is positions are never clear cut. According to John Brewer, the James Hackman case created an explosion of sentimental interest which would be re-worked in generations of succeeding poetry and drama. Yet if we turn to George Colman's *John Bull* (1803), we find almost the reverse.[170] In place of the *Wertherfieber* encouraging young men to dress

and act as Goethe's suicidal hero, we have the young man who is mercenary and mercantile. According to Shuffleton, an amour nowadays has
nothing to do with matrimony. 'We say "a good match" at the west end
of town, as they say "a good man" in the city; the phrase refers merely to
money'. Society has meanwhile improved. 'We have voted many qualities to be virtues now that they never thought of calling virtues formerly.
The rising generation wants a new dictionary, damnably'.[171]

Shuffleton's hard mercenary carelessness is ironically presented. It is
at an extreme end from the attenuated febrile sensibility of Sheridan's
Faulkland which will reach a neurasthenic extreme in Poe's Roderick
Usher.[172] A different form is the heightened emotion of much early Victorian romantic melodrama. Here love is often opposed to honour. Regularly, it is threatened by oppressive parents, dastardly rivals, and/or
divisions of class. This makes for strong theatre but is devoid of ironic and
sardonic nuances. Such applies in Bulwer-Lytton's *The Lady of Lyons;
or, Love and Pride*, first produced at Covent Garden (15 February 1838).
The plot – partly mirroring that of Victor Hugo's *Ruy Blas* – typically
revolves around love, betrayal, and reconciliation. There are two trig-
gers to it: (a) Pauline Deschapelles' jilting of the Marquis Beauséant and
(b) the love felt for Pauline by Claude Melnotte, the son of her gardener.

The development of *The Lady of Lyons* involves Beauséant persuad-
ing Melnotte to disguise himself as a foreign prince to trick Pauline into
marriage. This happens, but, on the discovery of the ruse, she has their
marriage annulled. Melnotte then enlists in the army to assuage his remorse, while Beauséant declares himself willing to save Pauline's father
from near-bankruptcy if the girl will marry him. The dénouement offers
a variant on the *Jane Eyre* mode of necessary atonement.[173] Specifically,
Melnotte becomes a war hero, whereupon Pauline realizes that she is
truly in love with him, after all.

The Lady of Lyons is in many ways comparatively formulaic. But it
does look in parts to Gilbert. In *The Ne-er-Do-Well* (later revised as *The
Vagabond*), the main plot of the tortured love relationship of Rollestone
and Marian (renamed Maud) again concerns issues of wealth and debt,
pride, and a love-triangle. Appointed as secretary to Gerard's pleasant,
almost bankrupt father, Rollestone soon learns that the old man is on
the verge of financial ruin and will lose his home unless his son marries
the wealthy Marion/Maud. He is then begged by his employer to put in
a good word for Gerard, so becoming torn between his love for the lady
and his gratitude to his benefactor.

The Gilbertian take on romantic melodrama does have some distinctive features, not least that it juxtaposes some (very enjoyable) comedy
with the melodramatic artifice. But the main mode is that of heightened
torment, with both soliloquies and dialogue expressing potent extremes
of emotion. When deprived of his early matrimonial hopes, Rollestone
(we are told) 'went mad and drank [himself] into a red hot fever that

lasted six weeks'. He then drank his way through Homburg and Baden, lost money at the gaming tables, went in desperation onto the stage, drank some more, wrote for low-class papers, betted, drank some more, worked in a billiard saloon, and is now (at the start of the play) more fit to serve as a scarecrow than as a model in a picturesque painting. The irony is that this man, like the equally dissipated Sydney Carton, has gentlemanly, even noble, instincts. At one point, he takes to himself the guilt of being the recipient of some indiscreet love-letters, even though this may scupper any future Marion/Maud relationship. The fact that he does so to exculpate Gerard is indicative. It again suggests a Sydney Carton-Charles Darnay link.

i.

The romantic melodrama mode had a long shelf life. Even by the late 19th century, it still has potency, particularly in dramas encapsulating religious uplift, as, for instance, in *The Sign of the Cross* (1895). This play – originally produced in Missouri but soon reaching London, and in May 1897 Sydney, Australia – centres on Marcus Superbus, an old Roman patrician who lusts after a young woman, Mercia, converts to Christianity at her inspiration, and joins her in sacrificing himself to the lions. The plot in some ways resembles that of *Quo Vadis,* but it also has strong links with *Measure for Measure*. The difference is that the Angelo figure sees and responds to the religious light, dying nobly and stalwartly with the girl he had attempted to seduce.

Loosely speaking, *The Sign of the Cross* does have ideas since it contrasts a pagan and Christian view of life. But there is little intellectual debate – it is more a question of spiritual feeling. Christian enlightenment is set against Roman barbarism, spiritual love against bodily lust. This familiar oppositional mode has various concomitants. Chief of them is a dialectic rigour of language, a condition which may apply even when the conflict is within a single breast. In *The Ne'er-Do-Well,* the oppositions are mainly in Rollestone. They are between two noble modes, brought into clashing conflict, one being gratitude and a sense of loyalty to Gerard and the other his equally noble love for Marion/Maud. One complication is the element of rather uneasy comedy within the stereotypical, as when the dismissed secretary Richard Quilt is bound hand and foot by the hero while caught trying to purloin the indiscreet letters. Quilt's 'arrest' here involves the use of a pipe brandished as – and assumed to be – a gun. This suggests not only the hero's resourcefulness but also his inherent gentlemanly constraint.

The danger of the highly charged tipping over into the ludicrous is seen far more potently in *The Lady of Lyons* where the language suggests emotional force rather than intellect. Rhetorical exclamation ('Torments and death!') here yields ultimately to sardonically vengeful invective, as in Beauseant's 'I wish you joy! Ha! ha! the gardener's son!'[174] Such hot-house attitudinizing partly explains a reaction. It augments the appeal of Tom Robertson's more colloquial domestic nuances. But there were other factors, one being a gradual broadening of moral outlook. When *The Ne'er-Do-Well* was written, the commissioning actor, E.A. Sothern, was concerned because Gilbert had made the heroine a widow. He feared that audiences would lose sympathy for the character if she were not a virgin. This contrasts with *Mrs. Dane's Defence* (1900) where, despite some highly rhetorical speeches, there is far less moral rigidity. Lady Eastney supports Mrs. Dane over the scandal-mongers even while knowing that Mrs. Dane is guilty of deception. Canon Bonsey ruefully laments the poor return he has gained for 'twenty-five years' management of the parish 'on the principle of the widest toleration for everybody's views in doctrine', and everybody's practices in morality.[175]

Mrs, Dane's Defence marks another change. Unlike (for instance) Paula Tanqueray, Mrs. Dane commits no final suicide – she suffers merely exile from the village without public exposure and the failure of her marital hopes. This marks a further development away from the extreme romantic melodrama mode of which even Wilde can be guilty. Lines such as Lady Windermere's:

> What do I bring him? Lips that have lost the note of joy, eyes that are blinded by tears, chill hands and icy heart.

seem too perfectly crafted and polished, while what follows

> That fatal letter! No! Lord Darlington leaves England tomorrow. I will go with him I have no choice.

appears artificial even in its brevity. Besides, would anyone really say 'leaves England tomorrow' in soliloquy? Even within the artificial medium, would not 'will be gone tomorrow' be a more credible alternative?[176]

ii.

The heightened emotion suggested in Lady Windermere is a special case. The product of a rather Puritanical upbringing, the character is very different from her society, most of whose members are witty, sophisticated, and either ruefully or sardonically worldly-wise. Nonetheless, even Wilde opts more for emotion than a theatre of ideas. Others go far further, one point about melodrama being that it was the chief social protest medium.[177] Hence, it was more likely to deal in stark oppositions than in reasoned nuance debate.

The other limitation in melodrama was a tendency to vitiate any serious intellectual content by humour and/or a lively indulgence in the sensational. Such applies in Boucicault's *The Poor of New York*, first performed at Wallack's Theatre, New York in 1857, but revived in Britain and Ireland with localized titles. The play derived from *Les Pauvres de Paris* by Edouard-Louis-Alexandre Brisbarre and Eugène Nus, revolving around the efforts of a middle-class family to survive against the machinations of a villainous banker. Boucicault adjusted the dates from the original 1840 and 1855 to 1827 and 1857, the better to coincide with the real New York financial crises. He also (he said) simplified the 'lengthy tear-stained narration' of the original, making the characters 'more vivid and amusing'.[178]

The Poor of New York is a good example of various Victorian theatrical excesses. One is the tendency to overload the misery. By the last two acts, nearly all the virtuous characters are starving. Puffy, the destitute baker, has been reduced to selling roasted chestnuts, and Paul, son of the wronged dead Captain Fairweather, is discovered crouching hungry and destitute. Nor are Paul's sister and mother Lucy and Mrs. Fairweather doing any better. They have failed to gain money, whether by needlework, selling their rings or begging. Hence, they decide separately to commit suicide by asphyxiation from the charcoal burner which they use to cook their almost non-existent food.

The extreme misery within the melodramatic mode is often parodied by Gilbert. In *The Frozen Deep,* Richard Wardour, stuck in the Arctic, proclaims: 'I am incensed – I know not why – and to relieve my feelings, I will break up the hut'. He then proceeds to chop up Frank Aldersly's berth, sees the letters E.B. on one of the planks, and nonsensically realizes 'at once' they must stand for his long-lost beloved Clara Vernon.[179] Equally targeted are rescue scenes. In *The Poor of New York,* a melodramatic death for Lucy and Mrs. Fairweather is forestalled by an even more melodramatic rescue scene. Such contrivance is mocked by Gilbert in *The Pirates of Penzance* where the police initially *fail* to save the Major General, having to rely on the unlikely Queen Victoria trump-card to extricate themselves from their own defeat.

The rescues in *The Poor of New York* give a good idea of the intellectual limitations of the drama. They are managed by Paul coming upon the ladies when they have succumbed to the lack of oxygen, as, to some extent, has the villain Badger, lodging conveniently in the next room. Paul's heroism causes Badger to undergo a change of heart. He reveals that he has evidence of the wicked banker's villainy, though he passes out before he can provide the written proof.[180] What follows wrenches us towards an unlikely happy ending. First, Badger rather amazingly nurses Lucy back to health. Then, we learn that in a fever she confessed to spurning her beloved Livingstone only so that he might regain his lost wealth by marrying the banker's daughter, Alida. Equivalent happy-ending contrivances occur in *The Colleen Bawn* and *Not Guilty*. In Gilbert's version of the latter, Mr. St. Clair's arrives at the last moment offering a free pardon to the good-hearted convict Jack Snipes for his 'amusing behaviour in the verandah during the Indian Mutiny'.[181]

The happy-ending contrivance usually requires one other preliminary ingredient, namely the sensation scene. Gilbert parodies this in his burlesque *Lost at Sea* where flames burst through the floor, consuming all the planking, only *eventually* to attract the hero's attention.[182] In *The Poor of New York*, fire is again central but is far more spectacular. On the very eve of the Alida-Livingstone marriage, Bloodgood the banker sets fire to the lodging house. Livingstone meanwhile repudiates Alida, having, among other things, gained access to her letters to her lover.

The sensational fire scene is a sign of yet more pandering to the visual sense rather than to the heart or (especially) the intellect. Originally, it involved the importation of a real fire engine and the use of a preparation called Quick Match, made of gunpowder, alcohol, and naphtha, to work upon window frames, themselves soaked in these materials. By now, intellectual debate has been completely abandoned but even earlier, the play's one polemical scene is of limited intellectual quality. What actually happens is that a small crowd assembles round Livingstone, taking him for an orator, and that one of them begins taking notes. This leads to a policeman entering, telling them 'This won't do', a phrase later used to interrupt protest in Act 2 of *Utopia Limited*. In the Boucicault case, the policeman's point is that no 'stumping to the population' can be allowed in the park. This causes Livingston immediately to rush off, without further radical comment.

It is quite unlikely that Gilbert was referencing *The Poor of New York* in King Paramount's use of one short phrase. But there is, nonetheless, a certain contextual irony. *Utopia* offers the famous satirical song in which it is fulsomely asserted that, in England, poverty is obsolete, hunger is abolished, and the middle classes, far from being oppressed, are in the ascendant.[183] This is the exact obverse of Livingstone's point. For him, the middle classes are those most to be pitied:

> These needy wretches are poorer than the poor, for they are obliged to conceal their poverty with the false mask of content – smoking a cigar to disguise their hunger as they drag from their pockets their last quarter, to cast it with studied carelessness, to the beggar, whose mattress at home is lined with gold.

Here, the conviction of the utterance is degraded by two things: the wider dramatic context, and the fact that there is no one present to put a counter-argument.[184]

iii.

The avoidance of serious debate has another linked aspect, that of plot forsaking likelihood, and sound structure being sacrificed for temporary thrills. This is something often attacked by Gilbert, as when he calls *Not Guilty* an unsatisfactory sprawling piece without beginning, middle, or end and with far too many superfluous irrelevant characters.[185] What annoys him even more is emotional string-pulling. Pathos allied to uplift becomes *The Triumph of Vice*. It becomes the satirical *Sensation Novel by a Small Boy*. In the latter, the narrator, a nine-year-old lad, falls in love with a woman of twenty-seven called Jane. He feels they have a deep understanding and is hence mortified when she slaps him for throwing himself at her feet and accidentally tearing the gathers in her dress. All this leads to a vow of deadly vengeance but when (presumably in atonement) the 'tigress' sends him some barley-sugar, both he and it melt, the latter mainly through its being worn close to his heart in the summer season. The next development is the appearance of a rival – James Jones – known mainly for his skills in skinning mice. He does, however, send some personally collected leeches when Jane falls ill, causing the narrator great agonies. Hence, when he discovers James purloining jam, he hits him on the head, apparently killing him. He then in the nick of time stuffs the body in the drawing-room grate behind the screen.

One of Gilbert's skills is to write from an unexpected viewpoint. Another is the use of small details to give verisimilitude in the midst of the exaggeratedly unconvincing. The fact that it is summer, for instance, is significant. It means that no fires are being lit. Another skill is to allow us to anticipate dénouements without spoiling the fun. When Jane moves in as governess, we know marriage with the father is imminent, the boy's delight being based on the false premise that it heralds his own wedding to the young lady. Meanwhile, the summer season is over and fires will be resumed. Fearing discovery of the body, he considers hiding it in his nursery play-box but fears that decay will have made it impossible to remove. This itself is a complete upturning of the more normal saintly child *motif*, reinforced, when, on learning the truth of the papa-Jane relationship, he goes mad with hysteria.

The rest of the story further mocks literary stereotypes. One is the boy's decision to drown in the Serpentine, only to be haunted by a 'dread apparition' gravely stalking towards him. It turns out to be James who, like George Talboys in *Lady Audley's Secret*, was not quite killed after all. He had merely lain low to avoid being denounced for the jam-stealing. The climax is the boy's second attempt. He thrusts James into the inky waters only for them to freeze, trapping his own arms until death. It is in this fixed but preparatory state that he is actually recounting these adventures.[186]

The trend of Gilbert's *Sensation Novel* is to mock both specific works and a whole novelistic and theatrical *genre*. In particular, it references

Lady Audley's attempt to drown her husband in a well, which becomes in Gilbert the fiasco in the Serpentine. What Gilbert does is to turn the lonely child from a creature of pathos to an amoral monster. This is augmented by two things: (a) the fact that there is no suddenly contrived remorse (unlike, say, with Hardress in *The Colleen Bawn*) and (b) that papa is not at all a wicked parent and the boy seems generally very much indulged.

iv.

The melodramatic and/or sentimental vacuity of much Victorian writing has one caveat. Together with a stripping away of domestic ideals, many works do suggest notable anxieties, not least about the anonymity of the city which is what gives Lady Audley the power to change her identity. Also notable are those dramas which *do* raise economic, social, and politic issues, the downside being the simplistic nature of the treatment. Such applies in *The Factory Lad* (1832) – a work that is more powerful than intellectually discriminating and in which the rights and wrongs tend to be absolute.

The Factory Lad essentially sets a mode of paternalistic industrial management against a new selfish but commercially profitable pragmatism. Squire Westwood's father would never have deserted his men or preferred steam machinery to honest labour. Nonetheless, having inherited the factory, the Squire 'feels obliged' to introduce steam looms and to dismiss his loyal workers. His reasons, however, are slanted towards class-viciousness. By dismissing his men he will save some 3,000 a year. Besides, the world is one where the fittest survive and everyone pursues his own best economic interest. 'Don't you buy where you please, at the cheapest place? ... Don't you, too, sow your garden as you please, and dig it as you please?' the hard-hearted capitalist asks.[187]

The heartlessness of Westwood is made all the more apparent because he *does* hear and even understands the men's fears. When they admit dreading being turned out to beg, starve, or steal, he comprehends but is unmoved: 'Sentiments in theory sound well, but not in practice'. Nor does he acknowledge the flaw in the 'Don't *you* do as you please?' argument, particularly when it is based on inequality of resources and unequal bargaining power. The result is that the men join forces with the poacher and outcast Will Rushton, a victim of the Poor Law and economic powerlessness whose arguments are 'harsh, embittered and uncompromising'.[188] Here, the denunciations, uttered in impeccable English, serve as a kind of justification. They give grounds for all the violence that follows.

What actually happens is that together the men take revenge on Westwood by setting fire to his factory and his home. The factory lad, George Allen, escapes arrest thanks to the daredevil bravery of Rushton, but eventually all end in court together. One notable aspect is the inclusion of pathos in the form of the innocently suffering Mrs. Allen and her children. Another is the rhetorical potency of all these mill-hands, sometimes with the sort of biblical echoes satirized in Rose's utterance in *Ruddygore*. When Hatfield bravely speaks out to his villainous employer, he does it thus:

> Then if ye will not hear a poor man's prayer, hear his curses! May thy endeavours be as sterile land, which the lightning has scath'd, bearing nor fruit, nor flower, nor blade, but never-dying thorns to pierce thee on thy pillow.

Here, the quasi-biblical tone and imagery add weight and dignity, while the fact that we never see Westwood with *his* wife and family sets the scales more on the side of the artisans.[189]

The climax of *The Factory Lad* continues the mode of one-sided argument. In court, the Judge is not only corrupt but is actually called 'Bias'. He commits all the lads to the local assizes, for an almost certain death sentence. When Allen's wife pleads to Westwood for mercy, she is spurned. This allows what follows to be a kind of justified retribution. Specifically, Rushton produces a pistol and shoots Westwood dramatically dead.

The polemical mode of *The Factory Lad* makes it still a powerful statement. But we do have to recognize how we are being manipulated. One method involves an invocation of family values which are given a kind of religious sanction. George Allen is responsible for the devoted support of a wife, three small children, and an aged mother. The children combine a sad barely comprehending vulnerability with protective loyalty towards their weeping mother and endangered dad. Heaven itself demands vengeance if the father is unable to feed these little angels.[190]

The danger to the family unit is reinforced by undeserved stress. The strain on George Allen causes him to trample the lace that his noble-hearted daughter has been producing, followed by instant remorse, with the child tearful rather than accusatory. Meanwhile, any hope of escape to a better life is discounted by one carefully planted example. When Will Rushton went abroad seeking work, his four children were slaughtered by the natives who hate white men and live on human flesh. His wife (George's sister-in-law) was borne away either for the same fate or perhaps worse. It is this that has rendered a former honest hard-working artisan 'crazed, heart-broken, a pauper and a poacher'. The stakes have been raised just at the point when – in the face of looming violence – we most need to feel sympathetic rather than alienated responses.

The lack of an intellectual centre is, then, clear. But it is also seen in another way: namely, that the men themselves act partly out of *sympathy*. They are aware that Rushton is half-mad, but compassion for the cause of it makes them readier to accept his violent leadership. Besides, his family's fate is a warning. Working abroad is dangerous. There is a deliberate arguing from the particular to the general, shutting down nuanced consideration, and accelerating the pace. Even before we know all the details, we – and the men – are being swept along by his literally incendiary rhetoric.[191]

It is, of course, perfectly justifiable to insist that emotion should play a part in dictating action, and that men with dependants will be particularly stressed. But this in itself is a manipulation. It offers a kind of exculpation for the Factory Lad who is carefully removed from the centre of violence. The other manipulative factor is the patriotic one which is really addressed to the audience. In Hatfield's words, a true English gentleman is one who feels for another and relieves his distress, not one who turns out the honest and hard-working so that he may keep his hunters and foreign wines. The word 'foreign' here becomes suspect. This is reinforced when Sims contemptuously speaks of men like Westwood as being themselves likely to travel to foreign parts.

v.

The patriotic card played in *The Factory Lad* is just one example of the sort of rhetoric regularly mocked by Gilbert. In *H.M.S. Pinafore,* there is also revolutionary socialistic talk, but it is undercut in several ways. One is the incidental byplay, with Dick Deadeye continually reviled for stating the most obvious of truthful platitudes. Another is the puzzled wondering tone in which some of the challenges are voiced, as when the Boatswain sadly remarks that the captain's daughter will have nothing to do with poor able seamen. Since *he* says it, this is accepted unanimously, but what follows (when Dick agrees with him) brings out the irony:

DICK: No, no. captain's daughters don't marry foremast hands.
ALL: *(recoiling from him)* – Shame! Shame!
BOATSWAIN: Dick Deadeye, them sentiments o' yourn are a disgrace to our common natur'.

Here, we note that the men's complete lack of sympathy for Dick undermines all talk of communal feeling. Gilbert meanwhile keeps Ralph sympathetic to the audience by having him divert onto his own puzzled thoughts, rather than joining in the general anti-Dick acrimony.

Even Ralph, however, dislikes Dick, again suggesting Gilbert's undercutting of ideals of human sympathy. One impression is that much depends upon the appearance and circumstances of the orator. Rushton, though wild-looking, is sympathetic because he has suffered. Dick (who seems to have no family to lose) has a bodily deformity which is taken to be emblematic of an internal viciousness. What is interesting is that Gilbert gives the most sensible remarks to the most (unjustifiably) alienated and alienating figure. In *H.M.S. Pinafore,* the outcast is turned by almost universal hostility to betray his messmates. He becomes as vile as they have painted him. In *The Factory Lad* the effect is the reverse. Rushton remains to the men a kind of flawed hero. At the same time – from the audience viewpoint – his wielding of the firebrand helps to distance the rest from the horrors of destruction.

vi.

Dick Deadeye's common-sense stance is not the only one that can be called loosely political. There is also the landlubber First Sea Lord declaring fatuously and hypocritically that a British seaman is any man's equal excepting his. The fact that the men lap this up in turn satirizes them, as does the Boatswain's form of patriotism which imputes merit in a matter that is purely arbitrary. By contrast, in *The Factory Lad,* the virtue of being born English is played straight, rather like that of being middle class in *The Poor of New York.* Englishmen, we are told:

> were happy when they knew naught but Englishmen; when they were plain, but, honest, upright and downright – the master an example to his servant, and both happy with the profits of their daily toil![192]

Against this may be set a sudden uprush of sympathy for an outsider villain. 'Stay! Mr. Bloodgood', says Paul, 'in the midst of your crime there was one virtue: you loved your child; even now your heart deplores her ruin – not your own'.[193]

The idea that everyone has some spark of goodness related to an accepted ideal is undoubtedly heart-warming. But in Gilbert, it is regularly undermined. In *The Burglar's Story*, the narrator actually begins with an inversion of conventional moral standards. In the first sentence, he refers proudly to his father as a '*distinguished* begging-letter imposter'. Then, when it becomes time for the Eton-educated lad to choose a profession, he and his father mutually decide on burglary, for which the boy undergoes a vigorous professional training after being formally articled. A year's probation then follows, during which he accompanies his trainer on several expeditions, in one of which (as he nonchalantly tells us) he accidentally shoots his mentor in the stomach, mistaking him for the master of the house. This causes the man (like *Ethel; or Only A Life*) to die on the grand piano. The trainer bears no malice, however. His dying wish is 'that his compliments might be conveyed to me'.[194]

The inversion by which criminal activity becomes a matter of professional training is far removed from the stern moral mode of much Victorian drama. In *The Poor of New York,* morality is combined with virtuous uplift. Paul, tearing up the evidence, ends by telling Bloodgood, 'I have no charge against you. Let him be released. Restore to me my fortune, and take the rest; go, follow your child; save her from ruin, and live a better life'.[195] This – used like Bloodgood's paternal love to engineer a happy ending – is the opposite of the mode in *The Burglar's Story* where the outwardly charming narrator combines increasing viciousness with commendably prudence, as shown in the choice of victim, a bachelor Evangelical, who, as well as being 'very feeble' and eccentric, is elderly, drinks and snores.[196]

The inversions in *The Burglar's Story* have another challenging aspect: they evince a complete and deliberate failure to follow orthodox patterns or revert to sentimental pathos. When the narrator, having made very precise orderly plans, breaks into the house of the old bachelor, he (and we) discover that the 'dear silver-haired old man' has a loaded revolver with which he confronts the apprehended thief. The silver hairs do not, however, mean that the thief is at all softened. 'My first impulse', he says, 'was to rush at and brain him with my life-preserver'. The dear old man is, however, well up to this. 'Don't move', he remarks, 'or you're a dead man'.

The rest of *The Burglar's Story* continues in the same vein. Far from being alarmed, the old bachelor (a designer of dados) is rather delighted at being broken into. He has 'often wished to have the pleasure of encountering a burglar'. He even promises in the name of his own honourable profession to let the man go if he will subject himself to a little experiment. The drawback is that, if the narrator defaults, he will be shot, as indeed he shortly is.

Overall, *The Burglar's Story* says much about Gilbert's delight in subverting literary and theatrical cliché. It is the sort of story that could easily become a sophisticated mini-drama or a sketch in a university review. The key point is that nobody behaves as expected. Even the policeman is unorthodox. His arrival comes after the narrator has been forced to strip naked, has tried and failed to cover himself with antimacassars, and has finally decided to give himself up. The constable, however, is impervious. 'Nonsense, sir', he says, '... you'd better go to bed'. Only with extreme reluctance is he induced to take the lad into custody. Even then he kindly covers him with his own greatcoat and lends him his personal handcuffs.

vii.

The mode of ironic reversal is in Gilbert a personal trademark. Essentially, it has two types. Either it consists of inversion and subversion or it exaggerates to the point of the ludicrous. In his burlesque version of *Jezebel,* Madame d'Artigues not only plans to marry and poison an old enemy but also to marry and poison the whole world. In *Sir Rockheart the Revengeful,* our hero, with no reason for vendetta, wars against the whole of society, boils his aunt, chops up his baby, strangles his daughter, and still manages to die loved and regretted by all.[197]

The deliberately exaggerating mode is even within itself inherently mocked. Madame'd'Artigues, for instance, undercuts her avowed fiendishness even as she expresses it: 'I am a female fiend, but I have reasons of my own for not wishing this to be generally known'. Elsewhere, apparently grim events are treated with casual nonchalance. In *The Burglar's Story*, after warming himself comfortably at the police station, the narrator seems quite happily (or at least without protest) to submit to ten years' penal servitude. It is true that the 'terrible hours' spent with the dear old gentleman have for years caused him to shudder in passing his house. However, fortunately (in another joke), he has now entirely forgotten the whole incident.

What then amid the mockery are Gilbert's main targets? One obviously is strong moral oppositions based on codes of rigorous orthodox conduct. But there is also satire of extremes of unlikely dialogue and plotting, structural incoherence, and over-emphatic playing for effect. All are satirized in *The Flying Scud*, as in this short scene at the Tattenham Club:

MEREDITH: I will play you – ar – for – ar – everything i – ar –possess – ar.
GOODGE: 'Tis well. [*Wins everything MEREDITH possesses.*
LORD WOODBIE: Goodge, I saw you cheating!
GOODGE: Ha! Presumptuous boy! [*Knocks him down.*
LORD W: We will fight at Calais! [Tableau.

Here, the staccato effects suggest the action of puppets, while the brevity of the dialogue only underlines the stagy attitudinizing of the sentiments.[198]

The satire of the rhetorical mode had one drawback. Rhetoric was itself in decline. Nonetheless, the parodies of real plays show that there remained numerous possibilities. One that is often mocked by Gilbert is the uplifting ending. This can be seen in the regularly revived *The Lady of Lyons* which ends with a kind of moral lesson addressed in apostrophe to the audience:

> Ah! the same love that tempts us into sin,
> If it be true love, works out its redemption;
> And he who seeks repentance for the Past
> Should woo the Angel Virtue in the Future.

Gilbert's contrasting approach is to rejoice in vice rewarded or virtue discomfited, as applies with the villainous Sir Rockheart.

Another of Gilbert's modes is to end on a throwaway note either of fatuous joy or dismissiveness. The former applies with his burlesque of *The Man o'Airlie,* which ends with the assertion that, if anyone can explain why the play is called by this title, there won't be a happier party in all Scotland than the lover, lady, and lunatic who took part in it. This contrasts with the play's *real* ending where the bard James Harebell 'sinks slowly into the silence and darkness and everlasting peace of death'. The more dismissive mode can be found at the end of the story-version of *Creatures of Impulse.* Here 'none of the personages…married each other', they being too annoyed at having made such fools of themselves.[199]

The Gilbertian tendency to demolish any sort of uplift is directly against the prevailing tendency. The 1871 Philadelphia printing of *The Man o'Airlie* informs us that 'The sadness which elevates our hearts is one of the purest of blessings'. The eyes of hope and of prayer are 'taught to look upwards'. The play is so full of tender sentiment and elevating pathos 'that it cannot fail to awaken interest, attract sympathy and diffuse refined pleasure and moral benefit'. Also mentioned are its character-interest, picturesque circumstances, and truth to life combined with a sense of the validity of the ideal. Gilbert would have mocked the whole thing. In *his* version, the sad, deranged poet is greeted (by all) with the words, 'Ha! It is James Harebell, gone daft from reading his own poems'. In *Creatures of Impulse,* the lack of a marital ending is the really curious part of the story since the rigours of happy endings usually insist on it.[200]

Mockery of the nature of the ending is one thing. But sometimes, Gilbert goes further, mocking sheer incomprehensibility. In a burlesque-critique of *Barnaby Rudge,* Miss Miggs' curtain line – spoken by an American actress – tells us that, if anyone can make head or tail out of the play, or get any gratification at all from it, 'there won't be a happier party in all England than *Harlequin Barnaby Rudge; or the Fairy Varden and the Yankee Gal from Down East'.* [201] Elsewhere, even apparently upbeat aspects are suspect. At the end of *Creatures of Impulse,* Peter (we are told) escaped the general shamed annoyance, having shown such undaunted courage that he deserved his inn-keeping promotion. However, he only acted bravely (or apparently bravely) under a bad fairy's compulsion. The ending is thus ironic, undermining the response.

There is one other point about Gilbertian endings, which is that they often deflate noble magnanimity and a heavenly apotheosis. Thereby, they mock works such as *The Corsican Brothers,* which dovetails a kind of stiff upper lip nobility with a hope for reunion in the afterlife. The strong curtain here is achieved by the ghostly emanation of one dead brother to another living one. This can be set against Gilbert's deliberate interweaving of the dead and the living, amid a wider mockery of ghost-human parameters.

Gilbert's ghost-human anomalies are easily illustrated. In *Ages Ago* (where the humans also play the ghosts), much fun is gained from the fact that, for a ghost emerging as an animated portrait, a picture painted in the 15th century when the sitter was seventeen may be simultaneously older and younger than the likeness of a descendant painted years later in mid-life. The reanimated seventeen-year-old Lady Maud is, in fact, the great great great great, great-grandmother of Lord Carnaby who appears as an elderly sixty-five. Equally interestingly, the ghosts' appearances are framed by the human contingent, making an interesting case of framed pictures being themselves framed by the main plot narrative.

The framed ghosts of *Ages Ago* are rather a special case because they do not directly interact with the living. But in Act 11 of *Ruddygore* ghosts and humans are more closely interwoven, the original ending involving the resuscitation of an entire ghostly portrait gallery. In Gilbert's version of *The Frozen Deep*, matters are made easier because there is only one ghost-figure. Initially, Lieutenant Frank's spectre is greeted with joy, but, when asked to explain himself, he generously, and with some embarrassment, passes the opportunity to Richard Wardour who has just been accused of eating him. This leads to exculpation of the cannibalism charge but also to questions as to why, lost and hungry in an arctic waste, the two did not consult the British consul. Then, with everybody unconvincingly reunited, Wardour proposes general revelry, after which he suddenly remembers he is dying and expires in excruciating agony.[202]

Gilbert's take on *The Frozen Deep* is, of course, a burlesque of one particular play. But he is also mocking *generically* unlikely and/or over-uplifting endings. In *The Factory Lad,* the ending works as a dramatic shock, but it remains inherently unlikely that Rushton, in a closely supervised magistrate's court, would suddenly be able to produce and brandish a pistol. Gilbert in *Notre* – mocks a happier example. Here, Gudule suddenly produces a shoe belonging to her daughter who was stolen seventeen years ago by gypsies. This leads Esmeralda immediately to retort: 'Ha! And here is its fellow!' showing that she is, after all, Gudule's long-lost child.[203]

The mockery of happy reunions has a long history. In Euripides' version of the Electra story, there is a parody of Aeschylus' treatment, Orestes being recognized from a scar he received on the forehead as a child. This is a mock-heroic allusion to a scene from Homer's *Odyssey* where Odysseus is recognized by a scar on his thigh, the cause being reduced from the effects of a heroic boar hunt to a semi-comic incident involving a fawn. Elsewhere, it is final joy that is burlesqued, one Gilbertian example being the parody ending of *Henry Dunbar*:

DUNBAR: I am about to die, and if our friends in front will only look
     kindly on my efforts, there will not be a happier old dog in England
     than Henry Dunbar [*Dies in great agony.*

Here, Gilbert is partly mocking J.B. Buckstone's idea that 'People like to see the principal actor or actress advance, and speak a sort of epilogue', this one involving dying in excruciating pain.[204]

* *

Stars, Subject-Matter, and the Production Approach

The nature of Gilbert's comedy is, then, partly explained by his context. But how far was his a unique response? The first thing to state is that Gilbert was not alone in his topsy-turvy inversions. Offenbach's *Les Brigands* (1869, revised 1878) is satirically not unlike *The Burglar's Story*, while in plotting, it has many similarities with *The Mountebanks*. In the French piece, a financially strapped robber-band undertakes a complex scheme to rob the court of Mantua, with the use of disguise to entrap a travelling Princess. In *The Mountebanks,* this becomes a disguise plot for the entrapment of a travelling Duke and Duchess. The setting is a similarly wild and rocky place; the brigand lieutenant is called Piétro, matching the leader of the mountebank troupe; and an innkeeper (Pipo in *Les Brigands*) plays a prominent part in both scenarios.

The plot of *Les Brigands* is of a type to appeal to Gilbert, not least because it involves the *motif* of royal substitution, used with variations in both *The Gondoliers* and *The Grand Duke*. In *Les Brigands*, a portrait of the Princesse de Grenade is replaced by that of the daughter of Falsacappa, the brigand chief, allowing for *motifs* of impersonation and identity confusion. As regards identity overlap, *The Gondoliers* offers the best example, but another occurs in the short story *Tom Poulton's Joke* (March, 1871), a tale partly inspired by Gilbert's real-life membership of his club, The Serious Family.

Tom Poulson's story has nothing to do with brigands, but it does show a kind of brigandage in everyday life. Tom himself is the Chairman, Treasurer, Secretary, and Trustee of a 'sociable club', also called the Serious Family. He commits a scam with the members' money and then, as a further joke, makes a will, leaves his non-existent wealth to the club members while taking the identity of a dying man with an identical name to his own.

The impetus for the *Tom Poulton* plot is financial. The dead man with the stolen identity proves to be secretly rich and dies intestate. Tom, his *alter ego*, having made the club members his legatees, now tries to resurrect himself but the members, greedily wanting the dead man's inheritance, claim not to know him, so that he finally has to accept the fiction that he is actually somebody else. The result is that he ends up as Major General Arthur Fitzpatrick, enrolled and subsidized annually by the club members, on condition that all mutually pursue the fiction that he never was the man that he actually still is.

The blending of identity substitution with monetary scams has other variants. It is also central to *Les Brigands*, which Gilbert translated for Boosey in 1871, purely, he said, to secure the British copyright. This links with the fact that in 1852, foreign writers had been granted five years' protection against unauthorized translation, a move extended in 1875 to cover adapted pieces. Then, in 1887, the Berne Convention

strengthened copyright arrangements between most European countries. One of Gilbert's objections regarding *Les Brigands* was to new
songs inserted in the piece written by another inferior lyricist.[205]

Gilbert's adaptation of *Les Brigands* was later to bear more fruit in
The Pirates of Penzance. It also contributed to *The Gondoliers*. In the
meantime, his arch lyrics, when finally performed, pleased the (admittedly rather small) audiences, who enjoyed seeing a rough-and-tumble
band of desperadoes speaking impeccable drawing-room English. Their
accounts of dastardly deeds in a context of gavottes, and musical romps
in three-quarter time, link with *Princess Toto*. Here, the brigands are
said by Caramel to dance the wild quadrille and maddening 'Sir Roger
de Coverley' in soirées which are attended by all the respectable brigands
for miles around.[206]

In many ways, the mode of *Les Brigands* ideally suited Gilbert since
the plot's immoralities were financial, not sexual. This makes it rather
odd that he cut some rather Gilbertian original passages, as, for instance,
one in which Falsacappa explains that he inherited the gang at the age of
three when his father was hanged, and that the faithful Piétro dutifully
held it in trust for him until he came of age. In another cut passage,
Falsacappa's daughter assures her father that, though her own feelings
about banditry are ambiguous, she honours his filial piety in continuing
a 'trade' gloriously exercised by his father. Nothing, she says, is more
respectable, and the example should be more frequently followed.

The treatment of robbery as a respectable way to earn a living matches
that in *The Burglar's Story*. It also links with ideas of coming of age
(and faithfully serving one's indentures) which are to be central to *The
Pirates of Penzance*. In *The Brigands*, as in *Gentle Alice Brown*, Gilbert
presents lawlessness as a kind of justifiable family business. This follows
the original. In one (actually cut) passage, Fiorella had told her brigand
father, 'I am proud to be your daughter – I should like to rob in your
footsteps'.

The inversion of professional and moral standards is a frequent Gilbertian technique. In Gentle Alice's world, ruthless bandit parents can
be morally horrified when their daughter shows a possibility of marrying
'out'. The priest who, for motives of profit, condones their villainy is
appalled when Alice confesses to a very mild moment of flirting with an
eligible and honest young acquaintance. *Les Brigands* similarly inverts
the norms. Fragoletto, a young farmer, falls in love with Fiorella not in
a situation offering normal romantic possibilities but when her father's
gang loots his home. He then boldly comes to the robbers' lair to ask her
father formally for her hand.

Gilbert's translation not only distils most of the original. It actually
augments the teasing subversions of Meilhac and Halévy. Gilbert's
Fragoletto claims to be deeply impressed by the brigand chief's values.
'They do credit to your head and your heart', he says. 'You are quite

right – you are a scoundrel of the deepest dye, and you want another scoundrel of the deepest dye for a son-in-law'. Later, his acceptance of the young man as a full gang member foreshadows *The Pirates*. Here, the decorous sherry-drinking corresponds to the 'judicious revel' welcoming Fragoletto's initiation in *Les Brigands*.[207]

The inter-linking of themes and *motifs* is, then, undeniable. *Princess Toto*, like *The Brigands*, offers us outlaw gatherings that are highly respectable, in this case with elderly ladies always on hand as chaperones.[208] One irony is that it is Toto herself who forces the criminal agenda, while Caramel, the imposter-leader, is actually horrified at the *lack* of respectability. Uttering the mildest of oaths ('Goodness gracious!'), he bitterly laments that the romantically-minded young princess is always urging him to stop mail-coaches and secure wealthy travellers.[209] This is a concept which already occurs in *Les Brigands* and is later to resurface in *The Mountebanks*.

i.

The links between Gilbert and other satirists suggest that he is not an isolated innovator. But in many ways, his approach *is* distinctive, not least in his concept of what constitutes a theatrical company. Here, one point is that there was an increasing tendency to celebrity culture, as shown in Jenny Lind's second London season. Here 'Jenny Lind' waltzes, quadrilles, polkas, and dances were immediately rushed into print. She was 'the talk of the town'. Butcher's meat was advertised as, like her, sweet and tender.[210] Equally popular was E.A. Sothern who was later to commission Gilbert's *The Ne'er-Do-Well* and whose success in *Our American Cousin* turned a minor role into a cult. In both New York and London, the idiotic aristocratic English buffoon, Lord Dundreary, stole the show. Not only did the whiskers he sported became known as 'Dundrearies'. His dressing room at the Haymarket was crowded with parcels sent by haberdashers, hoping that he would wear and indirectly endorse their offerings.[211]

Like most things, celebrity culture was not exactly new. There had already been Garrick, Siddons, Kean, and Macready. But it did in the Victorian period accelerate, and it certainly marked a great contrast to the limited lives of many penurious jobbing-actors. Dundreary adorned the cover sheets of at least sixteen pieces of sheet music. Silly jokes became known as 'Dundrearyisms'. Little books were sold on street corners telling not just of his own imaginary doings but also those of his relatives. The main point, however, is that Gilbert disliked a 'star' culture, his tendency being to groom a number of talented performers for whom, within an Ensemble, he devised appropriate tailor-made parts. One example is of Rutland Barrington whose appearances began with Dr. Daly, for which he received six pounds per week.[212] Thereafter, Gilbert carefully tailored roles to suit his assets, his limitations, and even his physique. In *Iolanthe,* a reference to his stoutness – almost an apology to prepare the audience – allows the massive Fairy Queen amusingly to remark, 'I see no objection to stoutness, in moderation'.[213]

The desire in Gilbert to limit acting egos came to a head in *The Gondoliers,* notably in a disagreement with Jessie Bond about salary which prompted the equality *motif* in the opera.[214] Indirectly, this relates to another point, which is his repudiation of Sothern-style ad-libbing. When his wife noted that, in the wooing trio from *The Yeomen of the Guard,* 'Ulmar and Bond were going a great deal too far in pinching and tickling Grossmith', his response was firm. He actually wrote to Carte on Christmas Day demanding that 'whatever they do should be done *neatly* & *Delicately* (sic)' without any exaggerated effect.[215]

The rigidity of Gilbert's methods is sometimes seen as a control-freak mechanism for stifling artistic creativity. Certainly, he stamped quickly on unwise initiative: 'I hear great complaint of Barrington's gagging', he wrote, '... The piece is, I think, quite good enough without extraneous embellishments ... Anyway it must be played exactly as I wrote it'.[216] David Eden links this with jealousy, self-importance, and a latently narcissistic complex, referring to Gilbert's pushing aside the actors to take the first bow at the première of *The Palace of Truth.* Actually, Gilbert insisted that author *and* actors were called for and indeed that he was pushed from behind.

Rumours of professional high-handedness did, however, persist, one relating to Gilbert's grudging response to Madge Kendal's triumph in *Pygmalion and Galatea.*[217] As regards gagging, his stance was clear: 'I won't have an outside word introduced by anybody ... it opens the door to any amount of tomfoolery'. Partly this reflects an awareness that he would be the one judged by the public. But it does also suggest a rigid belief in his own crystallized rightness, causing some to compare him to a marionette-master. Certainly, with his famous blocks of wood and his stern directorial eye, he controlled almost all aspects of production, stipulating, for example, that the arquebus that Wilfred Shadbolt has just fired must have smoke curling from the muzzle and that a Utopian chorus lady's costume must be cleaned.[218]

The fact remains that Gilbert usually achieved fine results. Mildred of the London *Figaro* went into raptures over his costume-design for the *Ruddygore* bridesmaids, while the elegant mediaevalism of *Princess Ida* was said by the *Sportsman* to encompass 'one of the most perfect landscapes ever put upon the stage'.[219] Perhaps, the most original aspect was his combination of authenticity with a content that was often surreal and parodic. Fairies go to Parliament. Pirates are apprenticed. The realism aspect is seen most notably in the second revival of *H.M.S. Pinafore.* When Mrs. Carte suggested flying a flag aboard, Gilbert insisted that it should be the White Ensign, 'not the Jack – which is essentially a merchant flag and is only flown on the bowsprit of a Man of War'.[220] Famously, before designing the first set, he visited Portsmouth to study the rigging of the *Victory*, making sketches of the ship to familiarize himself with every physical detail.

The Gilbertian demand for realism may seem a minor matter. But it is essential to his craft that the surreal and satirical should be set off by a contrasting basis in normality. Sometimes, this becomes an inversion. The fanciful is treated with a logic-chopping *gravitas* while the inverted pedestrian becomes supremely fanciful. Another variant lies in visual parody. In the 'curse of Rome' scene in Bulwer-Lytton's *Richelieu*, the Cardinal, defying the king's emissaries, and with Julie, his orphaned ward, clinging to him, exclaims:

> Mark where she stands, around her form I draw
> The awful circle of our solemn Church!
> Set but a foot within that holy ground,
> And on thy head – yea, though it wore a crown –
> I launch the curse of Rome!

This is part-parodied in *Ruddygore* where Richard Dauntless produces a Union Jack, waving it over Rose Maybud's head in a flamboyant protective gesture.[221]

Influences and Conclusions

We have seen, then, that Gilbert was frequently an innovator. But he did obviously learn from others, his Ensemble mode, for instance, referencing Tom Robertson and the Bancrofts. John Hollingshead, who in 1869 produced *Dreams* at the Gaiety, wrote glowingly of Robertson: 'The little school-children ... loved him. He took them, one after the other, tenderly by the hand and led them to their places on the stage'. Gilbert too was fond of children, but Hollingshead compared *him* to Oliver Cromwell. He was never a particularly kindly director, though he undoubtedly – and with acknowledgement – borrowed many of Robertson's stage-managing techniques.[222]

One area where Gilbert did owe Robertson a debt was in stage pairing and another linked one in Ensemble formations. This is seen, for instance, in the frequent balancing of two girls, one lively and feisty, one more quiet and self-contained. In *The Gondoliers,* Tessa and Gianetta may well derive their personalities from Robertson's Polly and Esther (in *Caste*), also looking back to pairings such as tall, athletic Rosalind and small, dainty Celia. Sometimes, one of the pair is more spiritual, as in *The Lord of The Manor* (1780) where the sensitive, lofty-minded Sophia is set against her more lively, common-sense sister. Elsewhere, the two-girl grouping may form a single unit, as in the jointly repressed Nekaya and Kalyba. In *The Gondoliers,* there is even a quartet formation, Tessa, Gianetta, Marco, and Giuseppe in their 'contemplative fashion' looking back choreographically to the Rosalind, Orlando, Phebe, Silvius inter-weaving in *As You Like It.*

The above is not the only area in which Gilbert drew on existing ex-amples. He did the same in relation to historical accuracy where the main model was not Robertson but Planché. The latter, says Donald Roy, 'was not slow to claim credit for the whole antiquarian movement', though he did recognize some abuses. Favouring Greek tunics for his classical pieces, he specifically prevented one comic lead from playing Prometheus 'dressed like a great lubberly boy in a red jacket and nan-keen, with a pinafore all besmeared with lollipop!'[223] This is part of a wider disparagement of the low comedian who in Gilbert's *Actors, Authors and Audiences* is berated for gagging and wearing an intrusive 'remarkably clever mechanical wig'. In *The Grand Duke,* this is mocked and referenced in Ludwig's wearing the authentic Greek dress but sur-mounted with a huge Louis Quatorze headpiece.

Another area where Planché and Gilbert cohere is in a concern for refinement. For the former, the theatrical aim was to provide a 'pretty story, humorous action, pointed and graceful dialogue, sweet music, beautiful scenery and tasteful costumes'. His main objection to *opéra bouffe* was not so much the burlesque approach as its lack of artistry and 'unmeaning buffoonery'.[224] Gilbert generally agreed but had a far sharper cutting edge and was less attracted to extravagant spectacle. He would probably have disdained Planché's attempts at replicating the 1825 coronation of Charles X of France and would never have sanc-tioned the interpolation of a pageant of the Lord Mayor's Show into Rowley's *A Woman Never Vext,* even if it *was* performed 'as it appeared in the reign of Henry V1'.[225]

One area where Gilbert and Planché *did* agree was in a sense of the value of a well-drilled chorus. 'All this requires animated gesture on part of chorus', Gilbert notes of the 'Go away, Madam' sequence in an early *Iolanthe* promptbook. Individual exhibitionism was, however, discour-aged. In an 1898 revival of *Trial by Jury,* Gilbert was, much vexed by a chorus man named Moss who not only overacted but also contrived to make himself conspicuous by appearing one night in a 'grotesque flaxen wig'. His demand was that Moss should be put in the back row at the furthest end from the stage. Thereby, he said, 'his exaggerations would cease to be important'.[226]

i.

The degree to which Gilbert was a martinet is a matter of debate. Some-times, we know, he incorporated good ideas – even interpolations – from talented players, one example being Pooh-Bah's 'I don't want any lunch'.

Equally, he was the first to capitalize on fortuitous accidents, the most famous example being the changing of 'Rapture!' to 'Modified Rapture!' for a limited joy in *The Mikado*.[227] Sometimes, he would allow a degree of high-spirited licence in dances while insisting on straight dialogue delivery. This applies in *H.M.S. Pinafore,* where the ship is a microcosm for exploring the absurdities of a rigid Victorian caste system, while also mocking the would-be levellers. Except in *Never Mind the Why and Wherefore*, Sir Joseph is unbending. This is necessary to show that the so-called radical is vain, pompous, and unwittingly hypocritical, a bonus being that his model W.H. Smith was so woefully inexperienced in seafaring matters.

The introduction of big star turns was undoubtedly not a Gilbertian tendency. But in his hands-on mode of control, he was quite close to Victorian norms. For much of the Victorian period, plays were specially commissioned or chosen by actor-managers who themselves might supervise stage-management and perform the leading roles. Augustus Harris dilates on his endless dealings with carpenters, lighting men, choreographers and the like, while from the 1860s dramatists took ever-more responsibility for the production of their own plays. Don Boucicault was widely known as a hard taskmaster. Pinero's martinet reputation lay in an insistence on obedience in respect of every single movement, gesture, inflection, stress, and occasional pause.[228]

As regards speech, Gilbert was in the Pinero camp. He had, for instance, strong feelings about blank verse, commenting on the 'lack of knowledge of the art of elocution apparent in many of our young actors'. To some extent, this matches Henry Irving, one of whose lectures stresses the importance of elocution. The difference is one of emphasis. Gilbert argues that actors should neither mispronounce words (apparently deliberately) nor speak Shakespearian lines 'as if they were a lesson in one syllable for little boys'. Irving – sometimes criticized for his delivery and for the extremes highs and lows in his cadences – advised differently. He told his audience to express *feelings* through words, which could justifiably mean 'a variation of sound not provided for by the laws of pronunciation'.[229]

Gilbert's concern with speech was partly practical. He was concerned with audibility, clarity, and coherence. But he also had a strong sense of rhythm and cadence and was concerned that standards of eloquence should not slip. Actors, he said, habitually deliver blank verse lines in a monotone, keeping to one note through the sentence and finishing a semi-tone higher or lower.[230] They also fail to sustain an arc, slicing up the iambic pentameter like sausages, when reasonable flexibility and variety could offset the rigidity of the mode.[231] Such views look back to the high value accorded in the 18th century to oratory, rhetoric, and voice-projection, but Gilbert is not merely hidebound. In an interview with Bram Stoker in January 1908, he praises the forward tendency of modern drama. The limitation is that he dismisses many modern plays as *pièces banales,* has little interest in Ibsen and Strindberg, and bemoans the modern tendency to put a great effect in the penultimate rather than the final act.

Not all Gilbert's ideas will now seem acceptable, but it is because he so much cared about the theatre that he warrants the above degree of attention. Steeped in theatrical precedent, Gilbert uses it, inverts it and sometimes breaks the mould in a manner prefiguring the Absurdists. He may have been pessimistic. He may in 1901 have told William Archer that he was now altogether left behind.[232] But what he was actually doing was looking forward – anticipating writers such as Waugh, Stoppard, Ayckbourn, and Simpson – while also gaining succour from the past.

* * * *

Notes

1 Smollett, Tobias, *The Miscellaneous Works of Tobias Smollett,* Vol. 5 (Mundell and Son, 1800), p. 51.
2 *Advice to a Son: Precepts of Lord Burleigh, Sir Walter Raleigh and Francis Osborne,* ed. Louis B. Wright (Cornell University Press).
3 Gladstone, Lowe, and Ayrton were, respectively, the Prime Minister, Chancellor of the Exchequer, and First Commissioner of Works (Public Buildings). The three characters were made up and costumed to look like the caricatures of them that had appeared in *Vanity Fair.* See also *W.S. Gilbert, A Mid-Victorian Aristophanes* by Edith Hamilton; *The English Aristophanes* by Walter Sichel; and *A Classic In Humour* by Max Beerbohm, edited 2011 by David Trutt, Los Angeles, California, U.S.A., Hamilton's essay is from the October 1927 issue of *Theatre Arts Monthly* and Walter Sichel's from the October 1911 issue of *The Fortnightly Review,* reprinted in the December 1911 issue of *The Living Age.*
4 Sometimes, there are also internal contrasts. Minnie's stockbroker-sharp business brain, for instance, adds a further dimension of contrast with her baby-talk mode of self-expression.
5 Aristophanes, *The Frogs,* http://classics.mit.ed/Arisophanes/frogs.html (translation online).
6 Quoted in Hamilton, Edith, *W.S. Gilbert A Mid-Victorian Aristophanes,* p. 12. Compare *The Mikado* in *The Complete Annotated Gilbert and Sullivan,* p. 567.
7 David, E., *Aristiophanes and Athenian Society of the Early Fourth Century* (E.J. Brill, 1984), p. 17.
8 Nelson, Stephanie, *Aristophanes and the Tragic Muse* (E.J. Brill, 2016), p. 202.
9 David, *Aristiophanes and Athenian Society of the Early Fourth Century,* p. 18.
10 Ibid., p. 19.
11 Julian, *Misopogon.* Translation by W.C. Wright (1913), available as Internet download, p. 7. See also *The Pirates of Penzance* in *The Complete Annotated Gilbert and Sullivan,* p. 246.

12 Chaucer, Geoffrey, The *General Prologue*, ll. 371–376 (available online – Poetry Foundation).

13 *Era*, 22 May 1870, p. 11.

14 *Gammer Gurton's Needle,* Act 2, sc 5. Friar Rush derives from a German narrative, where the devil enters a monastery posing as a man called *Bruder Rausch* (*Broder Ruus* and variants). The Early Modern German *Rusche, Rausch* is the term for a loud swooshing noise.

15 W.S. Gilbert, *Creatures of Impulse* (W.S. Gilbert Archive download), p. 14.

16 *Fun*, 3 August 1867; 16 March 1867.

17 *The Commedia dell'Arte of Flaminio Scala: A Translation and Analysis of 30 Scenarios*, ed. Andrews, Richard (Scarecrow Press, 2008), p. xxiv. See also Debrov, Gregory, Brill's *Companion to the Study of Greek Comedy* (E.J. Brill, 2000), pp. 490–491.

18 *H.M.S. Pinafore* in *The Complete Annotated Gilbert and Sullivan*, p. 161.

19 Hamilton, Edith, *W.S. Gilbert A Mid-Victorian Aristophanes*, p. 15. The sex point is true but Gilbert's social critique is stronger in the uncut versions of the libretti.

20 W.S. Gilbert. *The Gentleman in Black* (Word File, Internet download), pp. 22–23.

21 There are many legends of changelings and demon abductions and kidnaps from this area. One concerns Rübezahl, a mythical spirit of the Krkonoše Mountains, a mountain range along the border between the historical lands of Bohemia and Silesia. He is a prankster and the subject of many German folklore and legends. See Carl Maria von Weber, romantic opera *Rübezahl* (1805 Breslau). See also *Changelings, An Essay by* D. Ashliman, 1997 (Internet availability; Copyright material).

22 Pater, Walter, *Miscellaneous Studies*; *Apollo in Picardy*, The tale appeared in *Harper's Magazine* in November 1893. Reprinted 1895 in *Miscellaneous Studies*.

23 For this and other stories, see Sikes, Wirt, *British Goblins: The Realm of Faerie* (Felinfach: Llanerch, 1991).

24 See *Myth and Moor, Into the Woods, 10: Wild Children* (Internet, 11 June 2013). Usually, the abandoned child grows up, learns his true parentage, and fulfils his foreseen destiny. Cyrus, for instance, grows up, learns his true origins, and not only captures the Median throne but goes on to conquer most of Central and Southeast Asia. Similarly, Paris is born under a prophecy that he will one day cause the downfall of Troy. The baby is left on the side of Mount Ida but is suckled by a bear and manages to live – growing up to abduct Helen of Troy and spark the Trojan War.

25 Macbeth's kingly robes hang on him like a giant's garments on a dwarfish thief. The clothing imagery may have been inspired by references in the North Berwick witch trials. For *Eyes and No Eyes*, see Stedman, Jane W., *Gilbert before Sullivan* (London: Routledge and Kegan Paul, 1969), especially pp. 210–211.

26 This leads into the 'unaccommodated man' *motif* of *King Lear*. Hollowness is implied by Hector's stripping off of the golden armour of a Greek warrior in Act 5 of *Troilus and Cressida* to reveal putrefaction beneath.

27 Shakespeare, William, *All's Well That Ends Well*. In Act 3, sc. vi, Bertram's friends dare Paroles to go to the battlefield to retrieve his lost drum. In Act 4, sc. I, he quickly gets captured by some men, speaking an imaginary language, pretending to be enemy soldiers. In Act 4, sc. Iii, without hesitation, he betrays his friends and the Florentine army in exchange for his life. He is then disowned by his friends, including Bertram.

28　This is the divorce from Catherine of Aragon and marriage to Anne Boleyn. The queen suing for her head in *The Yeomen of the Guard* is probably
Anne Boleyn.

29　Shakespeare, William, *Richard III*, Act 1, sc. ii:

> Was ever woman in this humour woo'd?
> Was ever woman in this humour won?
> I'll have her; but I will not keep her long.

30　*Mankind,* See lines 471 et seq. (Lester, G.A., ed., *Three Late Medieval
Morality Plays*. The New Mermaids Series, London: A&C Black, 1981).

31　*The Mikado,* in *The Complete Annotated Gilbert and Sullivan*, p. 631.

32　This also applies in works such as *Die Zauberflöte*.

33　*The Mikado,* in *The Complete Annotated Gilbert and Sullivan*, p. 631.
Trial by Jury, pp. 21–23.

34　*The Mikado* in *The Complete Annotated Gilbert and Sullivan*, pp. 587–589.

35　W.S. Gilbert, *Creatures of Impulse*, p. 19.

36　Schironi, Francesca, *The Trickster Onstage: The Cunning Slave from
Plautus to Commedia dell'Arte* (Internet download), pp. 447–448.

37　W.S. Gilbert, *The Gentleman in Black*, p. 26.

38　W.S. Gilbert, *His Excellency* (W.S. Gilbert Archive, Word Download (unnumbered pages)).

39　Quoted in *Gilbert and Sullivan's Mystery Play* by Trevor Timpson BBC
News, 16 August 2011.

40　Shakespeare, William, *Henry 1V, Part 2*, Act 5, sc. iv.

41　Pater, Walter, *Gaston de Latour*. Five chapters were published in *Mac-
millan's Magazine* in May 1888, and a sixth, entitled *Giordano Bruno*
in the *Fortnightly Review* (Vol. XLVI, No. CCLXXII (1 August 1889),
pp. 234–244. Various fragments appeared thereafter.

42　*H.M.S. Pinafore*, in *The Complete Annotated Gilbert and Sullivan*, p. 141.

43　Ibid., pp. 129–131.

44　Shakespeare, William, *Much Ado about Nothing*, Act 2, sc. i.

45　W.S. Gilbert, *Only a Dancing Girl*; *Fun n.s. III*, 23 June 1866.

46　The essence here is fast-paced fun as when Figaro, as a last resort, tries to
save the situation by pretending it was he who jumped out of the window,
not Cherubino.

47　*The Pirates of Penzance*, in *The Complete Annotated Gilbert and Sullivan*,
p. 247.

48　Shakespeare, William, *A Midsummer Night's Dream*, Act V, sc. i.

49　Shakespeare, *As You Like It*, Act III, sc. ii.

50　*Patience*, in *The Complete Annotated Gilbert and Sullivan*, p. 287.

51　Jack Point's statement actually rebounds against him because the laughter
he notes is in response to his own ignorance about the real Colonel Fairfax
whom – to his face – he has labelled plaguey ill-looking (Act II, dialogue
before 'A man who would woo a fair maid'). Beatrice's command comes in
Much Ado, Act IV, sc.i.

52　Hicks, *Between Ourselves*, pp. 49–50.

53　W.S. Gilbert, *His Excellency,* Act II (W.S. Gilbert archive download).
Here, as elsewhere in dancing scenarios, there is a marionette allusion, the
soldiers becoming 'mincing marionettes, ha! ha!'

54　Shakespeare, William, *Twelfth Night*, Act II, sc. iv; Act III, sc. iv.

55　Usually, love triumphs but Gilbert has nuanced endings. Sergeant Meryll is
virtually tricked into marriage. Julia only takes Ernest on sufferance. Ko-ko
assures the deceived Katisha that he is the best bargain she can expect.

56 See Hager, Ian, *The Age of Milton: An Encyclopedia of Major 17th-century British and American Authors* (Greenwood Publishing Group, 2004), p. 104.

57 W.S. Gilbert, *A Hornpipe in Fetters* in the *Era Almanack and Annual*, 1879. On this, see pp. 91–92.

58 W.S. Gilbert, *Old Plays and New Plays*; *Era Almanack*, 1873.

59 *Illustrated Times*, January 1868.

60 Part 2 of *The Siege of Rhodes* followed in the 1657–1659 era, and was first published in 1663. The plot was based on the 1522 Siege of Rhodes, when the island was besieged by the Ottoman fleet of Suleiman the Magnificent. The score of the opera is believed to be lost. However, the original sketches by John Webb for the stage sets are extant.

61 *Illustrated Times* review, 15 May 1869.

62 Letter from Prince Pückler-Muskau, 23 November 1826. See Puckler's Progress: *The Adventures of Prince Puckler-Muskau* (sic) *in England, Wales & Ireland as Told in Letters to His Former Wife, 1826–1829* trans. Flora Brennan (Harper Collins, 1987).

63 Corneille, Pierre, *Of the Three Unities of Time, Place and Action* (*Discours du poème dramatique*, 1660). Liaison between the scenes is not specifically an Aristotelian requirement.

64 The original runs: Javert: Ten years ago – Jean Valjean was believed to be dead – so, the pardon was kept back – It is here – 'twas obtained by the President of Arras, for his good services as Maire of Montruil! Release him'.

65 *A Sensation Novel* in *Gilbert before Sullivan*, p. 144.

66 Ibid., p. 140. For *Oonagh*, see Stedman Jane: *W.S. Gilbert's Theatrical Criticism* (The Society for Theatrical Research, London, 2000), p. 59.

67 Marston, John Westland, *A Hero of Romance*. Quoted in *Gilbert's Theatrical Criticism*, p. 128.

68 Pepys' *Diary*, ed. Wheatley (G.R. Bell & Sons, 1920), Vol. VIII, p. 296.

69 See Restoration Drama – TheatreHistory.com

70 In *On Guard*, discussed further in my forthcoming work on Gilbert's themes, in the section *Sex, Gender and Marital Relationships*.

71 Carroll, Lewis, '*The Stage and the Spirit of Reverence*'. In Clement Scott, *The Theatre*, XI (Strand Publishing Company, January–June 1888), p. 291.

72 La Nippe is English. He 'took his foreign names upon his travels to save his master's reputation' – there is 'nothing so disgraceful nowadays as to be waited on by your own countrymen'. Among other things, he allows his master an hour every morning for yawning (Burgoyne, John, *The Lord of the Manor*, Act 1, Drury Lane, 1780).

73 W.S. Gilbert, *Era Almanack*, 1879: *A Hornpipe in Fetters*. See also Stedman Jane: *W.S. Gilbert's Theatrical Criticism*, p. 199.

74 Ibid.

75 The King himself loved to see beautiful women on stage, sometimes himself attending the theatre, rather than simply inviting acting companies to perform at court.

76 *Cambridge Companion to English Restoration Theatre*, ed. Deborah Payne Fisk (C.U.P., 2000), p. 6. It is not known who designed the new theatre building, though tradition ascribes it to Sir Christopher Wren. More likely perhaps is Robert Hooke.

77 The *Adelphi Guests* were the extras 'hired by the day' to swell out a scene or add a retinue. *Astley's Amphitheatre* was a performance venue in Lambeth, London opened by Philip Astley in 1773. With increasing prosperity and rebuilding after successive fires, it grew to become *Astley's Royal*

Amphitheatre, and this was the home of the circus. Astley's original circus was 62 ft (~19 m) in diameter and later he settled it at 42 ft (~13 m), which has been an international standard ever since.

78 This was during the run of *Secret Service.* Terriss was killed while entering the Theatre by the royal entrance in Maiden Lane which he used as a private through-way.

79 It was an acceptable part of audience behaviour to arrive an hour and a half late and then to talk all the way through the performance. One Regency wit allegedly complained that 'the trouble with the opera was they sang so loud one couldn't hear oneself talk'. See Murray, Venetia, *High Society: A Social History of the Regency Period, 1788–1830* (Viking, 1998), pp. 220–230.

80 Quoted in Wilson, Ben, *Decency and Disorder, The Age of Cant, 1789–1837* (Faber and Faber, 2007), p. 197. Decency still mattered to the middle classes. Mary Berry's *Fashionable Friends* (1801) was withdrawn after only three performances because of its lax morality. She had not accounted for the fact that the sexual innuendo and loose behaviour which the upper classes took for granted still shocked the general public.

81 See Wilson, *Decency and Disorder, The Age of Cant, 1789–1837,* pp. xiii–xiv. Significantly, Lady Sarah was rebuked by her prim grandchildren for uttering the word 'belly'. Sheridan's *A Trip to Scarborough* sets the trend, being a very sanitized version of Vanbrugh's 1696 comedy *The Relapse,* itself subtitled *Virtue in Danger.*

82 See Wilson, *Decency and Disorder, The Age of Cant, 1789–1837,* pp. xvii–xix. One extenuation is that Punch's violence toward his wife is prompted by her own violence toward him. In this aspect, he retains some of his previous hen-pecked persona. As for the baby, here the violence depends (a) on the irritating nature of its presence and squalling and (b) on the fact that he at least sees it as an extension of a domestic trap.

83 Dickens, Charles, Letter to Mary Tyler, 6 November 1849, from *The Letters of Charles Dickens Vol. V, 1847–1849.*

84 See *Pierre-Claude Nivelle de la Chausée* (Wikipedia article). *Mélanide* (1741) is the play that fully develops the *comédie larmoyante.* The new method found bitter enemies. Alexis Piron nicknamed the author 'le Reverend Père Chaussée'.

85 *Patience* in *The Complete Annotated Gilbert and Sullivan,* p. 323.

86 W.S. Gilbert, *Tom Cobb* (W.S. Gilbert Archive download, [PDF, 164KB]), pp. 7–9.

87 W.S. Gilbert, *His Excellency* (W.S. Gilbert Archive, Word Download (unnumbered pages)), Act 11 dialogue shortly before the final musical sections.

88 See Introduction to *Money* in *Nineteenth Century Plays,* ed. George Rowell (O.U.P., 1972), pp. 45–46.

89 The writer was actually Herbert Croft, a young Essex lawyer.

90 Darwin, Erasmus, *Zoonomia; or, The Laws of Organic Life* (1794–1796), quoted in Brewer John, *Sentimental Murder: Love and Madness in the Eighteenth Century* (Harper Perennial, 3 January 2005), pp. 186–188; 191.

91 Trotter, Thomas, *A View of the Nervous Temperament* (Second edition, 1807), pp. 49–51. See also pp. 225–226. Trotter saw many foods and drinks including tea as contributing to the malaise. Dr. Thomas Beddoes claimed that coffee produced a sense of intoxication and of enfeebled faculties. Even the fear of war was a sign of a weakened and nervous country. Defensive systems were a sign of cowardice.

92 *Scourge 11,* 1811, pp. 202 ff. *Scourge or Monthly Monitor,* a journal published in London is further quoted in *Decency and Disorder, The Age of Cant,* p. xiv.

93 The song covering this was the first to get an encore on the first night. See Bradley, Ian, *The Complete Annotated Gilbert and Sullivan*, 20th anniversary edition, p. 1062.

94 Quoted in *Decency and Disorder, The Age of Cant,* p. xxiv. For the sensibility of Sheridan and the Prince Regent, see Murray, *High Society: A Social History of the Regency Period, 1788–1830*, p. 20.

95 Murray, *High Society: A Social History of the Regency Period, 1788–1830*, p. 20. Tears, said Beau Brummell in a nonetheless sad farewell letter to a young French girl, may be counterfeited with a sponge and rose water.

96 Trotter, *A View of the Nervous Temperament*, p. 90. In the House of Usher inbreeding intensifies the febrility which is shared between house and inhabitants by a kind of osmosis.

97 Letter to Alice James in *Letters of Henry James*, ed. Percy Lubock, 2 vols. (London, 1920), pp. 16–19. See also Orlando, Emily J., *Edith Wharton and the Visual Arts* (University of Alabama Press, 2007), pp. 61–62.

98 Quoted in Parkins, Wendy, *Jane Morris: The Burden of History* (Edinburgh Critical Studies in Victorian Culture, 15 April 2013), p. 59.

99 *Scourge 11*, 1811, pp. 202 ff.

100 For *Creatures of Impulse*, see W.S. Gilbert Archive download copy (zipped word file), especially pp. 14–16. For Aristotle (pseudonym), see *Aristotle's Compleat Master Piece*; *The Works* (London, 1776), p. 42. This is a volume in four parts, the *Compleat Master Piece* being in the first.

101 Jerrold, Douglas, *Black-Eyed Susan*, Act 11, sc. ii in *Nineteenth Century Plays*, p. 22.

102 On this, see *Decency and Disorder, The Age of Cant*, pp. 167–168. Among the drivers, there were some noted 'characters' – Lord Dashalong, for instance, whose real name was Lord Sefton. The whole Barrymore family was infamous. The seventh earl – who haunted Vauxhall Pleasure Gardens – was so viciously immoral he was known as Hellgate. The eighth was Cripplegate because he had a club foot. Their sister was Billingsgate, named after the fish-market because of her continual swearing. The younger brother, a lustful clergyman, was Newgate because he was often kept held in the prison.

103 See *High Society: A Social History of the Regency Period, 1788–1830*, p. 61.

104 *The Plays of Richard Brinsley Sheridan*, ed. Ernest Rhys (Dent Everyman, 1933), pp. 352, 241.

105 *Princess Ida*, in *The Complete Annotated Gilbert and Sullivan*, p. 485.

106 *Decency and Disorder, The Age of Cant*, pp. 181–182.

107 *Patience* in *The Complete Annotated Gilbert and Sullivan*, p. 289.

108 Jesse, Captain William, *Beaux and Belles of England* (Athenaeum Press, 1900), Vol. 1, pp. 50–51. We also learn that his boots were polished 'au vin de Champagne', and 'the ties of his cravats designed by the first portrait painter in London, who only became the rage when Brummell had entrusted him with this delicate and sacred task'.

109 Coates, had arrived in England in 1807, hugely rich from an inheritance from a West Indian sugar plantation. See *High Society: A Social History of the Regency Period, 1788–1830*, p. 41.

110 Ibid., pp. 43–44.

111 Stedman, Jane W., *W.S. Gilbert, A Classic Victorian and His Theatre*, p. 309.

112 W.S. Gilbert, *Tom Cobb* (Act 111), p. 23.

113 Published in America by Louis P. Goullaud, Boston, 1874. Sung version available on C.D. *On the Boards: Songs from the Victorian Music Halls*.

114 *Austen Jane, Love and Friendship, LETTER the 13th LAURA in continuation.* There is a further joke in that Werther's waistcoat was yellow.

115 W.S. Gilbert, *Tom Cobb*, p. 23.

116 *John Bull Triumphant; British Museum Collection Online.* Museum Number 1851, 01901.22.

117 See Burwick, Frederick, *British Drama of the Industrial Revolution* (C.U.P., 2015), p. 103 and *High Society: A Social History of the Regency Period, 1788–1830*, p. 220.

118 When Lady Caroline Lamb writes to her mother with news of the illegitimate daughter of the Duke of Devonshire 'flirting at a play, she – a woman of culture – fails completely to mention what the play was, who was in it or whether it had any merit'.

119 Quoted from Henry Lytton's *Memoirs* in *The Complete Annotated Gilbert and Sullivan*, p. 722.

120 *The Kept Mistress*, pp. 109–110 (introduction to anonymous text in *Eighteenth Century Drama: Afterpieces*, O.U.P., 1970).

121 Ibid., pp. 132–133.

122 Quoted in *Decency and Disorder, The Age of Cant*, p. 212. Ben Wilson refers us to *Political Review*, 4 November 1809; *Times* 8 November 1809; and Anon, *Short Treatise on the Passion, Illustrative of the Human Mind. By a Lady*, Two vols (London, 1810), Vol. 1, pp. 65–66.

123 W.S. Gilbert, *The People of Pantomime; Fun*, 4 February–14 March 1863: *The Pantomime Prince*.

124 Information obtained from web-page 1832: *MacReady vs. Kean – Battle of the Lions.* See https://theatregoing.wordpress.com/tag/william-macready/

125 Otten, Terry, *The Deserted Stage* (Ohio University Press, 1972), p. 3.

126 Bancroft, Maria and Squire, *Mr. and Mrs. Bancroft on and Off the Stage* (London: Richard Bentley and Son, 1889), p. 136. Quoted in Catherine Pope's *A Storm in a Teacup? Evaluating T.W. Robertson's Impact on Victorian Theatre* (Internet download).

127 Barrett, Daniel, *T.W. Robertson and the Prince of Wales Theatre* (New York: Peter Lang Publishing, 1995), p. 70.

128 Quoted in Stephens, John Russell, *The Profession of the Playwright: British Theatre 1800–1900* (Cambridge University Press, 1992), p. 58.

129 For Sam Wild, see *The Profession of the Playwright: British Theatre 1800–1900*, p. 50. See also Compton, Piers, *Victorian Vortex* (Robert Hale, 1977), p. 139.

130 Crowther, *Gilbert of Gilbert and Sullivan*, p. 224. The ease of writing is denied elsewhere.

131 The view of Clement Scott, quoted in Barrett, *T.W. Robertson and the Prince of Wales Theatre*, p. 82.

132 *The Times*, 11 April 1867, p. 11.

133 Jenkins, Anthony, *The Making of Victorian Drama* (C.U.P., 1991), p. 132.

134 For Gilbert's view, see Archer, William, *Real Conversations*, p. 114. For Henry Arthur Jones, see Barrett, p. 131, For Buchanan, see *Essays on the Drama, The Stage of Today*, first published in the *New York Daily Tribune*, 21 December 1884, p. 4. For Yeats, see Styan, *Modern Drama n Theory and Practice 1: Realism and Naturalism* (C.U.P., 1981), p. 52.

135 Schlicke, Paul, *Dickens and Popular Entertainment* (London: Unwin Hyman, 1985 – paperback 1988), pp. 91–94.

136 *Fun*, 28 October 1865: *Musings in a Music Hall*/By a Young Man from the Country.

137 See *The Complete Annotated Gilbert and Sullivan*, p. 828 for a copy of the lyric. As well as 'Robin Hood' plays, Vernacular Plays, and Bible-based Morality Plays were popular. Strolling players would adapt their acts to

what was currently or locally popular, larger groups including singers and acrobats to vary the performances.

138 W.S. Gilbert, *Pantomimic Presentiments*. The men of property are stage-hands and property-men who also seem to be required to assist with the blacking up of the demon characters.

139 This is the view of John Pick in *The West End: Mismanagement and Snobbery*, quoted in Catherine Pope's *A Storm in a Teacup? Evaluating T.W. Robertson's Impact on Victorian Theatre*, p. 7.

140 See Fischler, Alan, 'Guano and Poetry: Payment for Playwriting in Victorian England'. *Modern Language Quarterly*, Vol. 62, Issue 1 (2002), pp. 43–52, 52.

141 W.S. Gilbert, *Era Almanack*; *A Hornpipe in Fetters*, quoted in Stedman J.W., *W.S. Gilbert's Theatrical Criticism*, p. 199.

142 Dickens, Charles, *The Life and Adventures of Nicholas Nickleby* (London, Chapman and Hall, 1866), p. 309.

143 Gautier, Théophile, *Historie de Part dramatique en France depuis vingt-cinq ans* (Leipzig, 1858–1859), pp. 15, 111. Gautier refers to Scribe as having 'an anti-poetical nature par excellence'.

144 G.B. Shaw, in the *Saturday Review*, 1 June 1895. For his comments on *Tosca*, see Baker Evan: *Sardou and Sardoodledom, Puccini and Tosca*; Programme Notes, San Francisco Opera, 2009.

145 W.S. Gilbert: Review of *Jezebel*; *Fun*, 24 December 1870. Boucicault's response to comments on *The Poor of New York* reflect the fact that it was written hastily in 1857, when he was desperately in need of money after the birth of his second child. The play was actually a collaboration between Boucicault and three journalists, Seymour, Goodrich, and Warden.

146 In 1879, the Bancrofts moved to the Haymarket Theatre. Productions included revival of *Money*, Sardou's *Odette* (for which they engaged Madame Helena Modjeska), *Fedora*, and Pinero's *Lords and Commons*. The comments on *Fedora* – which lost its accent – occurred in this context.

147 G.B. Shaw, in the *Saturday Review*, 1 June 1895. For his comments on *Tosca*, see Baker Evan: *Sardou and Sardoodledom, Puccini and Tosca*; Programme Notes, San Francisco Opera, 2009.

148 Quoted in *Meilhac and Halevy – and Gilbert: Comic Converses*, a Paper by George McElroy given at the 1970 International Gilbert and Sullivan Conference, ed. James Helyar (University of Kansas Libraries), p. 93.

149 Harris, Augustus, article in *The Magazine of Art*, quoted in STR lecture *John Ruskin and the British Pantomime* (19 February 2009, Art Workers' Guild, London) given by Jeffrey Richards.

150 Quoted in *Light Touches: Cultural Practice of Illumination, London 1780–1840*, thesis by Alice Barnaby submitted to Exeter University (2009), p. 284.

151 Ibid., p. 286.

152 Fitzgerald, Percy, *Principles of Comedy and Dramatic Effect* (Tinsley, 1870), pp. 89–90. Quoted in *Victorian Spectacular Theatre 1850–1910* by Michael R. Booth (Routledge and Kegan Paul, 1981), pp. 80–81.

153 Ibid., p. 82.

154 (*37) Hickory Wood and Collins, *Sleeping Beauty and the Beast*, quoted in *An old fairy tale told anew: Victorian Fairy Pantomime* p. 3 of 10 (Internet availability).

155 W.S. Gilbert, *What Is A Burlesque?* (*Belgravia Annual*, 1868).

156 *The Times*, Monday, 9 October 1893.

157 W.S. Gilbert, *The Fairy's Dilemma*, in *The Lost Stories of W.S. Gilbert*, p. 232.

158 Phillips, Watts, *Not Guilty* (reprint of Robert M. De Wit, 1869 edition), p. 37.

159 *The Gondoliers*, in *The Complete Annotated Gilbert and Sullivan*, p. 957.
160 The mechanisms of the *parallèle* are explained in M.J. Moynet's *L'Envers du théâtre* (1873), pp. 100–102. This was enlarged with extra illustrations by M. Glen Wilson and Allan S. Jackson in *French Theatrical Production in the Nineteenth Century* (State University of New York at Binghamton, 1976).
161 Article in *The World*, 1893, quoted in *John Ruskin and the British Pantomime*, p. 4.
162 *John Ruskin and the British Pantomime*, p. 4.
163 Ibid., p. 9. Ruskin's most sustained writings on pantomime come in *Fors Clavigera 39* (March 1874).
164 Ibid., p. 5.
165 Ibid., p. 11. The *Ali Baba* pantomime was written by Gilbert A Becket, subordinating the fairy-tale elements to contemporary references. The thieves' cave was an up-to-date London club complete with billiard tables. When the forty thief-girls proceeded to light forty cigars, the Great British Public burst into a spontaneous round of applause.
166 Harris, Augustus, article, 'Spectacle', in *The Magazine of Art*. See Newey K., Richards J., *John Ruskin and the Victorian Theatre* (Springer, 2010), p. 166.
167 O'Brien, John, *Harlequin Britain*, p. 218. O'Brien quotes the views of Henry Fielding in *An Enquiry in the Causes of the Late Increase of Robberies* (1751), p. 79.
168 *John Ruskin and the British Pantomime*, p. 13. For Paramount's song, see *The Complete Annotated Gilbert and Sullivan*; *Utopia Limited*, pp. 999–1003.
169 *The Times* (27 November 1882) refers not unsympathetically to the inclusion of a more serious note but goes on to damn the treatment: '… as this song is sung by Strephon, the aforesaid fairy M.P., and himself a fairy down to the waist … it cannot be said to be artistically very appropriate or morally very impressive'. Recent productions including the aria have suggested its viability.
170 On Sentiment, see Brewer, *Sentimental Murder: Love and Madness in the Eighteenth Century*.
171 Colman George (The Younger) John Bull, 1803, in The Magistrate and Other Nineteenth-Century Plays, ed. Michael Booth (O.U.P., 1974), p. 21.
172 Poe, Edgar Allan, *The Fall of the House of Usher* (reprint: *The Works of the Late Edgar Allan Poe*, Vol. 1) (New York: J.S. Redfield, Clinton Hall, 1850), pp. 291–309, 296.
173 In *Jane Eyre*, Rochester atones (a) by trying to save the life of his mad wife and (b) by repenting and humbling himself before God in advance of Jane's return. His maiming is a ritual punishment but her arrival, as a kind of Quester to a Wounded Fisher King, permits salvation.
174 Bulwer-Lytton, *The Lady of Lyons*, Last scene of 1857 version, available as an Internet download.
175 Jones, Henry Arthur, *Mrs. Dane's Defence* in *The Magistrate and Other Nineteenth-Century Plays*, p. 406.
176 Wilde, Oscar, *Lady Windermere's Fan*, opening speech in Act 111.
177 One possibility is that Wilde's more probing ideas are subordinate to his seeking a vehicle for his witty bon mots and brilliant capacity for elegant dialogue. *Vera*, an early work, does aim at political discourse, though again with melodrama effects and some amusingly sardonic epigrams.
178 Gerould, Daniel (1983). *American Melodrama; Performing Arts Journal Publication*, quoted in Wikipedia entry on the play.

179 *The Frozen Deep*; *Fun*, 17 November 1866.

180 The Captain had died of a heart-attack resulting from the banker's machinations.

181 Gilbert's parody-review of *Not Guilty* appeared in *Fun*, 6 March 1869 and there is an *Illustrated Times* review (20 February 1869).

182 *Lost at Sea*; *Fun*, 16 October 1869.

183 *Utopia Limited* in *The Complete Annotated Gilbert and Sullivan*, p. 1049.

184 *The Poor of New York*, End of Act 2, Scene 1 (1857 text). In the fire scene, the top of the building crumbles inwards and Badger is revealed in his old room. The building collapses further and Badger falls with it. Badger re-appears in the ground floor and drags himself from the ruins, on fire. The crowd rescues him. End Tableau.

185 Review of *Not Guilty*, appended to *Fun* parody. Quoted in *W.S. Gilbert's Theatrical Criticism*, p. 125.

186 W.S. Gilbert, *A Sensation Novel by a Small Boy* (*Fun Almanack*, 1866).

187 Walker, John, *The Factory Lad* in *The Magistrate and Other Nineteenth-Century Plays*, p. 125.

188 Ibid., p. 127.

189 Ibid., p. 126.

190 Ibid., p. 128.

191 Ibid.

192 Ibid, pp. 135–136. Contrast Dick Deadeye's quoted speech earlier where his 'plain' speech is greeted with hostility (*H.M.S. Pinafore in The Complete Annotated Gilbert and Sullivan*, p. 125.)

193 Closing speeches of *The Poor of New York*.

194 W.S. Gilbert, *The Burglar's Story* in *The Lost Stories of W.S. Gilbert*, p. 201.

195 Closing speeches of *The Poor of New York*.

196 The name 'Bloodgood' suggests the melodrama villain who rejoices in spilling blood but also perhaps hints at the natural blood-tie making him love his daughter.

197 *Fun*, 24 December 1870, and *Fun*, 11 November 1864.

198 *Fun*, 20 October 1866.

199 W.S. Gilbert, *Creatures of Impulse* in *The Lost Stories of W.S. Gilbert*, p. 142.

200 For the Lawrence Barrett printing, see Keeinger Legacy Reprints, *The Man o'Airlie, a Drama of the Affections* (from Ledger Steam-Power Printing Office, Philadelphia, 1871). For Gilbert's version, see *Fun*, 3 August 1867. For *Creatures of Impulse*, see *The Lost Stories of W.S. Gilbert*, p. 142.

201 *Fun*, 24 November 1866. In the original production, Mrs. Wood's last exit, carried off in a tub with her legs sticking out, induced intense hissing. An English-born American actress she was sternly critiqued by the *Illustrated Times* (17 November 1866), p. 311 Gilbert alludes to her 'Yankee' origins in the quoted extract. 'Down East' is a joke for 'Down South'.

202 *Fun*, 17 November 1866.

203 *Fun*, 29 April 1871.

204 *Fun*, 23 December 1865. Buckstone said this to the Italian actress Miss Binda, arguing that the conclusion to Fanny Kemble's *Mademoiselle de Belle Isle* was awkward because the closing address divided one sentence between two characters.

205 I have been unable to find out who this extra lyricist was but do know that the piece was not a huge success. *The Times* review tells us that 'Distinction there is none in Offenbach's melodies', though their vulgarity is infectious and irresistible. Gilbert was praised for 'excellent adaptation', but there was

a caveat. It was 'curious … to note how the false accents in the original – due … to Offenbach's imperfect appreciation of French – have been reproduced in the English version' (*Times* Review, 17 September 1889).

206 W.S. Gilbert, *Princess Toto,* in *Plays by W.S. Gilbert* (C.U.P., 1982), p. 105. The *Sir Roger de Coverley* is the name of an English country dance and a Scottish country dance (also known as *The Haymakers*), published in *The Dancing Master*, 9th edition (1695). The dance's steps are reminiscent of a hunted fox going in and out of cover. Nonetheless, it is very decorous by brigand standards.

207 This is called a 'small debauch' in the original. See *Meilhac and Halevy – and Gilbert: Comic Converses*, by George McElroy (University of Kansas Libraries), p. 95.

208 *The Grand Duke* in *The Complete Annotated Gilbert and Sullivan*, p. 1107; *Princess Toto* in *Plays by W.S. Gilbert*, p. 105.

209 *Princess Toto* in *Plays by W.S. Gilbert*, p. 114.

210 Diamond, Michael, *Victorian Sensation* (Anthem Press, 2003), pp. 252–258.

211 Ibid., pp. 265–268.

212 Quoted in Leslie, Baily, *The Gilbert and Sullivan Book* (Spring Books, London, 1952), p. 141.

213 *Iolanthe*, in *The Complete Annotated Gilbert and Sullivan*, p. 367.

214 Quoted in Leslie, *The Gilbert and Sullivan Book*, p. 331.

215 Quoted in *Gilbert's Stagecraft: Little Blocks of Wood*, a Paper by Jane W. Stedman given at the 1970 International Conference (collected papers, p. 197).

216 Ibid., p. 198.

217 Eden, David, *W.S. Gilbert – Appearance and Reality*, p. 140.

218 Stedman, *Gilbert's Stagecraft: Little Blocks of Wood*, pp. 195, 199. The blocks themselves were painted in various colours to indicate voice ranges and moved and grouped on a miniature stage. F.C. Burnand also used little models in planning his often bizarre stage business.

219 *The Sportsman*, 7 January 1884.

220 Stedman, *Gilbert's Stagecraft: Little Blocks of Wood*, p. 202.

221 Bradley, Ian, *The Complete Annotated Gilbert and Sullivan*; *Ruddygore*, p. 721.

222 Quoted in *Thomas William Robertson His Plays and Stagecraft*, Maynard Savin Brown University Providence, Rhode Island 195 822 R65ZS U 822. See *Robertson's Life*, p. 41.

223 Planché, J.R., *The Recollections and Reflections of J.R. Planché, A Professional Autobiography* (London, 1872), Vol. 1, p. 180. See also Stedman, *Gilbert's Stagecraft: Little Blocks of Wood*, p. 199.

224 Introduction to *Plays by James Robinson Planché*, p. 12.

225 Ibid., pp. 5–6. This was during his engagement at Covent Garden (1822–1828) so obviously preceded Victoria's accession. The movement for historical accuracy began with a production of *King John* (1823). The actors were deeply suspicious of the 'new and strange habiliments' nicknaming the flat-topped 12th-century helmets 'stewpans'.

226 Stedman, *Gilbert's Stagecraft: Little Blocks of Wood*, p. 197.

227 *The Mikado*, in, *The Complete Annotated Gilbert and Sullivan*, p. 583. Lely died in Glasgow on 29 February 1944, an appropriate date for a Gilbert tenor, given its significance to Frederic.

228 Booth, Michael, *Theatre in the Victorian Age* (C.U.P, 1991; 1995), p. 107.

229 Irving gave at least two lectures of acting, the first at Harvard in 1885, the second at the Philosophical Institution in Edinburgh in 1891. The complete

text was published in *The Drama Addresses* in 1893, later made available through Book on Demand publications (January 1901).

230 It is not clear whether Gilbert means individual ten-syllable lines or actual verse-sentences which may involve enjambement and caesura. His comment on countering monotony was made in an interview arranged to publicize his (actually prose) play *The Fortune Hunter* (October 1897). Edward Rose, the playwright, recalled Gilbert in his fairy plays seeking to 'reform the atrocious system of speaking verse which obtained a generation ago'. See Maud, Cyril, *The Haymarket Theatre: Some Records and Reminiscences* (London, 1903), p. 157.

231 *Fun*, 11 November 1865; *Moonshine*, 22 August 1891. See also Stedman, *W.S. Gilbert's Theatrical Criticism*, p. 202.

232 Among other things, he is thinking of the decline of the *pièce bien faite*, to which, for its structural skills, he still shows allegiance. Sardonically, he says: 'I know there has been progress by a very convincing proof – namely, that I find myself altogether left behind'. See Archer, William, *Real Conversations* (Conversation V); *Pall Mall Magazine*, 25 September 1901, pp. 88–98.

Part 3
Constraints and Limitations

For a man as pugnacious as Gilbert, constraints were never likely to be endured passively. In an interview with regard to the forthcoming *Ruddygore,* he tells the *Pall Mall Gazette*:

> It is quite true that you make merry at our secrecy, but I assure you we do not lock our doors. We must, however, protect ourselves. It is the American pirates for whom we have a deadly hatred. But we shall soon be even with them. At present, Massachusetts is the only state where we have absolute protection against them. In other states we have to fight ...[1]

This sets the tone for his customary resistance to any attempt by a state (or censor) to impose a superior will. It is a case of 'We have fought, we are fighting, and we intend to fight, cost what it may'. Nonetheless, there were certain constraints that Gilbert could not resist, not to mention others that he imposed upon himself.

What, then, was he fighting against and to what extent was this a reaction against curtailing impositions? In this section, I shall cover two main issues: licensing and censorship restrictions and theatrical and audience limitations. This in turn impinges on many other aspects, the main one being Gilbert's own writing persona, relevant to which is the significance of the child, the need for make-believe, and the purely theatrical influences which may have determined – and to some extent limited – his adult creativeness.

Section 1: Licensing, Censorship, Duplicity, and Artistic Conflict

a) The Pre-Gilbert Period

Where, then, does licensing start? Historically, one key date is 1559 when Elizabeth 1st banned unlicensed work, meaning that by 1572, touring companies had to obtain a separate licence in each town they visited. Two years later, the Master of the Revels was made the licenser of all plays and companies, while during the reigns of James 1st and Charles 1st, all London companies were licensed to members of the royal family. Charles 11's two monopoly patents (for Lincoln's Inn and Drury Lane) have already been discussed, but it is worth noting that in 1695 there was a split in the United Company which had a monopoly on performance at their two theatres. Dramatist and architect John Vanbrugh saw this as an opportunity to break the duopoly, and in 1703, at a cost of £2,000, acquired a former stable yard for the construction of a new theatre on the Haymarket. One incidental aim was to improve the share of profits going to playwrights and actors, the initial money for building having been raised by subscription, probably among members of the Kit-Kat Club. Vanbrugh was joined in the enterprise by two main collaborators: his principal associate and manager William Congreve and an actors' co-operative led by Thomas Betterton.[2]

The next stage was the obtaining of a royal licence. This was provided by Queen Anne by whose authority *a Company of Comedians* was formed on 14 December 1704, leading to the theatre's opening as the Queen's Theatre on the following 9 April. This featured imported Italian singers in *Gli amori d'Ergasto* (*The Loves of Ergasto*), an opera by Jakob Greber, with an epilogue by Congreve, which was the first Italian opera seen in London and which significantly failed. The first new play performed was *The Conquest of Spain* by Mary Pix.[3] This time, the theatre proved too large for actors' voices to carry across the auditorium, and the first season was essentially a flop. Congreve departed, Vanbrugh bought out his other partners, and the actors reopened the Lincoln's Inn Fields' theatre in the summer.

This, however, was not the end. Although early productions combined spoken dialogue with incidental music, a taste developed for through-sung Italian opera, and in December 1707, the Lord Chamberlain's Office ordered that 'all Operas and other Musicall presentments' (but no non-musical plays) 'be performed for the future only at Her Majesty's Theatre in the Hay Market'.[4] By this time, Vanbrugh's management had become increasingly chaotic, showing 'numerous signs of confusion, inefficiency, missed opportunities, and bad judgement'.[5] Hence, he had sold the lease at a loss to Owen Swiny.[6] After 1709, the theatre devoted itself to Italian opera, becoming informally known as the Haymarket Opera House. Here, a young Handel produced his English début, *Rinaldo*, on 24 February 1711. It featured two leading castrati, Nicolo Grimaldi and Valentino Urbani, and was the first Italian opera composed specifically for the London stage.

The fortunes of the Queen's (later King's) Theatre would make a book in themselves, including (for instance) Swiny's flight abroad to escape his creditors, a longer period of management by John James Heidegger,[7] and in 1778 the transfer of the lease to Richard Brinsley Sheridan and Thomas Harris, stage-manager of the Theatre Royal, Covent Garden.

What is really notable, however, is the hazard involved. Not only did Sheridan and Harris have to borrow £22,000 in a bidding war. Despite (or because of) extensive remodelling making the theatre 'light, elegant and pleasant', box office receipts consistently failed to match the outlay on the improvements.

The outcome of the above was the dissolving of the partnership. Sheridan bought out his partner but only with a mortgage on the theatre of £12,000 obtained from the banker Henry Hoare. There was more to come. Eventually, a former dancing master and company member, Giovanni Gallini, purchased the mortgage, having already been involved in the bidding war while enduring considerable xenophobia in the process. Meanwhile, Sheridan's woes were not over. Having placed the theatre's financial affairs in the hands of a lawyer, -manager, William Taylor, he quickly became bankrupt.[8]

The fate of the King's Theatre gives a good idea of the constraints operating in 18th-century theatre management. It took seven years of transfers of authority, forced declarations of bankruptcy, feuding trustees, and sheriff's sales before Gallini finally achieved control, and even then conditions were far from ideal. For one thing, he served as trustee for William Taylor, who loathed him, harassed him, and sued him continually. For another, he had to operate under a budget cap of £18,000 enforced by the Court of Chancery. For a third, the Lord Chamberlain, who regarded him as an undesirable foreigner, made him struggle to get a performing licence. Nonetheless, he prospered, importing German works and artistes, continuing the Italian programming, and surviving the riot of February 1789 when, despite the capable direction of ballet-master Jean-Georges Noverre, a vehement audience demanded that better foreign dancers be imported.[9]

Problems of staging and performance can of course occur in any age. Gilbert had some notorious litigious battles with Henrietta Hodson whose character informs aspects of Julia Jellicoe. Sullivan laments that even moderately good singers can now get as much for performing two or three songs at a concert 'as for singing through a long and difficult opera'. But Gilbert and Sullivan had at least two advantages. One was that, according to a letter to *The Nation*, Gilbert eliminated many potential problems by going down to rehearsal 'with every detail prearranged and set down upon paper'.[10] The other was that the partnership at least had good cultural credentials. Taylor, by contrast, had none. Although manager of his theatre for most of the period between 1781 and 1812, he is said to have never known 'a note of music or a word of any tongue but English'. Essentially he was just an adroit financial manipulator with no private resources. In 1783 he was imprisoned for debt, after which he spent a large part of the rest of his life in nominal confinement within the Rules of the King's Bench.

The above makes a good contrast with the considerable management skills of Richard D'Oyly Carte. Even Gilbert, who often crossed swords with him, refers to his 'exceptional ability, which 'has brought in a large return to the confederation'.[11] In the 18th century there was a much more cavalier aspect to theatre-management. While nominally in prison, Taylor somehow still contrived to indulge his favourite pastimes of fishing and practical joking, not to mention for five years (1797–1802) representing the Borough of Leominster in Parliament. John Ebers, a later manager, leaves his own damning pen-portrait:

> He quarrelled with every body, ridiculed every body, and hoaxed every body ... 'How can you conduct the management of the King's Theatre', I said to him one day, 'perpetually in durance as you are?' 'My dear fellow', he replied, 'how could I possibly conduct it if I were at liberty? I should be eaten up, Sir, devoured'.[12]

This at least suggests the greater professionalism of the best of the 19th century practitioners.

ii.

The rest of the pre-Gilbert period continues its catalogue of conflicts and disasters. As far as the King's Theatre is concerned, the hazards culminated on 17 June 1789. It was on this date that the roof was set deliberately on fire, dancers in rehearsal fleeing from the stage as a beam fell on it. Initially, Gallini schemed to found a new business in a new space with a different partner, but by December, he had broken away, joining forces with his former enemy William Taylor, who was rebuilding on the old site. Defying the Lord Chamberlain, they then, in Spring 1791, dangerously reopened without a licence.

The attempt to work outside the Lord Chamberlain's parameters was bound to cause repercussions. One involved no less a figure than Joseph Haydn who wrote an opera *L'anima del filosofo* for Gallini, only to have it banned. One reason is said to be a dispute over the matter between King George 111 and the Prince of Wales. Another may have been casting difficulties. Gallini had taken great pains to appoint superb singers with international reputations, but Haydn wrote in March to his mistress that one of them, Madame Lops, was 'a silly goose'. The main point, however, was the lack of a licence to stage Italian opera. The Lord Chamberlain, a supporter of the Pantheon theatre in Oxford Street (q.v.), was in no hurry to issue one, meaning that the company had to present operas and entertainments as 'rehearsals' without scenery, staging, lighting, or costumes. Negotiations with the Chamberlain meanwhile faltered, the theatre only finally presenting 'legal opera' in 1793.

Gallini was, in fact, more successful than most, not least because he did eventually retrieve money owed to him by Taylor. But theatre could still be a precarious business. At one point – and despite the presence of Haydn, the great tenor Giacomo Davide, and the dancers Vestris and son – the company lost £9,700 in five months. Gallini thereafter dropped out of opera management, contenting himself mainly with concerts at his Hanover Square Concert Rooms, and giving lessons in dance at which he was superb.

The fluctuations endured by the King's were replicated in other houses. Fire, for instance, was a constant hazard. On 24 February 1809 (despite some much vaunted 1774 safety precautions), Drury Lane Theatre burned to the ground. At least this afforded an occasion for wit. On being encountered drinking a glass of wine in the street outside, Sheridan allegedly remarked, 'A man may surely be allowed to take a glass of wine by his own fireside'.[13] His own involvement with the theatre had begun in 1776, by which time he had already earned enough money to buy his share of the patent along with Linley and the physician James Ford. Two years later, they were able to buy out Willoughby Lacy, Garrick's partner, leaving Sheridan as manager of the theatre for many years, later becoming sole owner with no managerial role.

If fire was a constant threat, a more predictable hazard was censorship, particularly in regard to political satire. One casualty was Samuel Foote, the background being that in 1758, Theophilus Cibber had obtained from the Lord Chamberlain a general licence under which Foote tried to establish the Haymarket as a regular summer theatre. Opening on 14 May 1767 as the Theatre Royal, it became the third patent theatre in London, but Foote, already suffering from ill-health, finally got into such difficulties by caricaturing well-known celebrities that in January 1777, he had to sell both the theatre and patent to George Colman Senior. Nor was this the end. One disaster occurred during the season of 1793–1794 when Drury Lane Theatre was being rebuilt and the Haymarket opened out of season under the Drury Lane Patent. Regrettably, on 3 February 1794, there was a 'Dreadful Accident'. 'Twenty Persons unfortunately lost their lives, and a great Number were dreadfully bruised', the cause being 'a great Crowd pressing to see his Majesty' who was attending a performance.[14]

The accident occurred only six months before, on 14 August, George Colman died, and the theatre descended to his son. This too was ruinous. Though successful both as playwright and manager, Colman the Younger dissipated his gains by his extravagance, for a time living in a room at the back of the theatre and being finally forced to sell his shares to his brother-in-law, David Morris. Monetary difficulties nonetheless increased, meaning that for many years he managed the theatre from the King's Bench Prison, where he too was confined for debt.[15]

iii.

In pre-Gilbert days, problems of theatrical debt were quite often compounded by a resort to the law. It was, for instance, the arrest of Taylor in May 1783 that led to the forced sale of the King's, with Harris purchasing the lease and many of the effects. Further legal action transferred the theatre interests to a board of trustees, including Novosielski, a celebrated

Polish scene-painter and architect, confusingly born in Rome, and by 1772 living in London's Golden Square. The problem lay in the personnel. The self-serving trustees acted with such a flagrant disregard for the needs of the theatre that in August 1785, the Lord Chamberlain assumed the overall running in the interests of the creditors. Although Gallini had meanwhile become manager, Novosielski pocketed the receipts, thereby limiting investment in future productions. This, plus wider misappropriation and endless litigation, resulted in amateur performers being employed, leading *The World* to comment: '... the dance, if such it can be called was like the movements of heavy cavalry. It was hissed very abundantly'.[16]

Audience dissatisfaction was indeed another constant threat. In 1749, a fraudster billed as The Bottle Conjuror was advertised to appear at the Little Theatre in the Haymarket. The publicity claimed that, while on stage, he would place his body inside an empty wine bottle, in full view of the audience. When the advertised act failed to appear, the audience rioted and gutted the theatre, the main blame falling on John Montagu, the second Duke as the most likely origin of the hoax.

Even Gallini was not exempt from audience diatribes. Several times, he had personally to defend himself as angry mobs charged the stage and destroyed the fittings, and the company ran for their lives.[17] Meanwhile, censorship controls continued and sometimes actually increased. Such applied under the aegis of George Colman who in 1824 had been released from gaol by George IV. He was given two appointments: Exon of the Yeomen of the Guard (which he sold to the highest bidder) and examiner of plays under licence from the Lord Chamberlain, the Duke of Montrose.[18] Although his own works had incurred criticism for indecency and profanity, Colman refused to pass even such words as 'heaven', 'providence', and 'angel', becoming by the time of his death hated by contemporary dramatists for his twelve-year illiberal dispensation.

The above was bad enough. But worse sometimes was sheer duplicity, augmented by personality conflict. At about the time of the fire, Gallini had fallen in with a law-student Robert Bray O'Reilly, who became his legal advisor. Initially, they worked without discord. When the King's Theatre was destroyed, they obtained a temporary licence from the Lord Chamberlain to perform operas at the Little Theatre and Covent Garden for the 1789 season. But what followed was strife. One problem arose when they attempted to obtain land in Leicester Fields for the erection of a permanent replacement house. O'Reilly did submit plans which by 20 November had met with 'Royal approbation', but the catch was that the land had to be purchased before the patent could be granted. Meanwhile, Taylor, in real or pretended ignorance of this rival scheme, had been making legal and financial arrangements for the rebuilding of the theatre on the old site.

Taylor did not merely plan to rebuild. In December, he wrote (twice) to the Lord Chamberlain protesting at the injustice of the proposed patent to Gallini and O'Reilly. Meanwhile, O'Reilly was pursuing his dream. Working (as he thought) for both himself and Gallini, he agreed to the purchase of the new site for £31,550, covenanting for his own part to pay £8,000 within a month. The trouble was that Gallini now decided to abandon O'Reilly, 'expecting by that means to become sole possessor of the Patent'.

The rest of this sorry saga has one clear element: it shows that Gilbert's notorious litigiousness was actually less extreme than the wheeler-dealing contrivances of the previous century. In Gallini's case one result was that he refused either to sign the agreement or to assist O'Reilly with any payment. Faced with ruin, O'Reilly applied to the Lord Chamberlain and was promised that he alone should have the patent. He then concluded the purchase, paid over the £8,000 and consolidated his position by a provisional agreement with Edward Vanbrugh. This involved a promise to purchase the latter's interest in the King's theatre after the expiry of Taylor's term, then scheduled for 1803.

Edward Vanbrugh was the son of Charles Vanbrugh, brother to Sir John, his importance being that he had been granted a succession of Crown leases, beginning in 1753–1754, and extended in 1777–1826. He did not, however, expect the furore that occurred. For one thing, Gallini now became O'Reilly's most violent opponent. For another, Taylor obtained the support of his creditors for the rebuilding of the theatre on the old site and joined the opposition which the proprietors of the Covent Garden and Drury Lane theatres were already raising to O'Reilly's proposed Patent.

Rather like Gilbert, Gallini was a tenacious opponent. As mortgagee he appears to have assisted by granting him possession of the ruins. This led to more developments. On 3 April 1790, eleven days before the hearing of the case against O'Reilly's Patent, the foundation stone of the new theatre in the Haymarket was laid. Taylor is alleged to have stated later that 'when I stood upon the reeking ruins, and laid the foundation stone, I had nothing in my pockets but both my hands'. He would, in fact, 'have given the world for one guinea'.[19]

Even now O'Reilly's troubles were not over. At the hearing against him (14th April) it very soon became clear that the Lord Chancellor would not recommend the Crown to make any grant which would involve other parties in heavy loss. O'Reilly, committed to the purchase of the ground in Leicester Fields, now 'saw no prospect but impending ruin'. He, therefore, took a lease of the Pantheon in Oxford Street at the enormous rent of 3000 guineas and on 30 June 1790 was granted a four-year licence for the performance there of Italian opera. One thing he did not know was that this was a theatre which in 1792 – and possibly by sabotage – would burn to the ground.[20]

The Pantheon licence was probably a sop. However, it certainly did not end O'Reilly's troubles. James Wyatt, the theatre's original architect, was employed to make the extensive alterations, and throughout the second half of 1790, there seems to have been intense rivalry in the completion of the Pantheon and the King's. In October, Novosielski's 'stupendous fabric' in the Haymarket seemed to be winning: it was 'actually covering in', but unfortunately then, the staircase collapsed. Gallini meanwhile 'formed a plan of monopolizing the Dancers' at the expense of the Pantheon, and, when this scheme failed, patched up another agreement with Taylor. A likely war of attrition was only avoided when O'Reilly's first season at the Pantheon failed miserably. This caused him to flee to Paris to avoid creditors, thereby also losing his provisional agreement with Edward Vanbrugh for the purchase of the reversionary interest in the King's.[21]

b) Gilbert's Contribution

The Byzantine dealings over the King's Theatre make Gilbert's own litigious troubles almost child's play. But they did exist, the most famous being focused in the notorious Carpet Quarrel. One problem here was the sheer quality in the Gilbert and Sullivan partnership. When Sullivan complained to Gilbert in 1889 about the artistic sacrifices necessary for the good of the operas, Gilbert replied, 'You are an adept in your profession, and I am an adept in mine. If we meet, it must be as master and master – not as master and servant'.[22] Sullivan nonetheless continued to feel underrepresented. The other factor was Richard D'Oyly Carte whose vision of an English Theatre devoted to the performance of English comic opera turned the duo into a triumvirate business. The commitment was formally recognized in a five-year agreement signed on 8 February 1883. In it, the collaborators undertook to provide Carte with a new opera at six months' notice.

Although financially beneficial, the agreement may have rankled as an enforcing trap. At any rate, the first really serious argument occurred within thirteen months starting in March 1884 when Sullivan (by now knighted) told Carte that 'it is impossible for me to do another piece of the character of those already written by Gilbert and myself'. To Gilbert he added that he had come to the end of his tether. His music was of necessity 'syllable-setting', thus never being allowed to rise and speak for itself. The main impetus, augmented by his new status, was a desire to escape from topsyturveydom and mechanical plots into areas of genuine emotional interest. Nonetheless, except in the jealously painful love-sickness of Katisha, *The Mikado*, premiered on 14 March 1885, hardly fulfilled his criteria.

Despite *The Mikado*'s brilliant success, conflict rumbled on. Not only did *Ruddygore* strike Sullivan as a play interspersed with a few songs and concerted pieces. In 1888, he demanded some 'rather important alterations' to Act 2 of *The Yeomen of the Guard*. By 1889, he was complaining, 'I am a cipher in the theatre', implying that he was doing nothing more than conforming to *Gilbert's* vision, staging, and directorial control. Not that Gilbert was any less touchy. When invited to provide the libretto for a new Grand Opera (later to become *Ivanhoe*), his refusal was grounded in the view that 'the librettist of a grand opera is always swamped in the composer'. Meanwhile, his relationship with

Carte, never untroubled, had worsened. Even as early as 1875, he had been writing sarcastically to Sullivan: 'It's astonishing how quickly these capitalists dry up under the magic influence of the words "cash down"'.[23]

The artistic divergence between Sullivan and Gilbert was probably increased by the idea of a new Grand Opera House, with Carte supporting Sullivan's higher musical aspirations. But Gilbert had long been suspicious as regards the financial management. Hence, it is not altogether surprising that on 22 April 1890, he wrote to Sullivan:

> I have had a difficulty with Carte ... 'I was appalled to learn from him that the preliminary expenses of the *Gondoliers* amounted to the stupendous sum of £4,500!!!' This seemed so utterly unaccountable that I asked to see the details and last night I received a resumé of them.

What most rankled was not the outlay for costumes and set but the £500 allocated for (italicized) new carpets *'for the front of the house*!' This related back to the 1883 contract, whereby the profits from the operas were to fund all expenses and charges for production and performance including 'repairs incidental to the performance', the remainder to be distributed equally between the triumvirate. Gilbert denied that the new carpets could fall within this remit. Indeed, by such an interpretation, liability for improvements might even extend to the lobbies, staircases, auditorium, or stage.

The escalation of this quarrel is variously reported. According to Helen D'Oyly Carte, it was Gilbert who first proposed a complete break, while Gilbert tells us, 'I left him with the remark that it was a mistake to kick down the ladder by which he had risen'. He was perhaps recalling a letter of June 1885 when Carte himself had written: 'I envy you your position, but I could never attain it. If I could be an author like you I would certainly not be the manager. I am simply the tradesman who sells your creations of art'.[24]

It is unlikely that Gilbert really wanted to sever all ties. But he did want what he would deem a fairer contract. Sullivan meanwhile opined that the dispute over expenses should be settled first. To him, the whole thing was merely a matter of 'a few miserable pounds', whereas to Gilbert, it was a shady transaction and a presumptuous incursion. In 1885, he had already informed the composer: 'When *we* manage the theatre for him (Carte), he succeeds splendidly. When he manages for himself, he fails'.[25] Perhaps, the most galling aspect was not the money but the challenge to his controlling pre-eminence. Carte himself insisted that Gilbert had mistaken the cost of the carpet; it was not £500 but only £140.

The Carpet Quarrel is a good example of a financial conflict that arises more deeply from artistic differences and questions of dominance. It led on 5 May 1890 to Gilbert writing to Sullivan that 'The time for putting an end to our collaboration has at last arrived'. Even before the *Utopia Limited* reunion, this was not the end of the contest. One significant factor was that the Savoy profits were allocated quarterly. When in July 1890 the next payment became due, Carte's solicitors decided that these could not be distributed until the dispute over the April account had been resolved. The result was that Gilbert issued a writ for the profits, Carte sent him £2,000, and Gilbert demurred, calculating his share to be at least £3,000. On his solicitor's advice, he then applied for a receiver to take action on the *Gondoliers* accounts.

The resulting law-case was brief. After two adjournments, it came before the court on 3 September 1890 and was settled the same day, Carte being instructed to pay Gilbert a further £1,000, and Gilbert's application for a receiver being refused. Surprisingly, Gilbert then sought a reconciliatory meeting, attended, not by an angry Richard D'Oyly Carte but by his wife. Here, Gilbert retracted some statements made in anger but added that he wanted all the Savoy accounts from 1883 onwards re-examined. Even though he soon dropped this demand, there were further ripples. When Sullivan too sought a reconciliation, Gilbert denied consent unless the composer retract an affidavit which had effectively accused him of perjury – a condition which the composer refused.

How far Gilbert is to be considered culpable in all the above is debatable. One revelation in court was that in the previous eleven years, Carte had already paid him £90,000. But the matter became for Gilbert more a battle of wills, besides which it *does* seem that Carte at the very least made some accounting blunders. On 28 May 1891, Gilbert wrote to Sullivan that Carte had admitted 'an unintentional overcharge of nearly £1000 in the electric lighting accounts alone'. Perhaps, he suspected more than this – perhaps he even detected 'the spark of a swindle'. This, in conjunction with Gilbert's irascible, litigious temperament would be quite enough to sour any productive professional relationship.

c) Legislation, Licensing and the Lord Chamberlain's Office

Personal conflict, then, is itself a limiting factor. But, outside this, one minefield for theatre managers was increasing legislation. In 1752, a new bill required the licensing of all places of public entertainment within twenty miles of London, while in 1788, this was extended to the whole country. One result was that the unrestricted Irish and United States stages increasingly welcomed British actors and companies unable to obtain home licences. The American position was later directly to affect Gilbert and Sullivan, but in the meantime what mattered was that the British Statute of Anne, instituting copyright regulation by the government and courts, did not apply to the American colonies, where only three private copyright acts were passed before 1783. Eventually, following a resolution by the Continental Congress, states were encouraged (not forced) to ensure that new works have copyright protection for not less than fourteen years, to be extended for another fourteen if the author was still alive.[26] Though most states followed this, five did not. They granted copyright for single terms of fourteen, twenty, or twenty-one years with no right to renew.

As far as Gilbert's early lifetime is concerned, one key act was the 1843 Theatres Act. Also known as the Theatre Regulation Act, this implemented proposals made by an 1832 select committee, the main effect being to modify the 1737 charter. By the latter, the Lord Chamberlain had had the right to vet the performance of any new plays, to prevent such performance, to demand modifications, and to insist that performances could only take place in licensed playhouses. He was not required to justify his decision, and theatre owners could be prosecuted for staging a play (or part of a play) that had not received prior approval. A licence, once granted, could also be withdrawn. In London, spoken drama was still to be limited to the patent theatres of Drury Lane and Covent Garden.

Even before the 1843 Act, there were occasional modifications and a few new licences. One related to the aforementioned Haymarket Theatre, founded in 1720 by the young carpenter John Potter on a site by the Cannon and Musket gun shop. Desperate to keep it afloat, Potter cast about for anything to put on stage, from concerts and amateur plays to the street entertainments already crowding at the entrance. Taking money at the door was, however, illegal, leading to constabulary intervention and regular closures.

For the Haymarket, the change came with a visit from the Continent. Arriving in London with a troupe of French actors and a play, 'La Fille À La Mode', the Duke of Montagu was vexed to find neither of the Patent Theatres willing to present a foreign language production. Hence, he turned to the Little Theatre in the Hay. In this case French influence was a blessing. Modest growth led in 1729 to a smash hit, 'Hurlothrumbo', a thirty-night theatrical spectacular, which proved vastly more successful than anything running at the patent houses. Then, when Samuel Foote acquired the lease, there were more successes, leading nineteen years later to the gaining of a royal patent to play legitimate drama during the summer. Notwithstanding Foote's decline, by Gilbert's time the Haymarket was well established, though by now located in different premises following a re-design in 1821 by John Nash.

The gradual widening of theatrical possibilities suggests a very slow relaxation of political and geographical restriction. One example was the Theatrical Representations Act of 1788 by which local magistrates were permitted to license occasional performances for a period of up to sixty days. This is not to say that there had been little provision before. In Manchester, one typical early theatre, located at King and Marsden Streets, housed a repertory company and occasionally offered concerts, oratorios, balls, and auctions. In the summer of 1762, it welcomed its first London actors, His Majesty's Servants, from the Theatres Royal. These performed three times a week from June to September, and every night during the August race meeting.

Apart from the London patent theatres, many theatrical venues were relatively austere. In 1764, the above-mentioned Manchester theatre was described by Thomas Wilks (sometimes Snagg) as 'plain and unadorned, having been newly built'. Accommodation facilities varied. Apparently, 'the manager had a room to himself; the first male performer likewise a separate room; the useful plebeians ... a general apartment for habiting (=dressing); the heroines and principal ladies likewise an attiring room; and the underlings the cockloft'. A boost was probably given during the following summer when an actress relatively new to London's Drury Lane joined the company. This was Mrs Baddeley, whom Wilks admired as extremely beautiful and who became *prima donna* in most comedies and operas, as well as playing tragic roles such as Ophelia. Wilks claims proudly to have often been 'allotted to be her lover before the curtain', bringing an intimacy, 'with many a cup of tea and private walk' during which he was 'charmed with her melodious voice'. Nonetheless, sustained success was not assured. Nearly a decade passed before the London players made a return trip to Manchester.[27]

The licensing of the provincial theatres is not always very clear and nor is that of actors themselves. We do know that in the 1750s, Liverpool's Drury Lane Theatre offered summer entertainment to prosperous visitors flocking in for the bathing season, but no playbills are extant, and little is understood about the company or performances. In 1756 there was a particular flurry, with newspapers alerting the public to the arrival of *'Comedians from the Theatres Royal'* for June, July and August to perform a variety of plays, the days of acting being Mondays, Wednesdays and Fridays. Manchester meanwhile had mixed fortunes. According to an 1896 article in the *Era*, the city's first theatre was erected in 1753 and was quickly engaged by an Irish itinerant company. This, however, was a damp squib. The authorities stepped in, ordering the company to leave town within twenty-four hours.[28] The theatre then remained closed, except for one concert and a performance of *Acis and Galatea*, until December 1759, when James Whitley brought his own company of comedians. In October of the following year, the 'London players' (unspecified) visited the town and, finding Whitley in situ, performed in the Riding School on the Salford bank of the River Irwell. The company even erected a wooden bridge for citizens' ease of access, this remaining in use for some sixty years.

How far local magistrates intervened when actors arrived is difficult to determine but presumably if they came from London patent theatres, they would be more welcome than if they were merely strolling companies. By the 1737 Act, non-licensed performers were to be deemed rogues and vagabonds, those permitted to perform needing 'letters patent from His Majesty, his heirs, successors or predecessors' or from the current Lord Chamberlain. Offenders against this were to be fined fifty pounds and to have any (illicit) 'rights' or licences rescinded. If they confessed their fault or were denounced by a credible witness, they were to be brought before two Justices of the Peace and those unable to pay the fine were to be jailed for six months. This was also to apply to those who performed in alehouses. At least in all cases, the prosecution had to be initiated within six months of the offence. In addition, there was a right of appeal, which, if successful, would result in the awarding of 'treble costs'.

The effect of the 1737 Act was to divide performances into what became known as legitimate and illegitimate theatre. The first essentially consisted of licensed spoken drama while non-patent theatres produced melodrama, ballad opera, and part-musical burlesque. Later by the 1843 Act, Justices of the Peace had more say. They could, for instance, licence local theatres, while the Lord Chamberlain retained power to license new ones in London, Westminster, and other named boroughs.

The gradual growth in provincial theatre is only patchily recorded but certain milestones do remain. One was the Act of Regulating Places of Public Entertainment (1755) which gave the force of statute law to the way magistrates in London, Westminster, and the Home Counties had licensed a wide variety of places of popular entertainment. The Enabling Act of 1788 extended this. It confirmed the powers which magistrates had already exercised in provincial England in respect of touring players and their repertoire. Restricted licences were meanwhile being issued for musical burlettas, ballad operas, and melodramas, as in London applied to the Olympic (1806), the Strand (1832), and the St. James (1835). Earlier, in 1787, John Palmer's Royalty Theatre was licensed for light entertainment by the magistrates of Tower Hamlets. Other London examples included Astley's Amphitheatre (1773), the Royal Circus (1782), and Royal Coburg (1816).

Although theatre was increasingly popular, it did require influential patronage and government approval. Such applied in the 1771 Act of Parliament providing letters patent for the Liverpool Theatre Royal and, four years later, in Lord Lyttelton's sponsoring of a bill for a Manchester equivalent. Lyttleton's aim was: 'to establish a Theatre … to keep a company of comedians for His Majesty's service, and to act such Tragedies, Plays, Operas, and Entertainments only as had been, or should be, licensed by the Lord Chamberlain of His Majesty's Household'. The licence was granted to Joseph Younger and George Mattocks (who already managed the Liverpool Theatre), subscriptions being raised to construct a brick building with boxes, pit, and gallery.

From the Manchester dispensation, we know a little of current repertoires and acting practices. The first production (5 June 1775) was *Othello*, performance nights being Monday, Wednesday, and Friday. Then in October, the regular season commenced, success being ratified towards the end of 1776 by performances from Sarah Siddons and her brother John Kemble, as well as from the Irish actress Elizabeth Farren and the playwright-actress Elizabeth Inchbald. Farren's case is interesting because provincial success preceded her metropolitan one. As a juvenile, she performed at Bath, while in 1774, in her early teens, with her mother and sisters she was singing and acting in Wakefield under Whitley. At about fifteen, she played Rosetta in *Love in a Village* in Liverpool, and subsequently her best known role of Lady Townly in *The Provoked Husband*. She first appeared on the London stage in 1777 as Kate Hardcastle, ultimately having over one hundred characters in her repertoire.

ii.

The matter of licensing – whether of performers or theatres – can hardly be considered out of the context of censorship which has generally conditioned it. The lowest point in England was during the Puritan interregnum (1642–1660) when all theatres were closed, but controls, still influential in Gilbert's day, applied long thereafter. The 1737 Stage Licensing Act required managers to submit new plays to the Lord Chamberlain's Office at least fourteen days before the first performance and made clear that:

> [It] shall and may be lawful to and for the said lord chamberlain, for the time being, from time to time, and when, and as often as he shall think fit, to prohibit the acting, performing, or representing any interlude, tragedy, comedy, opera, play, farce or other entertainment of the stage, or any act, scene, or part thereof, or any prologue, or epilogue.

Plays banned by the Chamberlain in Westminster and its environs might sometimes be acted elsewhere in the country where, especially after 1788, the licence to perform was vested in the local magistrates.

By the time of Gilbert's writing debut, matters had moved on, mainly owing to the 1843 Act which curtailed the Lord Chamberlain's powers. He was now able to prohibit performances only when he was convinced that 'It is fitting for the preservation of good manners, decorum, or of the public peace so to do'. The act also gave yet more powers to local authorities to license theatres, breaking the London patent theatre monopolies, and incidentally encouraging the development of saloon theatres attached to public houses and music halls. Whatever its limitations, the regime so established had a long life. Though it was considered by a select committee of the House of Commons in 1866 and two Parliamentary Joint Select Committees in 1909 and 1966, no changes were implemented until 1968 when the act was finally repealed.

iii.

The above does not provide the whole picture. Equally notable is the fact that, while reducing the Lord Chamberlain's scope, the 1843 edict did not limit his geographical reach. His voice was heard throughout the country, albeit with the advance submission requirement reduced to seven days. Also worth remembering is that the Chamberlain was far more often censored by the press for licensing plays than for banning them. Many of those passed were considered to offend against public decency, and often it was authors, not managers, who pushed for greater liberalism. John Hollingshead's view was that as a theatre manager he had 'nothing to do with the taste or even the morality of any drama produced under my management'. The government, he said:

> ... had kindly relieved me from this responsibility by appointing a reader and licenser of plays, and accepting a fee for this watch-dog work. When I had paid my one, two, or three guineas to the Lord Chamberlain's office I left him to justify the amusement he had officially sanctioned and I had provided for my public.[29]

Here, we may note that there is no criticism as regards aptitude for the office or the fact that the Lord Chamberlain was a political appointee with many other duties besides supervising the stage.

The preservation of good manners, decorum, and the public peace was in the act rather loosely defined, but it certainly included elements of sexual restraint. This is reflected in *The Realm of Joy* where Gilbert changes the cloakroom attendant from the French original into someone far more like Gladys and Ada, the cinema fans in Waugh's *The Balance*. In the source play, a sexually scandalous operetta, *Le Roi Candaule*, is being performed, the plot being based on a king so infatuated with his wife's naked beauty that he posted his lieutenant Gyges where he too could appreciate it. Unfortunately, this then led to his own overthrow by Gyges and the queen. The scenario is obviously unfit for a well-brought up young girl, and in the original, an attending bourgeois father shoos his own daughters into the passageway every time a risqué song begins. The problem is that two fashionable young men then pick up the girls, teaching them the lyrics. Meanwhile, two different male friends are evading each other because the first is accompanying his friend's mistress whom he hopes to seduce under the operetta's influence, while the second, with a similar intention, has brought along the first man's wife. The problem is that the box office has blunderingly sold both couples the same box, leading to a humorous array of dodges, discoveries, feints, and lamentations.

Under the British rules, it would be difficult to offer such a play in straight translation. Even the ending is 'immoral', for, though each man ends up seeing the play with his own lady, that lady slyly insists that his friend should be welcomed to dinner. Gilbert's solution is to sanitize the piece while adding an extra raft of jokes of his own. He makes the improper play which everyone wants to see his own *Happy Land* transparently paraphrased to *The Realm of Joy*. Moreover, it is objectionable *not* because of amorous frankness but because of political subversion. The would-be seducers also become less explicit in their intentions and are from the start both married.

The temporary banning of *The Happy Land* has already been described, but it is worth stressing that its use here offers a double parody since that play was already a burlesque of *The Wicked World*. The revised plot, however, eliminates much of the original fun. The scene, set in the Box Lobby, shows three box doors visible, as is the cloakwoman's room. Into this scenario enters the box-keeper, shoving two spectators into an already overcrowded box. He and the cloakroom attendant then discuss the scandalous success of the play, which (we are ironically told) holds up to mockery our most dearly loved public figures and is an affront to the Lord High Disinfectant. 'Society is furious, Society loves its Lord High Disinfectant' – but Society still flocks to the play, making the hypocrisy clearly evident.

The idea of a piece which itself shows an audience at a play reminds us of *Comedy and Tragedy*, both clearly appealing to Gilbert's concept of meta-theatre. But the British censorship laws do entail a reduction in the rakish elements. In Gilbert's version, the nearest we get to loucheness is in the two young rakes, Jopp and Quisby, who have come to this theatre night after night, not to see the play but to view the spectators. When the bourgeois Mr. and Mrs. Jellybag arrive with their daughters, the daughters are appraisingly described by Quisby as 'Not bad', without direct sexual development. One new joke is that political matters could be regarded as interesting – or even very corrupting – to two teenage girls. This is conveyed when Mr. Jellybag explains to the cloakwoman that he will protect his girls' morals by sending them out of the box whenever the dialogue becomes 'politically disgraceful'.

The best jokes in the Gilbertian version concern the characterization of the ancillary staff. In the French original, the box-opener is a practical woman, very proud of the show's success. It is the lewdest available with the least-dressed girls, producing huge receipts and (from the audience) an abundance of overcoats. Her only concession is that schoolgirls should not be allowed to hear the improper songs. In Gilbert's version, this is upended. The box-keeper sees the piece as a disgraceful attack on 'the most generally esteemed and unmistakeably indispensable of all our Court Functionaries'. The cloakwoman, weeping, agrees. She exhorts Mr. Jellybag to take away his daughters before it is too late: 'Oh sir, listen to the voice of a mother, have mercy on them and suffer them not to witness this horrible and demoralizing spectacle'.[30] The result is that at intervals during the rest of the play, the Jellybag daughters regularly pop out of the box to be looked after by the cloakwoman. Meanwhile, the parallel plot covers the quartet of potentially cheating couples, beginning with Wilkinson and Mrs. Scruby, who are enjoying a clandestine assignation while Mr. Scruby is allegedly away in Manchester.

There are undoubtedly some very good jokes in *The Realm of Joy*. One is that the ancillary staff members deplore the very thing from which they are profiting. Another is that their horror is exaggerated as if the unseen play (by Gilbert) were truly wicked, attacking God, the

Queen, the nation, and all traditional standards of acceptable morality. But the two couples plot, trimmed of much of it its amorality, is somewhat muted. In the Gilbert version, Wilkinson has excused himself with his own wife by telling her that he has had to go to Birmingham. This leads to Mr. Scruby's assignation with *Mrs.* Wilkinson. Given that they have been sold the same box as *Mr.* Wilkinson and *Mrs.* Scruby, it is inevitable that, after much shouting, running, and barricading of doors, the two couples should discover each other, embarking on a round of improbable explanations. The conclusion is that only by forgiving their spouses can they themselves be forgiven. Coinciding with the end of the unseen performance, this finishes their own play, depriving us, to its detriment, of Meilhac and Halévy's more sophisticated flourishes.

iv.

The fun to be gained from *The Realm of Joy* shows that, even in muted form and within the constraints of censorship, much humour can be obtained from adult hypocrisies. But the emphasis is different. There is a change from sexual to political impropriety, allowing for some amusing exaggeration of the ancillary staff's respectable working-class attitudes. Even the most prudish would in real life hardly have gone into hysterics over slurs on Her Majesty's highly unpopular ministers, particularly in language more appropriate to desecrations of religion and morality. What Gilbert is really doing is mocking the whole matter of control of people's moral responses. Included too is a revenge on the Lord Chamberlain for his handling of *The Happy Land*, though in fact it was the deputy Examiner of Plays to whom most such responsibilities were usually delegated.

The Examiner during the period of *The Happy Land* was William Donne, who had become permanent examiner in 1857. This was far from the only long-lasting appointment, for the 19th century saw thirty Lord Chamberlains but only seven Examiners. John Larpent, appointed in 1788, held the post for an astonishing forty-six years, His successor, George Colman, also felt secure, telling the 1832 Parliamentary Committee that he was not removable, except on grounds of notable misbehaviour. Nepotism seems here to have been a factor. Colman gained his post through the influence of his friend the Duke of York. On his death in 1836, he was replaced with the actor Charles Kemble who in turn delegated most of the work to his son, John Mitchell Kemble, the latter stepping into the post four years later.

Overall, we get a strong sense that Examiners were very difficult to remove. Four of the seven died in office, another only resigning when compelled by ill-health.[31] Nor, until Donne retired, was there any form of competition for the succession. Gilbert's main encounters were with Donne himself, Edward Frederick Smythe Piggott, and the latter's friend George Alexander Redford. Piggott, an Oxonian lawyer and journalist, occupied the post after Donne's 1874 retirement until dying in office in 1895. He was thus responsible for granting the licences to all the Savoy Operas except *The Grand Duke*. His successor (who had formerly been a bank manager) again succeeded through influence. Both Clement Scott and John Hollingshead were among the roughly seventy candidates who applied, but the incompetent Redford had already been enlisted as deputy by the ailing Piggott and it was he who duly gained the Lord Chamberlain's acquiescence.

What, then, do we know about the actual history of the censorship function? Essentially, the 1737 Act was meant to bolster Walpole, who was not only noted for bribery but also much harassed in dealing with anti-Hanoverian Tories and with Pulteney, Chesterfield and other discontented Whigs. Already *The Beggar's Opera* had satirized him as Robin (Robbing) of Bagshot, and used McHeath's bigamy to reference his own position vis-à-vis a wife and mistress. Henry Fielding's *Pasquin* and *The Historical Register for the Year 1736* (1736) merely compounded the attacks. The first play actually to be banned by the act was *Gustavus Vasa*. This was a historical work by Henry Brooke, a rising Irishman who has already translated the first two books of Tasso's *Jerusalem Delivered* and was acquainted with both Pope and Swift.

Initially, *Gustavus Vasa* seemed mercifully trouble-free. In 1738, the play was submitted to the Drury Lane management and was thoroughly rehearsed for five weeks. On the eve of performance, however, it was suddenly banned. The reason was clearly political: it invoked the Swedish Protestant king to castigate the purportedly corrupt, election-rigging Parliament of Walpole's administration. Brooke himself claimed innocence, insisting that he had meant only to write a historical drama. The furore caused Samuel Johnson to write a Swiftian satirical parody of the licensers, entitled *A Complete Vindication of the Licensers of the Stage* (1739), this being, not a vindication, but rather a *reductio ad absurdum*.

Gilbert's later complaint that old plays are automatically preferred to new ones indirectly relates to the above. One consequence of the controls was that any play that *did* pass the licensers was regarded with public suspicion. Hence, mid- and late 18th-century playhouses were more inclined to present old plays and pantomimes, even these having to avoid any relevance to contemporary politics. Another aspect was what Planché was later to define as the theft of words. This refers to the authors' lack of control of their own manuscripts. Early Examiners tended to regard play manuscripts as their own personal property. This is one reason why most of those submitted before 1824 no longer exist unless privately published by their authors.

A variant of the above was some kind of re-sale. When George Colman died, his widow sold the plays in his estate back to the Lord Chamberlain's Office for £100. Even Gilbert's plays proved vulnerable. No fewer than seven are known only from the Lord Chamberlain's Office copies or transcripts of the same. One is the Dickens-derived *Great Expectations,* which interestingly gives no acting part to Miss Havisham. The others are *Uncle Baby, Allow Me to Explain, The Realm of Joy, Highly Improbable, Our Island Home,* and *Committed for Trial.*

The fact that authorial manuscripts remained government property can be seen in two ways. It was a restriction, but it *did* ensure the survival of some pieces that might otherwise have perished. Less advantageous was the authorial position on copyright. In 1830, Planché convinced George Lamb, a Member of Parliament and fellow-playwright, to introduce a bill granting copyright protection to dramatists. This failed, but two years later Edward Bulwer Lytton was more successful. For all parties, the aim was to stop abuses of piracy. One popular pirating method was to purchase a copy of the prompt book from the prompter, and another to send in several agents to join the audience over a number of nights, each tasked with recording a particular character or characters. By the 1830s, the practice had evolved to sending in shorthand writers to take down the script as it was performed.

Given the above sharp practice, it is not surprising that Gilbert's own attitude to piracy is hostile. One of his stories is of an American impresario who wished to produce *The Mikado* without paying a fee and who came to Liberty's to purchase Japanese dresses. This led to a cat-and-mouse chase, with Liberty's refusing a sale and the man decamping to Paris, shadowed by D'Oyly Carte's emissary who secretly took the same boat and drove round all the Japanese shops to buy up material before him.[32] This and similar precautions were nothing new. In the 1760s, the actor-dramatist Charles Macklin had been forced into taking the precaution of never printing any copies of his play *Love à la Mode* and always taking the copy away from the prompter. In 1770, he sought an injunction from the Court of Chancery against theatrical theft, the defendants in this case not being a rival theatre company but the proprietors of a magazine called the *Court Miscellany.*

v.

The Charles Macklin case is an example of response to printed, rather than acted, theft. The magazine had apparently published the play's first act, promising that the second was to come. Macklin brought a bill seeking (a) an account of profits, (b) an injunction against further publication of the first act, and (c) a refusal of the promised publication of the second. The decision was deferred until the announcement of the result of another case, that of *Millar v. Taylor.* This is relevant for its links with the Statute of Anne (1709–1710), which was later to be tested regarding its music-theatre application.

The Statute of Anne is perhaps the first example of modern United Kingdom copyright law. At first, it was assumed not to cover printed music, but this was challenged by Johann Christian Bach whose works had been pirated by the London publisher James Longman. The case was filed in 1773 and was decided in Bach's favour, setting a precedent under which, after 1777, musical compositions were also covered. The results were twofold. One was that registrations of musical works for copyright soared, reaching to 1,828 in the 1790s. The other was that in 1842, English law was extended to include musical performance as well as publication rights.

The protections offered in England were not universal. In Germany, and in France before the Revolution, there was a privilege system. In France, *LeRoy & Ballard* had the exclusive right to publish *all* music from 1551 to 1713 and a *partial* right (shared with engravers) from 1713 to 1719. One problem was that, in some countries, such favour was bound up with feudal privilege. A privilege issued in Mainz, for example, would have little or no power to prevent piracy in Berlin, Munich, or Stuttgart, let alone Geneva or Paris.[33] In Republican France, the privilege system was replaced by a less restrictive copyright law, while in the United States, a copyright law of 1790 was extended eighty years later to include performance rights.

Gilbert's own attempts to establish copyright are well known. *The Pirates of Penzance* was premiered in New York rather than London, mainly in an (unsuccessful) attempt to secure the American copyright. Gilbert remarked in an 1887 interview that 'we are a pretty powerful trio, and are determined to do battle with every American manager who attempts to produce one of our plays without paying the fee'.[34] Perhaps, he knew of other past instances of difficulties. George Friedrich Händel suffered from such chronic piracy by John Walsh that, to contain the threat, he made Walsh his official publisher. Beethoven once complained to the Artaria house in Vienna that a pirated version of his Opus 29 sextet contained many errors. His solution was twofold. First he asked the owner to surrender the fifty pirated copies for correction. Thereupon he slashed giant X's across the pirate copy pages.[35]

vi.

It is impossible here to cover all the minutiae of copyright law but a few decisions do remain relevant. In the *Millar v. Taylor* case, the judgement sided with the publishers, stating that the common law rights were not extinguished by the Statute of Anne. Publishers had a perpetual right to publish a work for which they had acquired the rights and no amount of time would cause the work to pass to the public. The court's decision did not, however, extend to Scotland, where a reprint industry continued to thrive. All this was partially resolved in the landmark case of *Donaldson v. Beckett* (1774) with its decision that copyright in published works was not perpetual and was subject to statutory limits.

The resolution was, however, continually challenged, and Gilbert himself, in safeguarding his work, was driven to welcoming false reports:

'When it is said that because I go to Egypt, therefore I am writing an Egyptian opera, I do not contradict it. It misleads the Americans'.[36] On the legal side, he also took care to be well versed in cases of illicit piracy, one example being that of *Coleman (or Colman) v. Wathen*. The irony here is that Gilbert himself was later to be accused of piracy, this being in relation to *The Gentleman in Black* which the *Era* claimed to be derived from a story already printed in *Blackwood's Magazine*.

The *Era*'s accusation comes in what is actually rather a laudatory review, but it certainly suggests a purloining:

> Nearly fifty years ago, Dr. Robert Macnish introduced the readers of Blackwood to 'a little, meagre, brown-faced, elderly gentleman, in a snuff-coloured surtout, a scarlet waistcoat, black small-clothes, and a wooden leg', who, going beyond the length of the Pythagorean philosophy, not only believed but put into practice the doctrine that two living bodies may exchange souls with each other.

The assertion is that *The Gentleman in Black* borrows the idea, using 'caprices founded upon the same doctrine' to form the subject of 'a most mirth-provoking musical legend'. Whether this is plagiarism is debatable, but in any case Gilbert refuted the whole proposition:

> Sir, – Your dramatic critic, in his very kind notice of *The Gentleman in Black* at the Charing-cross Theatre, is mistaken in supposing that it is founded on the story of the same name that appeared in *Blackwood* many years ago. The piece is described in the housebill as 'original', a description that I should certainly not have appended to it if I had been indebted to *Blackwood* for the notion upon which it is founded.[37]

Here, we may note that the tone is not at all peremptory, though this may be mainly because the review itself was generally encouraging.

vii.

The rather confusing nature of copyright law remained vexatious not least because there had been so many interpretations. In the *Col(e)man v. Wathen* case, the background was a stronger version of the misappropriation alleged for *The Gentleman in Black*. Apparently, Colman, managing the Haymarket, had purchased the copyright of John O'Keeffe's *The Agreeable Surprise*, but Mr. Wathen, an ex-army officer now running the Richmond Theatre, had illicitly performed the piece. Thomas Erskine (later Lord Chancellor), acting for the plaintiff, argued that this certainly *was* illicit. A representation should amount to a publication, for, if it were not, 'all dramatic works might be pirated with impunity'. Lord Kenyon C.J., however, disagreed. He decided that the statute was limited to the publishing of the text itself, a move which may only be sanctioned 'by the author or his lawful assignees'.[38] Gilbert himself was very protective of his works, not just because he considered piracy illicit but because when others did produce his plays they were presented in inferior form. Sometimes, we find him expressing veiled glee in thwarting would-be buccaneers. He deliberately retains a veto on revealing the name of a forthcoming work; he is delighted that, on the slender and false rumour of a forthcoming Egyptian piece, 'more than one manager has already bought up Egyptian dresses'.[39]

Apart from cunning rumours, there were other ways of thwarting would-be piracy. Quite often the theatre managers would buy the 'copyright' in a play from the dramatist but, rather than printing, would secrete the manuscripts, both as protection for the text and as a long-term investment before much later sale to a publisher. This hoarding tendency also related to a new method of remuneration. The 18th-century system had involved authors taking a share of box office takings on the 'benefit' nights (the third, sixth, and ninth). By the early 19th century, this began to give way to the more reliable payment by a lump sum, which might include an allowance for the copyright and, in a long run, include bonus amounts on certain nights. The problem was that by the 1820s and 1830s, the theatres were in such general decline that this became reflected in decreasing amounts paid to the authors. According to Planché, John Murray refused to pay the entirely reasonable sum of ten pounds for the privilege of staging his drama *Charles XIIth*, pleading poverty. He then obtained an unauthorized copy and staged that instead.

Planché's own attempted reforms were not the first of their kind. In 1814, in the course of debate about so-called legal deposit, Davies Giddy, a scientist and MP for Bodmin, suddenly proposed a clause that would protect the interests of those authors writing plays 'intended merely for the closet'. This failed, however, and it was Bulwer Lytton who was most forceful in response. In his view, the original reason for suppressing the minor theatres – namely their disorderly state – no longer existed. The current system was the direct cause of a deterioration in the national drama. Moreover, he considered the censorship powers exercised by the Lord Chamberlain unconstitutional.

It is unlikely that Gilbert was as exercised as Lord Lytton by the evils of licensed, but he would have been aware of certain anomalies. The 1843 Act clearly contemplated that every word spoken on the stage must be licensed, also enshrining a fee structure of £2 for plays of three or more acts, £1 for pieces of one or two acts, and five shillings for a 'Song, Address, Prologue or Epilogue'.[40] Here, what is notable is that several Gilbert and Sullivan operas had songs introduced after licensing, without leaving any record of fresh application. Even the revised version of *The Sorcerer* has left no sign of any official submission. Possibly, conditions were not as rigid as we might assume. According to William

Donne, the checking of actual performance in the theatre was rare, and 'it was not three times in the year that there [was] any occasion for it'.[41]

Whatever the loopholes, authors were certainly becoming increasingly vociferous for their rights. In 1822, in the case of *Murray v. Elliston*, James Scarlett, argued forcibly that Lord Byron had expressly stated that he did *not* want his tragedy *Marino Faliero, Doge of Venice* to be performed. The play's possible failure would hurt the author's feelings as well as his fame. Later, such concerns were to be covered by Bulwer Lytton's successful bill of March 1833. This rated the penalty for representing a play without permission as fifty pounds for each performance, an amount amended in the House of Commons to forty shillings. On the matter of censorship, his Committee's recommendations were modest. Rather than abandoning the office of censor, it advocated extending the Lord Chamberlain's jurisdiction to cover the minor theatres, but removing the privileges of the patent theatres. This proved more contentious than the dramatic copyright bill and for a time had to be dropped.[42]

It is unlikely that Gilbert was greatly affected by many of the bill's repercussions. But he was certainly interested in the activities of the Dramatic Authors' Society, which was set up mainly to ease arrangements with provincial theatres. In London, dramatists usually granted a theatre the right to perform a play for a certain amount of time (or even forever), but dealing with non-metropolitan houses was harder. Initially, such venues were charged on a fixed scale according to the number of acts and the size and location of the theatre, but the arrangement was undermined by the preferential treatment given to Sheridan Knowles. The result was that by about 1866, the system had changed numerous times, the position now being that provincial managers were required to pay a certain (variable) sum, in return for which they could mount any play on the Society's list. Gilbert and others, however, were still asserting their independence, particularly in dealing with London managers. This led the Society yet again to revise its rules, allowing members to retain rights in popular plays for a certain period before the works (on payment of the fee) joined the list as more generally available.

viii.

Despite his relatively privileged position, the mixed skein of licensing and censorship law undoubtedly affected Gilbert. For one thing, there was the sexual limitation. It would have been impossible for Gilbert to produce a work such as Ben Elton's *Black Adder* where the perversions practised by the Bishop of Bath and Wells would have been prosecuted as blasphemous. Even in the late 20th century, prosecutions were brought against stage indecency as applied, for instance, with *The Romans in Britain*.[43] For Gilbert, sex was far more of a minefield, but political issues could also be contentious. One example occurred during the 1871–1872 pantomime season when William Donne banned all references to a recently introduced match tax. Gilbert's response was a letter to the *Daily News* (12 January 1872), supporting stage liberty and boasting that he himself often ignored the censor's cuts.

Gilbert's letter is a good example of controlled invective. In it he points out that Mr. Donne has three times taken objection to passages in his plays but that, considering himself just as well qualified to judge, he has systematically declined to take the slightest notice. He goes on:

> From my experience of the nature of Mr. Donne's exceptions, I have gathered the following facts:– 1. An actor may 'curse' as freely as he pleases; but he may not 'damn' under any provocation. 2. He may say, 'Heaven forbid that I should stand in my Pip's way', but he may not say 'Lord forbid that I should stand in my Pip's way'. 3. He may not use the German word 'sakrament', because it resembles the English word 'sacrament'. I may have done Mr. Donne an injustice, but I have always accounted for his objections on the theory that the existence of his office depends on his showing that it is of some practical value, and if he is unable to 'return' a satisfactory number of revisions, the Censorship of Plays will run some risk of abolition. I have no particular desire to bring about this catastrophe, but at the same time I am unwilling that it should be averted at my expense.[44]

Here, it is sarcasm that marks the tone, but later there could be downright invective, as applied with the six-week ban on *The Mikado*. This Gilbert calls an act of depredation, involving no discussion, losing potential receipts of about £10,000, and made all the more foolish by the fact that Japanese warships were actually playing the music.[45]

ix.

There is no doubt that censorship could at times be ridiculous. In his autobiography (1883), Gilbert tells that when he submitted *Great Expectations,* Magwitch's remark about Pip's chambers being fit for a Lord came back with the word 'Lord' struck out and 'Heaven' substituted in pencil. Nor was God the only figure to be reverenced. There was also considerable restriction on portraying notable or recently deceased persons, though this seems to have been winked at when living people were flattered by the publicity or when – as in Ko-ko's little list – reference was made by hints and gestures. One interesting mid-century ban was on mentioning Queen Victoria. This had been relaxed by 1879, giving extra piquancy to her invocation as an unseen *dea ex machine* in *The Pirates of Penzance.*

Although Gilbert often chafed against censorship, he would have been aware that his position was not universally shared. During the match tax fiasco, Charles Millward wrote to the papers in defence of Censorship, stating that he had written between thirty and forty pantomimes and never had a line expunged. When *The Orchestra* printed Gilbert's own letter, it was preceded by reference to this, including Millward's assertion that the Censor only intervened in cases of extreme offensiveness. Nonetheless, the journal sided with Gilbert, pointing out that he was a careful and pure writer, making it absurd that even *his* works should have been so restricted.[46]

c) The International Dimension and the Old Plays Debate

So far our censorship survey has been mainly England-centred. But there was, of course, a wider dimension, particularly in relation to international copyright and imported plays. The latter group seem to have been particularly suspect when they were French. In the 1840s, Victor Hugo's *Ruy Blas* was banned in Britain. The idea that a queen could be fooled by a lowly footman had implications for the royal family: 'playgoers [might] perceive in it, allusions to the choice of a husband her Majesty was about to make'.[47] Eventually, in 1858, one version was finally licensed, but only after alterations to ensure that the original social status of Ruy Blas was sufficiently elevated. Gilbert's mockery of both the ban and the tampering lies behind his own dramatization. He called it a 'Preposterous Piece of Nonsense For *Private* Representation', with airs 'chosen for the convenience of ... rough and ready amateurs', unless, of course, you write your own words.[48]

France was a key supplier of drama to the English, but it was not the only source of foreign dramatic imports. In the late 18th and early 19th centuries, the German *Sturm und Drang* Movement led to the translation and performance of plays such as *Pizarro* and *Lovers' Vows*, while in opera, Italian forms dominated. Colley Cibber was one of the most vocal to denounce the latter, telling us:

> The Italian Opera began first to steal into England; but in as rude a disguise, and unlike itself, as possible, in a lame, hobbling Translation, into our own Language, with false Quantities, or metre out of Measure, to its original Notes, sung by our own unskillful Voices, with Graces misapply'd to almost every Sentiment, and with Action, lifeless and unmeaning, through every Character.

Possibly, he recalled the hostility caused by the London performance of *Arsinoe*, the libretto for which had been taken directly from an older Italian opera, translated into English and given new music by the Englishman Thomas Clayton.[49]

Any feeling of native superiority felt by Cibber had a downside in a latent sense that, in opera at least, British participation might be rather deficient. So, for that matter, might British audiences. Like Gilbert,

Clayton was concerned that his audiences would not be equal to the quality of his work. He feared that 'The Musick being recitative, may not, at first, meet with that general acceptation, as is to be hoped for, from the audience's being better acquainted with it'.[50] He was also rather disparaging of his English singers, an idea later referenced and inverted in Gilbert's Utopian tenor who has to adopt an English name in order to win plaudits.

The sense of the national drama as under foreign siege did have some justification. During the 19th century, foreign publishers printed an increasing number of pirated British works, and Belgian and American reprints were also common. The 1842 Copyright Act instituted fines to address these concerns, and in 1878, a Paris Congress insisted on treating the author's right as a perpetual property entitlement. Then, from 1883 until 1886, the Swiss Government hosted annual conferences in Berne, with the purpose of creating a permanent international copyright law. The drawback for Gilbert was the absence of America which, because of its stance on copyright protection, failed to qualify for admission. Until the late 19th century, the U.S. government maintained the same stance on foreign copyrights as that introduced in 1790. The International Copyright Act of 1891 is the first U.S. congressional act to extend limited protection to foreign copyright holders from selected nations.

For Gilbert, the American copyright system was a permanent headache. In every state except Massachusetts, he said, 'we have to fight'. How far this drained his energies is difficult to evaluate, but his wider dislike both of *laissez-faire* piracy and its mirror opposite of inhibiting regulation persisted throughout. One indication of this comes in *Rosencrantz and Guildenstern* (1874) which, rather ironically, was refused for performance by Marie Litton because of the controversy produced by *The Happy Land*. Instead, it appeared in *Fun*, the *Argument* alone making clear that censorship lies at the heart of its meaning.

The background to *Rosencrantz and Guildenstern* is entirely theatre related. King Claudius confesses in blank verse a secret crime of his youth: not that of murdering anyone but, rather, of being guilty of writing a five-act tragedy. The play closed half way through the first act as a result of derisive laughter from the audience whereupon the humiliated Claudius decreed that anyone who mentioned the play must be executed. Rosencrantz's plan – formulated in alliance with Ophelia – is to get Hamlet to stage it, leading to Hamlet's banishment and their own marriage. The link with the Lord Chamberlain's office comes not just in the banning but also in the fact that Polonius is the official censor. Both aspects derive from the embargo placed on *The Happy Land,* but they may also reference William Donne's cutting of the seemingly innocuous line 'I wonder whether the Lord Chamberlain permits it' from a one-act farce a year earlier.[51]

The underlying joke about censorship is reinforced by much other comic material. Not only is there deliberately heightened and inflated language. In addition, the terror of the tremulous haunted maiden found in many a Gothic romance is transmuted to Ophelia's account of discovering the original play's manuscript:

> Last night I stole down from my room alone
> And sought my father's den. I entered it!
> The clock struck twelve and then – oh horrible! –
> From chest and cabinet there issued forth
> The mouldy spectres of five thousand plays,
> All dead and gone – and many of them damned!
> I shook with horror! They encompassed me,
> Chattering forth the scenes and parts of scenes
> Which my poor father wisely had cut out.
> Oh horrible – oh 'twas most horrible.[52]

Here the cod-Shakespearian language encapsulates a further joke relevant to the chamberlain's character. Shakespeare's Polonius is himself a chatterer, spouting a great deal of long-winded comment, so that his being appointed to cut and trim bombastic tragedies is farcical in itself.

ii.

The mockery of censorship has another aspect: it allows for another Gilbertian jibe about the preference for 'Old Plays'. In *Utopia Limited*, Scaphio and Phantis complain about Lord Dramaleigh in exactly these terms: 'Are you aware that the Lord Chamberlain, who has his own views as to the best means of elevating the national drama, has declined to license any play that is not in blank verse and three hundred years old – as in England?'. They are also aggrieved that the laws of libel have ruined the burlesque theatre, which, of course, threatens the scurrilous representations of King Paramount. A more indulgent reference appears in the next Savoy Opera where Ludwig alludes gleefully to the Greeks' rather risky dances 'which would shock that worthy gentleman, the Licenser of Plays'.[53] None of this is vehement satire, but censorship remained a serious business. When Helen Lenoir was in New York preparing for a simultaneous premiere for *Iolanthe*, Richard D'Oyly Carte wrote cautioning her not to reveal too much as the Lord Chamberlain's Office might 'come down bang and forbid it being done'.[54] This is because the sacred orders of the Garter, Thistle, Patrick, and Bath are 'going on the stage', a concern that looks forward to a later rebuke in relation to King Paramount's wearing of royal insignia in *Utopia Limited*.[55]

The Gilbertian response to censorship is not always hostile. In 1909, he gave evidence before a Joint Committee of the Lords and Commons stating that he was 'strongly of opinion that there should be a Censor'.

Even more strongly he felt that this should not be one person but a panel: 'one arbitrator appointed by the author, one by the Lord Chamberlain, and a third selected by those two'.[56] His reason for the support is, he says, that he is against unbridled polemic. He does not think that the stage is the proper pulpit from which to disseminate doctrines possibly of Anarchy, Socialism or Agnosticism or of adultery and free-love 'before an audience of all ages, sexes, conditions of life and varied degrees of education'. In addition, he is concerned for first-night audiences. He feels they have as much claim to be protected from outrage as any coming after them.

It is easy nowadays to mock such primness. But modern political correctness is creating its own racial and political taboos, while our (usually justified) concerns about sexual harassment are certainly affecting theatre productions. Gilbert's own argument includes drawing a distinction between what is read and what is shown. 'For instance', he argues, 'in a novel you might read that Eliza slipped off her dressing-gown and stepped into her bath, and no harm would be done, but if that were represented on the stage it would be a very different matter'.[57] One of the ironies in all this is that in his more mature judgement, he thought the Lord Chamberlain 'absolutely justified' to have interfered with the production of *The Happy Land* but – as we have seen – was infuriated by his temporary ban on *The Mikado*.[58] One wonders what he would make of the recent denunciations of *The Mikado* as racist Yellowface imperialism, but perhaps, it is best not to ask.

* *

Section 2: Constraints and Limitations in Theatre Performance

a) Company Structures and Issues of Celebrity

Censorship and licensing law were always for Gilbert an annoyance. But in areas of staging, company structures, and audiences he shows mixed attitudes. Sometimes he is harsh all round. His remark about attendees at *The Mountebanks* – that they have not realized how bad it is but it is at least good enough for them – suggests both self-contempt and disdain of the audience for accepting the second-rate. This, however, is somewhat offset by his actual insistence in various interviews on being a perfectionist and on a perfect rapport between him, Sullivan, and his audiences.

Gilbert's insistence on general harmony is conveyed in many of his interviews. In *'BLANK, BLANK', THE NEW OPERA AT THE SAVOY*, he talks of 'five hours a day for weeks drilling the company', further describing the use of wooden models (or blocks) to help him in grouping his choristers. His company, he says, has been accustomed to work with him for years, the twelve at the core making 'a very happy family'. He does not believe that there is any company 'so free as ours from those jealousies and heartburnings which abound in theatrical circles'. This sounds fine but is somewhat disingenuous, for the opera being rehearsed was *The Gondoliers*, for which Jessie Bond had already sought a pay rise. Indeed, the theme of equality had itself been selected partly as a means to counteract the rising egos of some of the cast.[59]

Gilbert's insistence on the great efforts required in writing and production directly belie occasional references to the libretti as easily scribbled trifles. The word used by the interviewer is 'labour' and Gilbert reinforces this, stressing that he first writes an elaborate narrative, working it out from all angles, while writing bits of dialogue 'on the opposite page as they occur to me'. He then begins again from the start. Last come the lyrics, which, says he, 'I polish and polish until I am satisfied', proving it by showing two verses which distil the essence of a dozen sheets of paper upon which he has tried 'every turn possible'. The conclusion – 'So, you see, I don't spare myself' – seems accurate enough, even though the actual writing time is restricted: 'I never do any work in the daytime, except rehearsals, but generally begin writing at 11 P.M. and go to bed at 2 or 3 …'.[60]

The thorough professionalism in Gilbert's approach is undeniable, but the assertion of trouble-free processes is misleading. In one conversation from 1906, he claims that he and Sullivan have always worked in perfect harmony – a view belied by arguments over the lozenge plot, by the Carpet Quarrel, by differences of opinion as to the desired character of Lady Sophy, and by Sullivan's exasperated agonies during the gestation of, and rehearsals for, *The Grand Duke*. As early as 1884, Sullivan writes to Gilbert that with *Princess Ida,* he has come to the end of his tether. His music needs a chance to 'act in its own proper sphere'. His tunes are in danger of becoming mere repetitions; his concerted movements are 'getting to possess a strong family likeness'. Gilbert's response seems genuinely surprised. Such reflections have caused him 'considerable pain', though he must generously assume that Sullivan wrote in haste. This does not suggest total harmony. It implies a creative imbalance, one of the problems being that, for the sake of the words, Sullivan is keeping down the music while Gilbert himself wants every well chiselled syllable to be heard.[61]

ii.

Apart from constraints of collaboration, there are also performing limitations. Rutland Barrington, for instance, was stout and tended to tire in the dancing. Grossmith on first nights could be horribly nervous. Audiences also could be difficult, as borne out by the catcalls during the premiere of *Ruddygore* demanding the return of *The Mikado*. The truth is that British audiences had a long-standing reputation for rowdiness, a point exemplified in a German resident's description of the Manchester theatre and its audiences in the 1780s:

> The gallery is here, as everywhere in England, unbearably un-ashamed; they throw apples, pomegranates, nut-shells on the stage, in the pit and the boxes they cry out and make a lot of noise; I know people who refuse to sit in the front seat of the boxes. With ladies they are more polite. Many years ago a flask flew from the gallery into the pit, striking a man's skull. This shrieking and din and all this bad behaviour is difficult in the intervals ... during the play itself the gallery is quieter than I have heard in any other place, and the applause and laughter in the middle of speeches does not last so long that one loses the thread or misses the climax ... Of battles and murders they are especially fond.[62]

Here, we may glimpse a foretaste of the famous Covent Garden Riots, while the Bancrofts' experience at the 'Dust-Hole' shows the mid-Victorians too as a hostile force to be reckoned with.

The Bancrofts' account of the Prince of Wales (or 'Dust-Hole') gives a pretty fair indication of the sort of audience Gilbert personally feared. Situated off Tottenham Court Road, it was initially an unfashionable establishment, notable for bringing even Madame Vestris to failure. Not surprisingly, therefore, Marie Bancroft's initial impressions were inauspicious:

> It was a well-conducted, clean little house, but oh, the audience! My heart sank! Some of the occupants of the stalls (the price of admission was, I think, a shilling) were engaged between the acts in devouring oranges (their faces being buried in them), and drinking ginger-beer. Babies were being rocked to sleep, or smacked to be quiet, which proceeding, in many cases, had an opposite effect! A woman looked up to our box, and seeing us staring aghast, with, I suppose an expression of horror upon my face, first of all 'took a sight' at us, and then shouted, 'Now, then, you three stuck-up ones, come out o' that, or I'll send this 'ere orange at your 'eds'.[63]

This, suggesting what Gilbert was trying to combat, further explains why he was so directorially meticulous. He wished to allow no chance for error, a caution which proved justified judging by the harsh criticism of the *Ruddygore* ghost-scene for a Saturday night failure in the machinery.[64]

iii.

Gilbert's sense of a need to cover all eventualities can be related to the very high standards he actually set himself. In 1906, he tells the *Pall Mall Gazette* that he has for the past twenty or thirty years never seen a performance from the front because he is never satisfied with his own work: 'I always feel that it might be very much better than it is'. This did not mean, however, that he undertook extensive revision: 'Except for some occasional modifications that may be made afterwards, my work is done as soon as I have finished superintending rehearsals'. Such remarks may suggest supreme self-satisfaction but may simply register a confidence in his authority. Gagging is forbidden. He objects to actors 'using the author's libretto as a sort of skeleton framework on which to hang their own eccentricities'. When he *does* allow for revision, as with the 1884 *Sorcerer*, it is on his and Sullivan's own terms. Elsewhere, his demand for the *dernier mot* is justified. He is, he says, responsible for the whole and 'don't care to be credited with the humour of other people'.[65]

The desire to stamp on company intransigence is recorded many times. A mild case was Rutland Barringon's wish to augment his part in *The Pirates,* duly recorded in his memoirs. After extolling Marion Hood as Mabel ('tall, slight, and graceful, a typical English girl with a wealth of fair hair which, I believe, was all her own') he goes on:

> I only appeared in the second act, and my song, 'The Enterprising Burglar', was such an immense success that I had always to repeat the last verse at least twice. It occurred to me that an encore verse would be very nice, and in a rash moment I one day presumed to ask Gilbert to give me one. He informed me that 'encore' meant 'sing it again'. I never made such a request again, but I heard it whispered that, years later, in a revival of the opera, the comedian playing the part was allowed to sing the last verse in three languages as an encore.

Perhaps, Gilbert liked the novelty of the three-language concept. He does say he would consider gags and novelty ideas submitted to him first, and even Barrington got away with a few inspired improvisations.[66]

The constraints demanded by Gilbert are one thing. But, of course, he too was subject to limitation. *Harlequin Wilkinson* roundly mocks the use of cumbersome scenic effects, and Gilbert's own comments on the production of *Harlequin Cock Robin* are a testament to his exasperation when spectacle overrides dramatic impetus, plot development, and common sense's rational parameters. Even less controllable was natural accident, one example causing the near-postponement of the premiere of *The Pirates*. This is recorded by Barrington in the following terms:

> The first performance of *Pirates* very nearly had to be postponed on account of an accident to Miss Everard, who was to have played the part of Ruth; she was delightful as Little Buttercup in *Pinafore*. She was standing in the centre of the stage at rehearsal one morning, when I noticed the front piece of a stack of scenery falling forward.

I called to her to run, and got my back against the falling wing and broke its force to a great extent, but it nevertheless caught her on the head, taking off a square of hair as neatly as if done with a razor. The shock and injury combined laid her up for some time, and there was consternation in view of a postponement. Fortunately I was able to suggest to Carte a clever and dear old friend of mine, by name Emily Cross, who I felt sure would be capable of replacing Miss Everard in the time. She was telegraphed for, and after much pressure she consented, and with only two days' study and rehearsal appeared and made a great success.

At least here the end-result was happy, as it was when Miss Cross – now playing Ariel – lifted her skirts above the mud to cross the street, only to be told by a street-urchin, 'Yow needn't be so particular about 'em, Emily; we can see 'em all any night for tuppence'.[67]

iv.

The growth in the popularity of the theatre was, in the 19th century, genuine but by no means consistent. Even in a successful piece, audiences might complain, demanding more opportunities for their favourite performer. In *Tame Cats; or The Triumph of Collette*, Gilbert hilariously lampoons the unruly behaviour of the claque vigorously supporting the star, pointing out too that his part is of very little importance. Much of the more significant action is actually omitted, because 'really, there is no reason why we should trouble our readers with dialogues between subordinate characters played by such insignificant artists as MISS MARIE WILTON and MR. BANCROFT'. Everything Collette says produces sensation, loud laughter, loud cheers, and thunderous applause. His most mundane remarks are hailed with 'extraordinary demonstrations of delight'. Collette is indeed 'our only joy', a point of which he himself must be aware judging by the ebullient responses of his fan club.

There is no doubt that a popular performer can affect a production. One probable reason for the cutting of the excellent song *When jealous torments* from *The Yeomen* was the temporary departure of Rutland Barrington into theatrical management, leaving the Shadbolt role to a Savoy newcomer. The alleged star-quality of Collette is more questionable but certainly raises the temperature:

Enter MR. COLLETTE. The Young Men in the Stalls stretch themselves and indicate in pantomime to Young Men in Private Boxes that here is something worth living for at last.

Even the last speech is passed over (except for the words 'Tame Cats'), the reason being that Collette himself is not speaking it.[68]

v.

Gilbert's mockery of a particular production does not necessarily indicate dislike for the actor. Charles Collette was genuinely successful in *Tame Cats*, later starring as Sir Oliver Surface in *The School for Scandal*, Mr. Puff in *The Critic, and* Autolycus in *The Winter's Tale*. He also appeared as Sergeant Jones in *Ours*, in various adaptations of Dickens' novels, and in his own musical play *Cryptoconchoidsyphonostomata* which was on the bill with the 1875 première of *Trial by Jury*.[69] What Gilbert really dislikes is the audience taking over the direction of the play. In the burlesque, Collette, being a gentleman, fails to respond to long calls for his appearance after the curtain. He is, says Gilbert, no doubt disgusted by the preposterous folly of his friends, this being yet another example of the undermining, not just of other actors, but also of authorial intention.

The undermining of the author is, for Gilbert, a particularly sore point. In *Actors, Authors, and Audiences*, the dramatist on trial asserts that the evidence shows conclusively that his original manuscript has been materially altered. This is an affront to his skills and his reputation and has arisen in the face of his earnest protest that

> ... as the play was put before the public in his name, the play should be his play, and not a modified version thereof, trimmed, altered, written up and cut down to suit the views of individual actors and actresses engaged in representing it. If he was incompetent to the task of writing a good practical play – and the events of the evening pointed to that conclusion – the manager's obvious course was to apply to a more skilful author, not to take upon himself, or to entrust to a deputy, the privilege of making alterations which, in the author's opinion, placed his work before the audience in a distorted light.

Here, the annoyance may be set beside the recommendations for improvements detailed in *A Stage Play* where in particular it is the lack of adequate rehearsals that is lambasted.

Gilbert's suggestions for improvements are many and various, but the main meat is in his last paragraph. Here he insists that:

> In the first place, every actor and every person engaged in the piece should have a perfect copy of the piece, and that copy should be *printed*, not written.

In addition:

> It is absolutely necessary that every actor should have the *context* of his scenes before his eyes as he studies them.

In addition:

> It is a monstrous shame and an unheard-of injustice to place three-act pieces on the stage with fewer than thirty rehearsals, in ten of which the scenes should be set as they will be set at night, and in five of which every soul engaged should be dressed and made up as they will be dressed and made up at night.

These modifications will not only show respect to the play (and the author) but also to the actors, some of whom need time to acclimatize themselves to their fellow-performers dressed in character. Interestingly, here, Gilbert actually praises the French system. There, he says, parts are distributed, learnt perfectly, and then rehearsed for six to eight weeks, sometimes extending to three months or even four.[70]

vi.

Gilbert's attitude to rehearsal says quite a lot about his view of acting as a craft. It is, he thinks, imitative and can be taught. In France, scene rehearsals and dress rehearsals occupy the last week of preparations. Actors and actresses *act* at rehearsal. This has been taught and required from the first, their art receiving 'microscopic investigation' from the stage-manager (=director) and the author. The consequence is that a bad actor becomes a reasonably good actor, and a reasonably good actor becomes an admirable one. The English system is deficient because it works against this. Jones rehearses briefly with Brown, a man about town. He is disconcerted on the first night to find Brown dressed as an Archbishop. Had Jones had the opportunity of rehearsing with Brown-the-Archbishop, instead of with Brown-the-Swell, and had the set for rehearsal been the Archbishop's Library, rather than an empty stage, Jones, instead of risking failure, might have become the talk of the town from the first.

The idea of practice making perfect sounds relatively easy. It may indeed be the reason why Gilbert signs the above article in the name of a *persona* he calls Facile. But one may doubt whether the imitative mode is enough to produce great performances. Gilbert, implying that it is, claims that the solution lies in numerous rehearsals with scenery, dresses, and make-up. They must be 'earnest rehearsals', with every expression and gesture in place, ready for performance. Otherwise, the English stage will never take the position justified by the intelligence of its players, the enterprise of its managers, and the talent of its authors. Notable here is the fact that Gilbert does praise all parties. It is the *system* which he regards as flawed, though he is particularly concerned with the injustice it heaps on the authors.

b) Public Taste, Stock Companies, and the Company of the Savoy

Although he often criticizes actors, the mature Gilbert could at least play a large part in choosing and moulding them. More problematical were the audience-members and, of course, the censor. The former were not only unpredictable. They were also often ill-educated and lacking in aesthetic discrimination. As early as *Hush-a-Bye Baby,* Gilbert lambastes the execrable taste exhibited in – and shown for – popular song. The refrain he introduces to his own topical musical item is 'Claptrap, Claptrap'. This – with its 'trap' reference parodying George Leybourne's lyrics for *The Mousetrap Man* – is quite virulent, ending with the words:

> Public will have and singers will cry,
> Claptrap will sell whilst we've patrons to buy.

One wonders what the addressed public thought and whether they realized how much they were being insulted.[71]

The unpleasing public taste for ridiculous novelty jingles is matched by the audience acceptance of doggerel pantomime and overblown, often ludicrously inapposite, spectacle. In Gilbert's own *Harlequin Cock Robin,* the Fish Ballet in the Forest is a case in point. If the audience would only refuse to accept such things – as, indeed, cumbersome effects such as the magical crystal fountain – the author could get on with developing a plot coherently and cogently in a sound structural format leading to an effective climax. Structural concerns matter to Gilbert. In reviewing *Tame Cats,* he calls it 'very disjointed' and not entirely intelligible. He also dislikes anticlimax. In 1901, he tells William Archer that he disapproves of a tendency for a play's fifth act to mark a tailing off. This, he says, applies even in such great works as *The Merchant of Venice* and *The School for Scandal.* But he cannot think it is sound art, confessing to 'a preference for finished form, even if the form, and perhaps the play itself, was borrowed from the French'.[72]

Gilbert's dislike of loose structure, interpolation, and excrescence can be found in many guises. In his parody of *Not Guilty* (which he subtitles *A Party by the name of Johnson*), he pours scorn on the contriving of a walk-on part for Johnson, the scene painter. Johnson's appearances, as we have seen, disconcert practically the whole cast, one example being that of Mrs. Armitage shrieking 'Avaunt!' as he makes yet another of his impromptu appearances. Elsewhere, it is scenery and costuming that are mocked. *Mazeppa,* to be fair, is well mounted, always worth seeing, and a 'fine old crusted absurdity'. But the tone of his critique is one of parody. MAZEPPA's dresses are 'in first and third acts worth (probably) millions; in second act, about fourpence-halfpenny'. Clearly, the reference is to Adah Menken's sensational fleshings. In the damning burlesque of *Tame Cats,* there is another approach. The last words – as if to denigrate all else – are: 'The scenery is capital'.

ii.

The vogue for the equestrian drama is a good example of the vogue for the sensational. But by 1867 – the performance date of *Mazeppa* – it was hardly a new phenomenon. We can trace it at least to John Philip Kemble's 1811 production of the younger George Colman's *Bluebeard* when its deployment was part of a campaign to revive Covent Garden's fortunes after losses from several unprofitable Shakespearian productions. About twenty performing horses were hired from Astley's Amphitheatre, first charging on in answer to Selim's bugle-call (Act 11, Scene 1) and later galloping back for the grand finale depicting a full-scale attack on Bluebeard's castle. The result earned the theatre thousands of pounds, being followed by an equally popular production of Matthew Lewis's *Timour the Tartar.*

The problem with Kemble's *hippodrama* was one of precedent. By staging this non-patented theatrical form at a legitimate venue, Kemble had eroded the distinction between legitimate and illegitimate theatre. Gilbert's mockery suggests a keen eye for the enjoyable absurdity of the whole mode. In his *Mazeppa*, the horse shies, trots slowly, and occasionally collapses. The hero's heroic ride is farcical, the stallion itself being notably nervous and instantly fainting when a shrub happens to fall on him.[73]

Gilbert's wit is not always appreciated. Reviews of the first night of *Thespis* suggested that its classical mythological background was somewhat above the audience's heads, making it harder for many to appreciate the jokes.[74] Perhaps too, they were unaccustomed to the mode of playing, and indeed Gilbert's company was hardly typical. In the 1860s, the norm was the use of a stock company with actors hired by the season to play a particular line of business. At the same time, the repertory system's long-term contract was being replaced by a 'single play, long run' policy. This goes against the former trend for stock parts to be often guarded for years. In *The Grand Duke*, one actress is said to 'claim all hoydens as her rights', having played them for thirty seasons. By contrast, Julia thinks of herself as a celebrity import, the Romantic Movement's idea of individual genius having given a further boost to a one-star (sometimes two-star) system.

iii.

The essence of stock companies was that they were troupes of actors performing regularly in a particular theatre, presenting a different play nightly from a repertory of prepared productions. Usually, the players specialized in dramatic types such as the tragedian, or leading man; the first lady or *prima donna*; the villain or 'heavy' lead; the old woman; the juvenile lead, who played the young lover or stalwart hero; the soubrette, or female second lead; and the low comedian of whom Gilbert's Ludwig is an example. In *The Grand Duke,* Gilbert mocks such dispositions while also showing some sympathy for the actor-manager who significantly is beaten by his own low comedian, thence becoming a technical ghost. The danger in stock company Ensemble playing was twofold. Sometimes the types became wooden, rather ritualized, caricatures. Sometimes those stuck with playing them became bored and started inventing their own unauthorized business.

The actor-manager as ghost is the obverse of Gilbert as controller, though, of course, Gilbert was not so much a manager as a creator-director. Traditionally, actor-managers worked with a permanent company, each choosing his or her own plays, taking a leading role, and handling most of the business and financial arrangements.[75] Already in the 18th century, successful actor-managers such as Colley Cibber and David Garrick were achieving performance standards superior to those associated with theatre owners who hired occasional casts for individual dramas. One downside was that the actor's most famous performance might be in an inferior work, as later applied with Henry Irving in *The Bells* (1871). Gilbert had his own spat with Irving who claimed that the librettist saw nothing but unworthiness in the press, the managers, the actors, and the public – in everyone, in fact, except the beleaguered dramatist.

The Gilbert-Irving spat was the result of an interview with Edinburgh's *Evening Dispatch.* Here, Gilbert not only denounced 'French plays, English translations, music hall, musical comedy, the press, the managers and the actors' but particularly lambasted Sydney Grundy (described as 'only a translator'), George Alexander, Beerbohm Tree, and Irving himself. Perhaps, he was misreported. Gilbert himself wrote to those he had most offended, explaining in a letter to the *Era* (16 October 1897) that had not meant what he appeared to say. Mr. Grundy in particular was a skilful practitioner, being, among adaptors, what Mr. Pinero was among original dramatists – *facile princeps.*[76]

Whether he was misreported or not, Gilbert's general demeanour does suggest how beleaguered he felt by the wider theatrical (and press) environment. With Irving, there may have been an element of professional jealousy, though what he highlights is the actor's dull monotony of delivery. Perhaps, this suggests that one part of Gilbert was an actor-manager manqué – that as well as writing and directing he coveted a great actor's star status. But the actor-manager was a dying breed. The late 19th-century trend was to more corporate ownership of theatres. One big constraint was financial, the cost of investing in new plays being increased by the need for a fresh combination of artistic personnel.

Gilbert himself did not exactly oppose the actor-manager system, but he disliked the star system when it distorted a piece through the exigencies – or sheet popularity – of a principal player. An example here was *Our American Cousin*, in which E.A. Sothern's initially minor role became hugely inflated. The irony is that Sothern had allegedly been tempted to throw up his stage career when Laura Keene, who had engaged him as a 'light eccentric comedian', insisted that he play a small part in a piece only being mounted as a stopgap.[77]

The problem with star performers was one experienced even by Gilbert. Jessie Bond in *Memories of an Old Savoyard* recalls the background: 'Gilbert snapped out that he was tired to death of artists who thought they were responsible for the success of the operas, and that he intended to put a stop to the whole thing'. The result was *The Gondoliers*. 'We'll have an opera', he exclaimed, 'in which there will be no principal parts. No character shall stand out more prominently than another'. A letter to his usually cosseted Jessie begins:

> I am distressed to learn that you decline to renew under £30 a week – distressed because, though nobody alive has a higher appreciation of your value as a most accomplished artist than I, no consideration would induce me to consent to such a rise.[78]

The problem of salary demands was only one of Gilbert's headaches. Another was the tantrums of those putting on airs because of their alleged star status. Later, Gilbert will satirize this through Julia Jellicoe – the *prima donna* in a work where theatrical contracts count for far more than marital ones. Here, Sullivan's music cleverly reflects the different status of leading lady and *seconda donna*, Julia's egocentric star turns making the most of what Sullivan himself called music's farmyard coloratura effects.[79]

Sullivan himself could resent aspects of theatre experience. He was greatly disappointed by 'the indifference of the public to the *Yeomen of the Guard*', believing that for years he had been 'sacrificing himself'. Whatever Gilbert's insistence on their equality of supremacy, it is clearly untrue that 'Whatever differences there were between us arose entirely outside the productions'.[80] In *The Gondoliers*, one latently barbed line is the assertion 'All shall equal be'. Another, suggesting the need for collaborative unity, is, 'Replying we sing as one individual'. Perhaps, this applies to Gilbert's ideal status for Sullivan and himself while also stressing the need for egalitarian unity in the company. The opposite is Julia's continual demand for centre stage, while the ultimate in regimented Ensemble is its *reductio ad absurdum* in the Prince of Monte Carlo's rote-performing suite.

Gilbert's sense of the value of teamwork is doubtless sincere. When Marco and Giuseppe, working 'as one individual', strike a pose with their arms around each other's shoulders, equality achieves a visual reinforcement.[81] Obviously, the ideal often jars with his martinet mode as director.

But he did genuinely see the need for a kind of overarching theatrical harmony, and – as in the case of Cousin Hebe at the end of *H.M.S. Pinafore* – he liked occasionally to bring a minor character into a brief moment of unexpected prominence.[82] Jessie Bond's stepping into this role – at what she then regarded as the princely salary of three pounds a week – was to result in long-term involvement but, though much favoured, she too recorded Gilbert's controlling and deflationary tendencies:

GILBERT: Miss –, why are you taking the centre of the stage? Did I not tell you to stand over there?

ACTRESS (INDIGNANTLY): Indeed, Mr. Gilbert, – I always took centre-stage in Italian opera.

GILBERT: Madam, this is not Italian opera. It is only a low burlesque of the worst possible kind.[83]

Here, Gilbert's disparagement of his own work is heavily sarcastic for it is the pretentious self-display that is actually being criticized.

iv.

Gilbert's hatred of posing and pretension is linked with other dislikes. One is the tendency to milk applause. Another is playing deliberately to a coterie and a third is disobeying his blocking. When in rehearsals one of the principals objected to being made to stand in a less than prominent position, his response was withering:

ACTRESS: 'Really, Mr. Gilbert, why should I stand here? I am not a chorus girl!

GILBERT: No, madam, your voice isn't strong enough, or you would be'.[84]

This can be related to a wider concern for theatrical balance, as when the Act 2 plan for the Grand Inquisitor to teach the gondolier-kings ritual etiquette was re-assigned to the Duke of Plaza-Toro on the grounds that Denny, the performer, already had a three-verse song in the same act.[85]

The above does not mean that Gilbert considered only himself. When the entire chorus begged him to reinstate Richard Temple's *Mikado's Song*, he yielded. When, in *The Gondoliers*, Sullivan preferred a gavotte to a minuet, this too was conceded. But Gilbert would never have allowed the laxity we find (for example) in E.A. Southern's exchanges with Laura Keene where his own condition was that he should be allowed to 'gag' to his heart's content. This, hardly suggesting artistic integrity, adds irony to Gilbert's admiration for Southern as a performer, particularly when *Our American Cousin* went on to make a small fortune for all concerned.

Despite Gilbert's admiration for Southern, star status did not necessarily lead to unstinting admiration. Writing to Sullivan to suggest that Grossmith be given a present of some kind on his departure, he includes the nonetheless spiteful assertion that he is 'a d-d (damned) bad actor'. Later, when Grossmith was giving songs-at-the-piano recitals in Torquay, Gilbert couched an alleged attempt to lure him back with the semi-sarcastic offer that 'You shall have a thousand a week and then the entire receipts'.[86] The plus side is that, despite or perhaps because of all his severities, Gilbert did help to raise artistic standards. By the end of the century, ad hoc companies were being hired in London for well-rehearsed single plays which were then taken on extensive tour. In addition, theatre was again respectable. This, already an aim at the Prince of Wales Theatre, is suggested by increasingly middle-class audiences at the Savoy and the Royal Command performance of *The Gondoliers*.

Looking back in 1899, Gilbert clearly noted the improvements. The Drama, he said, 'has made her fortune and is quite the lady'. She has 'endless hosts of highly cultured friends'. Plays now run for a year, houses are packed and actors get knighthoods. This, of course, is a slightly mocking generalization, as, even more, is his remark that earls and countesses are engaged to play 'utility'. Utility parts were, in fact, at the lowest end in the 'lines of business', a point made amply clear in the first duet for the wise men in *Utopia Limited*.[87]

c) Critics, Antagonists, and Foreign and Native Plays

The increasing status of the theatre as a venue for the respectable middle classes is undeniable. It is indeed the theme of *Gilbert and Sullivan's Respectable Capers* which argues that class distinction was preserved and encouraged by the Savoy's seat pricing system. Nonetheless, it would be simplistic to suggest that Gilbert had an easy time achieving acceptance or that he ever ceased railing against limiting conditions. In the preface to a privately printed *Pygmalion and Galatea*, he describes the piece as inferior to *On Guard* but infinitely more popular because it had been adequately rehearsed. When a copy of his grumble got into the hands of the daily press, it led, on 7 February 1872, to a long letter to the *Observer* pointing out that he was entitled to his own opinion, that his preface was not a public comment, and that *On Guard* had been hastily rehearsed with two other pieces on a stage half-occupied by carpenters. 'I was in the position of an artist who, having to paint a large picture, is permitted to see only six square inches of his canvas at a time', he remarked.[88]

The above would, perhaps, not have mattered very much but for the fact that Marie Litton (who had taken over the Royal Court on 25 January 1871) brought an action for libel. Gilbert then immediately called upon leading theatre people 'to prove that a three-act comedy and two farces cannot be efficiently rehearsed in ten days'. Ultimately, the action seems to have been dropped, but the farrago left Gilbert even more jaundiced. His own view was that *On Guard's* relative failure was due to poor rehearsal allocation, impercipient audiences, and hostile, unappreciative critics.

The reception of *On Guard* (28 October 1871) was certainly not encouraging. Even those critics who admitted the dialogue to be sometimes brilliant, claimed that it was too 'talky'. Righton, it was said, had overacted, the audience was irritable, and when Gilbert appeared at the curtain, there were cries of 'Cut it down!' Within the month the piece had been withdrawn, allegedly because of previous arrangements. 'Possibly the management arranged for a larger audience and they did not come', was the comment of the *Hornet* (22 November 1871).

The annoyance caused by audience and critics was augmented by Gilbert's sense that home-grown talent was underrated. He fumed at the critical assumption that French plays are innately superior and that 'Old Drama' must be better than new. Old Drama here includes Shakespeare where (changing tack) Gilbert complained that unaccountable liberties were often taken, leaving audiences with 'a trimmed and cocked and interpolated version of [the] play'. One thing he reviled was change to the sequence of scenes, and another, the dominance of the star performer. *Henry V111*, for instance, was normally played without the last two acts 'not because they were not written by Shakespeare but because the star-part Wolsey finishes in the last act but two'. 'What author', asks Gilbert, 'can be fairly judged by a play of which one half is deliberately suppressed?'[89] Actually, the play is not pure Shakespeare, but his complaint is generally just.

Gilbert's venom at the mistreatment of old plays is matched by rage at the denigration of the new. Quoting from Percy Fitzgerald's *Principles of Comedy and Dramatic Effect* (1870), he lambastes the 'reckless reverence' with which Fitzgerald quotes and approves passages from past plays and suggests that the critic try to 'work himself up into a state of frothy enthusiasm' for a contemporary dramatist. His aim should be to 'determine beforehand to make the very best of everything – to respectfully attribute *(sic)* all obvious blunders to a knowledge of human nature far deeper than even his (Mr. Fitzgerald's) own'. He will then be astonished to find 'how really excellent a modern dramatist such as James Albery may be'.[90]

Gilbert is not always critical. He does, for instance, concede that new plays may expect a more respectful treatment than Shakespeare, though even here he refers to the exceptions in 'ill-disciplined theatres when the actors are self-willed and opinionated, and the author a man of no influence'.[91] Elsewhere, it is the critics who are blamed, they being far too ready to damn modern originality. In 1870, he invited the critical killjoy to approach an old play that he considers faultless 'in the cold, sneering, captious, ready-made frame of mind in which he deals with a modern piece'. He will then 'be annoyed to find how thoroughly farcical and impossible, how vapid, how utterly idiotic' the old comedy may be made to appear.[92]

Another problem was that of foreign imports. The influence of the French drama was for Gilbert a considerable bête noire, though, of course, he himself frequently translated and adapted French models.

Particularly influential was the Théâtre du Palais-Royal, which already had a longish history, having started as a puppet theatre built in 1784 to the designs of the architect Victor Louis.

The Théâtre du Palais-Royal is a vivid example of the vicissitudes which Gilbert so much feared. In 1790, it was taken over by a Mademoiselle Montansier, becoming known as the Théâtre Montansier and enlarged in 1791 to increase both stage and audience capacity. However, in 1807, Napoleon's so-called decree on the theatres introduced significant constraints. From a diet of dramas and translated Italian operas, the theatre now became used for lighter fare, such as acrobatics, rope dancing, performing dogs, and Neapolitan puppets. In 1812, its fortunes sank further. It was converted into a café with shows.

The importance of the *Théâtre Montansier* comes, for us, from its afterlife. After the July Revolution, some of the earlier restrictions were relaxed, the theatre being reopened as the Théâtre du Palais-Royal. It now had a licence to present *comédies, vaudevilles,* and *comédies mêlées d'ariettes*, among which were some early works by Hervé, later its chief musical conductor. Then, in 1864, where the restrictions on genre were lifted, it began to present, not only comedies (including Feydeau farces) but also more ambitious productions including *opéras buffes* such as *La Vie parisienne*. Sophisticated French comedy with its hint of sauciness and clockwork construction was now a major European taste. Gilbert, with some misgivings, accepted this, twice adapting Meilhac and Halévy's *Le Réveillon,* first as *Committed for Trial* (1874) and then in 1877 as *On Bail*.

It would be unfair to call the fashion for French farce a constraint, but there were certainly limitations in making it acceptable for the British Lord Chamberlain. This is seen in Gilbert's adaptations of Le *Chapeau de Paille d'Italie*, in both versions of which sexual irregularity outside marriage is expunged. Interestingly, the *Times* critic regarded the second (musical) version as outmoded, or at least based on a 'somewhat old-fashioned farce'. Perhaps, Gilbert was not surprised. The French farce formulae, though financially profitable, were not specially to his taste. Writing of the success of *The Wedding March,* he tells us that he had been paid 'considerably more than £2,000 in return for two days' labour, although it was 'little more than a bald translation' and 'the dialogue was, in itself, contemptible'. A little earlier he had in the same spirit written his 'free and easy' version of Meilhac and Halévy's *Le Roi Candaule*. Here again a feeling that all this was pre-prepared hack work added to a wider artistic disgruntlement.

ii.

The use of French drama was for Gilbert never a matter of proselytizing. French farce was something he used, assimilated, and outgrew. What remains notable is that Victorian English drama was far less insular than people often believe. One borrowing was the distinctly risqué *Dominos Roses* which directly spawned *The Pink Dominos*, a farce in three acts by James Albery. This involves a plan by two wives to test their husbands' fidelity at a masked ball, with the complication of a mischievous maid who wears gowns similar to those of the spouses. What is notable is its degree of success. First performed in 31 March 1877, it ran for a record-setting 555 performances. This was far better than the artistically superior *Engaged*. Although Gilbert admired Albery, the difference rankled. Again it encouraged Gilbert to be mistrustful of audience taste.

One thing that Gilbert did value was the French idea of the well-made play. One reason for omitting Sergeant Meryll's 'Laughing Boy' aria from *The Yeomen of the Guard* was his sense that its inclusion held up the action. It prevented a sufficiently rapid onward thrust to the arrival of Jack Point and Elsie Maynard.[93] Elsewhere, his dislike of poor construction is shown frequently in his burlesque reviews targeting cliché-driven characterization, over-plotted construction, unlikely sensation, ridiculous dialogue, heavy-handed exposition, and impossible dénouement. These too reflect disdain for popular modes, though the wit and zest of the treatment gives them a buoyancy which limits any mordant effect.

One of Gilbert's frequent butts is Dion Boucicault whose *Jezebel* features many of the above, not least the stock sensation character, the Female Fiend, who needs no motivation for her wicked acts. In *A Sensation Drama,* she was to become the fiend with yellow hair (based on Lady Audley), but in the *Jezebel* parody, it is the extreme rapidity of decision, the intensity of expression, the total lack of nuance, and the lurching to ever-greater extremes that make her dialogue funny. Above all, Gilbert offers an implicit criticism of the unlikely stage device of a character blatantly telling an audience what is necessary (a) for understanding his/her nature and (b) for following the plot.

Artificial self-revelation is not always a fault. In farce, it may itself be a comic device, as it is in John Maddison Morton's *Drawing Rooms, Second Floor and Attics* (1864). Usually, however, it is part of a wider reliance on cliché of content and treatment. Often, in burlesque, humour is gained by the deliberate juxtapositions. Searing emotion (usually remorse) may be linked with (a) a precise time-sheet or (b) the material existence of solid objects brought into the emotion's orbit. In the parody of *Lost in London,* both apply, Nellie remarking:

> I almost wish I hadn't run away with Sir Gilbert. I really feel some remorse at having left poor Job – and I express it by fainting over the furniture every quarter of an hour.

Eventually, after doing this several times, she '*Dies over three-legged stool*', thereby echoing Ethel, the tragically unfortunate music mistress, who, discovering that her last matrimonial hope, Langdale is already married, similarly '*Falls over the grand piano and dies*'.

The humour in the Gilbertian parodies may hardly seem to suggest constraints, but it does suggest the clichéd theatre-world which he was seeking to combat. In Ethel's case, he does this by reducing the character to an archetype (*'Enter ETHEL; or Only A Life'*), and making her wretched sufferings an absurd cliché of disillusion and loss. Also mocked are the limitations imposed on sexual passion. The young love between Ethel and Hilton, the son of a retired linen-draper, is conveyed thus:

HILTON: Ethel, I have orange hair and no forehead to speak of, but I adore you.

ETHEL: I am a most superior young person, yet, cub as you are, I worship you.

From this, the plot moves by rapid, melodramatic transitions to a tableau of loneliness and insignificance, the humour lying (a) in a mix of direct exposition and irrelevant detail, and (b) in the blend of suppressed deep feeling with mundane information, knowledge of which seems to have been largely fortuitously acquired.[94]

Gilbert's admittedly amused impatience with theatrical conventions leads to his burlesquing romantic love altogether. Sexual attraction, lust, and emotional complexities cannot, for censorship reasons, be allowed on the public stage. In retaliation, he will mock the extreme and melodramatic positions to which playwrights are forced in lieu. Obviously, one could argue that Gilbert *himself* finds sexual representation difficult, in which case the 'constraint' is equally an opportunity. But he is also acutely aware of the mundane realities which limit emotional transcendence. In *Allow Me to Explain,* John Smith may be reckless to absurdity but, faced with the crunch of a full-scale elopement, even he cannot take the demands of the pressure:

ANNA: We will fly to –

SMITH: Putney!

ANNA: Putney! Nonsense. Petroleum!

SMITH: Petroleum!

ANNA: Yes – the Oil City!

CADDERBY: Oh, this is going too far![95]

Here, the fun makes a serious point. Rhapsodic enthusiasm is likely to evaporate in the face of common sense considerations but an audience, lapping up romantic melodramatic sensation, seems to be blind to it.

iii.

The limiting nature of audience taste means that Gilbert sees his comedy role essentially as one of subversion. 'Going too far' in the above is not just a pun. It is an actual expression of the ludicrous extremes to which the non-realistic theatre has moved. One undercutting technique is to weave the time-bound and mundane into emotional transcendence. Nellie's fainting 'every quarter of an hour' reduces torment to Pavlovian automatism. It is a variant of Casilda measuring by her watch the time intervals in her agonizing parting from Luiz. A linked device is to puncture the false or extreme with the likely and actual. This, notable in John Smith, also applies to Cadderby, Anna's husband, who, though not a party to her actually laudable motives, remains in his alarm prosily matter-of-fact.

The point about Cadderby is that he really believes his wife intends adultery. He anticipates her flight with the man on whom his annuity depends. At the same time, his response is both eminently practical and almost ruefully stoical. Though at one point he calls Smith an 'infernal ruffian', his concern is as much for his allowance as his marriage. Stunned by his wife's apparent romantic frenzy, he does not commit suicide, go mad, or fire a revolver. He takes steps to lock up her clothes.

The incursion of the prosaic and practical is in Gilbert a defiance. It is a way of mocking the impositions of theatrical excess. But in certain areas, the clichés – and the characters – become really irksome. One such is the singing chambermaid; another is the low comedian. The latter is the sort of 'comic footman in an exaggerated livery and impossible whiskers', whose only duty, according to *The British Playgoer*, is to 'announce names wrongly and to fall down with a tray of ices and apples'. Equally resented (though comically exploited) is the intrusive scene painter. This is interesting because Johnson's last act scenery for *Firefly* was, Gilbert admits, 'especially good'. Nonetheless, his incursion as a fictional character in *Not Guilty* is ridiculous. Gilbert, always disliking show-offs, liked the sets but in his critique clearly repudiates the painter's self-advertisement.

The caustic response to Johnson's egotism is well caught in a review in the *Illustrated Times* (20 February 1869). Here, Gilbert finds it 'impossible to give a clear outline of the plot' but highlights Johnson's taking the liberty of rushing on the stage four or five times whenever his sets are applauded. Behind this, there is again a serious point: set-changes often extended a show to unbearable lengths, demanding long hiatuses or routine filler-scenes before the curtain. Gilbert's use of a two-act structure for most of the Savoy Operas is an innovation aimed at avoiding such elongations, while also incidentally cutting down on scene-provision expense.

There were, it is true, ways of adding colour and excitement to technical necessity. One major scenic innovation was the panorama. This, first used on the London stage in 1792, was set up in a circular building where the audience, sitting on a central platform, was totally surrounded by a continuous painting. Later Daguerre went on to invent the diorama where the audience sat on a platform that revolved to show paintings on proscenium-like stages. Gilbert did not lambaste such developments, but his own approach was simpler, favouring contrasting locations. The sets for most of his operas are carefully contrasted – sun-lit rocky seashore followed by a ruined chapel by moonlight; exterior of a quaint sun-soaked fishing village followed by interior of a gloomy Gothic castle. What he did disdain was the scene-stealer, allowing him yet more shafts against Johnson. At one point, a party of convicts is heard to remark: 'Our punishment is severe enough without *his* constant presence'. Then, he turns up on a deserted battle field. Finally, after even the audience starts hissing, somebody suggests he should be chained to the wings. This presumably happens, for at the curtain call everyone appears except Johnson whose chains can be heard rattling as he endeavours in vain to escape.

iv.

The Gilbertian disdain for self-important personnel is matched by irritation at one other element: sheer incompetence. Here, apart from obvious matters such as forgetting lines or moves, what is most highlighted is a failure in the necessary art of voice-projection. Enunciation was, for Gilbert, a key requirement. It explains why he often listened to rehearsals from the top gallery. Reviewing *Barnaby Rudge* (24 November 1866), he informs us that 'A PARTY WITH FIGS IN HIS MOUTH' appears in the first act to say 'Chow chow, Popchip, chock chow chobbles', to which a Stranger answers, 'Terroo. The young a-man says a-well'. Nor is this the end. The alleged chewer remarks, 'Catchow cockchaw chop bow wow chick', later adding, 'Catchow cockchaw chop bow wow chick', all of which is accepted by the other characters as clear utterance. The most that can be said is that it is better than the enunciation of a character in the anonymous *Helen Douglas*. He, we are told, runs all his words together, giving us, for instance, 'Thencomeandstaywithusaslongasyoulike' and the even more unwieldy 'Howcanheprosecutehisplans *(gulp)* unlesslaskhim?'[96]

The play which most roused Gilbert's ire is, however, *East Lynne*, premiered at the Surrey Theatre on 5 February 1866. Adapted from Mrs. Henry Wood's best-seller, this had an apparently unintelligible Avonia Jones, in the star role of Lady Isabel Carlyle. Gilbert mocks her simply by the use of the word 'mumble' denoting inaudibility: 'Then I go. Mumble, mumble ... He does not meet his mumbles, for unexplained mumbles, in yonder mumble at mumble'. Gilbert's own rehearsal methods would have quickly ironed out such incompetence. Decima Moore, the first Casilda, tells us that the dramatist 'would read out a line of dialogue, clapping his hands between the words to emphasize their rhythm, thus:

"I've no patience *(clap)* with the presumption (clap) of persons *(clap)* in his plebeian *(clap)* position *(clap)*".

This shows his assertive sense of there being a clear right way to declaim a line, as also his love of alliteration to heighten the rhythms and dramatic emphasis.

It is impossible now to be sure how far the constraints and limitations really irked Gilbert and how far he saw them as a facilitator for his own satire. Sometimes, his response is simply to mock the ridiculous by taking it a stage further. It moves into the mad literalism of the surreal. In the *Ethel* review, when Mrs. Montgomery tells a character to avaunt, he avaunts. In *Nellie's Trials*, after doctors give Sprawley an electric shock by mistake, there is a tableau of 'SPRAWLEY *dressed in somebody else's electric shock*'. This – fortuitously looking forward to the notorious electric corset or electropathic belt – is more amusing than critical. It suggests pleasure in the ridiculous. But elsewhere there is real annoyance. In *Jezebel,* for the sake of visual effects, 'the scene is shifted for no necessary reason from South America to the Rhine ... [and] ... all the characters turn up together in different quarters of the globe without any sufficiently ostensible reason'. In other plays, almost everything is lampooned. The British playgoer, says Gilbert:

> ... must allow that young ladies of high distinction are in the habit of rambling alone in dismal forests, long after the rest of the family have gone to bed, and that, rambling under such circumstances, they always meet with a villain and a thunderstorm. He must accept the proposition that bad men are in the habit of revealing in soliloquies their most audacious projects, and that whenever they do so, a good man is crouching behind a bush, listening to them.

This is exasperation mixed with satire, mixed with fun, making a pretty good sample of Gilbert's mingled responses.[97]

Section 3: Gilbert's Writing Persona: Childhood and Theatrical Constraints

Apart from all we have covered, there is another aspect which must affect a writer's creative achievement. This is his own personality, augmented by early influences. In Gilbert's case, one factor was his father's periodic near-insanity and a prolonged law-suit over Joseph Gilbert's bequests.[98] But there were also various inner conflicts. There was both a need for a make-believe world and a recognition that one could not live in it. Also, there seems to have been a tendency to resist, yet be constrained by, the growing up process, which is one reason why child-adult dichotomies and inversions are such a frequent feature.

a) Children and Teenagers: Childhood and Theatrical Influences

Childhood was a major concern with W.S. Gilbert, but it is important not to exaggerate it. An interview of 1897 in *The Evening Dispatch* describes the writer as 'a genial, hearty gentleman', suggesting maturity, good nature, and a well-balanced adult personality. On the other hand, his extreme controlling tendencies hint at obsessive compulsion. They could even be a compensation for the inability to control elements of childhood trauma. Another possibility is that his adult addiction to theatre-magic reflects a desire to regain elements of childhood which he felt had been prematurely denied.

Childhood for Gilbert was very much a matter of being moved about. There was the decamping to Boulogne and soon afterwards a period of residence with the Seton Laings who were the sister and brother-in-law of Joseph's widow.[99] One constant, however, was the love of theatre and particularly of theatre pantomime. We do not know the name of the first pantomime seen by Gilbert but Drury Lane's *Harlequin and William Tell; or The Genius of the Ribstone Pippin* (26 December 1842), the afterpiece to Nicholas Rowe's *Jane Shore*, is a possibility. F.C. Burnand, who definitely *did* see it, was, like many children, only taken to his seat as the preceding tragedy was concluding. He remembered being 'considerably frightened by the awful noises, hootings, yellings and shouting' with which *Jane Shore's* last act was received. This in itself is a testimony to the rowdiness but also the enthusiasm of Boxing Night theatre audiences.[100]

Whether or not Gilbert saw the piece, it certainly gives an idea of the mode he was later to incorporate and modify. According to the *Lady's Magazine*, the show started with an allegory of the Regions of Slavery defeated by a 'very pretty little Britannia'. She overturned the fiend's power by the aid of a large detachment of little (i.e. infant) Blue Jackets and Red Jackets, which was (in the offensively deplorable language of the time) 'celebrated by a dance of emancipated 'Niggers'. This dance included – or led to – a transferring of the action to the valleys of Switzerland where William Tell embodies and sustains the liberty *motif*. Also present is a very annoying child who 'enjoys taunting his mother but also knows how to win her approval and forgiveness'. At one point, J.C. Smith playing Tell (and later doubling as Harlequin) decides to teach this lad how to use a bow and arrow. The careless use of the weapon causes it to 'find one of Tell's ears', leading, not surprisingly, to the instruction being terminated.[101]

The stage-use of children – and particularly girls such as little Miss Britannia – may in part account for the relatively juvenile and diminutive nature of many of Gilbert's characters. In *An Elixir of Love*, Jessie, the heroine, is a 'pretty little girl of eighteen' with 'soft brown eyes, and bright silky brown hair'. In *Diamonds*, the second section is called *Little Woman* and introduces us to another heroine, Mary Vyner, who writes in a 'girlish hand' and is, on the whole, 'a very good little girl'.[102] In *The Mikado*, the three little maids are fifteen-year-old schoolgirls, as, in a sense, are *Utopia Limited's* Nekaya and Kalyba. So what is going on? Is this a case of revelling in childhood innocence? Are we witnessing a writer of arrested sexual and emotional development, or is he simply following the mode of his childhood theatrical experiences?

A good case could be made that Gilbert did suffer from some kind of arrested development and perhaps a slightly prurient interest in barely pubescent girls. There is, for instance, the embarrassing photograph published in *The Tatler* in 1904, showing him staring avidly at the bare buttocks of a small statue of a reclining nymph.[103] But if he did feel such an attraction, it is at least as likely that he remained expressively inhibited; that he *liked* the idea of girlhood innocence; and that he found the restrictions on sexual depiction broadly in line with his own outlook, social conditioning, and innate temperament. Not all young females appeared as Britannia, a nymph or a fairy – we remember Ruskin's disgust at the smoking female thieves in *Ali Baba* – but usually, and certainly with writers such as Planché, charm was predominant.

The fact that children and teenagers were such a main feature of the pantomime undoubtedly affected Gilbert's later work. Even the men are often infantilized. Like Jenny Wren and Fortunio, Rose and Robin are a little maid and little man. Lisa is a child-bride who is also distinctly child-*like*. Also relevant are the Gilbert-controlled children's productions of *H.M. S. Pinafore* and *The Pirates*. Nonetheless, the child-adult is hardly all-pervasive. Even if we ignore the well-built heavy contraltos, there are plenty of Gilbertian females who are voluptuous and statuesque. Mary Vyner is set against Lady Julia Domner, a haughty imperious beauty with a marble face and copious blue-black hair. Lady Bertha in *The Triumph of Vice* is a 'magnificent animal', six-feet tall, with an imposing bust.

It is true that some of the above features are merely required for the story. Bertha's 'splendid proportions' are, for instance, necessary because the plot requires her to shrink. But even girls not so afflicted can be tall and commanding. Princess Zara was created by the naturally tall Nancy McIntosh who, despite performing deficiencies, was intended to appear decisive and forthright. Julia Jellicoe is both forceful and dominant. The point matters for two reasons. One is that Gilbert often worked in paired contrasts – Julia being set against Lisa; Lady Julia against Mary Vyner, the lively chattering Tessa against the more reticent Gianetta. The other is that some critics dismiss the Savoy Operas for the absence of a sexual element. Women, as in early Dickens, are either virgins or frumps.[104] One need only mention Little Buttercup or the modified Lady Sophy to refute this. Elsewhere, what are dismissed as marionette-like simplifications in the characterization may suggest faults in the playing. One difficulty with Gilbert and Sullivan is not to be vulgarly and overtly sexual but to be stylish enough to avoid the merely coy.

The idea of Gilbertian females as marionette-like may be related to two factors. One is the influence of *Commedia dell'arte* models, and the other is his own alleged emotional retardation. There is no doubt that his stage design, taking in every detail of set, costume, and movements (or 'drills', as he called them), involved the reduction of character to the type rather than the complex individual. But perhaps the approach is more military than reflective of arrested personal development. Much could be made of the fact that the blocks he uses to represent women are smaller than those representing men, but this reflected physical actualities in his company. His three little maids were, for instance, naturally petite, this in itself stimulating his scenario conceptions.

Gilbert's production methods are certainly strict. 'My method of stage management', he says,

> is to go down to rehearsal with every detail prearranged and set down upon paper. I work out the scenes by means of small wooden blocks on a miniature stage, on a half-inch scale. The blocks representing men are three inches in height, those representing women two and a half inches, and each block is one inch in breadth. The blocks for the principals are variously coloured, while for the male chorus they are black, for the female white.[105]

Here what one notices is that the overall picture supersedes the creative needs of the individual – a trait linked with, though different from, the fact that characters are rarely allowed to relate personally to the audience. There are rare exceptions – as when Mr. Cadderby makes an amusing last attempt to explain himself, or Ko-ko gives us a wry look, or the Duchess of Plaza-Toro directs a pointed criticism towards the band – but usually characters are kept strictly within the bounds of a pre-ordained enclosing scenario with the author-director definitively pulling the strings.

The controlling element may itself reflect a childlike aspect. Andrew Marvell's *To Little T.C. in a Prospect of Flowers* has a double implication. The title suggests a miniature portrait of the child (Theophila Cornwell), with her head set against an encircling floral background. But equally it suggests the pretty-as-a-picture sight of a little girl in the garden studiously talking to the flowers she has picked and high-handedly imagining – and decreeing – their destinies. One point here is that the girl herself is a fragile bud. She may herself be subject to the early frost of infant mortality. But what the poet is also showing is how rigidly controlling – and indeed imperious – children can be. Gilbert's controlling and organizing tendencies seem to have developed early, as shown by his single-handed management of a schoolboy production of his own *Guy Fawkes*. Whether this reflected an innate character trait or was a compensatory product of neglect is debatable. It does, however, produce a tension whereby his demand for naturalistic playing is set against extreme rigidity of initial concept.[106]

Even here, the constraints should not be exaggerated. George Grossmith almost certainly devised his own odd crouching gait for Mr. Wells during the Incantation, and sometimes a mix of the naturalistic and the highly choreographed can be doubly effective. What is not in doubt is that Gilbert struck many as more serious than droll. 'Is that

Mr. Gilbert? Why he doesn't look a bit funny!' was the remark of a lady overheard at a dinner. To some, he was a man 'whose very smiles were austere – a man with stern eyebrows, whose manner was all restraint, whose gestures were of the fewest, whose spoken humour was not a bit "rollicking"'. This is the reverse of the hearty genial Gilbert of the *Evening Despatch*, making the word 'Gilbertian' difficult to quantify. Gilbert himself affected to be unsure what it meant. The most he would concede was that there might be a general note running through a man's work which others – not he – might recognize as characteristic.[107]

The above is significant for two reasons. One is that it suggests an element of self-withdrawal – a refusal to give too much away. The other is that it implies an element of contradiction. We know that at children's parties, Gilbert could indeed be 'rollicking'. We also know that in private adult entertainments he could behave with a rather wild buffoonery, as he did at the Bancrofts' improvised mock-trials. The opposite is his dour acting of Harlequin compared by Hollingshead to a performance by Oliver Cromwell. Perhaps this suggests another limitation: that he could only allow his own character to breathe (a) in familiar company in privately staged conditions or (b) when – as at children's parties – he could relax and discard adult constraints while still retaining a controlling, organizing influence.

ii.

Given that Gilbert is no longer available to be psycho-analysed, our best clue to possible inhibition lies in the works. And here we find mixed signals. In both plays and stories, young girls are frequently idealized. Soft, sweet, non-sexualized femininity is enchanting. It suggests a Gilbert who is unhappy with post-pubescent female sexuality. Yet this view may be challenged in two respects. One is that (as in other authors) some constraints are due to censorship. The other is that many of his sweet young girls are in context strongly satirized. Some, like the outwardly charitable Rose Maybud, are shown to be selfish and mercenary. Others like the criminally disposed Alice Brown go considerably further, being both amoral and irredeemably vicious.

Undoubtedly, Gilbert feels greater freedom to develop the vicious and criminal elements in works not designed for the stage. But even non-staged written material could be heavily criticized, as happened with Hardy's *Jude the Obscure*. This text was renamed *Jude the Obscene* by the *Pall Mall Gazette*, whose critic branded it a work of 'naked squalor and ugliness'. The Bishop of Wakefield allegedly threw his copy into the fire. Even Edmund Gosse was moved to ask: 'What has Providence done to Mr Hardy that he should rise up in the arable land of Wessex and shake his fist at his creator?'[108] Nowadays, religious challenge and political danger-areas can still excite protest, as happened in 2006 in relation to Richard Bean's play *Up on Roof* at the Hull Truck Theatre. Set in a prison, the play – whose characters include Jesus – contained two or three references to Mohammed which, in the light of the Danish cartoon furore, Bean was advised to excise.[109] Another example is *My Name Is Rachel Corrie* which struggled to be seen in New York, finally – and despite Zionist efforts at prevention – being performed in 2006 by the Minetta Lane Theatre in Greenwich Village.[110]

Even though censorship was and remains a contentious area, it can at least help to limit self-indulgence. This is jocularly shown in Gilbert's poem *The Student* where editorial interference is mocked, even as the material being edited is lampooned. The poem starts with a lengthy account of what the idle student was *not* thinking of, leading to the following extended clarification:

> (Here in nineteen verses he explains his reasons for not thinking of the subjects enumerated in the preceding twenty-seven.)

One point here is that Gilbert presents *himself* as the student lawyer-writer. As with his burlesques of *Randall's Thumb* and *An Old Score*, the poem suggests that he can laugh at himself, though this need not imply that he would accept such mockery from other people.[111]

Whatever the degree of editorial constraints, Gilbert in print was well able to pursue themes of maidenly vice. What is notable, however, is that this is never sexual. Gentle Alice Brown's sexual expressiveness is limited to winking at a respectable young man who also winked at her. The humour lies in the horror this arouses (for instance, in her priest) when her deeds of murder and theft are passed over as immature frolics. The impression is of Gilbert being *selectively* subversive, highlighting the violence while subverting the sex. Possibly, the treatment also suits his own tendency. Is he perhaps keen to avoid issues of female sexuality? Does he even indirectly punish girls for having a sexual nature at all, through depictions of maidenly nastiness and viciousness?

There are various ways of considering the above. One view might be that maiden viciousness, for the perpetrator, is a compensation. It is a payback for repression of one's sexual identity, as applies to some degree in *The Crucible*.[112] But another view is much simpler. It is that beneath codes of imposed decorum and modest good manners young girls have just as many dark and prurient thoughts as young men. A hint of this comes in one of Gilbert's essays under the pen-name the Snarler. Here at a murder trial, young ladies are shown revelling in someone else's misfortune, possibly losing individual inhibition because they are part of a corporate audience.

The murder trial scenario is deliberately presented as a created spectacle. Everything is a cross between a stage show and a social occasion.

The Snarler himself is delighted: 'A more enjoyable day than that which I have just spent in the Turniptop Crown Court it has seldom been my lot to experience'.[113] The same applies, with reservations, to the charming audience of girls. Seating themselves in the gallery, with a look of beaming expectancy, they are disappointed that the star part – the murderer – is 'not much of a villain to look at, being small, dirty and unwholesome'. In addition, there is nothing really exciting or unusual about the killing. The man is charged with slaughtering 'his sweetheart (save the mark!) by kicking her on the head in the course of a drunken brawl'. The one advantage is that this simplifies the issue. It entirely removes 'any harrowing feeling of pity which a more refined or complicated murder would have aroused for the accused'.

The details of the Turniptop trial do place rather a big question mark over the Gilbertian view of Victorian maidenhood. The ladies fidget at the prospect of not hearing a death sentence, they grow bored with the witnesses and divert their attention to the young barristers, one of whom sketches a lady in the gallery, while another writes verses, and yet another makes a 'cork-man, with arms and legs of quill'. This, however, is not the end. As the cross-examination continues, 'Newspapers are produced and circulated', and papers of sandwiches and flasks of sherry are handed to the young ladies. A law-court gallery becomes itself the scene of a charming little improvised picnic.

Gilbert's depiction of the Turniptop trial is, of course, coloured by his own *persona*. Snarler, perhaps referencing Sheridan's Sneer, is a pseudonym which allows for deliberate cynicism and insensitivity. But there remains enough to suggest that Gilbert himself has no saccharine view of the fifteen-year-old maiden whom in other audience contexts he respects. Perhaps, he is merely satirizing actualities. At the Manning murder trial, many girls and women (including the Lady Mayoress) eagerly attended, while at the Courvoisier process fully one-half of those present were 'fashionably attired individuals of the feminine gender'. As for the theatrical link, this is shown later in the century at the Eleanor Pearcey trial. Here, *The News of the World* expressed surprise at the 'sympathetic interest taken by such a large number of the fairer sex', stating that they approached the matter as they might 'a theatrical sensational drama'.

The *News of the World* was not the only complainant about the true nature of ghoulish femininity. The *Pall Mall Gazette* was appalled that 'Wives came with their husbands, brothers brought the female members of their families, mothers sat side by side with their young daughters'. The *Evening News* went further. It said it would 'gladly publish the name of every woman who disgraces her sex by rushing to that wretched sight', comparing the glee of the occasion to attendance at 'the finest kind of raree show'. This takes us far from problems of Gilbert's psychology. It suggests a cross between a theatre spectacle and an exhibition of circus freaks.[114]

iii.

Gilbert's Turniptop scenario is not, then, even in a Snarler, a sign of a sadistic pathology. What it highlights is not so much bloodthirstiness as frivolity and flirtatiousness. Notable too is that Snarler includes himself among the satirized. He shares the gallery with the ladies and writes that they all enjoyed themselves exceedingly. By using the *persona*, Gilbert is able to enhance yet distance his own natural cynical tendency. This adds a double perspective, but it hardly suggests a personal disjunctive psychology.

The relative harmless of the Turniptop critique prevents our seeing it as reflecting deep childhood angst. But it still does hint at elements of mistrust. Maidens who might be idealized on stage become as *spectators* unpleasant, trivial and latently – perhaps vicariously – ghoulish. This may be a coded way of implying that audiences are always dangerous. At the Pearcey trial, the *Pall Mall Gazette* tells us:

> Hours after hour did these ghoulish women, armed with opera-glasses, sherry-flasks, and sandwich-boxes, hang with eager curiosity upon every movement and look of their miserable sister, whose fate was so firmly fixed from the outset. To the end they stayed, for the solemn closing scene had special attraction for them. These women were not the wives and daughters of labourers and coster-mongers, but ladies of gentle birth and no inconsiderate position.

Gilbert's approach is to exaggerate for the purposes of satire. Seeming to collude in something base or disagreeable, he actually highlights its vulgarities.

iv.

Gilbert's fear of audience reaction is bound up with his disparagement of audience taste. The fear is that they will fail to appreciate his work because they are ill-informed, vulgar, over-critical, and impervious to wit. More widely, there is a sense that the world cannot live up to his make-believe possibilities. He is disillusioned by reality. Perhaps, it is this which encourages his fondness for magical devices such as transformative lozenges. In the libretti, it works two ways. On the one hand, the magical transformations suggest dissatisfaction with the real. On the other, since the effects are usually disastrous, the escape hardly trumps the constraints.

The constraints of the real are indirectly suggested in Snarler's satire. The name Turniptop itself clearly suggest a backward-looking peasant community. It is the kind of 'primitive' rural place appropriate to the nature of the murderer and his unglamorous crime. This reflects one of

Gilbert's dualities: he both insists on reality and seeks to evade it. When the judge requests the verdict, the ladies rise. They leave the courtroom. They do not dare to hear the long-awaited death sentence. One target here is the whole cult of middle-class sensation, then emanating from lady novelists. Not only is sensation undercut. When drama becomes the reality, it turns human. We hence feel less free to enjoy it.

There is another aspect to the Snarler mode. It helps expose what Anne Tyler calls 'the heartbreaking silliness of everyday life'.[115] This, including frivolity, may also imply insensitivity and crassness in the face of real pain. When in Turniptop the sentence is pronounced, 'a shriek in the crowd at the back of the court tells that the sentence has gone home somewhere'. Another irony is that Gilbert still supplies a jocular ending. We are invited to think that a good time was had by all, though clearly the shriek implies the opposite.

The irony of the ending shows Gilbert in his mordant black comedy vein. This is the Gilbert we associate with Waugh, Joe Orton, and N.F. Simpson. But there is a further element because what the author is really contrasting is the false world of literature and the real one of actuality. In most sensation novels, the crimes occur in high society. There are nearly always attendant excitements such as madness, conflagrations, and dramatic tableau events. This is the sort of thing that, in *The Hooligan*, Gilbert was completely to undercut. The setting there is a cell, the crime is sordid and the culprit inadequate. In rural *Turniptop*, Gilbert satirizes sensation by suggesting its opposite. In *The Hooligan,* he actually reveals that opposite, doing so in an urban setting, devoid of satire, while giving an intricate study of the mind of the person condemned.

v.

Whatever the influences, personal and public, there is no doubt that Gilbert avoids highly sexualized treatments. The focus tends in other directions: to blushing virginal charm, to trivial, novelty-seeking inquisitiveness, or to selfish materialism, sometimes including actual criminality. The interesting thing is how much the modes overlap. Naivety overlies shrewdness. The blushingly modest may also be the self-seeking predatory, the former mode veiling the latter.

The exposure of hidden realities is in a sense Gilbert's moral mode. There is no preaching, but there is revelation by irony. This is why he needs an audience capable of picking up nuance. What perhaps he cannot face is female sexual vulgarity. At the (genuinely sensational) trial of Adelaide Bartlett, the women spectators were uninhibited. Hearing of sex and fetishism, they showed 'with careless mirth' that they were 'not at all in need of any protection'.[116] This would not please Gilbert. Even his frustrated Dames are never coarse. The loss is to rounded depictions. But the ironies do supply depth.

b) Make-Believe Worlds and the Harlequinade Aspect

We can guess, then, that Gilbert feels unease. He is aware but not pleased that ideal vision so often jars with the actuality. More prosaically, he disliked the excesses of stage treatments. In his account of *Ali Baba*, Ruskin enumerates 520 girls. This is before he even mentions those playing Oxford and Cambridge men or more picturesquely portraying forest flowers, chandelier lamps, or colours in the rainbow.[117] Obviously, spectacle increased during the last half of the century but even before that it had been lavish.

An example of the lavish mixed with the slapstick is the aforementioned *Harlequin and William Tell*. This included numerous crowd scenes, many featuring young girls, while the Harlequinade itself was a riot of novelty episodes. One of these had a set of tea kettles engaged in a concert for the benefit of the 'Tea-Total' Society. Another had the shooting off of the head of a gentleman in the upper circle and its return (by the 'approved method of a concatenation of bandanas'). There was also 'the precipitation of the Clown into the pit' and a lot of noisy interruption from people in the gallery who wanted the clown-figure to sing 'Hot Codlins'.[118] One interesting detail is the mention of a deputy clown. This was a three-legged gentleman from the Isle of Man who performed a jocular, presumably solo, *pas de trois*.[119]

The rowdiness of Victorian theatre may help to explain why Gilbert, fearing disruption, augmented his natural tendency to discipline and control.[120] Perhaps, indeed, it was fear of anarchy that encouraged the running of a relatively small company.[121] *Utopia Limited* admittedly makes considerable staging demands and has a large cast of principals, but this is nothing to the number required for the burgeoning pantomime. In 1880, Augustus Harris, preparing for *Mother Goose*, writes of the necessity of literally hundreds of interviews with property men, costumiers, scenic artists, ironsmiths, musicians, clowns, shoemakers, acting managers, advertisers, drapers, carpenters, rope-makers, and supers.[122] Besieged from morning till night, he is kept rushing for forty-eight hours at a time to places such as Newcastle, Birmingham, and Paris.[123] Gilbert's reaction, judging by his parodies, is against such excess. But also included is a dislike of the reduction of the Harlequinade. His own suggestion is that it be integrated with a more morally controlling ethical element. How far he really believes this is debatable because he usually conveys it through burlesque.

This moral concern requiring some kind of accountability has a double back-history. On the one hand, it links with the concept of pantomime as a medium for 'innocent instruction', which is favoured by Ruskin, Carroll, and Charles Dickens. On the other, it goes *against* the 18th-century trend where, even among the more lofty idealists, morality is hardly central. John Weaver's *Harlequin turn'd Judge* (1717) shows the rogue-dancer taking bribes from both sides 'without doing justice to either'. The *Harlequin Sheppard* pantomimes present him as a Jack-the-lad outlaw. This folk-hero element was not, however, entirely unchallenged. On 21 June 1731, the apprentice's annual show was famously changed from the bawdy and subversive *The London Cuckolds* to the more instructive *The London Merchant*. Equally, in Henry Fielding's *Eurydice Hiss'd* (1737), Honestus, who is the locus of moral virtue, urges his friend the author Pillage to:

> Give us a good tragedy for our money,
> And let not Harlequin still pick our pockets,
> With his low paltry tricks and juggling cheats
> Which any school-boy, was he on the stage,
> Could do as well as he.[124]

The advice looks to the Gilbert of *A Consistent Pantomime*, where, in a legal setting, Harlequin's magic is to be used to advance the satire of corruption in everyday life.[125]

Questions of morality may to some seem almost ironic, Gilbertian comedy being regarded merely a kid-glove enforcement of white male conservative values. But actually this is seldom the case. Only at the end is order restored. Only then do we get the final re-imposition of a status quo acceptable to a mainly middle-class bourgeois audience. Before that, the almost continual subversion is a more satirical form of the Clown's Harlequinade challenge. It is as if good order is itself in danger of being chased away, as occurs (for instance) in *The Sorcerer* where marital alliances become steadily less normative.

The Sorcerer is a good example of the slapstick mode of tea-kettle Harlequinades becoming a more sophisticated vehicle for literary and social satire. Mocking cup-and-saucer dramas, grand operatic banqueting and the aesthetic tea-pot ideal, the Brindisi may also include an allusion to the temperance tea-party scene in William Sewell's *Hawkstone* (1845). This is a novel supporting the authority of the High Anglican Church against a Roman Catholic temptation, associated by some with subversive forces hardly less dangerous than a sorcerer's magic. It also includes the character Marmaduke Brooks (a radical) who may well have been the ironic spur for the name of Gilbert's old-world baronet Sir Marmaduke.

Whether or not *Hawkstone* is directly referenced, the fact remains that variants on a gathering chaos are common in Gilbert. They are seen in the pantomimic collapse of order and decorum in *Thespis* and *The Grand Duke*, and in a stronger form in *Iolanthe* where Strephon's legislative reforms threaten a different, more radically political, overturn. Sometimes, the challenge itself provoked constraints. In *Iolanthe*, D'Oyly Carte was worried about possible offence from the wearing of regalia by the male chorus. In addition, the highly satirical de Belville song was cut, and there was press complaint about Strephon's aria linking crime with deprivation, *The Theatre* considering it 'jarring' for a fairy opera to include radical critique, especially in linking social disruption with a lack of personal nurture.

Not all of Gilbert's works suggest the dangers of chaos. The opposite mode is that of *Utopia Limited*. Here, too much good order and stable control is resented as bringing a merely dull prosperity. It offers a prospect of life without challenges. The ending (introducing a parliamentary party system to ensure prosperous chaos) is a joke, but it does include a quizzical questioning as to whether Britain and her splendid institutions are as admirable as the British like to assert.[126]

The quizzical doubt within his moral and social positives means that Gilbert can never be seen as a complacent, conservative optimist. Yet there is undoubtedly a core of allegiance to the fixed centre, without which chaos may indeed follow. One reason for his not being quite in the main stream was the popularity of the sentimental mode which was alien to his clinical subversions. Another was his use of a semi-surreal element rather than warm-hearted human interest and a deal of emotional utterance passing as character depth. The *Times* review of the revived *Engaged* refers grudgingly to some grotesque humour but regards the characters as 'mere incidental sketches'. Worse still, 'female interest' (as the critic terms it) 'even as Mr. Gilbert understands it, does not exist'. The other complaint rather paradoxically is about a lack of realism. Neither Mrs. Beerbohm Tree nor Miss Norreys, we are told are allowed 'for a moment to lapse into common sense'.[127]

Gilbert's revenge for the limitations of popular expectation is mainly seen in his withering parodies. Perhaps, like Honestus, he looks back to better times 'when better actors acted better plays' and, incidentally, 'the town paid less'. But more likely he is simply lampooning a dearth of current quality, using the already long-tried mode of criticism by parody. The *Lady*'s account of *Harlequin William Tell* refers to the 'funny parody' of the archery scene in Knowles' play and the jokes gained from the Gesler cap affair. The reference is to James Sheridan Knowles, the writer of the original *William Tell* play (premiered in 1825), where Gesler (actually, Gessler), the newly appointed *Vogt*, raises a pole under the village linden tree, hangs his hat on the top, and demands that everyone should bow to it.

How far Harlequinade characters were themselves a limiting factor is itself debatable. In his childhood, they influenced Gilbert deeply, but even here wonderment was tinged with a moral dye. On the one hand, for a young man or woman 'to be a Harlequin or Columbine was the summit of earthly happiness'. On the other, the condition of Clown or Pantaloon was a 'fitting purgatory in which to expiate the guilty deeds of a life misspent'.[128] The latter seems to glance at pre-Grimaldi modes where the Clown *was* routinely punished. Frequently, it was Harlequin who attacked him, beating him severely for boasting and cowardice, and thrusting him sometimes into the pit.

The traditional punishment of Clown was not confined to pantomime. It also occurred in *Punch and Judy* where he was often the owner of the Dog and his violence includes the killing of the baby. In this scenario, Punch often had his head struck off, matching the gentleman spectator in *Harlequin William Tell*.[129] What seems to have happened is that Grimaldi took various elements from the Scaramouche and zanni tradition and moulded them into an alternative creation. Clown, a lower-class servant of Pantaloon, dressed virtually in tatters, was elevated. He became the main initiator of the anarchy. Before Grimaldi, the character had mainly been significant as an antic device for slowing Pantaloon in his pursuit of the lovers.

The idea of Clown as a symbol of Anarchy is deliberately inverted in Gilbert's own *Harlequin Wilkinson*. But in reality, the change can be traced directly to one year – 1800. This was when Grimaldi starred at Sadlers Wells in Charles Dibdin's *Peter Wilkin; or Harlequin in the Flying World*, the name 'Wilkin' possibly being the source of Gilbert's 'Wilkin-son' spin-off. For the new more anarchic Clown, Dibdin introduced a costume variant, this being 'garishly colourful ... patterned with large diamonds and circles, and fringed with tassels and ruffs'. Later in the same year, the Drury Lane Harlequin also had a makeover. In *Harlequin-Amulet; or, The Magick of Mona*, he became romantic and mercurial, instead of mischievous. This left Grimaldi's Clown as the undisputed agent of chaos, which is how Gilbert too – with some misgivings – usually presented him.[130]

In some ways, the white-face agile satirical Grimaldi was the performing equivalent of Gilbert himself. Like Gilbert, though in more slapstick vein, he satirized contemporary British life, making comic mockery of absurdities in fashion and taste, as Gilbert would do in relation to the Aesthetic Movement. Nor was his influence swiftly dissipated. Dickens, we know, had seen him (in 1820, at the Star Theatre, Rochester), and after the clown's death, it was Dickens who edited and improved Thomas Egerton Wilks' clumsily written *Life*. One complaint about Gilbert's resurrection of the Clown figure was that it held him back. Dramas such as *The Fairy's Dilemma* were too full of old-fashioned tricks, lacking emotion and devoid of romantic interest.

Criticism of Gilbert often centred on a lack of spontaneity. In his serious works, he had hammered out hundreds of respectable lines, 'without striking any sacred fire'.[131] In the comedies, the accusation was of a lack of naturalness, this resulting from allegiance to a theatrical mode which had lost all its freshness. Also at fault was the limiting effect of his legal training: 'As somebody once well said, Mr. Gilbert never seemed able to shake the dust of Lincoln's-inn from his feet'. He has for a long time actually marred, if not spoiled, his works 'by ... quaint turns of fancy and love of verbal conceits'.[132] Whether this is true or not, Gilbert certainly looked back obsessively to Clown and Harlequin. It is Grimaldi's nickname 'Joey' that gives a double point to the song 'Not for Joe' mentioned in *Harlequin Wilkinson*. On the other hand, Gilbert was hardly alone in drawing on the legacy. The clown's catchphrase 'Here we are again!' was, for instance, revived in Henry James Byron's burlesque of *The Colleen Bawn*, the luckless Colleen shrieking it every time she bounced up again from yet another dip in the washing-tub.[133]

ii.

Gilbert, then, certainly drew upon his early Harlequinade experiences. But how did he relate to Clown and was it really such a limitation? Broadly speaking, what he did was to turn Clown's destructive physicality into a destructive wit. There is considerable physical violence in Gilbert scenarios, but usually, in the play scripts, it is not staged, simply alluded to. The exception is in the burlesque reviews. These are full of violence, the caveat being (a) that they are only an exaggeration of real performances and (b) that they were never actually meant to be staged.

The burlesque violence can be easily instanced. It occurs, for instance, in *Philomel* when Du Boulay and Adderley struggle with Judah, the first two falling over a cliff and catching at Judah's coat-tails which are then torn off as he holds on to a tree.[134] The comedy comes in the reaction. The whole horror is described by Judah in distinctly breezy terms: 'Here's a lark, they are smashed into little bits!' This effect is of a Clown devoid of the morality which elsewhere Gilbert seeks to impose. It leads to 'Great and comic joy of Judah at the awful death of two human beings', followed by a 'grand charivari of six or seven Comic Servants over the mutilated remains of the dead'.

It would be easy to complain at the heartlessness of the above but that would be entirely misguided. For one thing, it is a burlesque of an existing play by Henry Thornton Craven. For another, it was never meant to be acted. For a third, the horrors are presented in a context of such incongruous language that no one could take them seriously. What is most notable is the exuberant high spirits of the treatment, which again reflects the Clown influence. One exuberant example in the staged works is the 'Unction Junction' scene in *Thespis*, where, to an orchestral accompaniment including bells and whistles, the entire chorus in a kind of conga imitates a moving train. Another is the Christy Minstrels scene in *Utopia Limited*. A subtler variant is the duet 'Sing hey to you, Good day to you' in *Patience*. Here the namby-pamby nature of the oaths suits the effete aspects of Bunthorne, the fleshly poseur, while the vigour of the action (and the zestful quality of the music) add a clown-like dash of irrepressible high spirits.[135]

Judging from the above, the appeal of Clown can actually be a creative gain. Far from limiting Gilbert's talent, it releases it. Paradoxically, this may be because he is associated with a carefree *absence* of responsibility. In the unsigned but almost certainly Gilbertian *Getting Up a Pantomime*, we are told that 'The happiness of infancy lies in its total irresponsibility, its incapacity to distinguish between right and wrong, its general helplessness, its inability to argue rationally, and its having nothing whatever upon its half-born little mind'. These, we learn, are the privileges of Clown especially. The downside – given in a crushing sideswipe – is that they are equally 'the property of an idiot in a lunatic asylum'.[136]

The simultaneous lauding and denigration of both Clown and childhood is a typical Gilbert duality. His own view is of gain and loss. We 'advance in happiness as our intellectual powers expand', yet the gaining of awareness robs us of all magic. As a child, he says, he had accepted a fairy mythology almost as an incorporated part of religious faith. Now this is lost, and with it a belief in the reality of magical characters. 'I had no idea', he says, 'of a Harlequin who spent the day hours in a pair of trousers and a bad hat; I had not attempted to realize a Clown with an ordinary complexion, and walking inoffensively down Bow Street in a cheap suit'. Nor had he tried to grasp the possibility of Pantaloon being a mild but slangy twenty-two year-old or the girl dressed as Columbine paying rent 'like an ordinary lodger'.[137]

The practical aspects of theatre production, and the realities of acting life, are for Gilbert a problem. Always they conflict with the enchanted vision, being part of a mundane concern with hiring and firing, timing, and receipts. It is true that he claimed only to have written for money and expected total production control. But the former underestimates his driven quality, and the latter was in pursuit of a vision.[138] One constraint endured by Gilbert was the inability entirely to realize the inner intention. The other was the practical limitations already discussed.

iii.

Practical limitations, then, there were. But for George Augustus Sala at least there are some obvious remedies.[139] Writing in 1882, Sala suggests that managers should take a leaf out of the Hollingshead book. They should divide their pantomimes, like his burlesques, into three acts, thus ensuring 'brief intervals of rest' for both actors and audience. More generally, his view is that most pantomimes are too long, that the Harlequinade will soon be eliminated, and that audience dining times should be taken into account. Even with reform, however, success is not guaranteed. Writing of *Little Bo-Peep* (from whom Gilbert derived Peep-Bo) Sala is rueful. Splendid though it was in artistic arrangements, 'it is difficult to avoid the impression that pantomimes, properly so called, are, literally as well as figuratively speaking, on their last legs'.[140]

The sense of a dying mode is in a double sense relevant to Gilbert. This is a man who in his maturity seems to have become obsessed with both reinventing and restating the pantomime's glories. *The Grand Duke's* second act is a bacchanalian pantomime. Ludwig – winner of his position by cheating – is a comedy manifestation of both the Lord of Misrule and the Trickster. Elsewhere, the impression is more of breathing new life into old forms. The Harlequinade characters in *The Fairy's Dilemma* – though given the new twist of disorientation – hark back to the 1860s. They are a blast against a tide of modernity, including the modern spectacular. As early as 1882, Sala had suggested that the future lay, not with pantomime but with spectacular extravaganza. He also proposed that the Covent Garden and Drury Lane pantomimes should be preceded by a laughable farce or some other *lever de Rideau*. This would be a great gain. It would allow the habitual middle-class occupants of the boxes and stalls to miss it, having waited for their dinner before setting out.

iv.

The paradox that Gilbert is both old-fashioned and forward-looking is partly explained by his angle of vision. Pantomime and marionette-characters can be re-used. They may be recycled in an Absurdist or sur-real context. Nonetheless, in his latter years, he was seen as increasingly anachronistic. Certainly, he was not in tune with the rising movement towards 'Variety' or indeed to musical comedy where (in the days before Cole Porter) wit was not a notable prerequisite.

The attractions of the new is understandable, but this does not mean that that the older modes lack value. Harlequin's tricks reinvented can enforce a vision of life as itself a mechanical or soulless business. Slapstick blunders can suggest the machinery of life going wrong. The opposite is for pantomime to take the spectacular route towards the inflated overblown. 'Little Bo Peep' (according to Sala) 'begins at the unreasonable early hour of seven, and continues, *without the curtain once falling for a few minutes' interval*, for three hours and twenty minutes'. Gilbert at least never makes this error. In the operas, he favours a two-act structure, with a total performing time of well under three hours.[141] Occasionally, as in Act 2 of *The Gondoliers*, the plot may seem somewhat to stall, but even allowing for the long first act of *Utopia Limited*, there are few *longueurs*.[142] The essence of the playing is swift movement, lively variation, and keeping the audience wanting more.

v.

The generally swift pace of Gilbertian pieces may itself reflect Harlequin vigour. But the influence of the Harlequinade has another effect. It is able to suggest a double vision which possibly chimes with Gilbert's natural temperament. Both his innate pessimism and his high-spirited love of jokes do in fact find a chord in the main male *commedia* characters. They impart a degree of the mechanical to his vision but, by incorporating various character modes, allow for a rainbow of contrasting effects.

One of the modes we have already glanced at is that of disillusion. This in theatrical terms looks to Pierrot, who is usually seen as a French variant of the Italian Pedrolino. Originally, he seems to have been a 'second zanni', always on the periphery, dispensing advice that (to him, not us) seems sage, and bashfully, indecisively, and unsuccessfully courting Columbine, his master's daughter. One treatment comes in Molière's character, the lovelorn peasant Pierrot, in *Don Juan, or The Stone Guest* (1665), but many other French dramatists give Pierrot life. The most sensitive is Jean-François Regnard, famous not only as a playwright but also as a traveller, whose descriptions of the Sami people first introduced these pagan, often alcoholic, strangers to cultured Europe.[143]

There are three things that especially link Pierrot to Gilbert. The first is that increasingly he came to represent painful longing and a wistful sense of the futility of personal hope. Having at the early *Foires* been involved in general slapstick, by about 1700 he became poeticized.[144] This made him the subject, not only of poignant folksong (such as *Au clair de la lune*, sometimes attributed to Lully) but also of the art of Claude Gillot, Jean-Antoine Watteau, Nicolas Lancret, Jean-Baptiste Oudry, and Jean-Honoré Fragonard.[145] Gilbert often includes a yearning, wistful quality to his work, examples being his own version of songs to the moon, most particularly *The nightingale sighed for the moon's bright ray*, and *Fair Moon, to thee I sing*, in which it becomes a distant symbol of a greater calm. Sometimes, there is a soft yearning moment even within a context of zany burlesque farce. A particularly good instance is the moment when the model Major General, suddenly finding a lyrical Schubertian voice, offers us *Sighing softly to the river*. This is another lyric of hopeless, unrequited love where the breeze is the fickle free spirit.[146]

Another linked aspect comes when the character's wistfulness is a matter of lost or failed dreams. This applies in Princess Ida's *I Built upon a Rock*, musically enhanced by the alternation of plangent strings and heavy brass. It is also found in Julia Jellicoe's *All Is Darksome, All Is Dreary*, and on a more intimate level in Mad Margaret's *To a Garden Full of Posies*, expressing the disillusion resulting from abandonment. Although we should not make too much of it, all this is in line with some Pierrot interpretations. The Symbolists saw him as a lonely fellow-sufferer, crucified upon the rood of a soulful sensitivity, his only friend the distant moon. Meanwhile, his often frustrated pursuit of Columbine, coupled with an innate unworldly naïveté, conspired to lift him out of the *Commedia dell'Arte* into the larger realm of myth. 'I'm Pierrot', said David Bowie once, 'linking him to a suffering, poignant Everyman'.[147]

It would be absurd to make claims that Gilbert's sadder moments have a mythic significance. But they do have resonances. When Julia loses her dream of maintaining her starring Grand Duchess role, she genuinely – if briefly – contemplates suicide. In her case, a natural resilience and feisty optimism pull her through. But there is an oddly touching pathos in other examples – sometimes even in semi-comic ones, such as *Tit Willow* with its reference to Japanese blue plate designs. Whether Gilbert himself ever suffered such wistfulness of woe is debatable. But he did once say that, if his wife died, he would kill himself. Lucy, he told Mary Crawshay, was the centre of every bit of his happiness, his only peace, his safety, his unstintingly trusted guardian angel. Clearly, this is a marked dependence. Undoubtedly, a fear of losing her must have added a level of pain and anxiety to his existence.[148]

The third aspect linking with Pierrot comes when the personal extends to the more universal. One example here is *The World Is but a Broken Toy*, while a more neutral, more wondering, hint is to be found in *Comes a Train of Little Ladies*. Obviously, there are plenty of lyrics where optimism and love of life are highlighted, not least the Madrigal of the Seasons in *Ruddygore*. But the wistful note (found also in *Brightly Dawns Our Wedding Day*) seems a genuine one and hints at a latent romantic aspect in the writer's personal psyche.[149]

vi.

The links with Pierrot are, then, real, but one thing that is difficult to establish is how far they were conscious. We do know that the character is part of the tradition of the English pantomime. In 1717, as played by Mr. Griffin, he surfaces in *The Jealous Doctor; or, The Intriguing Dame*, and thereafter, he is a fairly regular feature, his most notable interpreter being Carlo Delpini (1740–1828). The limitation was that Delpini neglected the spiritual side. He 'kept strictly to the idea of a creature so stupid as to think that if he raised his leg level with his shoulder he could use it as a gun'.[150]

If Pierrot's theatrical influence is difficult to assess, there is no doubting the major impact of three other *commedia* characters. Of these, Harlequin is probably the most significant, for Gilbert revels in his tricks, his disguises, his light skipping ability to evade constraint, and his capacity for transforming one theatrical world into another. Pantaloon as an influence is less marked. Judging by *The Fairy's Dilemma*, he has associations of judicial anarchy, appealing to Gilbert's love of legal subversion but not matched in the traditional *commedia*, where he is a devious, greedy, elderly merchant, readily fooled by Harlequin's tricks. Shakespeare sees him as old and gullible, referring to him as 'lean and slippered'.[151] His near-cousin is the near-decrepit Notary in Act 2 of *The Sorcerer*, where again the link is with the law rather than merchant-trading.

By the time Gilbert was writing seriously, Pantaloon was already a diminishing figure. In the Harlequinade, he had traditionally tried to keep the young lovers separated but had been no match for Harlequin's cleverness, besides which the antics of Clown (his servant) slowed down his pursuit. Later, with the rise of Grimaldi, Pantaloon became Clown's assistant, and it was Clown and Harlequin who became more influential. Harlequin is the side of Gilbert associated with imaginative airy flight while Clown is his more destructive violent self, here linked with a cynical rather jaundiced personality.

Whatever the precise combinations, it is impossible to deny that Gilbertian comedy deals more in theatrical *commedia* types than rounded characterizations. But we should not see that as the whole of him. Even in childhood (and despite what he says about infant imbecility), Gilbert seems to have wanted a moral framework to his pantomime structures. Eventually, he began to see Harlequin as a rather tiresome bungler – one 'who delayed the fun while he danced in a meaningless way with a plain, stoutish person of mature age'. As Christmases rolled by, he also got to know some Clowns personally, and the result was not edifying. He 'was disgusted to find that they were, as a body, a humble and deferential class of men, who called me "sir" and accepted eleemosynary (charitable) brandy and water with civil thanks'.[152] The main body of *Getting Up A Pantomime* extends this disillusion, being devoted to descriptions of various personnel, none of whom emerges unscathed, not least the author. He is rather bitterly dismissed as 'by far the most *un*important of all his *collaborateurs*, writing simply to order, with dialogue framed upon the principle of telling as much as possible in the very fewest words'.

The constraints placed on the author bespeak Gilbert's sense of working in harness. But almost everybody is both constraining and constrained. Harlequin in *Getting Up a Pantomime* is the chief instructor of the corps de ballet. He addresses them individually 'with a curious combination of flowers of speech', collecting terms of endearment and expressions of abuse into a unique oratorical bouquet.[153] This seems jaundiced enough, but there is more, for the man is at the mercy of all the carpenters who are united in a conspiracy to let him break his neck if he fails to bribe them sufficiently. There is no glamour in this and no status. In the off-season he arranges ballets, teaches stage dancing, and may perhaps be driven to 'taking a music-hall engagement'.

The rather depressing view of pantomime life helps to explain the regular note of disillusion we detect beneath the high spirits. One example comes in *Patience*. Although Bunthorne here is highly satirized, his jaundiced assertion that we cannot have the Elysian Fields, and, if we could, would only let them out on building-lots, may be played almost straight. What indeed *is* the use of yearning for what we can never get? Also included is a sense of weariness with an old and tired world. Clown in *Getting Up a Pantomime* is presented as on the wane after his glory days, 'snubbed by the manager, ignored by the author and inconsiderately pooh-poohed by the stage-manager'. His scenes are pushed into a corner and have clearly succumbed to the far greater centrality of the transformation element. The modern clown is, in fact 'a dull and uninventive person', his attempts at innovation being limited 'to the introduction of dancing dogs or a musical solo on an unlikely instrument'. Reliant on outdated tired tricks and catchwords, he is a third-rate general entertainer, a talking Harlequin – in fact, 'anything but the rough-and-tumble Clown he ought to be'.[154]

It is ironic that Gilbert, accused of tired tricks, laments them so much in others, but his rather embittered view has its own interest. For one thing, it may explain his avowed low opinion of the Savoy Operas. To the extent that they show him at his most pantomimic, they belong to a tarnished world – one whose practical constraints mean that dream can never be made reality. The anomalies are twofold. One is that he remained extremely sensitive to criticism of his work by others, and the second that playing Harlequin was to him the achievement of a lifetime dream. Eagerness to do this may help to explain his extreme sensitivity to criticism. Criticism of himself was bound up with a criticism of his own theatrical Gondal. He is himself part of his own magical world.

vii.

Gilbert's appearance as Harlequin occurred on 13 February 1878. The occasion was the Gaiety Theatre's Wednesday Matinee performance of a pantomime burlesque, entitled *The Forty Thieves*. The performance, raising £700, was a charity production, produced by John Hollingshead and sponsored by celebrities from the Beefsteak Club whose membership included Gilbert and some two hundred of his literary-theatrical peers. But what the episode really shows is how much Gilbert related to the Harlequinade concept. He had himself contributed to the writing, collaborating with Robert Reece, F.C. Burnand, and Henry J. Byron, each writing a scene for the pre-transformation section. The choreography was by John D'Auban, Gilbert's friend and the ballet-master for most of the Savoy operas. The first performance was a sell-out, favoured by many dignitaries – including the Prince and Princess of Wales – all of whom had paid a charity-enhanced ticket-price.

Our knowledge of Gilbert's obsession with the Harlequin venture sufficiently indicates his theatrical preferences. He was 'tirelessly enthusiastic'. Many times he invited the cast for dinner demanding extra rehearsals before or after the meal. The question is, what does this suggest about him? Is it that he wanted to control the venture or that, as for Dickens, theatrical role-play was a release from the stringencies of Victorian 'white male' conformity? One odd thing is that, according to Madge Kendal, he was 'the worst actor I have ever seen'. Moreover, he disliked being among great male performers, especially handsome ones. He used to belittle them, accusing them of not being able to speak Shakespearean Blank Verse.[155]

Hollingshead's verdict – written in his book *My Lifetime* – tells us most of what we need to know about Gilbert's Harlequin obsession. 'The gem of the performance' he says, 'was the grimly earnest and determined Harlequin of W.S. Gilbert. It gave me an idea of what Oliver Cromwell would have made of the character'. This may be related to Gilbert's double-edged view of theatricality generally. On the one hand, his imagination rose at the concept of airy freedom – of soaring (or leaping) into another world where magic-dust prevailed over stucco and where human limitation was transcended. On the other, his rational mind disdained the artifice. This in itself helps to make him an Absurdist. He does ridiculous things but is himself dourly, if tacitly, aware of their ridiculousness.

The tension at the heart of Gilbert prevents a fully rounded generous humanity. But in other respects, it is an asset. It lends a tensile strength to the web of airy make-believe. The downside is that his immersion in the realities of theatrical life seems to have given him all too acute an awareness of the jarring gulf between on-stage merriment and off-stage struggle. This is reinforced by two indications. One is his often pained, frequently jaundiced commentary on characters and their appearance in the *Thumbnail Studies in the London Streets*.[156] The other is a short cartoon feature which can count as an embryonic summary of the conclusions to be reached.

The cartoon in question was printed in *Fun* in late January 1862 and is a drawing with captions. Entitled GETTING UP THE COMIC BUSINESS, it depicts Columbine, Clown, and Harlequin backstage, the last holding a frothing tankard. The accompanying dialogue suggests two performers (Clown and the Columbine, whose name is Maria) arguing about the *Harlequinade*. Each is egotistically seeking prominence, but the main point lies in dichotomy. It consists in setting the commonplace workaday aspects of the speakers against the half-magical creatures they are supposed to represent.

The implications of the cartoon are obvious. Theatre magic is entirely false. Reality is harsh, rough-edged, and selfish. This is made quite clear by the brief but telling dialogue:

No it's no use you jawing at me, Marier. I haint a-going to have my business dictated by anyone, let alone the likes of you.

Why, I haint a-jawing, nor yet a dictatin'. Only what I say is this, Ned – after you have killed the old woman, I must have time to finish off my *pas* properly before the perlice comes in.[157]

Already here we see a sense of disillusion. Already we have a casual reference to 'killing', hinting at what will become a moral problem for Gilbert – the representation of anarchic fun with an absence of adequate retribution.

It is not my case that this tiny example has earth-shattering significance. But it does, I think, suggest the essence of Gilbert's comedic thinking. Airy enchantment can be delightful, but it is a ruse. In a sense it is a confidence trick. This in turn may be applied to *all* the institutions by which the social and political wheels are oiled. Everything is a construct, and that construct is actually quite flimsy. It is sawdust and paint and quibbles and playing cards. The way to survive such dross is intellectually to despise it while accommodating oneself to its practical usefulness.

There is, however, another point and it is this. Even as we are seeing through it, the very theatricality of these false displays exerts an attraction. It makes the world itself a theatre, one that, like the stage-world, is essentially tawdry but can put on a good gloss. As for attitude, this too may be morally affected: if all the world is a sham, then perhaps it is *justifiable* to play with it – to use chop-logic and manipulative argument and to misdirect and mislead. Words themselves here have a double aspect. There is the literal meaning – the dictionary definition – and there is what they appear to show. By arrangement, exclusion, and manipulation, we can exploit and change their effect as we do that on stage by moving the scenery. It is a verbal sleight of hand. It is another use of the ubiquitous playing card.

What is lacking, of course, is emotion. However much we may use words – however much we rely on them for creating fun, or surviving attacks and overcoming vicissitudes – they do not constitute the heart of our humanity. So what place do feelings have in a cardboard and painted world? Must they really be contained and repressed, even if they are genuinely felt? Gilbert, we know, rarely made public – or perhaps even private – displays of emotion. But his devotion to his wife was absolute. She combined all the caring roles, including that of mother. Perhaps, indeed, the main constraint on Gilbert – personally and in what some see as the cynical heartlessness of his writing   is not that he could not feel but that has been trained in an adult role-play repression. If so, there is a final irony, for some of his training must be due to his father – a man of known explosive tendencies who himself mixed the engaging Harlequin all too readily with the unpredictable and sometimes dangerous Clown.

* *

Notes

1 *From 'Ruddygore: An Interview with Mr. Gilbert', Pall Mall Gazette*, 21 January 1887.
2 The Kit-Cat (or Kit-Kat) Club was an early 18th-century English club in London with strong political and literary associations, committed to the furtherance of Whig objectives, meeting at the Trumpet tavern in London and at Water Oakley in the Berkshire countryside.

3 Jakob Greber, who died in July 1731, was a German Baroque composer and musician. He was in London from 1702 to 1705. He died in Mannheim, where for many years he was *Kapellmeister* of the court orchestra. Mary Pix (1666–17 May 1709) was an English novelist and playwright. Church records indicate that she lived in London, marrying George Pix, a merchant tailor from Hawkhurst, in 1684.

4 *The Haymarket Opera House, Survey of London*, Volumes 29 and 30, St. James', Westminster. Part 1 (1960), pp. 223–250.

5 Vanbrugh never seems to have pursued those who owed him money, though he was scrupulous in paying his employees.

6 Owen Swiny (1676–1754) was an Irish art-dealer and impresario. In around 1749 he made a trip to Paris for John Rich, to arrange the London tour of Jean Monnet's troupe. He died in London and was buried in St. Martin's-in-the-Fields.

7 Heidegger (1666–1749) was a Swiss count and leading impresario of masquerades. His tenure was successful, not least because of his vigorous capacity for puffing.

8 Andrea Battista Gallini (7 January 1728–5 January 1805), later known as Sir John Andrew Gallini, was a Florentine dancer, choreographer, and impresario who was made a 'Knight of the Golden Spur' by the Pope following a successful performance. In a campaign to raise the intellectual respectability of dance, on 3 March 1762, he published *A Treatise on the Art of Dancing* which was followed *by Critical Observations on the Art of Dancing* (1770). These elegantly printed volumes were largely derivative, drawing on Weaver, Cahusac, and other sources, but they were important statements of philosophy, helping his professional career.

9 Jean-Georges Noverre (1727–1810) created the physically and emotionally expressive *ballet d'action*, itself a precursor of the narrative ballets of the 19th century. Garrick called him 'the Shakespeare of the Dance'.

10 *Workers and Their Work, Sir Arthur Sullivan* (*Daily News*, 10 January 1885) and letter to *The Nation*, by George H. Nettleton (3 August 1911).

11 *Workers and Their Work, Mr. W.S. Gilbert* (*Daily News*, 21 January 1885).

12 Ebers J., Seven Years of the King's Theatre, John Ebers, William Harrison Ainsworth, 1828. See also *Athenaeum Review*, p. 596 (*The Athenaeum: A Journal of Literature, Science, the Fine Arts, Music, and the Drama*: James Silk Buckingham, John Sterling, Frederick Denison Maurice, Charles Wentworth Dilke, Henry Stebbing, Thomas Kibble Hervey, William Hepworth Dixon, Norman Maccoll, Vernon Horace Rendall, John Middleton Murry, J. Francis, 1828).

13 Recorded in *The Oxford Dictionary of Quotations* (O.U.P., 1999). See https://quotefancy.com/quote/1411567/Richard-Brinsley-Sheridan.

14 *Survey of London*, p. 99. The Survey of London is an ongoing research project to produce a comprehensive architectural survey of the former County of London. It was founded in 1894 by Charles Robert Ashbee, an Arts-and-Crafts architect and social thinker, and was motivated by a desire to record and preserve London's ancient monuments. Originally published in 1912. Author: Walter Besant.

15 The King's Bench Prison was situated in Southwark and endured from medieval times until it closed in 1880. It took its name from the King's Bench court of law in which cases of defamation, bankruptcy, and other misdemeanours were heard; as such, the prison was often used as a debtors' prison until the practice was abolished in the 1860s. In 1842, it was renamed the Queen's Prison, and later became the Southwark Convict Prison. Colman

was forced to take sanctuary 'within the Rules of the King's Bench' – Rules meaning the parameters or immediate neighbourhood. Here, he resided for many years continuing to direct the affairs of his theatre.

16 Quoted in Bonderson, Jan, *The London Monster: A Sanguinary Tale* (University of Pennsylvania Press, 2001), p. 76.

17 Ibid.

18 Until the coronation of George III, Corporal was only another word for Exon, as may be seen on referring to the official programme of the Coronation, which mentions 'the *Corporals* or Exons of the Yeomen of the Guard'. The Exempt in the French Garde du corps always had charge of the Night Watch, and the Exon in the English Body Guard was especially appointed for that service.

19 BHO: British History Online: Architectural description of Vanbrugh's theatre. Taylor's finances are labyrinthine. We know that Gallini sold his share in the new building to Taylor but also that immediately before the dissolution of Parliament in 1802 Taylor fled to France to avoid his creditors. In 1803, he sold one-third of his interest in the theatre to Francis Goold (Gould) for £13,335; the management was to be vested in Goold during their joint lives, and in the survivor, should one die. In 1804, Taylor sold a further share to Goold, who also became mortgagee for the remainder of Taylor's share. There were almost endless further troubles, beginning after Goold's death on 17 January 1807 when Taylor resumed the management and refused to let Goold's executor, Edmund Waters, have any part in the running of the theatre.

20 *The Haymarket Opera House,* Survey of London, Volumes 29 and 30: St. James Westminster, Part 1 (1960), pp. 223–250. Gallini eventually sold his share in the new building to Taylor. In January 1808, arbitrators who had been appointed to settle the dispute between Taylor and Waters decided in favour of the latter, but Taylor seems to have ignored the award and continued as manager until 1813.

21 For more on this, see Appendix to Kelly, Michael, *Reminiscences of Michael Kelly of the King's Theatre and Theatre Royal* (Palala Press, 16 September 2015). Licencing was always a problem, as seen in the case of John Potter's Little Theatre at the Haymarket. From 1741 to 1747, Charles Macklin, Cibber, Samuel Foote, and others sometimes produced plays there, either by use of a temporary licence or by subterfuge. One advertisement, for instance, runs, '*At Cibber's Academy in the Haymarket, will be a Concert, after which, will be exhibited (gratis) a Rehearsal, in the form of a Play, called "Romeo and Juliet"'*. Foote's later royal licence was a permit to exhibit plays during four months in each year from May to September during his lifetime. Following the King's Theatre fire, Michael Kelly notes that 'operas commenced at the Little Theatre, Haymarket on 9 January 1790, and closed on 12 June, reopening at Covent Garden on 15 June until 17 July.

22 Letter of W.S. Gilbert, 19 March 1889 (Morgan Library).

23 This was in respect of the failure of a plan to revive *Thespis*.

24 Quoted by Andrew Crowther: W.S. Gilbert Archive: *The Carpet Quarrel*.

25 Ibid.

26 By the end of 1786 all states except Delaware had passed a copyright statute. Peter K., Yu, ed. Intellectual Property and Information Wealth: Copyright and Related Rights (Greenwood Publishing Group, 2007), p. 143.

27 Website: Mercia: Tuesday, 7 June 2016. *Playing the Provinces: 18th Century Actors on the Move, Part 1 (Liverpool & Manchester)*.

28 *The Era,* 4 January 1896.

29 Hollingshead, John, *Good Old Gaiety: An Historiette and Remembrance* (London: Gaiety Theatre Company, 1903), p. 26. Available on Internet archive.

30 See Mc. Elroy, George, *Meilhac and Halevy – and Gilbert: Comic Converses* (University of Kansas Conference Papers, 1970), p. 95.

31 Stephens, John Russell, *The Censorship of English Drama, 1824–1901* (Cambridge University Press, 1980), pp. 17–22.

32 Anecdote told by Gilbert in the interview: *Ruddygore and Savoy Operas* (*Pall Mall Gazette*, 21 January 1887, pp. 1–2.)

33 Scherer F.M., *The Emergence of Musical Copyright in Europe from 1709 to 1850* (Harvard Kennedy School. Faculty Research Working Papers Series, October 2008), p. 8.

34 *Ruddygore and Savoy Operas* (*Pall Mall Gazette*, 21 January 1887) pp. 1–2, under heading of The American Pirates.

35 Scherer F.M., *The Emergence of Musical Copyright in Europe from 1709 to 1850*, p. 6.

36 Interview: *Ruddygore and Savoy Operas*.

37 *Era*, 22 May 1870, p. 11.

38 According to the *Thespian Dictionary; Or, Dramatic Biography of the Eighteenth Century* (1802), Mr. Wathen eventually joined the opposition: 'having given up his unprofitable theatre at Richmond, he became a member of Mr. Colman's house; he was, likewise, engaged for the ensuing winter at Drury Lane'. His speciality was the playing of comic servants and rustics but eventually, war being declared, he re-entered the army.

39 Interview: *Ruddygore and Savoy Operas*.

40 Stephens, *The Censorship of English Drama, 1824–1901*, p. 12.

41 Shellard, Dominic, and Nicholson Steve: *The Lord Chamberlain Regrets … A History of British Theatre Censorship* (London: British Library, 2004), p. 17. Another limiting factor was that the sheer volume of plays reduced thoroughness of inspection and certainly prevented their all being viewed in performance. Marc Shepherd in *Lord Dramaleigh's Shadow* (*W.S. Gilbert Society Journal* Volume 6, Part 1, Issue 35, Autumn, 2014) tells us that by the 1880s William Piggott was reading 300 plays a year and by 1899 George Redford was reading 444 John Kemble told Donne that to view a dozen a month would be 'about the limit' (Stephens, p. 14.)

42 See *Re-Thinking the Age of Reform Britain*, 1780–1858 (C.U.P., 2003; ed. Arthur Burns), p. 246.

43 The Romans in Britain is a 1980 stage play by Howard Brenton that lambastes imperialism and the abuse of power. In 1982, it became the focus of an unsuccessful private prosecution by Christian morality campaigner Mary Whitehouse against the play's director Michael Bogdanov relating to the on-stage depiction of homosexual rape. This prosecution was defeated when Whitehouse's solicitor, Graham Ross-Cornes revealed under cross-examination that he had been sitting at the very back of the theatre when he saw what was claimed to be a penis. This led to the contention that Ross-Cornes could have witnessed the actor's thumb protruding from his fist. The case was ended after the Attorney-General entered a *nolle prosequi*.

44 Letter to the *Daily News*. 12 January 1872, p. 2. Also printed in *The Orchestra*, *No. 422* (12 January 1872), p. 236. See also *Gilbert, W.S. An Autobiography* (London, 1883), pp. 216–224.

45 Dark and Grey, *W.S. Gilbert: His Life and Letters*, pp. 148–149. Gilbert claimed that the ships were playing the music as 'a sort of musical comment

on the absurdity of the prohibition'. Gilbert does not blame the Examiner who 'had nothing to do with the matter'. It is the Lord High Disinfectant who is responsible.

46 WSG to the *Daily News*, 12 January 1872, also printed in *The Orchestra*. It had been written from the Junior Carlton Club on 10 January.

47 Quoted in Stephens, *The Censorship of English Drama, 1824–1901*, p. 51.

48 W.S. Gilbert, *Ruy Blas* (*Wayne's Christmas Annual*, 1866). The writing of your own words would be needed if you wanted a more operatic or concerted treatment.

49 According to Charles Burney, Italian singers, including *Francesca de l'Epine* (c.1680–1746) and Pier Francesco Tosi (1654–1732), began to arrive in London and excite English audience-goers with virtuosic Italian solo literature (sic) during the final decade of the seventeenth century. Next, Burney claimed, was *Arsinoe Queen of Cyprus* in 1705, which was the first 'musical drama that was wholly performed after the Italian manner, in recitative for the dialogue or narrative parts, and measured melody for the airs'.

50 The librettist for *Arsinoe* was Joseph Addison who ironically would become one of the most outspoken critics of Italian opera in England. The opera was roundly condemned. Clayton's remarks are quoted in Burney, Charles, *A General History of Music* (5 vols, New York: Dover Publications, 1957), p. 655.

51 Shellard and Nicholson, *The Lord Chamberlain Regrets … A History of British Theatre Censorship*, p. 39, n. 5.

52 W.S. Gilbert, *Rosencrantz and Guildenstern; Original Plays, Third Series*, p. 83. Also in *Plays by W.S. Gilbert*, ed. Rowell, p. 179.

53 *Utopia Limited* and *The Grand Duke* in *The Complete Annotated Gilbert and Sullivan*, pp. 1057 and 1153.

54 Quoted in Baily, Leslie, *The Gilbert and Sullivan Book* (revised edition), p. 234.

55 Ibid, p. 379. Letter from Gilbert to Sullivan (5 November 1893):

> I hear that the Prince of Wales took some exception to Barrington wearing the Order of the Garter … Several of the noblemen in *Iolanthe* wore the Garter and no objection was made – so I concluded, reasonably I think, that it might be permitted in *Utopia*. But I suppose the Field Marshal's Uniform makes it rather more personal to H.R.H.

56 Quoted in Dark and Grey, *W.S. Gilbert: His Life and Letters*, p. 147.

57 Ibid, p. 149.

58 Ibid., pp. 148–149.

59 Baily, Leslie, *The Gilbert and Sullivan Book*, p. 331.

60 Interview: *Ruddygore and Savoy Operas*. He says he finds lemon squash the best liquid to work on but adds nothing about what his wife may think of his nocturnal arrangements.

61 Letters quoted in *The Gilbert and Sullivan Book*, pp. 258–259. Perhaps, bruised egos were exacerbated by relative failure. In late March, Gilbert had already written that business for *Princess Ida* was dropping and (though it remains a fine work) each to some extent may have blamed the other.

62 Website: *Playing the Provinces: 18th Century Actors on the Move, Part 1 (Liverpool & Manchester)*.

63 Bancroft, Marie, and Squire Bancroft. *Mr and Mrs Bancroft on and Off the Stage* (London: Richard Bentley and Son, 1889), p. 86.

64 Quoted from the *Times* in *The Complete Annotated Gilbert and Sullivan*, pp. 722–724.

65 *The Revivals at the Savoy; Pall Mall Gazette.* 22 October 1906, p. 7 et seq. One sub-heading is 'No Gagging Allowed'.

66 *Rutland Barrington by Himself,* Chapter 3. Originally published, London: Grant Richards, 1911. Text available via W.S. Gilbert Archive.

67 Also quoted by Barrington in Chapter 3. The Ariel incident occurred in Grey Street, Newcastle-upon-Tyne.

68 Although Collette had his fans, *Tame Cats* was actually hissed by the audience. Gilbert's long serious discussion of the piece – printed in the *Illustrated Times*– suggests something of his own artistic stance. He starts with the problems faced by a novelist who turns to writing a play, claiming that he usually overcharges his dialogue with long soliloquies and tedious descriptions, producing a disjointed, slow-paced structure. In this play (by Edmund Yates), there is also an over-use of artificial devices: 'I really believe I am not exaggerating when I say that whenever a dialogue of any importance took place ... somebody, lying in ambush, overheard it all'. The review appeared on 19 December 1868, and the parody version in *Fun* on 26 December.

69 The subtitle of *Cryptoconchoidsyphonostomata* was the more manageable *While It's to Be Had.* Collette's song from the piece, 'What an Afternoon!' in which the title was regularly repeated, became independently popular, leading again to piracy. The unauthorized distribution of both words and music caused Collette successfully to sue a man named Goode, causing one paper to comment that the song should be re-titled 'What a Goode Afternoon'. Collette married Blanche Julia Wilton (1851–1934), the younger sister of Lady Bancroft, with whom he had one daughter.

70 The quotations from *A Stage Play* derive from an article so titled in *Hood's Comic Annual* (1873).

71 For the lyric of *Claptrap,* see Rees's *W.S. Gilbert and the London Pantomime Season on 1866* in the Kansas Conference Lectures (1970), p. 165.

72 See William Archer's *Real Conversations,* pp. 88–98; also to be found in *The Critic,* 39 (1901), pp. 106–131.

73 *Fun,* 2 November 1867.

74 Gilbert was aware of the low burlesque tastes of audiences. The mock-serious acting was also a new style for which there was little precedent. See Baily, *The Gilbert and Sullivan Book,* pp. 110–111. See also the reviews which include much praise but also a sense that the audience wanted something lighter, the *Era* (31 December), for instance, referring to a 'cold reception'. One of the problems for G. and S. has always been that some critics find the works too low-brow and others not low-brow enough.

75 The stock system had prevailed in England from the Elizabethan period and from the early 1800s was also to be found in the major American cities, though here the term 'stock company', distinguishing the permanent troupes from their touring competitors, was not used until the mid-century. In England, by the end of the Victorian period, most of the big-city stock companies had been ousted as a result of the long-running plays produced by touring companies. When touring companies ventured to outlying districts, regional stock companies again proved unable to compete.

76 The spat is described in full in Eden's *W.S. Gilbert – Appearance and Reality,* pp. 185–188.

77 Southern laid the script upon Miss Keane's desk, telling her 'that he absolutely declined to play it'. After a long exchange, she finally appealed to his chivalrous instincts or at least his generosity. Thereby, a degree of personal loyalty became responsible for the greatest and most surprising hit of his career.

78 Quoted in *The Gilbert and Sullivan Book*, pp. 333–334.
79 See 'The Revivals at the Savoy'. *Pall Mall Gazette*, 22 October 1906, p. 7. The remark may be true of the Carpet Quarrel but not of many other instances. See William Archer's *Real Conversations*. See also *The Gilbert and Sullivan Book*, p. 329.
80 *Rutland Barrington by Himself*, Chapter 3. Originally published, London: Grant Richards, 1911. Text available via W.S. Gilbert Archive.
81 *The Gondoliers*, in *The Complete Annotated Gilbert and Sullivan*, p. 909.
82 Hebe had actually originally been conceived as a rather larger part until Mrs. Howard Paul walked out, talking her dialogue with her. Jessie Bond was signed up for three years initially.
83 Quoted from *The Life of Jessie Bond* and George Grossmith's reminiscences in *The Gilbert and Sullivan Book*, p. 156. Grossmith says that Gilbert says this sort of thing in such a quiet and serious way that one scarcely knows whether he is joking or not.
84 Quoted in the 2016 Anniversary Edition of *The Complete Annotated Gilbert and Sullivan* which is the first to include *Thespis*. (See Act 11 Opening Scene, p. 40.) Sullivan stated that 'Until Gilbert took the matter in had, Choruses were dummy concerns'. The lady in this case was probably Mlle Clary.
85 This was 'There lived a King'. Gilbert re-wrote the lyric as shown in *The Gilbert and Sullivan Book*, pp. 338–339.
86 Quoted in *The Gilbert and Sullivan Book*, p. 333
87 See 'Miss Lydia Thompson's Farewell', *Pall Mall Gazette,* 3 May 1899, transcribed and posted on Savoynet by Arthur Robinson.
88 'Pygmalion'. WSG to *The Observer*, 11 February 1872, p. 2.
89 W.S. Gilbert, *Unappreciated Shakespeare*. Originally published in *Illustrated Sporting and Dramatic News*, Christmas Number, 9 December 1882 and reprinted in *Foggerty's Fairy and Other Tales*, London: George Routledge and Sons, 1890.
90 See *Era Almanack*, 1875: 'A Proposal for Elevating the Position of the Modern Drama'. Three years later in *An Appeal to the Press (Era Almanack and Annual)*, Gilbert argues that critics are too ready on first nights to believe that they are seeing 'an accurate embodiment of the author's intention'.
91 This comes from *Actors, Authors and Audiences*. Later, in a kind of back-handed compliment, the learned Judge tells the defendant-playwright:

> It is true that the plays of Shakespeare are frequently mutilated without apparent detriment to their attractive powers. But your light is not the light of Shakespeare. If I may so express myself, your night-light has been seen through a fog. (Printed in *Foggerty's Fairy and Other Tales*, London, George Routledge and Sons, 1890)

92 *Era Almanack*, 1875.
93 Wilfred's *When jealous torments* was also partly omitted for this reason. Both songs get occasional performances, the former – well orchestrated and gruesomely comic – adding considerably to Wilfred's characterization.
94 For Nelly and the parody of dialect plays, see the *Lost in London* parody text reprinted in Stedman's *W.S. Gilbert's Theatrical Criticism*, pp. 158–163. *Ethel; or, Only a Life* was reviewed by Gilbert on 27 October 1866. The full parody text is in *W.S. Gilbert's Theatrical Criticism*, pp. 104–109.
95 W.S. Gilbert, *Allow Me to Explain*, pp. 14–15.
96 See *Fun*, 30 July 1870.
97 For *Jezebel*, see *Fun*, 24 December 1870. For the British playgoer, see *The British Playgoer, Tinsley's Magazine,* January 1869, p. 638.

98 Joseph Gilbert was Gilbert's uncle. When he died, his sons were not expected to live and in the event of their deaths W.S. Gilbert would have been a beneficiary. Gilbert's father sought control of the young boys and was accused of cheating their widowed mother. Young Gilbert was meanwhile sent with the youngest of Joseph's sons to live with an aunt of the latter. Young Gilbert much resented the boy's pampered treatment.

99 For the Seton Laings, see Eden David, *A Tale of Two Kidnaps* (Sir Arthur Sullivan Society, 1988).

100 For more on this, see Crowther, *Gilbert of Gilbert and Sullivan*, pp. 18–19.

101 See website https://books.google.co.uk/books?id=3T0FAAAAQAAJ. *The Lady Magazine.*

102 W.S. Gilbert, *An Elixir of Love and Diamonds* in *The Lost Stories* of W.S. Gilbert, p. 108; pp. 96–97.

103 Eden, *W.S. Gilbert –Appearance and Reality*, p. 105.

104 For the idea of sexless creations, see *Guardian* Interview with Mike Leigh, 11 November 1999. Peter Hall, he says, called the operas 'sexless and camp'.

105 Interview with W.S. Gilbert: Salaman, *Cassell's Magazine*, 20 March 1900, pp. 413–421.

106 For *Guy Fawkes* and early home influences, see Rees, Terence, *Introduction to Uncle Baby.*

107 Interview with W.S. Gilbert: 'Mr. Gilbert Tells Some Anecdotes'; *Daily Mail*, Tuesday 30 October 1906, p. 5.

108 Edmund Gosse, 'Mr Hardy's New Novel', *Cosmopolis*, 1 (January 1896).

109 The cartoons showed visual depiction of The Prophet.

110 *My Name Is Rachel Corrie* is a play based on the diaries and emails of activist Rachel Corrie, who was killed by an Israeli soldier when she was 23. It was jointly edited by journalist Katharine Viner and actor Alan Rickman who also directed it. It was first performed in London on 7 April 2005 but struggled to be seen in New York.

111 W.S. Gilbert: *The Student; Fun*, 1 – 1 July 1865. Gilbert's parodies of his own plays may be found in *W.S. Gilbert's Theatrical Criticism*, pp. 184–196.

112 Other factors include the charisma of Abigail, as a focus and rallying point for the girls, the liberating effect of Tituba's conjuring, and the drudgery to which they are subjected by older married women fostering a desire for revenge.

113 *Fun*, 14 April 1866, p. 43.

114 *News of the World*, 7 December 1890, p. 4; *Pall Mall Gazette*, 4 December 1890, p. 2; *Evening News*, 4 November 1890, p. 2.

115 Comment on the novels of Barbara Pym: Front Cover: *Some Tame Gazelle* (Virago, 2009; reprint).

116 Quoted in Knelman, Judith, *Twisting in the Wind: The Murderess and the English Press* (University of Toronto Press, 1998), p. 237. The Judge, Sir Alfred Wills, had been shocked at the young women's keen interest in sex, fetishism, and murder.

117 Weltman, Sharon Aronofsky, *Performing the Victorian* (Ohio State University, 8 April 2007), p. 30.

118 The appropriateness is the link with apples, since William Tell allegedly shot an apple off his son's head. 'Hot Codlins' was probably Grimaldi's most popular song. It tells of an old lady who sold roast apples and drank too much gin. In the refrain, Grimaldi would stop before using the word 'gin' allowing the audience to yell it out, whereupon Grimaldi would look

at them and say 'Oh! For Shame!'. This song was one requested at his fare-well benefit performance.

119 Quoted in *The Lady*. The flag of the Isle of Man (Manx: *brattagh Vannin*) is a triskelion, composed of three armoured legs with golden spurs, upon a red background. It has been the official flag since 1 December 1932 and is based on the Manx coat of arms, which dates back to the 13th century.

120 The discipline and control and the advantage of a small company had been seen in Gilbert's observation of Tom Robertson's methods. See Catherine Pope's article: *Storm in a Teacup?*

121 The Chorus, for instance, was comparatively small – twenty love-sick maidens, twenty-four *contadine*, including Tessa and Gianetta.

122 Quoted in Booth, Michael, *Theatre in the Victorian Age* (C.U.P., 1991), pp. 29–30.

123 Ibid, pp. 29–30.

124 Quoted in O'Brien, John, *Harlequin Britain*, p. 205.

125 W.S. Gilbert, *A Consistent Pantomime* (*Graphic*, X1 (16 January 1875)), p. 62.

126 *Utopia Limited*, in *The Complete Annotated Gilbert and Sullivan*, p. 1079.

127 *Times* review of *Engaged* revival, 18 February 1886. By 'female interest' romantic love-interest is meant.

128 W.S. Gilbert, *Getting Up a Pantomime*, (London Society, 1868), pp. 50–51. Reprinted in *The Victorian Web* (Internet). For Honestus's days 'when bet-ter actors acted better plays', see O'Brien, John, *Harlequin Britain*, p. 205.

129 The *Punch and Judy* show has roots in the 16th-century Italian Commedia dell'arte, the figure of Punch deriving from the Neapolitan stock character of Pulcinella. The figure who later became Mr. Punch made his first re-corded appearance in England on 9 May 1662. The diarist Samuel Pepys observed a marionette show featuring an early version of the character in Covent Garden, describing the event as 'an Italian puppet play, that is within the rails there, which is very pretty'.

130 McConnell Stott, Andrew, *The Pantomime Life of Joseph Grimaldi* (Edin-burgh: Canongate Books, 2009), p. 109. Grimaldi played Punch and then Clown. This pantomime had many later variants. In *Harlequin-Amulet or, The Magic of Mona* by William Powell (1880) 'Pantaloon, an ancient gentleman with great land possession, wages a war of destruction against the Bards, for whom he holds a great hatred, aided by evil genius Morca, Lord of the Mines'. A Genius of Waters comes to the Bards' protection and creates a being called Harlequin to avenge their cause.

131 William Archer stated in 1881 that Gilbert had written 9,000 lines of blank verse, not one of which had the 'smallest metrical beauty'. See Eden, *W.S. Gilbert: Appearance and Reality*, p. 150 et seq.

132 *Era*, 2 October 1897. Quoted in *W.S. Gilbert: Appearance and Reality*, p. 184.

133 See Flanders, Judith, *The Invention of Murder* (Harper Press, 2011), p. 138.

134 *Fun*, 26 February 1870.

135 *Patience*, in *The Complete Annotated Gilbert and Sullivan*, pp. 333–335.

136 W.S. Gilbert (probably), *London Characters and the Humorous Side of London Life* (Stanley Rivers and Co. 1870/1871). It should be noted that George Augustus Henry Sala wrote a *Getting Up a Pantomime* in his '*Gas-light and Daylight*' journalism of 1859. Here, he records how much we love the old pantomimes still. 'Clowns steal the same sausages, and have been asked by the Pantaloon "how we were to-morrow?" for years and years ...'.

137 Ibid. The whole text of *Getting up a Pantomime* is available on the Victorian Web. This extract comes from page 1 of 4.

138 Gilbert often said money was the reason for his putting pen to paper ('Every line I ever wrote in verse was to order, and well paid for at that'), but he did sometimes have counterbalancing preoccupations. In his bitter spat with Henrietta Hodson, he wrote (of the play *Ought We to Visit Her?*): 'She shall not have the piece if she pays me £100 per night for it'. See *W.S. Gilbert – Appearance and Reality*, pp. 95 and 201.

139 Sala (24 November 1828–8 December 1895) was a journalist writing for *The Daily Telegraph, Household Words, All the Year Round*, and *The Illustrated London News*. His 1879 bawdy pantomime *Harlequin Prince Cherrytop* (adapted as a monologue sometimes called *The Sod's Opera*) is, oddly, occasionally falsely attributed to Gilbert.

140 Sala, George Augustus in *Living London* (article), 1882. See website: *Victorian London – Entertainment and Recreation*.

141 On the advantages of a two-act structure, see *How They Write Their Plays: Mr. W.S. Gilbert; St. James's Gazette*, 23 June 1893. As regards pace and timing, first night reviews of *Thespis* stated that it ended too late and that the audience was growing fidgety, but this is partly because it had been preceded by another work, leading to a late start and a finish at about 11 p.m.

142 Occasionally, Gilbert felt that a song slowed up the action and recommended its removal or excision. Such applies to the Duchess's (very good) song in Act 2 of *The Gondoliers*, which at one point Gilbert suggested be moved to the first act. Quite how it would have fitted is unclear.

143 Jean-François Regnard (7 February 1655–4 September 1709) was probably the most distinguished, after Molière, of the comic poets of the French 17th century. He is equally famous now for the travel diary he kept of a voyage in 1681. Earlier, on a return voyage from Italy in 1678 he was at the age of twenty-two captured by an Algerian pirate, sold as a slave in Algiers and taken to Constantinople, where the French consul paid a ransom for his release.

144 The main fairs (*foires*) were Saint-Germain and Saint Laurent. Here, Pierrot appeared in marionette theatres and motley entertainments. See Storey, Robert F., *Pierrot: a critical history* (Princeton University Press, 2014), especially p. 40.

145 Claude Gillot (27 April 1673–4 May 1722) was a French painter, printmaker, and illustrator, best known as the master of Watteau (baptized 10 October 1684–died 18 July 1721) and Lancret (22 January 1690–14 September 1743). Oudry (17 March 1686–30 April 1755) was a French Rococo painter, engraver, and tapestry designer, well known for his naturalistic pictures of animals and the hunt. Fragonard (April 1732–22 August 1806) was a French painter and printmaker whose late Rococo manner was distinguished by remarkable facility, exuberance, and hedonism.

146 See *The Complete Annotated Gilbert and Sullivan; H.M.S. Pinafore*, pp. 123, 155; *The Pirates of Penzance*, pp. 255–257.

147 *Daily Express*, 5 May 1976. Interview with Jean Rook, headed by '*Waiting for Bowie, and finding a genius who insists he's really a clown*'. Bowie often wore white make-up, and increasingly, Pierrot's physical insularity; his poignant lapses into mutism, his white face and costume, suggested not only innocence but the pallor of the dead. He was, however, fairly swiftly and naturally displaced by the native English Clown when the latter found a suitably brilliant interpreter in Grimaldi.

148 British Library, *The Gilbert Papers*, Add Mss, 49341, folio 144. The words are reported in a letter of condolence after Gilbert's death.

149 In the early 19th century, many Romantics claimed the figure of Pierrot as their own. For Jules Janin and Théophile Gautier, he was not a fool but an avatar of the post-Revolutionary people. He was the sad poetic spirit struggling, sometimes tragically, to secure a place in a bourgeois mercantile world.

150 Disher, Maurice Willson, *Clowns and Pantomimes* (London, 1925), p. 135.

151 Shakespeare, William, *As You Like It*: All the world's a stage (2.7.140–167).

152 W.S.Gilbert, *London Characters and the Humorous Side of London Life*, 1871. (Source: British Library, shelfmark C.133.g.71.)

153 W.S. Gilbert, *Getting Up a Pantomime*, *Victorian Web* reprint, p. 1.

154 Ibid., p. 3. For Bunthorne and the Elysian Fields, see *Patience* in *The Complete Annotated Gilbert and Sullivan*, p. 295.

155 For Madge Kendal's comment and others about Gilbert's dislike of Shakespeare and handsome men, see *W.S. Gilbert – Appearance and Reality*, p. 86. See also Kendal: *Dame Madge Kendal by Herself*, pp. 167–168. For Hollingshead's comments, see Hollingshead, John, *My Lifetime* (London: Sampson Low, Marston and Co. Ltd., 1895), Volume 2, p. 124.

156 *London Characters and the Humorous Side of London Life*. The characters are by no means all sufferers. 'There are few, very few, who are so unhappy, so isolated, as not to be the absolute centre around which some one's thoughts revolve'. However, the picture of humanity is not genial. We hear, for instance, of the Reform Gathering in Hyde Park:

> Here are thirty thousand people vindicating their claim to a franchise, some by talking windily to a mob who can't hear them, others by an interchange of gentle chaff, others by going to sleep in their backs on the grass.

The crowd are called noodles for thinking that the cause of reform can be advanced by such means. Among others, few are entirely praiseworthy. There is reference to swindlers, betting thieves, liars, and wife-beaters. The gay old bachelor in particular is described as being of 'drivelling imbecility', though the actress, going quietly to perform as a burlesque prince is sympathetically presented: 'a good quiet girl enough, with a bedridden mother and three or four clean but seedy (unhealthy) little children dependent on her weekly salary'.

157 *Fun*, January, 1862, quoted in Stedman, J.W., *W.S. Gilbert's Theatrical Criticism*, p. 15.

Part 4
Skills and Legacy

* *

Skills

It may seem rather late in the day to assess Gilbert's skills. Surely, these are the main reason why many of his works are still staged and why we remember them. But it is precisely these skills which show him as an influence on later writers. Sometimes, this may be more a matter of temperamental compatibility than of imitation. Often, it is a mixture of the two, a writer being temperamentally inclined to a mode which is found stimulatingly in the work of an earlier author.

One skill which I would stress is that of structural competence. This includes matters of pacing, the ordering of events, and, of course, the build-up to a powerful and arresting climax. Gilbert himself was forthright about what does and does not make a good play. In a subsequently notorious interview, he tells the *Edinburgh Evening Dispatch* that 'We ought to leave the French stage alone. They have good actors and atrociously bad plays'. The 'badness' lies partly in their being too analytically written and too much in the mode of novels. Sardou, for instance, writes plays which might be pages of Thackeray turned into French. One further problem is that their longer speeches are beyond the capabilities of British actors. French actors he says:

> can so speak and deliver speeches as to claim the attention of the audience, while ours – why, we have no actors who can make a thirty line speech interesting! Whoever heard in this country 'All the world's a stage' declaimed by a Jacques who did not in every line make it plain he had learned it off by heart?[1]

Gilbert's rather ill-tempered outburst against British performers (including Irving and Beerbohm Tree whom he blames for dull monotony) was in part later retracted, but it is nonetheless instructive. It suggests his concern for pace, momentum, and variety with plenty of stage action and movement rather than analytical exposition of character and motive. His comments in his diaries (ironically often in French) about the plays he saw in the early 20th century are frequently dismissive. They are *pièces banales* without any sense of magic, illusion, or specifically theatrical excitement. In conversation with William Archer, he remarks that in a positive sense, plays are artificial and should exploit the fact. Always he is aware of the need to keep the audience entertained. Speaking to Bram Stoker of the popularity of the music hall, he remarks:

> My impression is that people go to places of amusement to be amused; and somehow the music-hall often fits better into the social structure than does the theatre. You need not give up a whole evening to it. It is more facile in its ways; at whatever hour you go in, you can take up at once whatever is going on.[2]

The above may seem to suggest an anti-intellectual stance. Rather, it is a case of not overestimating the intellectual capacities of your audience. When he is asked whether the theatre has a function beyond mere amusement, he replies, 'It should have, but it rarely pays to attempt anything beyond mere entertainment. My own experience is that the higher the literary quality of the play, the greater its chance of failure'. In another interview, he states that intellectual cleverness has very little to do with any success of his own. A knowledge of stagecraft is the greater attribute.[3] When he is told that the French critic Filon had found 'something almost of Swift's *saeva indignatio* underlying the playful topsy-turvy of his fancy', he remarks gently, 'And they call that dramatic criticism in France, do they? Could any one have misconceived *Engaged* more perfectly?'[4]

Gilbert's comments on others give us an idea of the criteria by which he might expect us to judge of his skills. *Engaged* is a play of 'whimsical absurdity'. It is not – and should not be seen as – 'a bitter and cruel caricature of mankind'. If it were, it would alienate an audience who must be kept happy, entertained, and satisfied that they have experienced a well-structured piece with a clear beginning, middle, and end. While admitting that there are classical precedents for anti-climax, Gilbert dislikes this, lamenting an increasing tendency to put the 'great effect' in the penultimate rather than the final act. In constructing a play, he says, one is not justified in misplacing the climactic moments or trailing off into the indeterminate. A good many recent plays, though otherwise of great ability, seem to him to come to a helpless, makeshift, essentially feeble end. He cannot think that this is sound art, and, equally importantly, it leaves an audience dissatisfied.

The dislike of the premature climax relates to Gilbert's sense that a play is not life – a paradoxical view, given that he often suggests similarities. The explanation is that he is thinking structurally. The difference between *play* and *life* is that in real life, no curtain descends to tell you that the story is over. Indeed, for the duration of one's lifetime it never is. Audiences, though they may not articulate the need, though they may not even be consciously aware of it, are entitled to expect dénouements and conclusions. In constructing a play, he says, you must reach conclusions. You are 'not justified in interesting your audiences in the adventures of a group of personages unless you are prepared to furnish those audiences with some information as to what becomes of that group'.[5]

Gilbert's preference for 'finished form' is one of his key theoretical contentions. Look at nearly every 'classical five-act comedy', he remarks, 'and you will find that the last act is, as a rule, merely perfunctory'. This should not be. In something of a turnabout, he admits to preferring a sense of climax and completion 'even if the form, and perhaps the play itself, was borrowed from the French'. This is a reference to the concept of the well-made play, the *pièce bien faite*, a concept mainly attributed to Eugène Scribe who, in about 1825, developed a technical formula calling for complex and highly artificial plotting, a build-up of suspense, a climactic scene in which all problems are resolved, and a brisk happy ending.

Gilbert's attitude to the *pièce bien faite* is not entirely laudatory. Into his own form of it he injects wit, an element of cynicism, and, above all, a penchant for the topsy-turvy. Nonetheless, many of his most characteristic comedies do have this sort of outline. According to Scribe, conventional romantic conflicts were to be a staple subject, one example being that of a pretty girl who must choose between a wealthy, unscrupulous suitor and a poor but honest young man. Although Sir Joseph Porter is not exactly unscrupulous, this triangular arrangement is a lynchpin in *H.M.S. Pinafore*. Scribe's other requirements include suspense created by misunderstandings between characters, mistaken identities, secret information (as when the poor young man turns out to be nobly born), and lost or stolen documents. In *H.M.S. Pinafore*, Ralph turns out to be nobly born. In *Ages Ago*, there is much concern about missing title-deeds, and in many works, feigned or mistaken identities, such as that of Robin Oakapple, the Prince Regent, and Nanki-Poo, are a commonplace.

It may well be thought that Gilbert's allegiance to the *pièce bien faite* is a matter of capitulation. But structure is itself an aspect of control compatible with his temperament, besides which one may always tweak the material within the conventions. Ideally, this will appeal to the more perceptive in the audience, while not alienating the obtuse. It will also give the author a perverse personal intellectual satisfaction. In *Ruddygore*, the Robin-Rose-Richard triangle is conventional, but it has a reverse aspect because it is the poorer of the two suitors who is unscrupulous, subverting the conventional moral superiority of the poor but honest mariner. Another challenge is that the uncharacteristic virtuous prosperous landowner should by rights be performing a daily villainy. Not only does Gilbert turn the more usual bad wealthy suitor into a good one. He contrives that that good one ought by conscience and duty to be wicked, a role he has basely transferred to his unfortunate (innately virtuous) younger brother.

Much the same applies to the more satirized of the female characters. In *Ruddygore*, the pretty young girl has all the external trapping of virtue and sweetness without the actuality. Not only are her charitable gifts entirely unsuitable for the recipient. Her conduct is allied to instruction from a book of etiquette, which is actually at odds with her mercenary instincts. On one level, Rose Maybud is a workhouse child, abandoned probably because she was illegitimate. On another, she is the blameless niece of a virtuous aunt who in unexplained ways allowed her to be abandoned and then adopted her. The background here lies outside the opera's parameters, and Gilbert is quite right not to explain it. But a perceptive audience might nonetheless note the incongruity. Exploiting Scribe's formula of mistaken or hidden identities and a triangular love-plot, the playwright nonetheless subverts it. He also immerses the whole thing in a satire of the sensation-melodrama which was no part of Scribe's original intention.

The well-made play was even in its heyday sometimes ridiculed, and by the time of *Ruddygore*, it was increasingly discredited. Both Émile Zola and George Bernard Shaw denounced Scribe's work (and indeed that of Victorien Sardou, his successor), claiming that it exalted the mechanics of playmaking at the expense of honest characterizations and serious content. Gilbert's intention seems to have been to infuse seriousness – or at least satirical debunking – by the element of subversion. At the same time, he does not throw out the baby of a tried and tested formula with the bathwater. Like Charles Reade in the novel, he could 'Make 'em laugh; make em cry; make em wait'. He knew that Scribe, with the aid of assistants, had written hundreds of plays and libretti which had been profitably translated, adapted, and imitated all over Europe.[6]

i.

Gilbert's skill in using but re-working popular formulae is on a par with the tendency of many of his playwright contemporaries. Both Henry Arthur Jones and Pinero successfully used conventional ingredients, while augmenting aspects of social critique, characterization, and emotional tension. Gilbert's own attitude was not to disparage modern experiment but to seek to ground it in solid principles of sound construction and effective *motifs*. In 1908, he told Bram Stoker that the tendency of the modern stage was 'Forward! Distinctly forward', and that ever since the days of *Thespis*, there had been a continual development of 'a better class of play'.[7] Judging by *The Hooligan*, he was not averse to tackling dark material in concentrated form, and he had no complaint with those such as Émile Augier and Alexandre Dumas *fils* who combined polished structural techniques with the exploration of social conditions, such as prostitution and female emancipation. What he *did* dislike was structural incompetence, making it odd perhaps that he disliked the term 'playwright' and that in *On Guard*, he contrasts the admirable Denis' rough-hewn quality with the more artificial structure of polished furniture. In many ways to Gilbert, constructing a play *was* a craft. He *was* a maker. In this, he looks forward to writers such as Lillian Hellman and Terence Rattigan, both of whom provide challenging material within the parameters of the well-made play.

The Gilbert who can admire solid structures is at the same time the Gilbert who sometimes thinks he is in the wake or back-current of the times. Talking in 1901 to William Archer (and taking, Archer thought, a very liberal view), he remarks, 'I know there has been progress by the very convincing proof – namely, that I find myself altogether left behind'.[8] Perhaps, he had been stung by critical references to his old-fashioned bag of tricks. But equally, he may have felt that his structural skills were just a little too rigid and his characters too much conceived on his principle that acting was an imitative art. The implication here would be that his characters were of a rather marionette kind, limited in range and manipulated to exhibit merely stock Cartesian responses.

In fact, the above can be variously contested. First, we might argue that the stock character – derived partly from burlesque and extravaganza – was by no means a dead letter. It was to be newly exploited in experimental modes, as, for instance, in Ionesco's *The Future Is in Eggs* and Bahram Beyza's *The Marionettes*. In the former, the stock conventions, demands, and expectations of bourgeois life are subject to a hysterically surreal conveyor-belt variant. In the latter, the playwright draws both on Absurdism and on the traditional Iranian *kheymeh shab bazi* (puppet theatre), the twist being that the marionettes are – and are enacted *by* – human actors.

The Marionettes is a good example of a play combining ancient and modern. Drawing on native traditions – in which music would be an ingredient and a professional entertainer might have as many as eighty puppets – the piece also references Pirandello and Absurdist treatments of religion, politics, society, and philosophy. Yet it is managed by a Puppet-Master and peopled by figures familiar from Iranian tradition including a knightly hero; a monster (or *div*) for the hero to fight; a girl for him to love; and a cleric, a merchant, and a poet who are representative of the society he is defending. The effect is not unlike Gilbert's reinterpretations of Harlequin and Clown which were later to be more challengingly, less nostalgically, incorporated into Absurdist drama. Though his late plays – notably *The Fairy's Dilemma* – did strike some as regressive, there was novelty within the recapitulation. Not only was the Harlequinade shown as having personal and moral consequences. The playwright burlesqued even its own burlesque elements, this kind of reinvention later becoming a common Absurdist technique.

Gilbert's injection of the critical-surreal into traditional transformations is undoubtedly capable of further progression. It applies in *The Future Is in Eggs* where, in a grotesque parody of plays centred on bourgeois love and marriage, a pregnant mother morphs into a battery hen, being pelted with eggs by her genetically driven, socially programmed, and racially conditioned wider family. Gilbert, of course, does not go to these extremes but he does break bounds, not least in the *Bab Ballads* where conventional modes may be challenged more ruthlessly (a) because there is no danger of corporate audience alienation, and (b) because things shown are always more physically striking than things read about.[9]

There are, however, other reasons why Gilbert's 'old-fashioned' elements remain acceptable. One is that they are often used for parody, as is the case with the Cartesian behaviour of the Adelphi Guests in the Prince of Monte Carlo's suite. Another is that within the conventions, Gilbert produces some striking variants. Julia Jellicoe, Pooh-Bah, the Mikado, Wilfred, John Wellington Wells, Sir Joseph, Rose Maybud, King Gama, and numerous others are strikingly original figures. Mr. Wells combines the accoutrements of sorcery with the professional conduct of a respectful but easily offended lower-middle-class tradesman-moralist. Julia may be the traditional temperamental limelight-seeking *prima donna*, but she speaks English-German in a Hungarian accent, sings Italianate music, and combines an alleged emotional intensity with a coolly appraising business head. Pooh-Bah is a haughty nobleman whose pride consists in tracing himself back to the most primitive of organisms. The Mikado is a sadist who proposes horrific punishments in a tone of notable politeness, humanely insisting that he is not a bit angry.

There is another point about Gilbert's characterization – namely, that it often intentionally mocks a literary type. We cannot expect Richard Dauntless to be 'fully rounded' since he is essentially a subversive burlesque. A richer result occurs when the treatment involves both literary form and a more human psychological form of satire. Rose is a satirical version of the romantic melodrama's pure young maiden. Yet she is equally *any* girl hiding a selfish, gold-digging, agenda under a mask of expected socially programmed decorousness. Her romantic soliloquy consists of the bald statement that Robin – for whose unacknowledged love she is allegedly growing thin and pale – 'would do as well as another'. Nonetheless, his corn and oil do at least provide an extra incentive.

Gilbert's ability to mock conventional modes is everywhere apparent. Mabel (nominally) wins Frederic's heart only because she is the one girl who is plain enough to accept him. This acknowledgement, in the context of the entry of the *prima donna*, is itself deeply subverting. So, in a different way, is the allocation to Ralph of the language of courtly hyperbole, described by Josephine as 'simple eloquence'. It mocks the plain but honest diction of the traditional tar set against the false flights of oratory with which in *The Kept Mistress* it is contrasted. Sometimes, there are extra ingredients such as the mock-heroic or the use of irony. Princess Ida's address to her neophytes is remarkable in using both hyperbolic and deflationary techniques. She speaks hyperbolically but is deflated by the triviality of (for instance) her concept of chaos, which is presented as exhibiting, not intellectual acumen, but the limitations of the feminine mind and its narrow (mainly shopping-based) range of interests.

Princess Ida's oration is one of only two or three really long speeches in the Savoy operas, another being Robin's appeal to the portraits of his ancestors and a third Rudolph's response to the reading of his detective's letter. This is in line with Gilbert's desire to avoid Sardou's tendency to lengthy self-revelatory utterance, but it also shows a distinct advance on the mode of earlier farces (including his own) in which characters frequently have long soliloquies directly addressed to the audience. When a character has a longish speech in the Savoy operas, it is usually addressed to others and given a semblance of a realistic context. One example is that of Mr. Wells who, on first appearing, sets out his stall to Aline and Alexis. This is entirely in character for, as a conscientious tradesman in quest of business, he is anxious from the first to establish his reliable professional credentials. It is also very funny in its combination of business jargon with surreal elements. Such applies with the patent Hag who comes out and prophesies disasters and with his almost rueful, account of the unpopularity of his 'very superior blessings'. Apparently, only one of these has been sold – to a gentleman to bestow on his mother-in-law, the purchaser turning out not to be right in the head.[10]

The ability to accumulate a range of jokes within one sentence is of almost Shakespearian skill. It reminds us of the concentration of effects – though, this time, of horror – in the lines

> Finger of birth-strangled babe
> Ditch-deliver'd by a drab' – [11]

Such richness of invention may also include elements of comic juxtaposition. Such applies in the reference to a love-potion described as a Patent Oxy-Hydrogen Love-at-first-sight-Philtre, where business elements (the patent) jostle with science (Oxy-Hydrogen) and the romantic notion of immediate passion. Here again, Gilbert draws on traditional *motifs*, for the love-at-first-sight magic derives, via a flower of purple dye, from *A Midsummer Night's Dream* and stories such as that of Tristan and Isolde. Interestingly, a 'wicked advertisement' for a love-philtre ('The famous Love-Powder, or Love-Drops') was in the 18th century sold 'for five shillings a bottle at the Golden-Ball, in Stone-Cutters-Street, Fleet-Market'. Mary Blandy, tried and hanged for the murder of her father, claimed that the poison he ingested was a form of this, meant to make him more affectionate and amiable to her suitor.[12]

ii.

As with the love-potion, so with much else. Scribe was by no means the first playwright to suggest such elements as cross-current love-conflict, mistaken identity, overhearing, and planted or misappropriated letters. But the stock ingredients of comedy drama may be given an extra boost by a number of well-tried techniques. In *The Yeomen of the Guard*, there is mirth to be gained from the irony of the jealous Wilfred's allowing Fairfax continually to kiss Phoebe in the mistaken belief that he is her brother. The tormenter's paranoia – more fully revealed if he regains his Act 1 aria – makes him both repellent and oddly endearing. He is a tormenter tormented. We see his vulnerability, recognizing both his emotional simplicity and the intellectual limitations which are no match for Phoebe's cleverness.

The dualities in Wilfred are part of a wider 'oppositional' technique. In *The Pirates*, Frederic's 'Oh is there not one maiden breast?' has a high-minded appeal to moral duty followed by one to maiden desperation. In *Iolanthe*, a verse one invocation of the classical Ovid is followed by one to the leader of the London Fire Brigade. In terms of characterization, not only does Wilfred's dancing-bear stupidity offset his reputation for vicious torturing. The torturing is in any case kept carefully out of sight. Thereby Gilbert prevents any complete alienation of our sympathies, successfully suggesting the mix of brutality and sentimentality often found in a mind ill-tuned to subtlety or the meshes of emotional nuance.

Wilfred's song is a good example of Gilbert's concern for sustained pace in an overall structure. One reason for its omission (and certainly the reason for the cutting of Sergeant Meryll's aria) is the need to maintain a well-paced momentum towards the entrance of Point and Elsie. In Wilfred's case, there are considerable arguments for re-inclusion, both in further establishing his character and in providing a better balance between dialogue and music. Sullivan, we know, complained that *Ruddygore* was in danger of becoming a play with incidental songs, and just occasionally, a re-inclusion of 'lost' songs is a bonus.

Despite the caveats, Gilbert's judgement in such matters is usually very astute, not just overall but in terms of balancing solo arias, duets, and ensembles and including a substantial chorus contribution. Sometimes, he conveys plot developments or necessary background information through song. Such applies in Pish-Tish's *Our Great Mikado* and in Ludwig's *By the Mystic Regulation*. In *The Mountebanks*, important plot developments are conveyed in music during an ongoing quarrel.[13] Other variants are for two developments to occur at once or for an apparent irrelevance to contribute to a wider ambience. In *Utopia Limited*, Fitzbattleaxe's relationship with Zara is economically established within the wider Ensemble of her return from England. In *The Grand Duke*, an apparently irrelevant though lively number – the Roulette Song – actually contributes significantly to the *motif* of power-structures and prosperity as related to game-play and the random rules of chance.

iii.

The variety of effects used for plot developments is in Gilbert impressive. But so too is the way he recycles traditional elements to give them both satirical interest and a new validity. Works such as Handel's *Ottone* and Rossini's *Demetrio e Polibio* include many stock mechanical plot and character ingredients, looking forward (for instance) to *The Pirates* and *The Gondoliers*. The difference is that Gilbert's treatment mocks the very contrivances, particularly the lack of plausibility. In *Ottone*, the title character is attacked by a convoy of pirates, one of whom is arrested and held in chains. Only after three acts of concealing what he knows does he turn out to be the brother of the heroine. In *Demetrio e Polibio*, there is an embedded (partly false) tale of a stolen royal baby whose bride, when he grows up, is kidnapped by his disguised father. The father, foiled of kidnapping his son, kidnaps the bride. She and her supporters then resourcefully attack him, leading to a split-second rescue by his son, causing him to be so touched that he immediately forgives all hurts.

The lack of structural skill in many musically impressive works is precisely what Gilbert simultaneously mocks and corrects. In *Demetrio e Polibio*, the heroine's attack on her kidnapper, his rescue, and the happy Finale all occur within a few brief minutes. There is no sense of dramatic climax and no extended development. By contrast, in the sort of number parodied in 'Go, ye heroes', the heroine Lisinga had previously sung an extended aria, backed by her supporters, vowing at great length to go out on the attack.

The ability to parody existing modes would not in itself be enough to make a viable structure. But Gilbert is also adept at telling a story by a range of compatible means. It can be conveyed in dialogue; reinforced, after initial summary in a musical number; or developed in song with a ironical sting-in-the-tale, as happens in Don Alhambra's *I Stole a Prince*. Also common is a deliberate juxtaposition of contrasting effects. In *Ruddygore*, no sooner has Robin finally resolved on 'a regular course of Old Bailey' than Margaret and the reformed Despard enter, prim, and quaintly demure, to dissuade and undermine him. What adds to the effect is these characters' transformation. In a comic *volte face*, Margaret, in particular, has turned from mad wild-child to black-garbed schoolteacher with the bonus that the old wildness occasionally resurfaces. This is then suppressed by the happily chosen utterance of 'Basingstoke', a word which teems with the hidden meaning of having recently come to prominence in a local 1887 by-election.

The Pavlovian use of the word 'Basingstoke' is rather like the Fairy Queen's reference to Captain Shaw. Nowadays, it needs footnotes for the joke to be clarified. Nonetheless, it can work simply on the basis of its apparently harmless irrelevance – the use of a bland term to curtail insane vehemence. Elsewhere, structural juxtapositions are particularly notable in sustained musical sequences. In Act 2 of *Princess Ida*, Hilarion's romantic aria of love-despair is juxtaposed to the dramatic arrival of Hildebrand's army leading into a double chorus setting anguished female wailing against military intransigence. In *The Grand Duke*, the general rejoicing at Ludwig's defeat of Rudolph and accession to his title is dramatically interrupted by a deliberately ostentatious Julia claiming him from Lisa and demanding to be his bride. Almost always, Sullivan aids the contrasts by appropriate music. In *Princess Ida*, Hilarion's aria is moving but not slow-paced, (a) because this would reduce the momentum of an ongoing sequence and (b) because the appeal includes an element of desperation in what is, after all, a critical and rapidly developing conflict. In *The Grand Duke*, Julia's high-flown Queen of the Night star-turn suggests the element of display which is part of her nature. It reflects a falsity within her alleged reluctance, a desire to take centre stage, and a determination *not* to be overlooked. Here, the Italianate *prima donna* mode gains piquancy in the Germanic setting, while the music makes an effective contrast to the greater simplicity (and sincerity) of the melodies allocated to Lisa.

The above has one concomitant: Sullivan's contribution should not be taken out of its theatrical context, for fear of ensuing misjudgements. Gervase Hughes criticizes the 'lack of invention' in the chorus entries responding to Ludwig's account of his revelation of the conspiracy. In fact, the treatment is excellent. The rapid sequencing of the voice-part entries aptly suggests a buzz of concerned gossip sparking through the crowd, continuing until the awful revelation that it was none other than Rudolph's detective whom Ludwig addressed. This then leads to a pause, a communal intake of breath, and a horrified *concerted* response.

Skills with choruses are, in fact, a Gilbert and Sullivan trademark. In *Utopia Limited*, there are no fewer than three Act 1 chorus-arrivals, but they are treated differently, the middle one including a lazy lilting yet over-arching melody which is in direct contrast to the march announcing Scaphio and Phantis (itself in a jauntier time signature on its repeat) and the brassy military mode of the First Life Guards. In *The Grand Duke*, there is equal skill. In the Act 1 Finale, Julia's histrionics are cleverly undercut by a cynically downbeat setting of the Chorus' responses, while later in the Herald's Song, we have a sense of the same people trying to make sense of what is happening, repeating his words to each other as if seeking clarification and assurance. This is an example of the composer's psychological acuity. It is a musical depiction of people gradually taking in and assimilating the unexpected, also offering a sobering moment in their drunken Dionysiac excess.

iv.

Gilbert's (and Sullivan's) skill in dramatic sequencing is everywhere apparent, but it is particularly shown in the Savoy Operas' extended Act 1 Finales. Many of these have sudden dramatic interruptions, as when

Josephine stays Ralph's hand from a suicidal shooting, Hildebrand's soldiers invade the grounds of Castle Adamant, Sir Despard bursts in on the wedding of Rose and Robin, and (more subtly and initially in low-key manner) Grosvenor wanders in reading, causing havoc as the rapturous maidens divert instantly to him from Bunthorne. In *The Mikado*, the effect is particularly fine not only because ebullient joy is set against a terrifying blight but also because, in terms of plot requirements, Katisha need not appear here at all. In practical terms, not much develops. She utters a challenge and is merely repelled.

Why then is Katisha's intervention so potent? Obviously, the dramatic mood-change is striking. It provides a real audience-shock. But there are other validations. One is that the intrusion dramatically and instantly establishes a major powerful character. Another is that the rejection intensifies her determination to inform the Mikado, thereby increasing the suspenseful anticipation as we await his long-delayed appearance. A third is that it justifies, and is a culmination of, what Nanki-Poo has told Yum-Yum of the threat Katisha poses. As for longer delayed arrivals, these are a well-tried technique. In *The Critic*, Mr. Puff boasts that Queen Elizabeth is to be talked of forever but never actually appear. In operas such as *Princess Ida* and *The Mikado*, a much vaunted principal does appear but only after a sustained build-up, making all the more impact after the accumulation of suspense.

The ability to manage climaxes is not confined to Act 1 Finales. In *The Sorcerer*, in Act 2, the inappropriate couplings rise in a kind of steady crescendo leading ultimately to the sorcerer being hoist by his own petard (in being assailed by an amorous Lady Sangazure) and the man who hired him finding his own fiancée in a passionate embrace with the vicar. In *Foggerty's Fairy*, the accumulating disasters afflicting the main character rise to a comedy crescendo of arrest as a madman. A variant is for there to be a number of peaks rather than a steady crescendo. In *The Palace of Truth*, there is not one climax but four of them, all well crafted so that each eclipses its predecessor in power and importance.

The four climaxes in *The Palace of Truth* deserve a repeated mention. The first comes when the King is caught out in a lie, proving that the box he holds is a fake. The second follows when the Prince finds a page of Mirza's diary avowing her love for him. The third, in logical development, shows the genuinely noble Princess yielding her own claim. The fourth and highest occurs when Mirza, the allegedly pure and lofty, is exposed as having stolen the genuine talisman. Not only is this last climax powerful in itself. It is also managed dramatically. Asked, at the moment of her greatest success, for a love-token from the Prince, she brings forth a handkerchief and the crystal box tumbles out in the process. This incidentally is almost a mirror opposite of the rigged production of an apparently winning card in the Act 1 Finale of *The Grand Duke*. In one case, an article is unintentionally produced, accidentally exposing a cheat. In the other, a cheat deliberately plants something to be exposed, so that, by prearranged artifice, a desired outcome may be enforced.

The effective treatment of the climax is an undoubted authorial skill, but it is not only in the big dramatic moments, or indeed in the big dramatic character-parts, that Gilbert shows his abilities. Sometimes, a cameo role such as that of the plodding yet linguistically pedantic Private Willis can be as memorable as much more major contributors such as the Lord Chancellor, the Pirate King, Bunthorne, and Ko-ko. Willis utters platitudes as if they were searing insights. He is pompous and rather stupid yet is also gallant and reliable. In the quartet *In Friendship's Name*, he enters late but prominently as if he has had to be slowly wound up for his contribution. He is also effectively shown as a man who believes that polysyllables equate with learning or at least register an appropriate attitude for thoughtful solemnity. The heavy rigid use of polysyllables in his song is an ingenious variant on the mode of rapid unintelligible patter with which polysyllables are usually associated. Willis' version is characteristically solemn and four-square like his marching to and fro outside the House. Nothing in Act 1 has prepared us for this character yet his appearance – stolid, steady, and reassuring – out of a fairy landscape adds the novelty of a new character while providing a completely different tone from the lively ebullient challenges which closed the first act.

The ability to gain humour from character is not only notable in the musical works. Characters such as the unapologetically Irish Matilda in *Tom Cobb* are notably funny, again all the more because of deliberate juxtapositions. In this case, a down-to-earth, rather casual, borderline slovenly character is deliberately set against the ineffably lofty-minded, nobly exalted (but even more poverty-stricken) Caroline Effingham. Caroline herself probably derives from the more earnest *personae* in *The Serious Family*, a work in which Aminadab Sleek's exalted rhetoric and appeals to 'the disciples of true benevolence' combine with a mercenary concern for the profit-motive. Caroline is less odious but cut from similar cloth. She too combines lofty moralizing with a financial interest, a point shown in her very practical sending to a solicitor of all the letters from her high-souled but absconding fiancé.

The use of similar *motifs* suggests that Gilbert hones his skills within established theatrical parameters. Sometimes, this may lead to a degree of misinterpretation. The usually perceptive Carolyn Williams writes of *Little Maid of Arcady* as an immoral song, maintaining that 'the fable clearly argues that inconstancy and change of sexual partners is only natural, even for women'.[14] This surely is an overstatement. The song – charmingly set – is more like a marionette number in which one character sits down, moves, and is replaced by another. It is not meant to pose a serious moral challenge, though it *is* used to justify the idea of a change of partners. One point here is that the characters within it are deliberately infantilized. They are Little Man and Little Maid in a context of pre-pubescent nursery fantasy. The very fact that the singer Sparkeion was a man played by a woman, far from adding any naughtiness, removes the material from the world of adult sexuality altogether.

The need to bear in mind the prevailing modes has another aspect, which is the degree of cross-reference that exists between a range of dramatic authors. In *The Serious Family*, high seriousness and benevolence consort with an exhausted lassitude and 'world-worn spirits'. This is exactly what is referenced by the lofty-minded but materially depressed Effinghams, as when Bulstrode remarks, 'How nobly he looks when, sickened with the world, he turns his eyes inward to gaze upon his hidden self'.[15] Benevolence meanwhile also has some linked associations. It is associated by Tom Cobb with long hair, which in turn in *Patience* is associated with high aestheticism. In both cases, the long hair makes the apparent nobility suspect, but the main point I am making is that of interconnectedness. *The Serious Family* influenced *Tom Cobb* which inspired *The Colonel* which in turn is related to *Patience*. Literary connections are everywhere, some of them doubtless lost to us or yet awaiting re-discovery.

The above brings us to the question of what *in particular* is unique to the Gilbert repertoire. And here we must avoid exaggeration. Many of Gilbert's devices are time-honoured and long practised. His tendency to balance two characters against each other is, for instance, prefigured by Shakespeare. Short, fiery Hermia and tall, willowy Helena are in structural terms precursors of the melodramatic, flamboyant Belinda and the non-emphatic, childlike (yet mentally razor-sharp) Minnie in *Engaged*. In each case, two girls are juxtaposed in a love-conflict where their mirror-opposite characters and temperaments are highlighted by the contrast. The irony in *Engaged* is that they are actually two sides of the same coin, both being actuated by the financial motivations which drive virtually all the characters.

The fact that Gilbert is part of a tradition prevents our hailing him as a total innovator. Many of his skills mark a refinement of the mode of burlesque and extravaganza, including the latter's sub-genres of the 'classical' and the 'fairy'. One of Carolyn Williams' observations is that extravaganza depends for its fundamental structure on the juxtaposition of a present-day metropolis with a more mythical word of fairy or classical myth. Gilbert certainly follows this pattern, with *Iolanthe*, featuring a fairy-filled Arcady juxtaposed to the Houses of Parliament, and *The Grand Duke* incorporating Ancient Greece in an 18th-century German setting inspired partly by the current Hanoverians. One difference is that he imposes a far tighter structure than most extravaganza writers. Another is that he introduces a philosophical element. He takes, that is to say, a point of view, as, for instance, in the idea of life as an acted sham and hierarchy and authority as a game-playing pretence.

Gilbert's vision – his particular 'take' on the world – is something we must consider within the bounds of a sense of proportion. The very fact that characters are acting could mean that we don't have to take them – or their unpleasantness – seriously. On the other hand, there are clear pointers to later darker treatments. When in *The Balcony*, Genet's false judge calls the false Queen 'Irma', he is momentarily astonished at his own effrontery. Yet at the same time one part of him still knows she is a brothel-keeper and a collaborator in false images.[16] This is an insight shared by Gilbert. Court cards in *The Grand Duke* are merely cards yet we do impute value to them. Here in another plot of revolution and Establishment substitution, we are caught between two stools of belief and non-belief. Given that all authority may be sham, we too may half-acknowledge a validity in the elaborately painted surface.

The fact that Gilbert does have a vision is a point to add to his skills and qualities. It is something we must add to his sometimes brilliant word-play, great rhythmic variety, sound structures, and effective satirical inversions. In addition, we must add, I think, two things. One is the ability to conjure strong tableaux and striking situations. And the other is a refusal to be satisfied with the second best. Scenes such as that in which Princess Ida defies a threatening soldiery from her battlements are potent Act Drop tableaux. The tense drama held within the stage picture is augmented by the fact that nearly all around are begging her to yield. As against this, we might set the mid-act zaniness of episodes such as *Iolanthe's* 'If you go in' trio or *Utopia's* Christy minstrels. These provide not so much a tableau as a moving diorama. They are all life and zest, the essence lying in pomposity being made to throw off all constraints. The effect is of Hamlet playing the Clown. But it is also a way of showing the absurdity of all Establishment structures, reducing them to vaudeville knockabout. This is where Gilbert scores. He can infuse wit into slapstick. He can make a point even within a mode of apparently nonsensical irreverence.

The ability to create striking episodes is in Gilbert everywhere apparent. We see it in the soldiers transformed into aesthetes, in Mad Margaret and Despard transformed into eccentrically dancing but highly respectable automata, even in Constance arriving as the first main example of love at first sight, tied unwillingly to a decrepit old notary. The last case is, it is true, hardly side-splitting. Nonetheless, it is a small example of Gilbert's ability to create amusing stage pictures including a 'surprise' or unexpected element.

The ability to surprise us with the unexpected – ballet-dancing hussars in *His Excellency* or a tradesman-sorcerer amorously pursued by a lady of quality – can be set against smaller effects where the emphasis is on a human situation and a genuine – though comically contained – emotion. When Mrs. Partlett tries to push Constance's claim to be noticed by Dr. Daly, there is the following small exchange:

DR. DALY: Oh, I take you. To be sure. But there's plenty of time for that. Four or five years hence, Mrs. Parlet, four or five years hence. But when the time does come, I shall have much pleasure in marrying her myself –
CONSTANCE: *[aside]* – Oh, mother!
DR. DALY: To some strapping young fellow in her own rank of life.

(*15)

Here without Constance's interjection, the joke would be lost. As it is, there is a double effect. We get the joke without losing sight of Constance's genuine distress. Dr. Daly may 'take' Mrs. Partlett (i.e. he may understand her meaning), but there seems to be all too little chance of his ever *taking* the hand in marriage of her pretty little daughter.[17]

Gilbert's achievement in creating both large-scale comic episodes and tiny incidental effects leads to my last aspect which is that of a concern for excellence. This is difficult to prove or to quantify, but it is seen, for instance, in his willingness to cut, trim, change, and amend. *Thespis*, we know, was originally too long but was made more popular by some judicious cutting and rearrangement.[18] In *Patience*, rival curates were turned into rival poets when Gilbert recognized that censorship constraints were likely to cramp his invention. Sometimes, a whole characterization changes over the course of composition. The swashbuckling but gentlemanly Pirate King, for instance, started life in a much more timid manner, the irony being that so gloriously romantic a figure should be seen to act 'as a genial help in a humble way', cleaning knives, blacking boots, and endlessly responding to his crewmen's importunate ringing for room service.[19] Obviously, not all changes or cuts are advisable, some after a difficult first night suggesting panic rather than a judicious reappraisal. But usually, Gilbert got it right. In the case of the Pirate King, there is a need that in Act 2, we should believe in a degree of gentlemanly ruthlessness. This would hardly apply in the milksop version. The threats to Frederic leading to the violent *Away, Away* trio would here have involved too great a wrenching of character to be either plausible or dramatically effective.

The skills we have seen in Gilbert can be frequently illustrated. But the last thing I would stress is that underlying all the surreal and zany elements his comedy gains by an element of the real. This can be seen at a simple level in accuracy of setting, as in the case of *H.M.S. Pinafore*, famously rigged out with more than merely artistic verisimilitude. But it also lies in the hint of genuine emotion even within an ironic and satirical context. Obviously, in some of the big arias, an emotional height is reached partly by the inspirational quality of the music, as applies, for instance, in *I built upon a rock*. But even in little ways one can see a human heart beating. When Dr. Daly turns to Constance for verification that he is a very old fogy, the irony is obvious. But his tones are convincingly human for someone of his well-bred benevolent type. Constance's responses in which humility and shame rob her of eloquence – are also heart-felt. Perhaps, after all, this is what crafts-manship is. It is a matter of achieving a local effect while integrating the created concept into a wider whole. It is also – as with the revised Pirate King – a matter of shaping and re-shaping, while also coping even with the intrusively unexpected or apparently self-generating, to make it a part of your art.

Legacy

Gilbert's skills, then, are not in doubt. But what effect did he have on later generations, was it a beneficial one and is it still extending its feel-ers? One relevant point here is that of the Janus face. It is a matter of Gilbert's being – or becoming – simultaneously *behind* his theatrical times and *ahead* of them. In some people's critical estimation, he *did* become old-fashioned yet paradoxically it is the old-fashioned qualities which most look to the further progress of fun.

The presence of the old-fashioned element is noted frequently in Gilbert's own lifetime. It can be found, for instance, in the *Era*'s review of *The Fortune Hunter* (2 October 1897). Here we are told, the first act is so obviously expository that 'people can feel the dolls being wound up', in order that they may 'begin to work in earnest later on'. In addition, the rather sparse action is delayed. It is interrupted by 'bits of Gilbertian hu-mour, suggesting a lack of consistent intellectual purpose'.[20] The overall implication is of a lack of modal consistency, an old complaint, found at least as early as *The Ne-er-Do-Well*, to which the *Era* had been equally unforgiving. In the earlier case, the reviewer scorns 'the hop skip and jump burglar and the maiden lady who snaps at every man like a trout at a later summer fly'. It repudiates 'the Magistrate who enquires of how his case ought to be conducted'. These, it says, are an anomaly. They come 'too near the region of burlesque to be tolerated in a serious play'.[21]

There are, in fact, ways of justifying humour within seriousness, as, for instance, in *Romeo and Juliet*, but perhaps one drawback is that the humour is intermittent – that, rather than being strictly disciplined within the formal design, it intrudes amid the apparently serious.[22] Boucicault often committed the same fault, but his serious work – the 'guano' he could produce to order – claimed less for itself than the seri-ous plays attempted by Gilbert. These last, according to the *Era*, could never escape 'the realms of fantasy and topsyturveydom'. He may, in *The Fortune Hunter*, have 'made a very strenuous effort to be natural and true to human nature' but 'People who like to be amused and interested will avoid *The Fortune Hunter* as they would their pet aversion'.[23]

The idea that Gilbert was really no more than a clever bag of tricks is to my mind a gross denigration. But even in his own day it linked him with a slowly dying world of melodrama, mock-melodrama, and burlesque. In addition, he lacked two increasingly valued qualities: an imaginative poetic expansiveness and a keen insight into the meshes of sensitivity in other people's hearts. This, to some, limits him to the mechanical. A fundamental pedestrianism, says David Eden, confined his creative range 'to works in which human emotion, in the proper sense, is not involved'.[24]

If the above is conceded, it helps to explain the nature of Gilbert's most successful work. It does not (unlike Pooh-Bah) attempt verisimilitude. It deals in subversion, inversion, and the kind of legal quibble that treats truth more as a matter of words – of ingenious topsy-turvy logic – than of facts or emotional realities. Another point is that he subverts traditional modes even while including them. Traditionally, extravaganza exploits the juxtaposition of present with past and reality with myth. It emphasized the urban and modern while also offering escape from it. In Gilbert's work, *both* are satirized, so that, for instance, Fairy Rosebud's offered escapes are more like purgatory for those who suffer them. Similarly, Fairy Rebecca's intrusion into Foggerty's life ends, not with escape, but with his being apprehended as a madman and himself imagining he has been involved in a murder.

Despite the above, the charge of outdated tiredness did strike a nerve. In 1934, Edward Ricketts, who provided the incidental music for *The Fairy's Dilemma*, published an account in the *New York Times*, part of which runs as follows:

> My task was to provide an overture, a ballet, and much 'incidental music', all of which was to be selected either from the music of the Sixties or in the manner of that period ... I instituted a sort of house-to-house search of the old music-publishing firms, and I shall not forget Gilbert's delight when at last I dug out of a dust-covered shelf in Charing Cross Road a parcel of long-forgotten melodies which included such gems as 'Champagne Charlie', 'Villikins and his Dinah' and others of the sort which formed the basis of the music of the piece. Nor shall I forget the first night. I never before or since saw in a theatre such a concourse of gray-beards and bald heads. I can only suppose that the gathering consisted of all those old admirers of Gilbert and Sullivan who had followed their work from their first association thirty years before. Never were there such rapturous receptions of mere tunes as those old songs received. Indeed, the éclat of that first night could only be equalled by the puzzled silence of their reception by subsequent audiences, who had not the least idea what they were, or why they were.[25]

The implications here are of a time warp. The piece, for all its merits, is the product of a stalled mind – one, which, says David Eden, 'having failed to match Pinero and even the despised Grundy in moving with the times, had returned to its roots'.[26]

This brings us to the question of how the comedic process progresses. Are there such things as dead ends or does theatre obey Lady Blanche's concept of time, offering a cyclic sense of endless recapitulation?[27] Personally, I err towards the latter view, not least because there are only a few basic comedy *motifs*, affording many examples of a self-perpetuating borrowing. One example here might be that of the strawberry mark used as a sign (or not) of a kinship identity. In John Maddison Morton's *Box and Cox* (Royal Lyceum, 1847), we encounter the following dialogue:

BOX: Cox! *[About to embrace – Box stops, seizes Cox's hand, and looks eagerly in his face.]* You'll excuse the apparent insanity of the remark, but the more I gaze on your features, the more I'm convinced that you're my long lost brother.

COX: The very observation I was going to make to you!

BOX: Ah – tell me – in mercy tell me – have you such a thing as a strawberry mark on your left arm?

COX: No!

BOX: Then it is he! *[They rush into each other's arms.*

Later in *La Vivandière*, the idea is resurrected – indeed, plagiarized – by Gilbert, in the following:

SERGEANT: *[to Lord Margate]* –
    Say, are you covered, pardon the allusion,
    With strawberry marks in prodigal profusion?
    Two on each shoulder, on your bosom four;
    Twelve on your back, on each arm seven more;
    Three on your left foot, nine upon each knee;
    Five on your calves, upon each elbow three,
    Just sixty six in all.

LORD MARGATE: *(rapidly counting.)* –
                        Exactly so.

SERGEANT: –
Then you are *not* the Earl of Margate!

MARCHIONESS: *[surprised.]* –
                        No!

SERGEANT: –
    No peer of Margate, young, old, short, or tall,
    Had ever any strawberry marks at all.

TONIO· *[suddenly]* –
    I have no strawberry marks.

SERGEANT: –

Ha! Then I see
The rightful Earl of Margate you must be;
I can't help saying, for so well I knows yer,
This is a most *extrawberry* disclosure.

Here, the humour is gained first by the hyperbolic proliferation of straw-berry marks and, second, by the red herrings whereby recognition be-comes a matter of a negative. Also included is a socially subversive twist in that a humble Chamounix guide turns out to be actually an English nobleman mainly through a *lack* or *absence* which must be shared by most of the wider population.[28]

The above is in itself not especially important. As Carolyn Williams points out, such satire of the staple recognition scene had preceded *Box and Cox*. It was adapted from *Une chamber à deux lits* (1846), a French farce by Charles Varin and Charles Lefèvre which itself was a deriva-tive.[29] But the point I really wish to make is another one. It is that this idea of the comedy negative – the *lack* or *absence* element – finds its way into the work of one of Gilbert's avowed legatees N.F. Simpson. In the Absurdist world of *One Way Pendulum*, it is regarded as highly suspicious that Mr. Groomkirby happened on the 23 August to be in Chester-le-Street interviewing Myra Gantry. It is amazing because there must have been any number of places from which he absented himself in order to be in that particular spot. He could have been in London or Paris or Rome or Reykjavik yet incredibly be abstracted himself from all of them. The prosecutor's case is that this is incredible. It is ludicrous to claim that, in order to be present in one place, the witness deliberately absented himself from a whole host of places which only an expert ge-ographer could possibly be presumed to have known about. The flaw in the logic is obvious. Mr. Groomkirby did not deliberately absent himself from other places. He simply chose to go to Chester-le-Street. One inter-esting thing here is how Simpson, like Gilbert, so often exploits a legal framework and a technical quibble. He also gives his characters a delib-erately mechanical or marionette aspect, as notably in the circuit judge who (in an electricity pun) is literally switched on in order to perform.

As a concept the mechanical character is very often disparaged, fre-quently being further linked to mechanical plotting. In fact, both Gilbert and Simpson transform traditional stock scenarios, one example being *One Way Pendulum*'s surreal reinvention of the trial-at-law drama found in works such as *Cause Célèbre* and *Witness for the Prosecution*. It is true that Gilbert does sometimes create mechanical figures, both as characters (as in *The Mountebanks*) and as dramatic personae in their own right.[30] But this can be an asset. It can comically suggest how much the human personality is constrained and controlled, while also allow-ing for piquant stage effects. In *The Mountebanks*, this is carried to an extreme. Here, an actor playing an actor (Bartolo) plays Hamlet as a slot-machine figure. Moreover, he had originally turned to clowning because he had failed effectively to bring the character to life in a straight theatrical performance.[31]

i.

The mechanical aspects of Gilbert's art can, then, be justified. But there is another case brought against them. Often, they are said to have extended to his directorial methods. Certainly, he exerted an iron control, but this too may be a valid feature – even a means to a vision. Recently, Terry Teachout writing of Joe Orton's *What the Butler Saw*, remarked:

> Farce is the most paradoxical of all genres of comedy. It requires high discipline on the part of the director, the actors and their off-stage collaborators to set in motion the whirligig of seeming onstage chaos that is farce at its best. Without split-second control, everything falls apart ... Joe Orton's *What the Butler Saw*, a four-door farce of transcendent indelicacy, is as funny a play as has ever been written, but it won't play itself: It must be staged to the hilt, unobtrusively but decisively and in precise accordance with Orton's explicit requirement that the actors behave as though they have no idea that their plight is preposterous. 'Unless it's real', he wrote, 'it won't be funny'.[32]

Gilbert may have excluded Orton's strong sexual element but his often macabre treatment of death, pain, and torture precisely looks forward to the Orton mode, also demanding strict seriousness of playing to spark the sharply comic effects.

The Joe Orton mode is one, I think, that Gilbert would have understood. For one thing, both realized that seriousness of playing in the face of the horrific or preposterous actually adds to the piquancy of the comedy. It makes the horror more striking – even more memorable – by the dichotomy. Secondly, Orton's *motifs* – apart from sex – are precisely those favoured by Gilbert. Orton himself claimed revenge to be one of his strongest, and in Gilbert too, it has prominence. Ranging from vengeful babies through deceived pirates to vindictive Katishas and disgruntled Utopians, it has its most surreal form in some of the play-parodies. One example is *Gemma di Vergy*. Here Gemma, vowing to kill her sister for loving her husband, finds that she merely 'likes him as a brother-in-law'. She therefore instantly decides to take the poison herself, making the avenger into a victim, turning the revenge on herself.

Orton's fondness for revenge *motifs* is linked with another Gilbertian characteristic – that of an avoidance of sentimentality. *Engaged*, famously, was criticized by Filon and Shaw as heartless. It had the detachment which Orton would later claim to have acquired in prison. Admittedly, Gilbert's own assessment of the play is very different from Filon's, but many of Orton's lines do recall the slightly surreal darkness we often locate in Gilbert. The line 'You've lost nothing. You began the day with a dead wife, you end it with a dead wife' has a *Bab Ballads* cynicism. Also, Gilbertian is the faintly bemused 'I like to know where I stand in relation to the number of limbs a man has', and the epigrammatic 'All classes are criminal today. We live in an age of equality'.[33]

The detached cynicism of Joe Orton has yet another Gilbertian feature, which is that of latent cruelty. The *Daily Telegraph*'s initial response to *Entertaining Mr. Sloane* was that it was shameless and repulsive. Not only were the characters and their dealings gross and degraded. There was cruelty in their very creation. Gilbert was often similarly accused and, like Orton, was said to be misogynistic. When Mike Leigh's *Pirates* was produced by English National Opera, Fiona Maddocks in *The Observer* highlighted the 'cruel and misogynistic' aspects of the plot. Stuart Jeffries, interviewing Leigh for *The Guardian*, wrote of the unremitting sexism of *Iolanthe*. Rupert Christiansen in the *Daily Telegraph* referred dismissively (and rather lazily) to Gilbert as a 'classically terrible old sexist'.[34]

It might seem rather perverse to discuss fun's progress in terms of such a backward-looking psychology. But comedy is not bound by law to be politically correct, and in some cases, the criticisms fall wide of the mark. *Princess Ida*, for instance, has been called 'one long joke at the expense of the idea of women getting educated', but much of the humour is relatively impartial.[35] King Gama contemptuously dismisses Cyril's knowledge compared to the superior learning of the ladies. Lady Psyche places men firmly among the apes. At the same time, she is satirized herself, being exposed for not realizing that women too share that dubious distinction.

The truth is, revulsion is too easy a critical stance. It is not difficult to find misogynistic and disparaging attitudes in all sorts of writing, both serious and comedic. *Cosi fan tutte* has as its springboard the idea that women are changeable and faithless. Noel Coward opined that 'Certain women should be struck regularly like gongs'. To some extent, comedy actually *thrives* on moral indifference. Either that or it rejoices in the skewing of the best-laid schemes. In *The Mikado*, Ko-ko, Pitti-Sing, and Pooh-Bah find that they have fictitiously killed the Mikado's son and are doomed to death for it. In Orton's *Good and Faithful Servant*, poisoned water kills those it is meant to aid. Sometimes, evil deeds are actually given a spurious moral validity. In *One Way Pendulum*, Kirby Groomkirby only kills people so that he can go into mourning, though, to be sure, that is mainly because he likes an excuse for the wearing of black.

The moral indifference of black comedy means that we are rarely allowed to involve ourselves emotionally. In *The Mikado*, the imminent execution of the three victims is distanced by jokes about waiting till after luncheon and Pooh-Bah nor wanting any.[36] In *Ruddygore*, the abduction of a shrieking maiden is made funny by the maiden's mature years, stout-hearted defiance, and intimidation of her assailant. Sometimes, in Gilbert's successors, really dark material is included. In *Black Mischief*, Evelyn Waugh manages to make Basil's inadvertent eating of his own fiancée as much amusing as macabre. In *Funeral Games*, as Tessa puts a cake for tea on a doily, Caulfield is seen laying down a meat cleaver while carrying a human head.

The examples of Waugh and Orton suggest that anything cruel in Gilbert can at least be matched by those who follow him. In *Funeral Games*, the introduction of the head severed above the wrist, and wrapped in sacking, leads not to shock or horror but, rather, to a music-hall pun:

CAULFIELD: – I couldn't get her head off. It must be glued on.
MCCORQUODALE: – She was always a headstrong woman.

In Gilbert, beheading is also made darkly amusing, as when Nanki-Poo calls Ko-ko's bluff by bidding him instantly decapitate him. This, in the face of Ko-ko's hesitation, provokes from Pooh-Bah an impatient, unfeeling 'Chop it off! Chop it off!'[37]

An ability to exploit yet undercut the macabre involves various techniques. Sometimes, the jokes lie in a distorted scale of values. The ghosts threatening (and later torturing) Robin are, for instance, quite impressed by his admission of shooting a fox but give no quarter when he prissily declines to carry off a lady. More common are puns and an element of unlikelihood. It is unlikely, for instance, that anyone would smoothly and politely discuss luncheon in a context of imminent and terrible slaughter, or that Yum-Yum – in a pun – would content herself with objecting to burial alive as stuffy. Often included too is an element of visual or linguistic bathos. In *Utopia Limited*, a potential killing of the King with dynamite is presaged by an almost childlike rehearsal with explosive crackers. In *The Grand Duke*, Rudolph tries to encourage Ludwig to be blown up in his place by remarking, 'I daresay being blown up is not nearly as unpleasant as one thinks'.[38]

The refusal to be disorientated by death is a mark of comic resilience. In *The Good and Faithful Servant*, the poisoning at the well – itself referencing old accusations from the time of the Black Death – is made funny by the defensive, rather lofty exculpations of the killer: 'He meant no harm – it was an accident. The sanitary system of an alien country killed them'.[39] A variant is understatement made almost pedestrian, as when Dame Hannah greets Sir Roderick's return from death almost casually, then asks him if – in the grave – he is 'pretty comfortable'. In many cases, homely detail and colloquial language or puns increase the humour. Tess's doily stands in stark gentility against 'I couldn't get her head off' and the 'headstrong' pun. It matches the Mikado's precise use of the elegant term 'luncheon' in relation to a beheading.

ii.

Gilbert's legacy of dark understatement, punning horror and macabre exuberance has another aspect relevant to the English Absurdists. It is a consciously theatrical matter. Often the characters seem to know that they are in a play or to *act* their own selves rather than *being* them. In Gilbert's parodies, this is seen in a deliberate element of self-consciousness, as when, in a burlesque of Tom Taylor's *Lessons for Life*, we are giving a mocking demonstration of the effort required to achieve an impressive stage picture. In this 'pretty piece' (which, says Gilbert, is 'too goody two-shoes in sentiment') the climax comes when an erring son falls penitent at his father's feet. Thereupon, the heroine, entering with graceful assurance, cries, 'A tableau of two? Most inartistic! Let me join you. The pyramidical is the only true form of composition!'[40]

The idea of staging oneself is clearly linked with that of knowing one is in a play and being conscious of the artificiality of the construct. In *A Resounding Tinkle*, this is conveyed when Mr. and Mrs. Paradock discuss their own contribution:

MR. PARADOCK: – My lines seem to be coming to me in bits. Or what seem to be bits ...
MRS. PARADOCK: – What you can't remember you can make up.
MR. PARADOCK: – And what I can't make up can go unsaid.
MRS. PARADOCK: – No one minds with this kind of play. No one notices ...
    So don't, for God's sake start having any qualms over remembering your lines or anybody else's lines ...

Later, there is a direct discussion of the play as a performance in which the pretentious critical comments by scripted observers may be directly related to those in *The Real Inspector Hound*.[41]

Stoppard's crossing of play-world/real-world boundaries may link with Simpson, but essentially, it looks back to Gilbert in whom the overlapping and sometimes deliberate blurring of the bounds between performance and lived reality are part of his proto-Absurdist influence. In *A Resounding Tinkle*, the author appears as a character. He points out that 'The actors are as much the audience as the audience themselves, in precisely the same way that the audience are as much the actors as the actors themselves'. We are all spectators of one another, 'mutual witnesses of each other's discomfiture'.[42] Gilbert in his parodies takes this equally far, at one point allowing a speaking curtain to ring itself down in disgust at the shortcomings of the drama it is framing.[43] What he does *not* notably do is include an element of menace, which very often accompanies Absurdist scenarios. In Pinter's *The Room*, there is a strong sense of the threatening unknowable, as indeed of the danger of invasion by threatening forces. This is a fact which some critics attribute to the author's growing up as a Jew in a period when non-Aryans might well be presented with a Gestapo knock on the door.

The inclusion of this negative point – of what Gilbert does *not* offer – is important because we have to admit that 'legacy' is sometimes difficult to attribute, not least because of the inclusion of personal psychological and artistic factors. In *The Room*, many statements, unimportant in themselves, acquire strangeness because they suddenly have doubt thrown at them. After the landlord, Kidd, has talked quite matter-of-factly about his mother and sister, Rose suddenly says, 'I don't believe he had a sister, ever'. When a young couple arrive, they are looking for the landlord but firmly deny that his name is Kidd. Could there possibly be two landlords? Is Mr. Kidd kidding? And why should they be convinced that the room is vacant, when we can see perfectly well that it is occupied? There is even some doubt about how they approached it – going up or going down, a point which, taken with their name, Sands – suggesting shifting sands of possibility – itself implies the difficulty of getting our bearings.

Taken together, Pinter and Simpson offer a good guide for evaluating both the links and limits in making Gilbertian connections. Gilbert himself frequently uses an invasion plot. Works as diverse as *The Wicked World, The Gentleman in Black* and *Iolanthe* all feature a person or group encroaching on others' territory. Even the arrival of Major General's daughters on a remote rocky seashore is a kind of invasion of piratical territory. More sinister later developments include an electrically operated circuit judge appearing, with full court accoutrements, in a suburban living room, and a sinister music-hall double act invading a mysteriously bizarre seaside guesthouse in *The Birthday Party*. In the latter, the multiple game-playing of Goldberg and McCann may remind us of the games *motif* in *The Grand Duke*, while the role-play element links with the frequent identity changes and ambiguities in *The Gentleman in Black*. One obvious difference is that Pinter omits the supernatural, and another is that both his and Simpson's plays include issues of their own period. In *One Way Pendulum*, the Old Bailey replica constructed by Mr. Groomkirby has its own remit. Surreally, it references the 1960s Do-It-Yourself craze while also suggesting the existence of guilt and criminal secrets at the heart of the apparently innocuous bourgeois community.

Differences, then, there are. As with sugar in tea, new ingredients stirred in do alter the flavour of the mix. But there remains an essential connection. In some respects, Mr. Groomkirby's Old Bailey is the equivalent of the corpse in the garden in *The Waste Land*.[44] It suggests guilty secrets, though in this case without resonances of vegetation myth.

Invasion too nearly always unsettles an existing status quo, though treatments may be widely diverse. In *Iolanthe*, it results in a threat to the whole governing establishment. In *The Room*, it ends in multiple question marks. This is shown at the end when Rose's partner suddenly beats up (possibly murders) a blind Negro intruder, and Rose, by a kind of sympathetic magic is struck blind. What has happened here, we wonder. Is it meant to suggest Rose's latent biological kinship with the intruder or is the implication that we too will remain forever blind to the reality of motivations and backstory behind what has happened?

The *motif* of invasion is a good example of a concept that can be variously twisted. In Pinter, the impression is that no one can be sure about anything. Is there indeed any absolute truth? Motives are unknowable – or, at any rate they are not to be told to us. Maybe the beating was merely a matter of rage at the invasion, incursive forces (as in *Streetcar*) being dangerous in threatening an existing social and psychological balance.[45] In Gilbert, the invasion is usually resolved not by destruction or expulsion but by reconciliation. But this is not inevitable. At the end of *Thespis*, the comedic actors are expelled, being cursed to become eminent tragedians whom no one watches. In *The Wicked World*, as the mortal men disappear, the fairies seem to be awakening from a dream. They regain their true, virtuous selves and are ashamed of their former sexually motivated antagonisms.

The possibility even in Gilbert that all will not be mildly resolved is a sign that he too has disconcerting aspects to his vision. In *Pygmalion and Galatea*, Galatea finds no place in the world of actuality and has to revert to stone. In *The Sorcerer*, Mr. Wells has to be sacrificed. None of these endings poses anything like the metaphysical challenges we find in Pinter, but even the *Thespis* expulsion – lightly satirical though it be – suggests that total harmony is impossible. As in the case of Blanche Dubois, as in that of Pinter's ultimately voiceless Stanley, there will always in life be an element of selection, rejection, repudiation, and loss.

iii.

The lack of menace as a Gilbertian black-comedy ingredient does not, of course, eliminate direct and quantifiable threat. In *The Gentleman in Black*, the power to effect a swapping of souls has devastating, if amusingly treated, results. In *Iolanthe*, the Peers' invasion leads to a furious stand-off, with the Fairy Queen finally pronouncing the doom of the system of hereditary privilege. What is deliberately omitted is the kind of *unspoken* menace that is usually in inverse proportion to its degree of particularization. The 20th-century Absurdists often suggest that, the more defined the threat is, the more we may be able to fight it. Indeed, we may even find it does not apply to us. Gilbert, by contrast, always makes the threat element quite clear. Even in the nightmare song, the inversions and distortions seem rooted in daytime awareness. They suggest the subconscious fear of a regulated daytime system and scale of values veering out of control. The references to bizarre modes and forms of travel augment this: they suggest life departing from its normal route – from its planned, regulated, and rational daylight course.

The rooting of fear in the actual means that in one respect Gilbert falls short of those he may influence. His work lacks any comedic exploitation of the terror of the unknown. In Pinter, the less the threat is clear, the more we can read into it. It may become a repository for all the semi-conscious fears and traumas which lie beneath our rational, controlling surface. In Gilbert, fear is a rational response, to be comically exploited. It is the threat of dynamite or of a stuffy death by burial alive. Admittedly in *The Grand Duke*, Ludwig knows that he will *not* be blown up, but the Grand Duke himself has no such knowledge, producing humour in the aforementioned scene when Ludwig offers to take his place:

RUDOLPH: – Well, really, that's very handsome. I daresay being blown up
    is not nearly as unpleasant as one would think.
LUDWIG: – Oh yes it is. It mixes one up, awfully.[46]

This is the mirror-opposite effect to that of pain existing within a humorous context. When, in *A Handful of Dust*, the cool, efficient Mrs. Rafferty plays Animal Snap with a suddenly bereaved father, the effect of the near-Absurdism is not to mock but actually to *increase* the pathos.

The use of comedy to enforce pathos can be shown in various ways. In the above case, the very fact that 'it's a child's game' augments the effect, as, of course, does the fact that the dead little boy was killed by an *animal* and that his mother is away cavorting in Belgravia. When that mother finally does hear of John's death, she is for a second selfishly relieved that the John referred to is her son rather than her lover, the worthless and parasitical John Beaver. The implication – of a lack of maternalism or indeed any decent human emotion – recalls Julia Jellicoe but goes well beyond Gilbertian heartlessness. In context, it only increases an awareness of the hopelessness of humanity and the tragedy at the centre of existence.

Waugh's comedic approach is in many ways paradoxically serious. It is Agatha Runcible literally driving herself too fast and going off the rails to her death. Sometimes, indeed, comedy is dispensed with altogether. John Andrew's fatal and totally unexpected accident is deliberately presented in a no-nonsense journalistic style. It comes like the jarring of two tectonic plates – the level of the everyday and uncaringly straightforward meeting that of the personally and (ultimately) metaphysically horrific. Gilbert rarely juxtaposes the comedic and serious so potently but he *does* often show simultaneous double modes. The Madrigal *Brightly Dawns Our Wedding Day* ends in tears, while elsewhere the comic can graze the side of the serious and vice versa. In *Patience*, Bunthorne's hilarious posturing does not negate his being 'so unkind' to the heroine that it turns her selfless love to a bitterly plaintive song. In *The Grand Duke*, Lisa's selfless dedication to Ludwig manages to be simultaneously both funny *and* touching, the latter predominating in her Act 2 aria where her gentle submissiveness is directly set against Julia's highly dramatic centre-stage self-glorification.

The wistful sadness within humour is a Gilbertian speciality. Mad Margaret's Act 1 dialogue with Rose Maybud, highlighting love's (and insanity's) obsessiveness, is surreal, sad, and funny all at once. The line 'I once made an affidavit but it died' latently references Despard's love for her which has died likewise. Lisa's case also has various levels. On the one hand, her self-abasement makes an amusing contrast with Julia's near-contempt and dominatrix tendencies. On the other, it has genuine pathos because of the unselfishness of her subservience. Soothing Ludwig when he is 'cross with pain', is, after all, only her tactful way of excusing his irascible temper.[47]

The moments of feminine pathos do at least suggest that Gilbert was more than merely misogynistic. But far more characteristic is the sharpness of his forensic exposure. Nowadays, his mockery of the Law, the House of Peers, and the Establishment may be dismissed as saccharine but originally it packed quite a punch. Disraeli, we know, was made 'quite sick' by *H.M.S. Pinafore*: (a) because of its satire of his appointee, the bookselling First Lord, William Henry Smith, and (b) because of its mockery of the attempt to introduce into the navy new codes of humane discipline and politeness. This was a move already spurred by novels such as *Mr. Midshipman Easy*, but it also has a foreshadowing aspect. Specifically, it looks forward to the less subtle but equally debunking line in radio series such as *The Navy Lark*.

The Navy Lark is an example of Gilbertian deflation of a still well-loved institution. Running from 1959 to 1977, it was an immensely popular sit-com about life aboard a British Royal Navy named *H.M.S. Troutbridge*, a joke version of *H.M.S. Troubridge*, a real Royal Navy destroyer. The ship, like *H.M.S. Pinafore*, was said to be based in Portsmouth, and the treatment was satirical. The difference was that it was more geared to the inversion of strict naval discipline. It included ideas based on actual excuses for late return and other misdemeanours found in extant *H.M.S. Troubridge* bulletins.

Both *The Navy Lark* and *H.M.S. Pinafore* tend to emasculate actual naval rigour. In Gilbert's case, he reduces Government reforms to the level of near effeteness.[48] Thereby, he undermines traditional naval punishments which had been harsh in the face of frequent discontent. In 1797, when the crews of the Spithead and Nore fleets refused to obey their officers, the result was a '*Floating Republic*'. Admittedly, at Spithead, there was a promise of improvements in conditions, but at the Nore, the result was the hanging of twenty-nine mutineers. Interestingly, neither of the mutinies included the cat o' nine tails or impressment in their list of grievances. On the contrary, the mutineers themselves continued the practice of flogging, feeling it necessary for maintaining discipline, once their rejected officers had been sent ashore.[49]

The satire in *H.M.S. Pinafore* is an example of something that has necessarily lost force over the years. In early 1878, it would have been the more striking because the fleet was preparing to go east to prevent a Russian seizure of the Ottoman Empire. In the music halls, the rousing refrain was: 'We don't want to fight, but, by jingo, if we do,/We've got the ships, we've got the men, we've got the money too'. Gilbert, in a serious moment, provided the tars with a more potent alternative – the Glee entitled *A British Tar Is a Soaring Soul*. The irony is that this is provided by the landlubber Sir Joseph – a man who generally goes below in bad weather and has never remotely experienced war service.[50]

iv.

The plot developments in *H.M.S. Pinafore* show that Sir Joseph's reforms belong to fantasy-land. Even the kindly Captain is driven to threatening the cat o' nine tails, while Sir Joseph is seen sending his love-rival to the dungeon. The impression is an authorial cynicism not unlike that of Waugh and Orton, the difference being that there are certain areas which Gilbert cannot infiltrate. Religion and the Church, for instance, are difficult, even the inclusion of the rather charming rector in *The Sorcerer* being criticized by (for instance) the reviewer of *The Monthly Musical Review* (1 January 1878), who sniffily informs us that 'the class of the clergy represented by "Dr. Daly" might have been left untouched, for no good could be done by holding it up to ridicule'. Even before this, Gilbert has changed aspects of his own source story, omitting the young mathematically minded clergyman, possibly based on Lewis Carroll, and expunging the related satire on his absentee superior, the Rev. and Honourable Mortimer de Becheville.[51] Writers such as Joe Orton have a freer hand. In *Funeral Games*, mockery of the church, its ministers, and Christian charities is part of a larger package attacking a wider hypocrisy and middle-class morality. All include black humour, outrageously vicious characters, deliberate bad taste, and surreally presented situations.

The limitations hedging Gilbert's satire mean that he often sets it nominally in the past. *Iolanthe* takes place between 1750 and 1882. *The Grand Duke* is ostensibly set around 1750. This, though effective as distancing, does not do much to disguise the contemporary satire on (for instance) current Government policy, Queen Victoria's Hanoverian relations, the rise of the brewing and cotton lords, and the prevailing Establishment generally. Nor does it prevent real people, such as Captain Shaw, being directly mentioned or even addressed. Sometimes, the pushing back into past time has a variant in that a modern period actually acquires old-fashioned trappings. Judging by Frederic's birthdays, *The*

Pirates of Penzance is nominally set in about 1873, but the pirates themselves are anachronistic, the Pirate King being a rather disillusioned, out-of-time survival from a more romantic, less mercantile age. This is one reason why he should not be played (as he often is) as young and athletic. Wearing his out-of-date wig, and almost courtly in his gravely decorous manners, he represents a vanished world. His gentlemanly qualities and allegiances are precisely the reason for his Act 2 development. So outraged is he at the Major General's ungentlemanly deceptions that his conduct transmutes to a comic form of potentially blood-curdling violence.

v.

Gilbert's ability to make capital of – or distance – certain imposed restrictions means that he achieves subversion even within limitation. But there remain some no-go areas. Roger's self-castration in *The Balcony* would for him be impossible, though the play, like *The Grand Duke*, challenges hierarchical symbolic roles within a revolutionary context. Moreover, even its horror has a burlesque aspect. Roger's blood on the carpet infuriates Irma. It is shed just after he is told that his time for masquerading as the Police Chief is up. One interpretation of the emasculation is that he wilfully destroys what he cannot lastingly be. Since the Chief is monumentally representing himself as a giant phallus, this is a doubly symbolic way of undercutting him.

There is another reason why Gilbert eschews extremes. Temperamentally, he feels the need to shore up the social fabric even if its institutions are hollow and their value contrived. Chaos must after all be avoided. Better a gradual reform than out-and-out anarchy. The law in fact looks two ways: it is both a support and sometimes the reverse, serving as an embodiment or agent of a corrupt system. This applies too in N.F. Simpson where, however, it is the paradoxically anarchic associations that are stressed. In *One Way Pendulum*, the Judge plays cards – three-handed whist – in a game where he himself plays Mr. Groomkirby's hand. The treatment is an extreme variant of aspects of *The Grand Duke*, the deceptive playing card *motif* obviously being common to both.

Even mid-20th-century writers did not have total licence. But their parameters were notably wider. In *Funeral Games*, a cult leader, preacher, and con-artist called Pringle hires the thuggish criminal Caulfield to investigate an anonymous report that his wife Tessa is having an affair with McCorquodale, a defrocked Catholic priest. This seems to be false witness, but the non-celibate McCorquodale really *has* killed his own wife, burying her in the cellar. Only in the more macabre of the *Bab Ballads* does Gilbert venture into this sort of territory, and even *there* the sexual elements are limited. By contrast, in the Orton play, Pringle still maintains a wish to kill Tessa, being encouraged in it by a whole congregation, including the mysterious Lady of the Wand. The humble and the meek, says he, are thirsting for blood. Later when he has come within an inch of shooting her, Caulfield tells Tessa, in a mockery of Christian charity generally, that he was prompted to it by the Fathers of Love.[52]

The comedic involvement of a religious sect in potential murder would, in Gilbert's day, have been unthinkable. But there still remain strong links. In Orton's play, Pringle decides to tell people that his wife has 'gone away', a classic ploy intended here to help him gain respect as a killer and to appease his bloodthirsty cult members. This is a variant on Gilbert's own use of inverted respect for criminality, as occurs in *Princess Toto*, *Gentle Alice Brown*, *The Brigands*, and *The Burglar's Story*. Another link is that the *mésalliances* and inverted values relate to Bakhtin's concept of the carnivalesque.[53] Carnival, in Bakhtin's view, was a social institution – it was an inversion of which *grotesque realism* was the literary mode. Orton and Gilbert often invert the apparently normative, but this does not necessarily make the treatments *unreal*. What they are doing is showing the human underside, unveiling those 'interested motives' and wells of viciousness which are, in fact, the latent truth.

vi.

The revelation of the latent reality is essentially a defiance. It strikes at an accepted superstructure of socially convenient lies. This in turn can threaten a power base, an idea also canvassed by Bakhtin when, writing of laughter, he stresses its therapeutic and liberating force, arguing that 'laughing truth ... degrades power'.[54] Gilbert might well agree, though his scope to display it is limited. True, Alice Brown's priest is shown as collusive with murderers. But this is only in a short burlesque poem. There are no stage-works by Gilbert containing lines such as 'A mendicant monk objected to something I'd said. Made a terrible mess of my face with his crucifix'.[55] In the theatre – watched over by the Lord High Disinfectant – more decorum must necessarily be observed.

Faced with incipient censorship, Gilbert clearly had to tread carefully. Nonetheless, he found various ways to combine the subversive with the acceptable. One is to distance any apparently lauded viciousness from contemporary everyday life. Princess Toto lives nowhere in no-time and is, in any case, a fantasist. Her brigand-chief is actually the effete Prince Caramel seeking to impress her by indulging her fantasies. Other outlaws, brigands, and marauders are either removed to exotic settings such as the mountains of Sicily or given the fatal flaw of a tender sentimentality. What *remains* similar with the Orton approach is the technique of inversion. In *Funeral Games*, Pringle's ploy of being suspected of murder in order to gain respect actually works. It causes the membership of the Brotherhood to increase. This is very like the mood of *Gentle Alice Brown*, where objectionable conduct is embraced and morally commendable behaviour implicitly vilified.

The inversion of the norm is in Gilbertian comedy a consistent feature. In *Topsyturveydom*, England (a land hitherto unheard of by the
topsy-turvy monarch) is described as a barbaric region where everything
is done on inverted principles. Babies are born young and ignorant,
growing gradually old and wise; ugly is pretty, pretty is ugly; all the men
are women and all the women men. Here, one of the ironies is that our
norm is presented as abnormal. To Crapolee, the King's Prime Minister,
England itself is Upsidownia. Such *Topsyturveydom* is the stuff of Orton.
When a reporter, seeking to prove Pringle innocent, sends him a note to
that effect, Pringle is outraged. He bemoans there being 'no end to the
malice of people'. Vowing to seek professional advice from his lawyer,
he pronounces it a clear case of a private citizen being persecuted by the
Press. It embodies defamation of character. 'What's to be done?' he says.
'Think of the scandal. I'd never live it down if I were found innocent'.[56]

vii.

The links between Gilbert and later writers suggest his sustained influence. But this does not necessarily mean that there is direct imitation,
nor does it deny antecedents. Looking back to Aristophanes, Ben Jonson,
Goldsmith, and Sheridan, he also looks forward to Waugh, Auden, Isherwood, Simpson, Stoppard, Orton, and in lesser degree to Pinter and Alan
Bennett. Among other shared features the most notable is the mockery of
authority and Establishment figures. There is also much mockery of classic human flaws such as vanity, pride, and love of display, though – as in
the treatment of Katisha's pride in her elbow – these are given a new twist.

It is, however, in the treatment of the Establishment that a more specific link can be found. In the semi-surreal, semi-naturalistic *The Ascent
of F6*, Lady Isabel, one of the authority figures, addresses the nation
with the words, 'The Englishman is reserved. He does not wear his heart
on his sleeve'. Yet later, at the climax, she, Lord Stagmantle, and General
Sir Dellaby-Couch, seeking to gain a better hearing, are seen jostling
each other, jumping on each other's shoulders and 'behaving in general
like the Marx Brothers'.[57] The effect is to reduce the Establishment to a
vaudeville, as also happens with *Utopia*'s Christy Minstrels. In *Topsyturveydom*, the implications are even more extreme. One example comes
when Satis, M.P. for Ballotville, states that he would particularly like to
witness the deliberations of the country's collective wisdom. This leads
to the following dialogue:

KING: – The collective wisdom?
SATIS: – Yes. I mean I should like to be present at a sitting of the House.
KING: – Oh, I know what you mean. It's an odd request: we only admit
    the most learned and intellectual men in the kingdom into our House.
SATIS: – Oh, so do we. This place is not so topsy-turvy, after all!
KING: – Poor devils!

SATIS: – Poor devils?

KING: – Yes, they're all inventors and writers and men of science – in fact, paupers.

SATIS: – Do you mean to say you entrust the making of your laws to paupers?

KING: – My dear sir! These people don't make our laws.

SATIS: – But I asked to see –

KING: – The House –

SATIS: – Yes – the House of Commons.

KING: – Oh, I beg your pardon. You asked to see the collective wisdom of our country. I thought you meant the workhouse. Our Parliament is composed principally of wealthy donkeys who are elected partly because they are wealthy and partly because they are donkeys.

SATIS: – In my country, Members are elected because they represent most faithfully the opinions of their constituents.

KING: – Oh, in my country seats are bought and paid for.[58]

Here there is no need for vaudeville slapstick. Whether House of Commons or House of Peers, the implication (by mirror-opposite reversal) is that the King is actually talking of a farcically managed Great Britain.

viii.

The mockery of the Establishment certainly links Gilbert with his satirical successors. But there are differences. Lady Isabel, the General, and Stagmantle (based on Lord Beaverbrook) are cunning manipulators. They present a politically expedient mission to conquer a mountain as a patriotic endeavour, downplaying the fact that it is weapon in an Anglo-German war of diplomacy. Gilbert by contrast suggests government ignorance. He suggests incompetence. What links the two plays is an attack on privilege which in Gilbert involves a concept of inverted values seen through the prism of two worlds. The irony is that they are mirror opposites and simultaneously identical. *Topsyturveydom is* Great Britain. Just because people walk on ceilings and are born old and grow young, this does not mean that politically there are not closely related motivations and structures.

The suggestion of unity in opposition links with another of Gilbert's techniques, which is unexpectedly to *conflate* two different worlds or modes of thought. When the choristers in *The Mikado* sing 'The Japanese equivalent for Hear! Hear! Hear!' they are revealing what this libretto really is: not so much a patronizing 'Yellowface' piece of cod-Orientalism as a satirical ridiculing of British attitudes and institutions, with the exoticism serving as picturesque window dressing. Below lies burlesque critique, the targets ranging from self-important town councillors, to small town politics, to lady novelists, to contemporary politicians to (inverted) Darwinian theory. Generally speaking, everything is devalued, though, of course, value itself is ambiguous. In *The Grand Duke*, a double zero in Roulette is the lowest denomination, but for the bank, it is a winner. In the statutory duel, the lowest card is a loser, though the ace – its embodiment – had earlier been seen as the winning highest.

As against conflation, there is an opposite mode of ironic juxtaposition, the humour depending not on collage or blending but on tonal clash. This approach is generally expressed linguistically. In *An Old Score*, Colonel Calthorpe, coming upon Ethel quarrelling with Casby, tries to get them to make up by asking rather coyly, 'What do little birds do in their nests, James?' James is nonplussed but doubtfully hazards, 'Lay eggs?' This is not at all what the Colonel meant: 'They *agree*, James – they *agree*', doing so 'by mutual concession under crowding circumstances'. Here the biological, almost pedestrian laying of eggs is set against something very different. It is comically commandeered for the uplifting idea of the birds seemingly intent on giving us 'a beautiful lesson'.[59]

The double-tone or overlap technique is, deliberately or fortuitously, followed by many of Gilbert's successors. In Alan Bennett's *Her Big Chance*, a would-be movie star is told by the porn-film director, 'At last we're cooking with gas'. She asks, 'Is that good?' and, when told that it is, replies, 'Oh. Because I prefer electricity'. In *A Chip in the Sugar*, Graham's elderly mother befriends the attendant in the disabled toilet. When he asks what they were talking about, she answers 'Hanging', adding that the kindly woman is in favour of stiffer sentences for minor offences. Here, the combination of kindly help with ruthless ideas makes for a comic effect also found in the Mikado. It is seen in his matching of exquisite politeness with extreme sadism as he calmly and painstakingly points out his lack of anger in enforcing an ill-drawn law's excruciating punishments.

The unexpected response, or the mixing of the metaphorical with the actual, has another effect. It adds a minor surrealism to even the most ordinary of conversations. In *An Old Score*, the Colonel follows up his beautiful lesson by suggesting that Ethel and Casby should do as the little birds do and shake hands. In *Funeral Games*, Tessa absurdly suggests that she 'shall deny that [she is] alive', whereupon McCorquodale responds, 'I'll kill you then'. In all such cases, language is being used as a game, encapsulating impossibilities (birds shaking hands) or such extreme unlikelihoods as living people expecting to be believed in proclaiming they are dead. Sullivan disliked it. He prefers a story of human interest and probability, disliking what he calls 'fantastical devices'.[60]

ix.

It is impossible here to indicate all the ways in which Gilbertian humour is a precursor. But in my view, it is the English branch of Absurdism which is his main bequest. What, then, is it, and to what extent is his foundation later built upon and extended by his successors?

The term 'Theatre of the Absurd' appeared for the first time in 1961, its characteristics being summed up in 1968 by Irving Wardle as:

> substitution of an inner landscape for the outer world; the lack of any clear division between fantasy and fact; a free attitude towards time, which can expand or contract according to subjective requirements; a fluid environment which projects conditions in the form of visual metaphors; and an iron precision of language and construction as the writer's only defence against the chaos of living experience.

The impression is of a kid-glove reversal. The subconscious becomes externalized, showing its workings, the Gilbertian paradox being that, if the outer self is an acted self, there may be an inversion even in *that*. Another ingredient is the de-regulating of Time. Time, says Wardle, may expand or contract according to subjective requirements. It is fundamentally arbitrary. This – an idea already mooted in *The Mikado*, *Ages Ago* and *The Gentleman in Black* – may link with a sense of the environment projecting conditions in the form of visual metaphors. Gilbert's environments may admittedly seem solid enough. But the visual metaphor is there. Often, it is that of the playing card world. Equally, it may be a reformed parliamentary system from which *Iolanthe* proposes that we should escape sky-high.[61]

The need to escape from our existing environment suggests in Gilbert a tension – that between control and release. On the one hand, he values order and sees the point in hierarchy. In *The Sorcerer*, the old rural class-based calibrated structures ultimately defeat the world of the intrusive urban tradesman upstart. Yet there is some flexibility. Lowly Constance does, after all, win the vicar. And beyond that there is a sense of the abyss. Life is a joke in which we are all bit-players. On the one hand, we are each alone in a condition which sours the temper, thins the tresses, and shows us mutually at the mercy of Time. On the other, we are all in it together. We may, therefore, feel a need to work together to shore up fragments against our ruin.[62]

There is another way in which Gilbert fits the Absurdist definition. This is in his dual response to flexibility and precision. Life may be shifting but language use is precise. It is, as King Paramount puts it, more the rapier than the bludgeon. One Absurdist aspect is that this precision may itself be at the service of false logic, based on a surreal premise. At the end of *The Mikado*, the false logic is based on the idea that the Mikado's word is law. When he says 'Let a thing be done', it is as good as done and, if it is done, why not say so? Such an argument, applied to the false report of Nanki-Poo's death, makes that death real, although it never happened. When the Mikado bids the killing of a gentleman, he is in effect already dead.[63] One of many flaws in this argument is that there is in reality a lapse between an order and its commission, but, here again, time is distorted so that the will may be taken for the deed.

The twisting of legal logic is part of a wider Absurdism whereby everything is both ruthlessly pinned down and continually shifting. This can be linked with Gilbert's obsession with the law. Gilbert was a failed barrister in his youth and a lay magistrate in his old age. He loved the legal world, not least for its theatricality, and he was compulsively – even maniacally – litigious. Law – as Thomas More tells us – underpins order and, like Degree, imparts a structure on the potentially meaningless. Yet many of its rules are arbitrary and some (as at the end of *Iolanthe*) can be changed at the flick of a pen and inverted to their opposite.

The double face of the Law helps to explain why an Absurdist world may be both fixed and fluid. Ionesco in *Rhinoceros* often exploits a kind of mad linguistic logic and Simpson makes it a major part of his technique. The other point is that the law is not everything. Behind its structures and rituals and allusion to precedent, there may also be a strong sense of the insubstantial. Ionesco's earliest coherent memories were not of order, even of a mad inverted kind, but of a kind of living-dead phantasmagoria: 'On the sidewalks [were] sombre silhouettes in agitated movement, people in a hurry – phantom-like, hallucinatory shadows'. This is a grim transmutation of Gilbert's shadow of a shade. For Ionesco, 'When that image of that street comes to life again in my memory, when I think that almost all those people are now dead, everything seems a shadow, evanescence. I am seized by a vertigo of anxiety'.[64]

The idea of a context of underlying chaos means perhaps that language is a weapon. It either keeps the chaos at bay or traps and disempowers it by rigid definition. In Gilbert, language use is usually precisely forensic. Gilbert the gentleman is also Gilbert the revelatory cynic. Joe Orton's cynicism is more overt (and perhaps less surprising), and it is also more wide-ranging. Nonetheless, the mode is the same. Both deconstruct the edifices built by the controlling power base. In Mike Leigh's view, Gilbert was a natural subversive: 'His merciless lampooning of the heartless constraints of laws and etiquette reveal him, underneath it all, to have been a genuine free spirit and a true anarchist'.[65]

The anarchism in Gilbert is matched by a devious cunning, also seen in his approach to his own law-suits. Here, the tendency was borderline Machiavellian: it was to seek to evade uncomfortable truths by resorting to legal quibbles. Deep down, this suggests that the law – the great embodiment of the nation's moral, ethical, and social values – is a kid glove capable of being turned inside out, manipulated or multifariously construed. *One Way Pendulum* gives us an electric judge who is a manic, manipulative extension of the cunningly arbitrary one in *Trial by Jury*. Joe Orton's *Loot* is more direct. In that play, Inspector Truscott's response to a youthful challenge to his authority is to swear to 'kick those teeth through the back of your head'. The Absurdist aspect is seen in some of the inversions: 'I've fixed everything to my satisfaction. My men will be here shortly. They're perfectly capable of causing damage unsupervised'.[66]

Another aspect here is that of role-play. Many Absurdist dramas – and some that are basically realistic but include Absurdist possibilities – suggest the idea of life as enactment. Gilbert too suggests this, his tendency being to draw deliberate attention to the artificiality of a willing suspension of disbelief. When Bunthorne asks, 'Am I alone and unobserved? I am', he is intended, before the last two words, to glance slyly and quizzically at the audience, the joke being that he is *not* unobserved, for the audience is watching him. This is quite unlike the soliloquy mode in (say) *Hamlet, Macbeth*, or even in the Malvolio of *Twelfth Night*. It does, however, link with the mode of *A Resounding Tinkle*, where the author (an actor) immediately highlights the artificiality by directly addressing the audience.

The direct address mode is, in fact, less common in Gilbert than such para-theatrical devices as the 'Japanese equivalent' for an English exclamation. In later Absurdist writing, the breaking of the illusion tends to be more overt. Simpson's actor-playwright tells the audience:

> There is no desire, no intention on my part, or on the part of any of us on this side of the footlights, to impose on you any ready-made idea of our own as to what this play ought to turn out to be. So often the author – we have all known him – moves invisibly among his audience nudging one and distracting another, muttering and mouthing among his betters. Or he leans forward from time to time to make simultaneous overtures of sumptuous impropriety to every Aunt Edna in the house. Such has never been my conception of the relationship that should exist between us. No. It is together that we must shape the experience which is the play we shall all of us have shared.[67]

The implication here is that nothing is fixed or certain. The play exists in a kind of fluidity. Each audience, indeed each individual member of each audience, constructs the experience of the play from the materials offered by author and actors.

The idea of the fluidity of theatrical possibilities is brought to centrality in *The Grand Duke*. In that piece, Ludwig has one conception of the Grand Duchess role while Julia, who will play it, envisages the mirror opposite. The snag is that the script in Absurdist drama is actually fixed. It rejects the improvisational mode of the *Commedia dell'Arte*. Hence, freedom of expression becomes something of an illusion with the characters dancing like puppets to the tune of given words. Julia's apparent advantage is that she intends to devise her own script, but this is impossible because she is contained within a drama written by Gilbert. The mode is that of the editor-character in *The Athenian Murders*. More directly it anticipates the Theatre of the Absurd where characters often jib at the roles authors assign to them.

Resistance to one's role is not, however, anything new. Hamlet finds it hard to narrow himself down to playing a revenger's part, talking in theatrical terms of the motive and cue for passion. In Absurdist drama, this may become a more sinister sense of a bewildering enactment. In *The Birthday Party*, Goldberg's line 'Play up, play up and play the game' seems to include the idea of role-play in life itself, he and McCann being part of a staged (and shifting) music-hall double act.[68] In the first version of *A Resounding Tinkle*, there is a similar unexpected arrival when someone suddenly appears at the door to invite Bro to form a government. This – an example of an imposed role – leads to resistance expressed strictly in terms of logic and common sense: 'How can I start forming a government at six o'clock in the evening?' The obviously bigger question is why anyone should expect a suburban householder to undertake such a responsibility in the first place.[69]

A Resounding Tinkle is a good example of Gilbertian duality. The logic-based jokes exist in defiance of a total *ill*ogicality – a kind of inspired zaniness – in the actual *situations*. Before the government-forming scenario, the Paradocks have been complaining that the elephant which they have just had delivered is too big. On the other hand, their neighbour's snake is too small. Hence – with illogical logic – they decide to exchange pets. Shortly afterwards, there is an even odder exchange-variant. Uncle Ted comes in as a dazzling blonde, having had a sex-change on a journey from Inverness whence he has come (to South London) to hear the radio news. Here, the treatment of unexpected gender-change recalls *Happy Arcadia*, while the jokes based on travelling recall *Utopia Limited*. In particular, Ted's tremendously long journey just to hear the news makes fun of the eclipsing of distance. It matches Zara's comment on the Flowers of Progress washing their hands after their very lengthy and apparently stormy crossing to reach Utopia.[70]

The bizarre jokes within allegedly real situations bespeak another way in which Gilbert looks to later comedy theatre. This is the grounding of fantasy or absurdity within an apparently authentic context. Bro and his wife may have harboured an elephant, but this is only an extreme version of the well-known suburban English tendency to keep pets. In Gilbert, authentic or at least realistic detail often 'grounds' the flights of fancy. In *H.M.S. Pinafore*, the baby-swap plot (satirizing *Il Trovatore*) is absurd. It would make Ralph and the Captain roughly equivalent in age. Yet Josephine's reference to the interior of the Captain's luxurious house and her grim view of poverty in a back street blasted with the noise of barrel organs adds a kind of comedy realism. The expression of the ideas may be amusing, but the pictures in the mind are real. Another point is that, when the absurd *does* happen, no one is much surprised. Such is the case when Hannah meets Roderick's ghost, and when Uncle Ted enters as a nubile woman. Both cases suggest the play's self-contained parameters. Both are themselves a source of the comedy of bizarre acceptances.

x.

If Absurdist comedy roots itself in the actual, the same applies when it inverts and undermines it. In *One Way Pendulum*, the paid employment of an immensely fat woman to come and eat excess family food is a satire on Western waste, Western consumerism, and the existence, even within prosperous societies, of the institutions which we now call food banks. In Gilbert's *Engaged*, there is a mirror opposite. In that play, the outwardly expansive and generous Cheviot Hill suggests to his bride a fireside game of thinking up the cheapest possible dinner for nine-pence and the next day having it. Both examples suggest implicit criticism of the attitudes revealed. So too does the presentation of Angus Macalister whose ways of making an honest living include poaching, running an illicit whisky still, and throwing trains off railway lines. This last has a strongly economic point. It is so that the poor distracted passengers will spend their money being fed and bandaged by his fiancée and the latter's elderly mother.[71]

Of all the role-playing inversions, the most potent concerns human relationships and family life. Frequently, in Gilbert, babies are swapped, identities are confused, and there is an odd theatricality in bonding relationships. In *Thespis*, mythological role-play cuts across family genealogy and even marital ties. In *The Grand Duke*, Julia lives her entire life as role-play, a mode which she says will eventually extend to marital love and (faked) maternalism.[72] Later plays may seriously and comically cover the same territory. In *Who's Afraid of Virginia Woolf?* Martha enacts an increasingly desperate maternal fantasy with an imaginary son. In *The American Dream*, Mommy, Daddy, and Grandma, seeking a replacement for the adopted child that 'went wrong and died', purchase a replacement who is dead inside, drained of genuine feeling and the capacity for experience. He will do anything for money – even to the extent of role-playing a family member.

The golden or god-like external concealing a void or a moral emptiness has many variants. In *Troilus and Cressida*, refracted through the sickly, shrivelled man in golden armour, it becomes an image of the war itself. Elsewhere what is highlighted is family and social dysfunction. Ionesco was much influenced by the Punch and Judy shows which he saw at the Luxembourg Gardens, themselves linked with 18th-century puppet theatre and the mode of the *Commedia dell'Arte*. Puppets talking, moving, and clubbing each other were for him dysfunction made visible: 'It was the spectacle of the world itself, which, unusual, improbable, but truer than truth, presented itself to me in an infinitely simplified and caricatured form'. It underlined the grotesque and brutal truth – the essential savagery of life.[73] In Gilbert, violence tends to be more suggested that enacted, but it is sometimes shown and frequently latent. In *Gentle Alice Brown*, the young blameless sorter at the Customs Office is bludgeoned, slaughtered, and dissected. In *Ruy Blas*, Don Sallust is horribly killed but manages to resurrect himself for the all-singing, all-dancing Finale.

The turning of a conception of life into actual physical violence is particularly notable in Pinter. Bert's vicious assault on the negro intruder suggests another vicious intrusion – that of the irrational – though motivations remain as clouded as Rose's sight. The impression is of hidden secrets and a backstory we are not permitted to know. Everybody has secrets. Everybody is fundamentally a mystery to others. The violence itself may suggest the snapping of a pent-up force in a man long crushed by his wife's obsessive garrulousness. Her blindness may suggest an unwillingness to face the reality of what she has seen. Alternatively, it could be a kind of identification with the now permanently unseeing victim who in some interpretations is her father, guilty in the past of incest.

The violence that shockingly ends *The Room* cannot be fully interpreted. It may reflect sexual jealousy or racial hostility. It may be a response to the fear that Riley is about to reveal some secret regarding Rose's birth.[74] In Gilbert's treatments, there may be a similar perversity, but usually, there will be a precise cause to blame. The Mikado blames the shoddy drawing up of the law. It is this that accounts for his need to pursue – without anger – a very macabre range of punishments. In Pinter, the matter is more extreme because there is no explained reason for the assault. Perhaps, violence is endemic in all of us. Perhaps, all it needs is a trigger. One implication of the play is that the floors of the apartment building relates to different levels of consciousness, the basement hinting at latent violence, dark hidden forces, and primal desires. Meanwhile, the room itself – suggesting also *womb*, *tomb*, *doom*, and a kind of jarred *home* – hints at the small contained area of our lives suspended in a possibly meaningless space.

The path from Gilbert to Pinter is towards greater bleakness. Yet even Gilbert can be pretty macabre. Mike Leigh argues that the Savoy pieces are by no means 'light' operas. They are not soft-centred romantic offerings, any more than they are operettas, which are 'frilly, frothy affairs, devoid of any shade of the dark side'. His own suggestion (which I endorse) is that they be called grotesque and/or Absurdist.[75] The very fact that the Mikado is 'not a bit angry' at the alleged death of his only son points towards an extreme heartlessness. The blaming of the law suggests a tyrant-sadist's devious diversionist tactics. What tends to be *lacking* is a cosmic metaphysical dimension. This – related in Pinter to menace – has a long Fantasy-Absurdist history that considerably predates W.S. Gilbert.

The examples from the past show that Fantasy-Absurdism did not start with Alfred Jarry. *Gulliver's Travels* is one borderline case, but even more striking is *The Blazing World* which preceded it. What these works share with Gilbert is comic vitality. They show that alienation and a sense of life's lack of meaning or purpose need not deny fantastical invention and lively exuberance. *The Blazing World* is probably *too* randomly exuberant and is certainly no masterpiece. But it does anchor the vitality of comic invention in a context of fantasy lands and in a small way is proto-Absurdist in playing with different levels of metaphysical reality.

The Blazing World was written in 1666 by Margaret Cavendish, Duchess of Newcastle. The world itself is a region found by a Lady who has been carried away in a boat, blasted into the icy sea and left, surrounded by dead men drifting she knows not where. Luckily, things improve. She finds herself in a strange place among 'a wonderful kind of creatures' which excite fear and awe. Instead of houses, the inhabitants live in caves under the ground. They can create wind (not of the bilious variety) which they use to propel boats and which serves as a battering ram. Their Emperor's ships are pure gold and his palace shines with precious stones. This, however, is a very class-based and not altogether comfortable society. No one is allowed to wear gold but those of the imperial race. Priests and governors are castrated so that they will concentrate on serving the realm better. Non-royal people meanwhile take various odd shapes and sizes – there are worm-men, fish-men, spider-men, bird-men, fly-men, and so on. One of the Lady's pleasures is to cross-question these creatures. She asks the bird-men, for instance, about the nature of thunder and lightning, opining that it might be caused by slivers of ice falling upon each other.

The Duchess's Blazing World is only one of many fantasy places, beginning (as far as records can tell) with the Ancient Egyptian island of the Holy Snake.[76] But it is interesting to us because of its Gilbertian *modus operandi*, its recourse to dubious logic, and its use of inversion as a critique of social and political actualities. One of the syllogisms advanced is: 'Every politician is wise. Every knave is a politician. Therefore every knave is wise'. This is immediately countered with 'No politician is wise. Every knave is a politician. Therefore no knave is wise'.[77]

The plot of *The Blazing World* is essentially feminist. The Lady-heroine, by marrying the Emperor, becomes the Empress, the most glittering being in a glittering world. The metaphysical aspect – developed in a rather muddled way – relates to soul-existence which is not exactly absent from Gilbert but is treated differently. In *The Gentleman in Black*, souls are exchanged, but this is more a matter of personality and temperament than linked to a spiritual or abstract dimension. In *Princess Toto*, the Princess has two worlds, one of the imagination and one of reality, but only in Lady Blanche do we get a (heavily satirized) treatment of the nature of existence and the soul and the mysteries of Time.

The difference between soul as temperament and soul as metaphysical emanation is most easily illustrated by an example. In one section of *The Blazing World*, the Lady, now the Empress, sends for the soul of the Duchess of Newcastle (this being the writer) and is persuaded by the Duchess to make an imaginary world of her own. This she does, filling it with all kinds of creatures and with admirable laws. However, she is still restless. She wishes to see the Duchess's *English* world and travels, in soul-form, with the Duchess all over the place, even going to court and the theatre where she finds the music and the dancing more pleasant than the play.

The above is all rather episodic, but some sort of a climax is reached when the Duke's soul manages to intrude itself, generously entertaining the Empress's soul with 'scenes, songs, music, witty discourse and pleasant recreations'. Meanwhile, the Duchess and the Empress reinforce each other. Together they make a super-powerful Womanhood which, although expressed with rambling discursiveness, raises notable metaphysical issues. Power here has to depend partly on a kind of magic. It is through the miraculous abandonment of the body that the two – who are really aspects of one – are able to commune with each other, working almost as platonic lovers.

The linking of games, fantasy, and the metaphysical suggests a thin but traceable line extending from the Duchess of Newcastle to 20th-century Absurdism. On the way this takes in Gilbert, not so much in the metaphysical dimension as in the sense that the dream-world sections imply the need for make-believe – for fantasy ideals of better possibilities.

Another link is that of sheer theatricality. Even the Duchess's real (English) world sustains an overall theatrical mode, since it is mainly a pageant of songs, shows and multifaceted masquerades. Where differences arise, it is mainly in viewpoint and the lack of a subverting wit. The Duchess's Blazing World is, to those of aristocratic, self-aggrandizing propensities, a kind of Utopia. It is in its very nature extravagantly elitist. One difference from 20th-century Absurdism is that the dangers are far more solidly envisaged than anything (say) in Ionesco's savage nothingness or Pinter's undefined menace. In the second part, the Blazing World is threatened by very tangible wars and rebellion, these being conflicts which the soul of the Duchess of Newcastle is inevitably called upon to sort out.

The two-souls, two-world model is (without the latent sexual element) directly relevant to Gilbert. But, except when satirizing its pompous vacuity, Gilbert avoids any metaphysical or indeed much philosophical dimension. This is unlike the Duchess who specifically tells us, '... concerning the Philosophical-world, I am Empress of it my self'. What much more interests Gilbert is the *human* dimension. Just as Strephon is split between fairy and mortal, Gilbert suggests a human duality. All of us, he implies, may be split between reality and fantasy, the poetic and the prosaic, the power of the imagination and the rule of law. Gilbert, that is, rarely considers our place in eternity. The nearest he gets to it is in hinting that we may just be living in a void, rolling, uncaring universe.

The uncaring universe idea is most clearly and simply conveyed in *To the Terrestrial Globe*, a verse which may be inspired by the fifty-second quatrain in Fitzgerald's *Rubáiyát* where we read of the sky rolling impotently on 'as Thou or I'.[78] This, however, is not the whole picture. It is partly offset by *Eheu! Fugaces* where the Book of the Earth suggests a message of seasonal growth and decline and of some kind of meaning to the process, albeit with an emphasis on dissolution.[79] There are also less linear treatments. Lady Blanche posits a cyclic mode, while in *Topsyturveydom*, there is a strong sense that things change according to how we look at them. One point worth remembering is that comedic treatments do not necessarily suggest authorial belief, particularly in a satirized character. In addition, the requirements of a prose narrative (such as *The Blazing World*) may be very different from those of a stage work. Often indeed, the treatment of the contents is itself affected by the medium.

Whatever we make of the Absurdist line, there is no doubt that a sense of split and of life's unfathomable mystery is a part of the material. *One Way Pendulum* sets the normal against the abnormal, the real against the surreal, within one single suburban living room. It is a world where the person with the keenest desire to travel is wheelchair-bound and cannot go anywhere. Surreal imaginative fantasies of going on roller-skates to Outer Space by moonlight are indulged by a dependant relative who is in reality a little-old-lady cripple. Perhaps, this is a metaphor for the lack of progress possible for the human species. We seek to soar but are bound, like Hamlet, in a prison. Another possibility is that life, the world, and we as human beings *do* have meaning and even a purpose, but that our capacities are too limited – too wheelchair-bound – to be sure how to interpret it.

The difficulty of interpretation – of clarifying what Gilbert in *The Gondoliers* is content to leave as an enigma – is suggested by Simpson's short play *The Hole*. This is a work which suggests we are all separated entities, though some of us do seek social acceptance and a wider inclusion. One interesting aspect is its use of a game-playing and playing card *motif*. Another is its Gilbertian exploitation of inversions and opposites. In a conversation between two women, we learn that one has a husband who does all he can to be different from others, while the husband of the other does all he can to be the same. Against this is set the unchanging vision of the Visionary who lives in a world of his own. In between the recurrence of these *motifs*, there are interludes in which three widely contrasting people come along and, having examined a hole in a road, proceed to explore a succession of different possible interpretations.

The possibilities within different interpretations *do* sometimes arise in Gilbert. In *Topsyturveydom*, Satis's discomfiture at tables and chairs being placed on the ceiling leads to opposing interpretations of 'up' and 'down', leading to:

KING: – Do you know where the earth is?

SATIS: – Of course – under my feet.

KING: – Oh, no – open that window. [*They go to window and look out.* KING *indicates the ground above them.*] Look there.

SATIS: – Now, that's one of the most remarkable things I've seen for a long time. Now, that's all *up* with us in England.

CRAPOLEE: – It will be all up with you here if you ridicule our institutions. In those chairs and tables our guardian spirits dwell.

SATIS: – Spirits in chairs and tables? This is without exception the very maddest people on the face of the earth! Then I really am standing head downwards! It sounds awkward, but it's easy enough when you come to try it.[80]

This clearly suggests relativities, hinting at other ways of developing religious and metaphysical notions. Nonetheless, it hardly develops much beyond the jocular.

Compared to the above, *The Hole* offers far greater scope. The everyday is juxtaposed to the infinite surreal. Suburbia clashes with a metaphysical eternity. This is reinforced by the fact that the Visionary is waiting for an imminent religious event – the solemn unveiling of a great window whose many-coloured glass will eventually stain even the white radiance of eternity. In some ways, the world of Simpson's dark underground hole is the opposite of a blazing world of light. Yet the very fact that the Visionary's transcendental moment can be associated with something so 'low' again points to a cosmic split.

The dualities within Simpson's scenario suggest a Gilbertian ambivalence. Darkness is the source, yet just possibly it too may produce the blazing light. One point here is that, although the visionary is a creature apart, he has a desire to share his dream or perhaps to impose it egotistically. He had indeed once hoped to have a queue stretching away from him in every known direction of the compass. Though the dual *mode* is Gilbertian, there are here metaphysical areas and questions of prophetic motivation on which he barely touches.

The sharing of a dream *is*, however, a Gilbertian concept. It is familiar to us from Alexis and Princess Ida. The latter had hoped to join all women in her maiden throng, while Alexis (like his predecessor, the mathematical curate) had desired to fill his world with the blessings of marital love. The real point, however, is that in Simpson, there are bigger issues. We are asked to consider what makes for transcendental experience and whether it may be real, based on error, a symptom of delusion or founded on fraud. As the Visionary sits waiting on his camp-stool, various other characters project their own preoccupations onto the blank darkness of the mysterious opening. On one level, we are considering universal and timeless questions. On another, it is merely a snapshot survey of the fantasy life of the unremarkable inhabitants of an English suburb.

Suburban fantasy sounds a fairly limited field. But in *The Hole*, speculation gets ever wilder, increasingly focused on crime and criminals, and including (among the members of the Puritan backlash) violent demands for more torture and punishment. It is at this point that a workman emerges from the interior and informs the bystanders that it contains nothing more significant than a junction box of the electricity supply. Blazing light is after all a factor. Thereafter, there are rival approaches as to how to treat the knowledge. These break down into two main modes: an attempt to treat the information prosaically, and (alternatively) an attempt to invest it with mysterious resonances of poetry and enchantment.

The division between enchantment and reality is not unknown in Gilbert. When Strephon asks the Lord Chancellor, 'And have you the heart to apply the prosaic rules of evidence to a case that bubbles over with poetical emotion?' the Chancellor's response is that he most distinctly has.[81] Nor – without an affidavit from a thunderstorm or a few words on oath from a heavy shower – is he to be convinced that 'chorused nature' takes any interest in the matter. The difference is that *The Hole* takes such oppositions and makes them metaphysical-philosophical. Not only is meaning itself subjective and partial; it may also be derived from the empty and blank. This leads to the possibility that the whole universe is – not a Blazing World – but no more than a great black hole to which we try vainly to give undue significance.

The scenario of *The Hole* helps to show us how Gilbert both strongly links with later Absurdists and how in some areas he falls short. Like Simpson, he *does* have a concept of more than one world. Princess Toto has a world of dreams and a world of reality. Strephon inhabits two worlds at once. But nowhere are we asked to explore the possible interpretations of transcendental experience. In *The Hole*, the negative aspects are offset by a kind of hope. We may be all in the gutter but some of us are seeking the stars. In Gilbert, the nearest approach to this is in numbers such as *Eagle High in Cloudland Soaring*, reminding us of Edward Fitzgerald's 'Better a live Sparrow than a stuffed Eagle'.[82] However, it is not really metaphysical. Part-satirical, it is more about the value of aspiration than of an ultimate meaning to life.

The developments in the Theatre of the Absurd suggest that Gilbert is not the end of any journey. But his own links with it *do* suggest how later Absurdist may have learned from him, and why, for instance, writers such as Samuel Beckett have been Gilbert and Sullivan aficionados. In *The Hole*, the potential positive is that Man cannot – and does not wish to – live by the empirical alone. The downside is that the non-empirical can be exploited and/or lead to delusion. Gilbert, though always aware of dichotomy, passes by on the other side of such matters. In comedy, at least it is more a case of 'Life's a pleasant institution. Let us take it as it comes'.[83]

The pleasures of life are, however, not all that there is to Gilbert. His other mode is to stress the painted surface, the false appearance, the darker underlay. What he does *not* do is go as far as his legatees. Never within a comedy does he imply that the universe is itself a hole or that it is empty of any significance beyond that which we wrongly impute to it. Never (understandably for his time) does he enter speculations of a type to suggest that cosmic black holes into which our world may one day disappear are a heavenly equivalent to the sort of black hole which Simpson presents in the earth.

The above suggests a final conclusion – namely, that Gilbert is perhaps more a staging-post than a destination. Nonetheless, he does brilliantly pin-point human selfishness, human deceit, and the willingness of many to be duped. In *The Hole*, a character called Soma gradually starts to exploit the potentialities of power (electrical and personal) and mass emotion. Turning the technological facts back into an emotional mumbo-jumbo, he trans-forms the hole-viewing into a celebration of the religious rites of electrical generation. But it cannot last. By the late 20th century, unity is impossible. No longer may we hold hands down the middle, trusting to convergence of thought.[84] For the 20th-century Absurdists (as, before them, for Poe), society and its fantasies are only briefly made corporate.[85] The visionary stays alone in his waiting. The glass and the dream do not come.[86]

* * * * * *

Notes

1 *Interview with Mr. W.S. Gilbert: The Press, the Play, and the Players*: *Edinburgh Evening Dispatch*. Tuesday 5 October 1897, p. 2 et seq.

2 Stoker, Bram, *The Tendency of the Modern Stage: A Talk with Sir W.S. Gilbert on Things Theatrical; Daily Chronicle*, 2 January 1908, p. 8 et seq.

3 *Collaborating with Sir Arthur Sullivan: A Chat with Mr. W.S. Gilbert; Cassell's Saturday Journal*, 21 March 1894, p. 522.

4 Nettleton, George H., *A Visit to Sir William Gilbert*, from correspondence column of *The Nation* 93.2405 (3 August 1911).

5 Archer, William, *Real Conversations* (London: Heinemann, 1904/1905), p. 111. See *Pall Mall Magazine* (September 1901).

6 Scribe wrote dramas, vaudevilles, comedies, tragedies, and opera libretti. To the *Gymnase* theatre alone he is said to have furnished 150 pieces before 1830. He had a number of co-workers (Scribe's 'factory'), one of whom supplied the story, another the dialogue, a third the jokes, and so on. He is said in some cases to have sent sums of money for 'copyright in ideas' to men who were unaware that he had taken suggestions from their work. Among his numerous collaborators were Jean Henri Dupin (1787–1887), Germain Delavigne, Xavier Saintine, and Ernest Legouvé.

7 Stoker, Bram, *Daily Chronicle Interview* (2 January 1908).

8 Interview with Archer, *Real Conversations*.

9 This is a point Gilbert makes in his evidence on Censorship, where he mentions the difference in impact – and embarrassment – between showing Eliza slipping off her dressing-gown and stepping into her bath and writing about it.

10 *The Sorcerer*, in *The Complete Annotated Gilbert and Sullivan*, p. 69.

11 Shakespeare, William, *Macbeth*, Act 1V, sc. i. (The cauldron scene).

12 Mary was hanged in 1752. See Roughead, William, *The Trial of Mary Blandy*, BiblioBazaar, copyright 2006 from 1914 original.

13 This occurs when Elvino announces that the Duke and Duchess are going to stay at his inn in the midst of a quarrel between Ultrice and Teresa ('Upon my word, miss ... Oh, it's you, miss!').

14 Williams, Carolyn, *Gilbert and Sullivan: Gender, Genre, Parody*, pp. 46–47.

15 W.S. Gilbert, *Tom Cobb*, p. 21 (Opening dialogue in Act 3).

16 Genet, *The Balcony*, trans. Bernard Frechtman (Faber and Faber, 1962 revision), p. 71.

17 *The Sorcerer*, in *The Complete Annotated Gilbert and Sullivan*, pp. 51–53.

18 The piece was of course preceded by another, making for a late start. Had it been the sole item on the programme, the audience might not towards the end have become so restless.

19 See *The Complete Annotated Gilbert and Sullivan*, pp. 194 and 196 where the omitted and altered lyrics are included.

20 *Era*, 2 October 1897.

21 *Era*, 3 March 1878.

22 In *Romeo and Juliet* the Nurse is carefully excluded from the climax in the vault. The action deepens to overall seriousness after the unexpected death of Mercutio, a grim structural pivot like that of Polonius.

23 *Era*, 2 October 1897.

24 Eden, *W.S. Gilbert – Appearance and Reality*, back cover.

25 *New York Times*, 1 April 1934.

26 Eden, *W.S. Gilbert –Appearance and Reality*, p. 189.

27 See *Princess Ida*, in *The Complete Annotated Gilbert and Sullivan;* p. 487.

28 W.S. Gilbert, *La Vivandière: Or True To The Corps!* First Produced at St. James's Hall, Liverpool, Saturday, 15 June 1867. Available as W.S. Gilbert Archive download, p. 29.

29 See Williams, Carolyn, *Gilbert and Sullivan: Gender, Genre, Parody*, pp. 14–15.

30 This is the gist of David Eden's argument summarized on the back cover of *W.S. Gilbert – Appearance and Reality*.

31 W.S. Gilbert, *The Mountebanks*, p. 387. Bartolo's failure to elicit anything but laughter when playing Hamlet had led to his reinvention as Clown. As Clown, he plays a mechanical Hamlet, which is both a satire on the mechanical sawing gestures of some enactments (possibly Irving's) and a comment on an increasingly machine-dominated, machine-run society.

32 *Wall Street Journal*, 15 September 2017, in context of New Jersey revival of *What the Butler Saw* (Wisconsin's American Players Theatre).

33 Orton Joe, *Complete Plays* (Bloomsbury, 1976), *Loot*, p. 264; *The Good and Faithful Servant*, p. 165; *Funeral Games*, p. 345.

34 Quoted and collated in article in *The Guardian* by Andrew Crowther, 20 November 2015.

35 Andrew Crowther's made the 'one long joke' statement in the above article. I don't deny that it *is* a joke but feel that it is more nuanced in treatment.

36 One of Barrington's interpolations.

37 *The Mikado*, in *The Complete Annotated Gilbert and Sullivan*, p. 617.

38 *The Mikado*, p. 613; *Utopia Limited*, p. 977; *The Grand Duke*, p. 1131.

39 Orton, Joe, *Complete Plays*; *The Good and Faithful Servant*, p. 155.

40 *Fun*, 19 January 1867.

41 Stoppard, like Gilbert, plays with the concept of identity. Both are fascinated by a real life and theatrical identity overlap – with the added aspect that the 'real life' is that of a created character.

42 Simpson, N.F., *A Resounding Tinkle* (In *N.F. Simpson: The Collected Plays*, Faber and Faber, 2013), p. 39.

43 See *Fun*, 17 February 1866: *East Lynne*.

44 This is referenced in the scene of the commuters crossing London Bridge. The corpse that may be sprouting references both the idea of seasonal regeneration and a concealed domestic murder – the fact that it is attributed to Stetson (Ezra Pound) adding a macabre private joke.

45 In *Streetcar* Stanley refers what is within and what is outside his working 'territory'. But the flat is also – he feels – his territory with Stella, Blanche there being an invader. The territory of his mind is noticeably less flexible and more restricted than that of the imaginative, sensitive Blanche.

46 *The Grand Duke*, in *The Complete Annotated Gilbert and Sullivan;* p. 1131.

47 Ibid., p. 1157.

48 Dickens follows the same mode in his mockery of the 'soft' new model prisons to which Uriah Heap is sent in *David Copperfield*.

49 *Wikipedia*, entry under *Spithead and Nore Mutinies*. The phrase 'by Jingo' in the 1878 case comes from a long-established minced oath used to avoid saying 'by Jesus'. The specific term 'jingoism' was coined as a political label by the prominent British radical George Holyoake in a letter to the *Daily News* on 13 March 1878.

50 *H.M.S. Pinafore*, in *The Complete Annotated Gilbert and Sullivan;* p. 135.

51 *An Elixir of Love* in *The Lost Stories of W.S. Gilbert*.

52 Orton, *Complete Plays, Funeral Games*, p. 359.

53 Mikhail Mikhailovich Bakhtin (17 November [O.S. 5 November] 1895–7 March 1975) was a Russian philosopher, literary critics, semiotician, and scholar who worked on literary theory, ethics, and the philosophy of language. 'Carnivalesque' is a term used in the English translations of works written by Bakhtin. It originated as *'carnival'* in his *Dostoevsky's Problem of Poetics* and was explicated as a concept in his *Rabelais and His World*.

54 See *Studies in Scottish Literature*, Column 26, Issue 1, Article 31, 1-1-1991: *Bakhtin's Literary Carnivalesque and Dunbar's 'Fastemis Evin in Hell'* by Deanna Delmar Evans.

55 Orton, *Complete Plays, Funeral Games*, pp. 327–328.

56 Orton *Complete Plays, Funeral Games*, p. 345.

57 Auden and Isherwood, *The Ascent of F6* (Faber and Faber, no date), p. 115.

58 W.S. Gilbert, *Topsyturveydom*, first performed at the Criterion Theatre, 21 March 1874. Available as a download from the W.S. Gilbert Archive.

59 W.S. Gilbert, *An Old Score*, Act 1, p. 7. (W.S. Gilbert Archive download).

60 An example is his rejection in 1884 of the lozenge plot. Sullivan's views and letters containing them may be found in Baily, Leslie, *The Gilbert and Sullivan Book*, pp. 255–257.

61 See Esslin, Martin, *The Theatre of the Absurd*, (Methuen Drama, republished in 3rd edition, Vintage, 2001), p. 102.

62 This is the message of the end of *The Waste Land*. The soured temper and thinning hair derive from King Paramount's Song about life (*Utopia Limited*, pp. 999–1003.)

63 *The Mikado*, in *The Complete Annotated Gilbert and Sullivan*, p. 649.

64 Quoted in Esslin, Martin, *The Theatre of the Absurd*, p. 102. Wardle links this to the term *Comedy of Menace*, referring to a body of plays written by David Campton, Nigel Dennis, N.F. Simpson, and Harold Pinter. The term was borrowed by Wardle from the subtitle of Campton's play *The Lunatic View: A Comedy of Menace*. He coined it in reviewing Pinter's and Campton's plays in *Encore* in 1958. Campton's subtitle *Comedy of Menace* is a jocular play-on-words derived from *comedy of manners – menace* being

manners pronounced with 'somewhat of a Judeo-English accent'. *See New English Dramatists 12: Radio Plays* (Penguin Paperback, 1 January 1968).

65 Quoted in *True Anarchists* (*Guardian* article, 4 November 2006).

66 Orton, *Complete Plays, Loot*, p. 268.

67 N.F. Simpson, *A Resounding Tinkle* (Samuel French Ltd; Reprint edition (1 June. 1958): See the belated Authorial introduction, pp. 38–40.

68 Pinter, Harold, *The Birthday Party* (Faber and Faber, 1991), p. 77.

69 Simpson, *A Resounding Tinkle*, pp. 13–15.

70 *Utopia Limited,* in *The Complete Annotated Gilbert and Sullivan*, p. 1025.

71 W.S. Gilbert, *Engaged* in Plays by W.S. Gilbert (ed. Rowell) (C.U.P., 1982), p. 156; p. 139.

72 *The Grand Duke,* in The *Complete Annotated Gilbert and Sullivan*, p. 1101.

73 Quoted in Esslin, Martin, *The Theatre of the Absurd*, pp. 102–103.

74 Rose's identity is mysterious. Even her name varies, as she is sometimes called Sal. (Perhaps, her name is Rosalie.) The blinding by sympathetic magic suggests that there is a genuine link between her and Riley – perhaps even a genetic one and that now at last she is being made to acknowledge it. Perhaps, she had hidden the fact that she had negro blood in her but now admits the fact. Her touching of Riley's eyes before the beating certainly hints at this. There may too be hints that she has blinded the world to her links with Riley and is now being punished for it. The fact that Riley emerges from the dark basement has its own resonance. It suggests his association with hidden depths – of secrets and of consciousness. Is he the skeleton in the cupboard? Is he the suppressed knowledge – even in a way the identity – that Rose has buried not only from others but also from herself? Whatever the truth, Rose's blinding can be seen as positive or negative – or both – in its symbolic resonances emanating from the ambiguous treatment of Riley's revelations.

75 *True Anarchists, Guardian* article, 4 November 2006.

76 See *The Faber Book of Utopias*, ed. Carey (Faber and Faber, 1999), p. 1–8.

77 Ibid., pp. 78–80. See also Internet. The whole text may be downloaded. The overall impression is that the Blazing World would not to many of us be a Utopia. It strongly endorses tyranny, aristocratic privilege, opulence, and self-aggrandisement. In the end, the Lady returns to the real world, taking with her a Blazing World army and supplies of a Blazing World chemical that ignites on contact with water. With this, she systemically and ruthlessly burns the fleets and cities of every nation that will not pay tribute to her king.

78 Hamlet sometimes expresses a similar jaundiced mood, suggesting personal powerlessness. See Shakespeare, W., *Hamlet*, 3, i. (lines 126–128).

79 For *Eheu Fugaces*, see *The Dark Blue*, 111, April 1872.

80 W.S. Gilbert, *Topsyturveydom*, Internet Download from W.S. Gilbert Archive.

81 *Iolanthe*, in *The Complete Annotated Gilbert and Sullivan*, p. 387.

82 Letter to E. B. Cowell (4/27/1859). This is in regard to his translation of the *Rubáiyát*.

83 *The Gondoliers*, in *The Complete Annotated Gilbert and Sullivan*, p. 895.

84 Ibid., p. 895.

85 Poe was obsessed with the idea of the original unity of the Universe but of the collapse of the wholeness. One of his preoccupations is the need for the artist to restore the original unity to the chaos which surrounds the poetic spirit. Little atoms struggle back towards the 'absolutely ... irrelatively ... unconditionally One'. In *Eureka*, we can see Poe's description of what he believes gravity is (see Poe, Edgar Allan, *Eureka*, 1848).

86 See also *The Harvard Crimson*, 5 July 1960, where James Sharaf writes: 'The hole is the mind of man, the history of humbuggery, and, most particularly, ideas of God'.

Index

Note: Page numbers followed by "n" denote endnotes.

For Product Safety Concerns and Information please contact our EU
representative GPSR@taylorandfrancis.com
Taylor & Francis Verlag GmbH, Kaufingerstraße 24, 80331 München, Germany

www.ingramcontent.com/pod-product-compliance
Lightning Source LLC
Chambersburg PA
CBHW071453110726
47908CB00003B/597